Yr friend & bro.
W. Sparrow.

THE

LIFE AND CORRESPONDENCE

OF

REV. WILLIAM SPARROW, D. D.,

LATE PROFESSOR OF SYSTEMATIC DIVINITY AND EVIDENCES, IN THE EPISCOPAL THEOLOGICAL SEMINARY OF VIRGINIA.

BY

REV. CORNELIUS WALKER, D. D.,

PROFESSOR OF CHURCH HISTORY AND CANON LAW.

PHILADELPHIA:
JAMES HAMMOND, No. 1224 CHESTNUT STREET.
1876.

TABLE OF CONTENTS.

PREFACE.

In the preparation of the following Memoir, regard has been had more especially to the desires and wishes of one class, the largest among those who will give it a perusal, the pupils of Dr. Sparrow, the survivors of the different generations of students who, for nearly half a century, in Ohio and in Virginia, were under his instruction. Details, perhaps of little interest to others, but of much to these, have thus been introduced, portions of correspondence inserted that might have been otherwise omitted, and points amplified which might have been more briefly treated. As belonging to this brotherhood, the writer has had no difficulty in deciding what he would have desired from any one else engaged in his undertaking. What, therefore, he would have wished for himself, he has endeavored to provide for his fellow-pupils.

And yet the features of most interest to this class are those that will be apt to prove of interest to others. The hope may not unreasonably be indulged that outside of this peculiar circle, and among acquaintances of other classes, as among those who know of its subject only by name, this memoir may be productive of instruction and benefit. It only needed contact to make manifest Dr. Sparrow's intellectual greatness. His moral greatness, however, his simplicity, his integrity, his unfeigned and earnest piety, his devotion to the will of God, and to the real welfare of his fellow-men, these, not so immediately noted, nor so much estimated, have their higher value in the way of influence, and can scarcely fail, in a record of this kind, to be recognized. Such record cannot be studied without benefit. The individual, to use the thought of another, constitutes, while living, a demonstration of the power and truth of Christianity; and being dead, he yet speaks, proclaiming that God is faithful, that the promises of His grace have had their personal verification.

It remains that acknowledgment be made to the kind friends, and brethren in the ministry, by whom material, in the way of correspondence and otherwise, has been furnished. Where there are so many, it is difficult to specify; and the writer would, therefore, make his general, but no less grateful, acknowledgment for the essential aid thus afforded. As to the correspondence, the largest, and perhaps the most important, is that with Professor Wing, with Rev. E. W. Syle, Rev. E. H. Canfield, D. D., and Rev. J. A. Jerome. Single letters, however, to other correspondents, will be found of deep interest, and full of practical instruction.

The Reminiscences of Rev. Mr. Syle, containing some of the choicest material of the volume, were received only after the book was in the hands of the printer. Perhaps it is better that they should be in their present form, rather than arranged in the order of time, in the narrative, as might have been the case if received at an earlier period.

The Address, at the Commencement following the death of Dr. Sparrow, has, at the suggestion of brethren present at its delivery, been inserted. Its subject makes it supplemental to the Memoir.

The Fragments are selections from brief sketches, many of which, of a similar character, are found among the Doctor's papers. Some of tnem were manifestly intended for Faculty meeting addresses, some for sermons, others for articles, and some, doubtless, as analytical of subjects with which his mind at the time was interested.

It was in prospect to have included several of the most striking of his Commencement addresses; but this, in view of the size of the volume, was found to be not practicable.

MEMOIR

OF

WILLIAM SPARROW, D.D.

CHAPTER I.

EARLY LIFE IN IRELAND.

"The generations of men succeed one another, like the waves of the sea. They have no permanence. They are here for a little time, and then gone forever. The most that one generation can do for another must have reference to the eternity which lies beyond the grave."

These sentences were written by the subject of this memoir, during a voyage across the Atlantic, more than a quarter of a century ago. Their opening comparison was doubtless suggested by what was daily before his eyes, and, perhaps, at the moment he was writing—"the waves of the sea," over which he was returning to the home of his childhood. Their closing thought gives us the key-note as to the proper object of our undertaking, and, indeed, of all religious biography—that of spiritual benefit to survivors and readers. It should have "reference to the eternity which lies beyond," and so influence the present life as to fit it for the higher life of Heavenly existence. Other and subordinate objects, connected with such undertaking, may, of course, be sought and attained. But this should never be forgotten. While we gratefully recall the traits of personal character which gave charm to the intercourse of friendship and daily life, and draw our hearts to the departed in affectionate regard and veneration; while we thank God in every remembrance of the privilege of such association, yet there is this higher object, to which all these others should have regard. It is as the life, in its particulars, and in its general result, bears upon other lives, "with reference to the eternity beyond;" in other words, as it constitutes an illustration of the grace of God, bringing honor to Him and blessing to His creatures, that it specially claims our regard and imitation. We thus trace the Divine lineaments of the Master in the life of His follower; find inducements, for ourselves, to greater spiritual earnestness and activity. If in any degree we shall succeed in accomplishing what was the habitual desire of him of whom we are writing, it will be in making this record subservient to these great purposes.

William, the first son of Samuel Sparrow and Mary Roe, was born in Charlestown, Massachusetts, March 12th, 1801. His father, a native of Ireland, had been residing in this country only a few years, at this time. He had left Ireland in consequence of implication in the Rebellion of 1798, coming to America, where he remained until the year 1805. In that year he returned to Ireland, and remained until 1817, when he again came to America, making it his permanent home until his death, in Ohio, in 1838.

His father, the grandfather of the subject of this memoir, William Sparrow, of the town of Gorey, Wexford County, Ireland, was the descendant of a family of English stock, who settled in Wexford during the Protectorate of Cromwell. Quite a number of the name, mostly of the Society of Friends, were to be found in that neighborhood, as also in the town of Enniscorthy, about the beginning of the present century. William Sparrow was what was termed a middle man; that is, he was the holder of long leases on large tracts of land, which, on the system of tenantry then prevailing, he rented out in smaller parcels to the actual tenants. He was also, at various times, engaged in mercantile pursuits. Soon after the return of his son to Ireland, in 1805, his grandson and namesake, the subject of our memoir, became an inmate in his household, and there remained during the most of his boyhood. Dr. McElroy, who was acquainted with Dr. Sparrow and his father in Ohio, states that the intention of his grandfather was to have made him his heir, and at the time of his death had prepared him for entrance into Trinity College, Dublin. Whether change of determination, or sudden death without specific provision in his will to that effect, prevented the carrying out of this design, is not known. It probably secured the primary training and habits of study which stood him in such good stead during his subsequent life. It was here that he obtained his impressions of Irish character, and gathered up that stock of incident, in referring to which, in after life, he found so much pleasure. Those who have heard him allude to these incidents will deeply regret that an undertaking upon which he once entered was not carried out to its completion, that of an autobiography, for the benefit and instruction of his children. The fragment, commenced in 1848, during his voyage from this country to Europe, has already been alluded to, and a portion used as introducing our narrative. The rest of it may here be most appropriately inserted:

"I have often thought, dear children, that it might be profitable to both you and me, that I should address some thoughts, and narrate some facts to you, not to be read till after my decease. And now, here, in the midst of the Atlantic, on this third day of July, 1848, I begin my task.

"The generations of men succeed one another, like the waves of the sea. They have no permanence. They are seen for a time, and then gone forever. The most that one generation can do for another must have reference to the eternity which lies beyond the grave. The mutual services which we may render, which are limited to their influence in this life, are comparatively of small account. What I write, therefore, is designed chiefly to bear upon that other world in which we must all, however old I may be and however young you, soon be assembled. If, through God's mercy in Christ, anything can be made instrumental in bringing us together in a happy immortality, our songs of praise shall never cease. But while the heavenly inheritance is the chief thing to be sought after, it is pleasing to reflect that the pursuit of it in no way interferes with present happiness; nay, that God has so ordered things that the earnest pursuit of heaven will cause a man, as the Saviour has it, 'to inherit the earth.' In reference to your temporal interests I should have no manner of apprehension, if I were sure your spiritual interests would be duly attended to. The nature of true religion is such that it gives a man those qualities which, according to the laws that obtain in society and human life, naturally result in earthly prosperity. But besides this, God, who is above nature, has promised that they that seek Him shall never lack.

"Let me make, first, a few statements about my family. Family pride, like purse pride, pride of office, pride of talent, and all other kinds of pride, is a weakness. However the world may look upon it, the spirit of Christianity condemns it; it is inconsistent in a Christian. Even philosophy has pointed out its unsoundness. But family *affection* is a different thing. It is the best of all our natural affections; less low and selfish than any other, and prepares the way for higher and better things. With a view, therefore, to lay a foundation for this, let me say a few words about your ancestry a couple of generations back, first making the general remark, as I do with some satisfaction, that I know nothing discreditable of any of them. As far as my information goes they were persons of respectability and morality, and many of them lived and died in the faith, and hope, and charity of the Gospel.

"Both of my grandfathers, and one of my grandmothers, I saw and knew, to my fifteenth year. My grandfather Sparrow I lived with, from my fifth year. His wife was named Harrison, and died in the prime of life. My grandfather continued a widower to the end of his life, which lasted for thirty years after. He was a man of deep affections, too much reserve, and high integrity. He lived in a small house in Gorey, county Wexford, he and I and two servants making up the family. He was of very retired habits when I knew him. Probably he was of a different disposition. He was charitable to the poor, and read his Bible and Prayer-book; but, by a singular and gross inconsistency, he never went to the Parish Church, in my day. This arose out of a dispute with a former rector, a very unworthy man; and when another man was brought in his place, the habit of non-attendance was so fixed, that my grandfather never broke through it. His sin in this particular he confessed, and deeply lamented, to my mother, on his death-bed. It is a fearful sin to forsake the house of God, so conveying to the world the impression that we do, and can, and think it fit to, live 'without God in the world.'

"In early life my grandfather Sparrow had been a man of business; when I knew him, he was living on an income of fifteen or twenty hundred dollars, from a life interest which he held in some land belonging to Lord Fitznorris. While in trade, and ever after, he bore a high character for uprightness and honor. My grandmother Sparrow I never saw. She was most highly spoken of, as a most excellent woman, wife and mother. Her family name was Harrison. After her my sister Susan was called—Susan Harrison Sparrow.

"My grandfathers Sparrow and Roe were originally from the same county, Wexford, and the same town, Gorey; though the latter spent the last twenty years of his life in Dublin. Both families were large in the county of Wexford. The Sparrows are said to have removed to it, from England, in the time of Cromwell. Most of them are Quakers, and quite a thrifty people. When the Roes removed from England, to the Pale, I have not learned. They were a numerous and respectable family about Gorey and its neighborhood. In the Rebellion, my grandfather, Henry Roe, removed his family, for security, to Dublin; and when the Rebellion was over and peace restored, found such prospects opening before him in the capital, that he was induced to settle there for life. My grandmother's maiden name was Woodrofe, also of a family in Gorey, respectable in themselves, and respectably connected, though, like most of the gentry in Ireland, of that day, they had too high a style of living for their means.

"The families of both my grandfathers were large. That of my grandfather Sparrow was cut off as soon as they reached maturity, all but—" his son Samuel, we may add, to fill up the sentence, who married Mary Roe, daughter of Dr. Henry Roe, and whose relations to our subject have already been indicated.

"About my own history," to quote from another fragment, written, perhaps, some ten or fifteen years later, "it may be well to speak this much. My father came over from Ireland to this country soon after the Rebellion of '98, and settled in Massachusetts, near Boston. There two sisters, older than myself, and I, were born. About 1805 my father returned, with his family, to Ireland, at the request of my grandfather, and remained there until after his death. In about a year after that event we returned to the United States, settling first in Utica, New York, and ultimately in Ohio. The family then consisted of my father and mother, my sister Susan, myself, and my brother Edward. Three had been buried in Ireland. Two more were afterward added, Anna Maria, born in Utica, and Thomas, born in Ohio.

"Let me now confine myself to my own history. I might speak of my school-boy days in Ireland. I was a boarder, for three years or so, in the best boarding school in our section. It was near Arklow, at the opening of the vale of Avoca, in which the scholars often rambled. When I call to mind the evil influences I was exposed to, I at once thank God that I escaped with no greater detriment from the bad example and principles of my companions;

and it saddens me to think that youths from moral and pious families have to pass through such an ordeal to get an education. The school, I am persuaded, was no worse than the generality, whether in Ireland or in this country. But a public school is, at best, a necessary evil. If I could, I would have a private tutor instead; though even that method of preparing youth for the university is attended with its disadvantages; but they are not, in my judgment, so serious or difficult of prevention. The instruction was good, but the text books were naught; far inferior to those now used. The discipline was rigid but not despotic. The head of the school was a clergyman, a scholar, and a gentleman; but too much sought after by the neighboring gentry, on account of his social qualities, to leave him as devoted as he should have been to the interests of the school. He always treated me with kindness, and his influence upon my course in life proved salutary."

Thus, at his grandfather's as his home, but with the interval already mentioned, of the boarding school, it would seem, he continued until near the time of the departure of his father and the family to this country, in 1817, say until the neighborhood of his sixteenth year; the period of life to which he always recurred with unfailing interest and affection. His love of Ireland was that of one whose freshest years of life had been spent there, and under circumstances and associations pleasant, in after times, to be remembered. He was old enough to acquire the tastes and feelings of a native, and in all his subsequent career they were clearly distinguishable. One of these was very strikingly exhibited in his admiration of the then poet of Ireland. Some of Moore's melodies, doubtless read as they came out, with all the enthusiasm of youth and of national predilection, he was able to repeat late in life, and with a pathos and beauty which showed that they were thoroughly appreciated. Among these there was one, descriptive of the localities over which he had rambled in boyhood, connected with a later experience of a deeply interesting character. Twenty-one years after leaving Ireland, in the year 1838, he revisited the home of his childhood, as also the place of his early education. "I was," said he, speaking of it many years afterward, "a good part of a day traveling in the stage up the vale of Avoca, returning, after a long interval, to my old home. More than once I found myself thinking of those lines of Moore, so descriptive of my feelings under the circumstances. Many of those of whom I thus thought, and whom I expected to see at the end of my journey, I found were gone." The opening and closing stanzas of the passage, thus associated with that day's travel, with the anticipations and the failure to realize them at its close, will show their singular appropriateness to the circumstances under which they were thus recalled:—

"'There is not in the wide world a valley so sweet
As that vale in whose bosom the bright waters meet;
Oh! the last ray of feeling and life must depart
Ere the bloom of that valley shall fade from my heart.

"'Sweet vale of Avoca! how calm would I rest
In thy bosom of shade, with the friends I love best;
When the storms that we feel in this cold world should cease,
And our souls, like thy waters, be mingled, with peace.'"

It was in such feelings and associations that the subject of this memoir, although American born, was so largely Irish in his sympathies and character. The impressions of those early days were fresh and pleasant with him to the end. A considerable portion of his last visit to the Old World, in 1871, was made to the neighborhood in which he had spent his days of boyhood, and on the very last day of his life, but with no intimation that the end was so near, he made a playful allusion to some of his early experiences, as illustrative of a matter of which he was conversing.

Among the reminiscences of this early period, so pleasant as they manifestly were to the narrator, and so genial in their narration to the listener, a few may be recalled in this connection. One of the earliest was connected with a visit made to himself by his parents, after he had gone to live at his grandfather's. It was mentioned to illustrate the carefulness of the system, then prevalent, for guarding children against the danger of taking cold. "I slept," said he, "in a feather bed, with close curtains and an abundance of covering, and was, besides, protected with flannel. Once, when my father and mother arrived after night, 'the boy,' with a woolen comforter wrapped around his neck and shoulders, was set up in the bed to receive them; and after being duly admired and caressed, was again covered up and curtained in safety."

"Nobody," said he again, in speaking of another topic, "nobody could understand the beggary of Ireland except by living in the country. At our house each member of the family had his or her particular beggar to be remembered; and when he came he looked to his patron for relief." This was bringing in the principle of patronage, as also that of the division of labor and responsibility. "I had my beggar," said he, "and when he made his appearance I tried to have something for him." In this respect the old feeling exerted its influence in after life. An Irish beggar who knocked at the door of the Doctor's study, at the Seminary, was allowed to have his talk, sometimes was asked some questions about his home over the sea, and never sent away empty. Irish workmen, if engaged upon repairs of the buildings, or otherwise, were apt to be found out; and delineations of Irish character, such, for instance, as those of Charles Lever, were keenly appreciated. "Trench's Sketches of the Irish Peasantry" was one of the books which helped to relieve the tedium of confinement after his severe sickness, in the spring of 1873. It was a topic ever fresh and full of interest, and bringing up to his mind and heart grateful memories of the people and home of his childhood.

There was not in this interest, however, that kind of influence which affected his judgment as to the real troubles under which Ireland was suffering. His remedy, and the only one in which he had any confidence, for the troubles there, as for those of Spain, and Italy, and Mexico, was a Christianity based upon Scriptural intelligence, in other words, genuine Protestantism. His hopes for the population with which his early life had brought him in contact, rested not upon any proposed or possible change in the relations of that population to its rulers at home or in England, but in a change of their relations to their religious teachers. Most strikingly was his sagacity exhibited in an opinion called forth in recitation, during the year 1844, when the Temperance movement, under Father Matthew, was making such wonderful progress. The question was asked in class, "whether this great movement, which promised so much of moral amelioration, carried on by a Catholic Priest, would not tend to the still greater advancement of that system." The prompt reply was, "no; that everything which had the effect of enlightening and elevating a population would have the additional effect of weakening the influence of the Romish and increasing that of the Protestant system." The wonderful movement in that country during the next fifteen years fully justified the opinion thus expressed.

Very little has been mentioned specially, as to his earlier religious life. His allusion to his grandfather's relations to the Church is a very brief one, and throws no light upon his own feelings at that time, or as to any peculiar influences that were brought to bear upon him in the formation of his religious character. He was confirmed in Ireland, of course, before his sixteenth year, but the year is unknown; and there is no evidence as to how soon the question of entering the ministry became one of personal interest and definite consideration. He once incidentally mentioned, in a Thursday evening meeting, that early in life he had been led to regard the position of an English Rector as, perhaps, one of the most desirable that could be thought of, so far as regarded mere earthly comfort and happiness. But whether the thought went beyond this at the time, or further shaped itself into personal desire and anticipation for the higher work of the ministry, and with reference to its spiritual objects and results, he gave no intimation. The probabilities, however, are, that at a very early period he came under decided religious influence, and that to this there was an early response of sanctified impression. His uncle, the Rev. Peter Roe, was one of the most earnest of the Irish clergy of that day, of decided Evangelical views and sympathies, and largely instrumental in giving start and direction to a powerful religious awakening, the fruits of which have since been abundantly enjoyed. It is hardly probable that such a man would have failed to exercise some religious influence upon a sister's child at the time of Confirmation. We find the uncle and nephew in communication after the arrival of the latter in this country, and on matters connected with religion. The deep tenderness, too, with which he always spoke of his mother, and of her influence in the formation of his character, and the devoted affection with which he cherished her memory, would indicate that the sister and brother were of like mind and heart upon this subject. In all probability, her love and prayers first consecrated him to the Lord, and sought those spiritual blessings which he afterwards so richly enjoyed. During a season of special religious interest in one of the Dissenting churches, he was taken by some of the servants, without his grandfather's knowledge, to attend the services, and subsequently described himself as having been deeply impressed by what he saw and heard. Whether at this or at some other time, is not known, but during some portion of his boyhood his mind and heart were so impressed, that, as the prayers of the Liturgy were read, during service, on Sunday morning, he found it impossible to restrain his feelings—would sometimes be in tears, during the whole of the prayers. "I remember," said he, speaking of this same period, "that there was a man in the neighborhood whose mind had lost its balance, especially on religious subjects. Among other things, he endeavored to live, in various outward respects, like our Lord and His Apostles. I was very much impressed by his earnestness. In spite of his mental unsoundness, there was much in his bearing that rebuked the Christianity of many who looked upon him with compassion."

These are but fragments, but they show, even in boyhood, certain traits of character which were fully developed and exhibited in his subsequent career: deep thoughtfulness, going to the realities of things; religious susceptibility, and that peculiar power of sympathy which rendered him so thoroughly appreciative as to the feelings of his fellow creatures.

This portion of his life, as we have seen, terminates with the departure of his father and his family to America. His grandfather died in 1816, and the grandson returned to his father's home at Enniscorthy. Before this, and during the subsequent interval between his grandfather's death and the removal to this country, he seems to have been at the school mentioned in the autobiographical fragment already quoted. His preparation was sufficient to enable him to take charge of an Academy in Utica, within the first eighteen months after his arrival in America, and to enter Columbia College the year after, 1819. No particulars are accessible as to the instructions of this early period, beyond those given by himself, in the extract just quoted. Among those to whom his thoughts recurred during the day's journey in the vale of Avoca, he mentioned especially his old teacher, and spoke of his sadness, at its termination, to find that he was no longer living. To this unknown teacher, a "scholar and a gentleman," was, in all probability, due the first intellectual awakening and the habits of accurate mastery by which, in after life, he was characterized. Very considerable progress must have been made, both in training and acquisition, to enable him to take the position which he did a year or two afterwards, and to sustain himself in it successfully. "My teacher," said he, on a certain occasion, insisting upon the importance of mathematics in intellectual culture, and of the necessity of thoroughness, to secure its benefits, "my teacher would never accept an imperfect recitation. 'Sit down honey,' 'sit down honey,' was his standing order, at anything like hesitation, confusion, or haziness, in the demonstration, and there was no appeal." The lessons were thus thoroughly mastered. And the pupil, in this particular instance, regarded it as the most important part of his early training. Whether the teacher thus alluded to was the one in Ireland, or one of a later date, is uncertain. It is more probable that it was the former.

We are thus brought to the close of his life in Ireland. In 1817 his father's family, consisting of the parents and three children, one sister and two brothers, removed to this country, and settled at Utica, Western New York.

The following communication from Rev. Dr. McElroy, while repeating some of the facts already mentioned and partly derived from it, contains also other matter which will be of interest in connection with this portion of our narrative.

"SANTA CLARA, CALIFORNIA,
"August 28, 1874.

"REV. AND DEAR BROTHER :—

"In reply to yours of the 19th, I communicate, with great pleasure, what information I possess of the late Rev. Dr. Sparrow's boyhood, and of his parents. He was a native of Massachusetts, and three years old when taken to Ireland by his parents, on their return to their native land. He was for several years at school in Ireland, but whether as a day scholar or boarder I cannot say. He often, in his conversations with me, reverted to the thorough drill in Latin, Greek, history and mathematics, in the school which he attended, and to the ability and accurate scholarship of his teachers. The school was, I think, at Enniscorthy. When his parents returned to America, he had mastered the extensive preparatory courses of Latin and Greek, for entrance at Trinity College, Dublin. Either immediately on their return to America, or very soon after, the family settled at Utica, New York; he, advised and encouraged by his mother, became, youthful stranger as he was, a candidate at a competitive examination for the position of classical teacher in the principal academy of the city. He more than once dwelt with graphic interest upon that incident in his life, and the happiness which his success and appointment yielded to his mother.

"During the whole of his boyhood in Ireland the Irish Episcopal Church was in a fervid glow of revived spiritual life and activity; and doubtless he received, from infancy, faithful and discriminating Evangelical instruction. But by what means and instrumentalities he was brought to our Lord, and led openly to confirm his baptismal vows, or from what bishop he received the ordinance of Confirmation, I cannot with certainty say. My impression, however, as to the bishop, although not very satisfactory and distinct, is that Bishop Burke, the father of a Captain Burke, who in his day was a noted and efficient Evangelical layman, was the bishop to whose diocese Enniscorthy belonged in Dr. Sparrow's boyhood. An anecdote, emanating from a highly respectable source, was told of this bishop, which sheds some light upon the condition of the Irish Episcopal Church during the school-boy days of William Sparrow, at Enniscorthy. The bishop and his son were in Dublin during the anniversary week of the Irish great Evangelical societies. As Captain Burke passed the Rotunda of Sackville street, he noticed in front of it a long row of carriages, and on his return home inquired of his father what it meant. The bishop replied that it was a meeting of religiously frenzied and fanatical people. The son said that it must be a respectable assemblage, for he noticed some coronets upon the carriages, and that he would go and see what it was. The Rev. Dr. Singer, a senior fellow of Trinity College, who has since died Bishop of Meath, was speaking when the Captain entered the Rotunda. The latter was struck with the respectability of the assembly; but his attention was arrested and riveted by the speaker. He returned to his home with new views, under deep convictions of sin, deeply depressed and thoroughly wretched. The case was entirely new to the father. He became alarmed for his son, feared madness in his case, and sent hurriedly for his family physician. The physician represented to the father that nothing but religious anxiety was the matter with his son, and advised that Rev. Dr. Singer should be sent for. This the bishop, after great opposition, was prevailed upon to do. The son soon found peace in believing, and became known as an active, winning, and effective co-worker in the revival of the spiritual life of the Church. The conversion of such men, and of whole families, was a common event in all the Irish dioceses, in Dr. Sparrow's boyhood. The reading and preaching of the truth as it is in Jesus, in the Irish pulpit, was attended, at the time, with a mighty power, and it could hardly be otherwise but that William Sparrow, in his mature boyhood, became a subject of gracious and heavenly influence, and with renewed heart received the laying on of hands in Confirmation. I will simply add of Bishop Burke, that he became reconciled to the new views of his son. A secretary of the Irish Church Missionary Society informed me that the bishop had invited him to preach in the Cathedral, in behalf of the Society, an evidence of the happy influence of the bishop's son.

"That Doctor Sparrow's early religious instruction was particularly Evangelical and discriminating, and that his sympathies in youthful manhood were ardently with those known in his day as the Evangelical clergy, is very evident from the fact, upon which he often dwelt in conversation, of his enjoyment of the services at St. George's, in New York, and particularly of Dr. Milnor's Wednesday evening lectures and services, while he was a student of Columbia College, although he was personally unknown to the Doctor, and a stranger to every one present. When I last lectured for Doctor Milnor, at the lecture room of old St. George's, I thought of the youthful stranger and student, who had there, a few years before, without any human sympathy, enjoyed the holy influences for which that sacred room had so often been remarkable.

"As to Dr. Sparrow's parents, I knew his father quite intimately, but I never saw his mother. His father belonged to the class styled gentry, in Ireland, and was very respectably connected. He was a gentleman of vigorous intellect, of extensive reading, particularly in the department of human rights, popular and national interests, and political economy; and he impressed me as one well qualified to advise and direct in the education of his children. In my earlier and later preaching tours in the diocese of Ohio, I occasionally spent a Sunday in the neighborhood where Mr. Sparrow (the father) and family settled; and I occasionally met with ladies who had known the family intimately. They remembered Mrs. Sparrow with great interest and affection; spoke of her as a lady of great refinement, of exquisite grace and polish, and of most lovely and winning character; that, at first, she endured, with great fortitude and resignation, the deprivations of the wilderness and the pioneer life, but at last her health failed under its hardships, and she died, beloved and lamented by the whole community. But whether, equally with her sister and eminently useful brother, the Rev. Peter Roe, whom I had known, she inherited the mental energy and capacity of her family, I have had no satisfactory opportunity of learning. And yet I have never doubted, from what I did learn of the mother, that her distinguished son owed, under God, his early piety and subsequent greatness to her influence.

"Very affectionately, yours in Christ,

"James McElroy."

CHAPTER II.

FROM ARRIVAL IN AMERICA TO TIME OF ORDINATION.

The information of this portion of our narrative, that extending from the arrival in America until the ordination to the ministry of its subject, from 1817 to 1826, is more scant than any other with which we shall be occupied. Soon after this arrival, we find his father's family at Utica, Western New York. In this city, or more properly town, at that time, William, then only in his seventeenth year, as mentioned by Dr. McElroy, under some peculiar stress of circumstances in the affairs of the institution, was placed in charge of an academy of some considerable size, and carried it on successfully; at first alone, and afterward aided by an associate. The special vocation of his life was thus entered upon at a very early period. And it would seem to have been the only one, in some of its forms, either from the professorial chair or from the pulpit, in which he was ever engaged—that of a teacher. Some of the facts mentioned above were incidentally imparted by himself, and as illustrative of a point upon which at the moment he was insisting, that if students, of any kind, were not interested in their studies, the defect must be largely in the instructor. He evidently regarded himself as having succeeded, in this difficult post, not only in securing the interest, but the orderly obedience of his pupils. Probably an extract from a letter of one of his oldest living pupils, not in Utica, but in Ohio, a few years afterward, Rev. Erastus Burr, D.D., will help, not only to explain his success in this first essay as an instructor, but also to show that there was little deviation, in his subsequent life, from the course then adopted. "I commenced my studies of Latin, Greek and mathematics under him, and have always been thankful that I had this privilege. He laid well the best foundations. He was very exacting, and yet it was easier to prepare, and I felt happier in preparing, for his recitation, than for those of any other. There was no let off, no chance of shirking, and the good hard work he demanded brought its reward."

One incident, of some interest, connected with his first position in the academy at Utica, he alluded to in after life. There was doubtless anxiety and solicitude with some of the patrons, whether there was not risk with such a youthful teacher, whether the effort would be successful. One form in which such feeling found expression, was in the prayer of the Presbyterian clergyman of the place, on the first Sunday following, for divine aid and support in behalf of the youthful instructor. Whatever its effect upon the minds of others, it made a profound impression, when told of it, upon the mind of him for whom the prayer was offered. Looking over the course thus begun, and thinking of it, as it went on for the fifty-five or six years following, of the Divine blessing and success connected with it, was ever prayer more abundantly answered?

The work of this position, however, was only temporary, not more than a session and a half, perhaps only one session. In the year 1819 he entered Columbia College, where he seems to have remained during the sessions 1819–20, and 1820–21. During this time, his father, in the year 1820, with his family, consisting now of four children, including William, moved from Utica to Huron county, Ohio. William continued at college until 1821 or 1822, when he rejoined the family in Ohio. During this interval, and it would seem, in his absence, the home circle was broken, by the death of his mother, in Ohio, in 1821. Whether this event had any connection with the close of his college life, does not appear. Very soon after it he joined the rest of the family, and we may easily imagine, under the circumstances, the sadness and tenderness of their meeting.

At Columbia College, as indicative of the doctrinal and ecclesiastical preferences of the young student, we have seen that he was an attendant upon the ministry of the Rev. Dr. Milnor. He would, from him, hear the same Evangelical truths which gave power and unction to the preaching of his uncle, Mr. Roe, in Ireland. He was thus unconsciously systematizing, and confirming in his own mind the doctrinal truths and principles which, in after life, controlled his own thinking and action. Of the ministry of Dr. Milnor he had, in subsequent life, the highest estimate, looking back gratefully to his youthful attendance upon it, especially that portion of it constituting his weekly lectures.

The intellectual portion of this period was, doubtless, faithfully improved. The experience of the previous year in Utica had manifested the power of knowledge, had, doubtless, at the same time, revealed many deficiencies, the importance of more extensive and thorough attainment, of broader and deeper cultivation. Of one of his instructors, Dr. Charles Anthon, he was accustomed to speak in terms of grateful appreciation. The interest increased, if not excited, through his instructions in the Greek language and literature became a permanent one, and to the close of life a source of pleasure. Only a few years before his death, the tutor in the preparatory department of the Seminary was, from sickness, unable to meet his classes, and for several weeks Dr. Sparrow took the class in Greek, greatly to the delight of the students, some of whom spoke of the peculiar interest which his instruction had excited in their studies. In this department, as in that of mathematics, his anxiety and effort was more with reference to the quality than the quantity demanded from the student; on the principle that if the quality were properly insisted upon, in its proper place, the quantity would not be deficient. The allusion to his mathematical training, in the previous chapter, will be remembered; and his effort was to carry out, as far as possible, the same kind of instruction in languages. To use a distinction made by him elsewhere, the student, under this severe yet bracing discipline, found out the difference between merely *understanding* and thoroughly *possessing* the material of his information.

What terminated his college life, whether, indeed, it went beyond the close of the second session, no materials are attainable for ascertaining. In 1822 he rejoined his father's family in Ohio, and after remaining there a few months went with his younger brother, Edward, to Worthington, where Bishop Chase was then living. The bishop, at this time, in addition to his Episcopal duties, had pastoral charge of the church at Worthington, having connection also with a classical school, carried on by his son, Rev. Philander Chase, Jr. Mr. Sparrow became a teacher, for a short time, in this school, and an inmate in the bishop's family. About the same time, also, we find the name of his father, Samuel Sparrow, as a lay delegate in the diocesan convention. One of Mr. Sparrow's pupils, the Rev. Dr. Erastus Burr, of Portsmouth, Ohio, still survives; and his language has already been quoted, as exhibiting his youthful teacher's mode of instruction. His reputation as a teacher and manager of a school, based upon his success at Utica, it seems, had preceded him, and his pupil tells us that he was the

3

same unassuming yet dignified gentleman then, that he was ever afterward. "It was," says he, "a matter of talk with us boys, that so young a man could be capable of teaching and managing in an academy. I was too young to have much knowledge of his religious life. He seemed to me to be a man of uncommon sobriety of mind and manners. I cannot remember him as different, in this respect, at twenty-one, from what he was at thirty or forty. He seemed the same dignified, serious, Christiàn gentleman that he appeared in later life. I think," says he, "that Dr. Sparrow was more cheerful and hopeful in early life than he seemed afterward. Perhaps this" want of cheerfulness latterly "was owing, in good part, to ill health, and the near prospect in which he lived, of being soon called away. Perhaps, also, to a habit of self depreciation, to which he gave way. He always put a low price on himself and his work." An extract from a letter, written many years afterward, to this his old friend and pupil, will not only throw light upon his feelings and expectations at an earlier period, but also upon the spirit in which those feelings and expectations were remembered: "You hint at old times. It struck a chord deep down in my heart. Your letter just came as I was entering upon my seventieth year. Oh how long a life, and how little to show as the result! How long a life, too, for one so feeble and frail! For twenty years after you and I first met I never dreamed it *possible* I should attain such an age. And yet how many of my contemporaries have I seen pass away! I begin to feel quite lonely in the world, in that regard. In Ohio, where I was familiar with and to so many, I am unknowing and unknown. Even here, two of those who were my colleagues in this Institution have been taken, whilst I have been left; and of other acquaintances, multitudes. Thanks be to God, Christ is always with us, the same yesterday, to-day, and forever."

It is to be observed, in passing, as will appear more fully hereafter, that the twenty years thus alluded to, including the life in Ohio, were years of overwork, largely of perplexing work, at times a work of strife; and that feeble health and occasional depression of spirits, were the natural consequences. Whether from change of climate, work, or circumstances, there was a gradual change in health for the better, after his arrival in Virginia, and with this, increased cheerfulness and geniality. The Ohio headaches eventually passed away, and there were fewer recitations lost by slight ailments, during the last than during the first five years of his residence at the Virginia Seminary.

Within the year of his arrival at Worthington, Mr. Sparrow left for Cincinnati College, of which Bishop Chase had been elected President. In this Institution he was a teacher until soon after the bishop, in the autumn of 1823, went to England, to solicit aid for his contemplated theological seminary and college. This latter event seems to have terminated Mr. Sparrow's connection with the institution at Cincinnati, and we find him, not long after, a tutor at Miami University. His attention, meantime, had been drawn to the work of the ministry; the following record is contained in the report of Bishop Chase, in 1824, to the Convention: "There are, at present, two candidates for Holy Orders in this diocese. Mr. William Sparrow,* admitted last year, and Mr. George Roe, admitted at the present Convention. Several others, cheered with the prospects before us, are prepared to enter our seminary when established." This was the seminary in prospect, for which the means of erection had just been secured, in which the interests of one of the candidates thus mentioned would be so largely connected, and for the advancement of which his energies would be so largely devoted. At this same Convention, in Chillicothe, 1824, and in that of the next year, 1825, at Zanesville, Mr. William Sparrow appears as lay delegate, from St. Matthew's Church, Hamilton. No connection of his name with committees, or with action having reference to the proposed seminary, is found in the journal. In the appendix of the journal of 1825, he appears as Secretary of the Diocesan Missionary Society.

During this time, that is, the interval between his departure from Cincinnati and his second residence at Worthington, he was occupied, first as teacher of Latin and Greek at Miami University, and subsequently, at the close of his first six months' residence there, was elected full professor. The argument used with him, by Bishop Chase, for leaving this position and taking the less desirable one at Worthington, at nearly one-third less salary, was that of duty to the Church; that "no young man could then be found in

* One little incident, occurring during the candidateship of Mr. Sparrow, he more than once alluded to afterwards, as illustrative of a certain mode of dealing with doctrinal difficulties. It seems that he was perplexed with portions of the Baptismal Service, and went to a clergyman, a Doctor of Divinity, for relief. "O, Mr. Sparrow," was the reply, "you will get rid of all these difficulties when you get into the Ministry!"

Ohio, in the Episcopal Church, to fill the station, and that the Institution was too poor to call one from the East." To this argument he yielded, at the sacrifice, as we have seen, of income, and also of comfort. It was passing from a well-founded institution, with comparatively light duty, to the drudgery of seven or eight hours of daily teaching, in what was little more than a grammar school. The position was accepted, and the following note of entrance upon its duties, appears in the report of Bishop Chase, in the journal: "Authorized by the Board of Trustees, which met immediately after the Convention of last year, in Zanesville, I appointed Mr. William Sparrow, late Professor in the Miami University, Professor of the languages in this Institution, and also to the duty, for the present, of Professor of mathematics; and Mr. Gideon McMillan a teacher of the grammar school. Two small buildings, very temporary in their nature, were erected, at my own expense, which, together with my own dwelling and farm house, we thought would accommodate all the students that would offer this year. But we have found it otherwise. Our present number is thirty, and had we buildings and other means to enlarge our establishment, that number would be doubled many times."

From the statement thus made, some conception may be obtained of the nature of the undertaking thus entered upon at Worthington. It was, in prospect, essentially and primarily a theological seminary. Incidentally and secondarily to this, and also like it, in prospect, was a college, in which the usual course of classical and scientific studies could be pursued, but still, in some mode, included in the seminary, or subordinate to it. As a beginning, however, to these contemplated results, and as an actual fact, there was a classical school, in which pupils of all kinds, candidates for the ministry included, could receive instruction, and where the latter, as they might increase, and need it, could be aided in their theological studies. The predominant idea, however, with Bishop Chase, and his friends and contributors, as of the diocesan convention, with reference to the new institution, was that of a theological seminary; an institution to provide for a supply, in the opening West, of a properly prepared ministry. With the subsequent difficulties in the working out of this theory we are not here or elsewhere concerned, except so far as they come directly in connection with our object. But it is important, just here, to have a definite view of the nature of the undertaking entered upon; of what seems to have been the peculiar interest, both of Bishop Chase and of Mr. Sparrow, in that undertaking. As the latter himself distinctly stated, at a later period, it was a matter, with him, not of interest, but of pecuniary sacrifice; not of comfort or ease, but of increased and unpleasant labor; not of inclination, but of a sense of duty, to meet an existing want, and to make provision for its removal.

Included within this plan already described, and one in which Mr. Sparrow felt the deepest interest, as appears from portions of his subsequent correspondence, was that of providing a collegiate education for the sons of farmers and settlers, at a moderate rate; one which would enable these classes to avail themselves of the benefits of the Institution. We shall find, at a later date, that he resisted a new and more expensive style of living and doing, as tending to defeat the original design with which the Institution was established. It was but one of many instances of that practical wisdom, in which he was so pre-eminent, to look for and insist upon tangible beneficial results, rather than appearances.

When Mr. Sparrow entered upon his duties at Worthington he was still a candidate for the ministry. His ordination took place the year following, at the Convention in Columbus, Wednesday, June 7th, 1826, when he was ordained Deacon; and on Sunday, the 11th of the same month, four days afterward, at Worthington, he was ordained Presbyter. The record in each case is as follows: "At the time and place, agreeable to Constitution and adjournment, the Convention of the Protestant Episcopal Church, in the Diocese of Ohio, assembled. Morning Service was performed by the Rev. Intrepid Morse, and after an address, the ordination to the Holy Order of Deacons, of Messrs. C. P. Bronson and William Sparrow, who were presented by the Rev. Samuel Johnston, and the administration of the Communion by the bishop, the following clergy took their seats. On Sunday, June 11th, in Worthington, Mr. Gideon McMillan was admitted, by Rev. P. Chase, to the Holy Order of Deacons, and the Rev. William Sparrow, Deacon, to that of Priests; the former presented by the Rev. J. Hall, the latter by the Rev. Intrepid Morse."

Of this Convention, Mr. Sparrow was elected Secretary, as he was, also, a member of the Board of Trustees of the Institution with which he was connected.

His ministerial work, additional to that in the Institution, for this first year, is thus reported: "The Rev. William Sparrow reports, that from the time of his ordination, last Convention, till Christmas, he continued to preach every Sabbath, devoting one-third of that period to Columbus, another to Worthington, and dividing the remainder between Delaware and Berkshire, excepting one Sunday spent, by invitation, in Rushville. Since Christmas he has been prevented, by his official duties in the Literary Institution of the Diocese, and rather infirm health, from officiating more than seven weeks this summer. In Rushville he baptized one child; in Columbus two; in Worthington six; and administered the Communion three times. Of the spiritual condition of the parishes in which he has preached he cannot speak from personal knowledge, not having had time for parochial visitations; but if kindness and liberality to himself be any proof of their receiving the truth in the love thereof, that proof has been abundantly afforded. The people in Berkshire are contemplating to erect a church as soon as possible; and they in Worthington are actually engaged in the pious undertaking. Heaven smile upon the effort, and grant that while thus occupied in building the house of the Lord, they may themselves 'be builded together for a habitation of God, through the Spirit.'"

His more especial work in the Institution, during this and the few years following, will form the material of the next chapter.

CHAPTER III.

FIRST YEARS AT WORTHINGTON AND GAMBIER.

The nature of that work, to some degree, has already been indicated in the description of the character of the Institution. It was, first, to bring an existing grammar-school up to the position of a college; at the same time, during this intermediate stage, and subsequently, to make provision for candidates for the ministry; alike for their preparatory, classical, and scientific, as for their subsequent and more specific theological training. This undertaking, begun at Worthington, was eventually transferred, in 1823, to Gambier, when the founding of Kenyon College was fairly commenced. For the first four years, however, the work in both localities was substantially the same, and it was only as material was prepared in the training of the school, that there could be anything like arrangement of college classes. For the first session or two, therefore, say 1826–1827, and 1827–1828, this preparatory process was going on. Mr. Sparrow, during this period, if not an actual inmate in the family of Bishop Chase, formed part of the large household included in the boarding establishment for the school, conducted by Mrs. Chase. Of the first of those years we have no specific information, beyond the brief statement of Dr. Burr, who was at Worthington when Mr. Sparrow arrived. "I was," says he, "a pupil of his, the whole time of his occupancy of the Seminary," that is of his position at Worthington, both before and after his residence at Cincinnati, "and before his return from Miami University. I was one of a few pupils gathered by Bishop Chase, and taught by him until Mr. Sparrow came. I commenced my study of Latin, Greek and mathematics under Mr. Sparrow; and have always been thankful that I had this privilege. I recollect with great pleasure a kind of Bible class which he established for a Sunday morning exercise. He furnished us with objections, written, of the most popular objectors, to the truths of the Christian Scriptures, and expected us to answer them in the best manner we could, helping us, to some extent, to authorities, but leaving much to our own research. I cannot estimate how much benefit this was to me. He led, also, a class in history. This was aside from regular lessons, and entirely voluntary. At Gambier he established a Bible class for the many artisans and other workmen there employed. I have heard some of them, some old men, speak with enthusiasm of the pleasure and profit of those exercises."

One event of special interest, in its bearing upon the whole tenor of his subsequent life, demands record at this point. This was his marriage to Miss Frances Ingraham, on the 13th of February, 1827; the beginning of that life companionship of confiding affection, of common trial, and sorrow, and joy, which lasted for nearly half a century. Of one who was so much to the subject of our biography, and for his whole subsequent career, it would not be proper to speak in only a passing notice. In the labors and painful responsibilities of his position she proved a true helpmeet, and her life of unselfish devotion to her husband and their children found its desired reward in their comfort and welfare, as in their affection and veneration. It was her effort to take from him the burden of other things—household cares, pecuniary expenditures—so as to enable him, without distraction, to go forward successfully in his own peculiar work and duties. How efficiently and cheerfully this was done was best known in her own peculiar circle—that sacred inner circle where her retiring and diffident nature could only be fully appreciated. "God loveth a cheerful giver," was her remark, as expressive of the spirit in which she herself, and her household, should consecrate a beloved daughter to Christ's work among the heathen. The spirit of this remark ran through her whole life of loving and cheerful exertion. At the same time, while thus taking the burden in these respects, she was his adviser and sympathizing companion in matters of his more peculiar walk, those more purely literary and intellectual. No proper estimate of Dr. Sparrow's life and work, beginning at Worthington and closing in Virginia, can be made without taking into account that of this his companion, whom God gave to be with him during nearly the whole of its performance. "Mrs. Sparrow," to use the language of one who knew her intimately in Ohio, "was a very unselfish woman. By relieving the doctor of every possible care, she enabled him to devote his time to his literary labors, while her judgment was so sound, and her intellect so cultivated, that she was his counsellor on all matters. As a wife and mother, she had few equals; and I feel safe in saying, that not one woman in ten thousand possessed such a variety of intelligence as she did."

Miss Ingraham was closely related to Mrs. Chase, and it was probably in the bishop's family that the acquaintanceship was made, and the subsequent engagement with Mr. Sparrow took place. Only one little incident, in the course of the acquaintanceship, related by the doctor, in Mrs. Sparrow's presence, many years afterward, is at our disposal. "We were traveling," said he, "Mrs. Chase, Miss Ingraham, and myself, in a carriage, to one of the towns in Ohio, when we encountered a stream, which seemed to be too much swollen for fording. Leaving my companions in the carriage, I went over to a man who was working in a field near by, and asked him, 'can I ford?' 'Yes,' said he, looking at me, and I was thinner then, and looked taller than I do now, 'yes, I reckon *you* can!'"

During the year after his marriage, 1828, he was joined in his work by Mr. Preston, and at a later date, by Mr. McElroy. Their communications, which follow, will enable us more fully to understand the circumstances and peculiar duties of Mr. Sparrow at this time. "I went," says Mr. Preston, "to Worthington, early in 1828, to teach mathematics, where I found brothers Sparrow and Wing, and fifty or sixty students, about half of them in college classes. There were no theological students, so Mr. Sparrow taught the classics in the college. He was a very warm friend and supporter of the bishop, and stood very high as a preacher. I found him one of the best friends I have ever had, alike in his capacity as a scholar and adviser, and also in the warmth and cordiality of his friendship. He was one of the most faultless men I ever knew; ever seemed to feel the deepest interest in the success of the bishop and the welfare of the college. I graduated at Yale, and I confidently say that I found no officer there whom I thought his equal, in his capacity to teach and govern young men, and in the good influence he acquired over them."

"On a Sunday morning in September, 1828," says Dr. McElroy, speaking of this period, "I reached Mount Vernon, from Sandusky, and having taken a room at the principal tavern of the pleasant village and nascent city in the woods, I soon learned that Professor Sparrow, from Gambier, would, that afternoon, at three o'clock, officiate and preach in the Court Room. The information was particularly grateful, for I had a letter to him, from the Rector of St. Mary's, Kilkenny, Ireland, the Rev. Peter Roe, his mother's brother, with whom I had become acquainted at my home, a few miles distant from his residence, and through whose instrumentality I had come to cast my lot with Bishop Chase in his great work. I was very anxious to see Professor Sparrow. His uncle, just mentioned, who was a leading man in the Church of Ireland, and very decidedly of the school of Venn and Simeon, had shown me Professor Sparrow's last letter to him, and impressed me with his very exalted views of the capacity and excellence of his nephew. I expected, therefore, to meet with no ordinary man. When I entered the Court Room the service had already commenced. I was somewhat distracted by the novelty of appearances. The room was dingy, the clergyman was in his plain citizen's dress, the congregation, with a few exceptions, wore a very unkempt look; few had prayer-books, and the responses were feebly rendered. But the earnestness of the clergyman soon arrested my attention, and brought me under the influence of his fervor, making me at home amidst the strange scene. From the moment the text was announced, to the close of the sermon, the attention of the audience was breathless and riveted. I had seldom or ever heard, before, such a sermon; so able, so full of truth, so clear, transparent, beautiful and impressive. At this long distance of time the whole scene is vividly before me; the preacher, with his sweet and distinct voice, his modest yet commanding mien, his soft yet brilliant and penetrating eye, his gleaming and expressive features, and his whole countenance, betimes, one brilliant blaze of light. The congregation were enchained, enrapt; and I cannot describe my own delight, surprise, astonishment, and gratitude to the Great Head of the Church, that among the pioneers in the wilderness, for Christ and His work, there was one so profound, eloquent and Evangelical.

"Professor Sparrow, was at this time, I imagine, about twenty-eight years of age; and in my work of instruction in the grammar school, in the college, and to a class in the theological department, I had an early opportunity of judging of his scholarship. His learning was very accurate, and, at his age, I think, unusually extensive. He was a highly respectable general scholar, specially able, even at that early age, in the mental and moral philosophies. He had thoroughly mastered every able book on those subjects that had, at the time, been published; and my impression was that he was fully equal to write, on either, a better book than any on the subject then extant. His health was always feeble, and he seldom preached; but when it was by some means noised abroad that he was to occupy the chapel pulpit on Sunday morning, there was always, from Mount Vernon and the adjacent neighborhood, a large and overcrowded attendance. Even the common people heard him gladly. Gambier, at that time, was a delightful residence for a Churchman who loved Christ in spirit and in truth. The intellectual atmosphere of the college was pervaded by an air of sweet and warm devotion; and the communion of saints was realized there more generally, and to a higher extent, than it is usually enjoyed among us. While I was there personally resident, there were one or two years of extraordinary religious attention and fervor, during which a large number of the students were hopefully born of God, making large accessions to our ministry. Professor Sparrow always tenderly sympathized with all such revived attention to religion. He never doubted that it was a most gracious evidence of God's blessing upon the devout services of our Church, and upon the Word preached from the college pulpit; and he, therefore, always prayed fervently and labored earnestly for a return of such a blessed season. On a certain occasion, one of our college preachers repeated, extemporaneously, in the afternoon, to his forest congregation, the sermon which he had preached from the manuscript at the college chapel in the morning, from the text, 'Search the Scriptures.' He had usually lively attention from these forest people, but upon this occasion they listened with restless indifference. The preacher suddenly stopped and inquired of each person present if he could read, and had a Bible. There were sixty married people present, and fifty-nine reported themselves without Bibles or Testaments. Professor Sparrow took great interest in the organization of a college Bible Society, auxiliary to the American Bible Society, to supply this destitution. In this good work no one was more deeply interested than Bishop Chase. He and Professor Sparrow devoted themselves, with unflagging interest, to the supply; and I often noticed the Professor's eyes suffused with tears, as our college colporteurs reported the touching instances of gratitude and piety which they met in the cabins in the forest. While I was associated with him his relations with his brother-in-law, Bishop Chase, were cordial and intimate. He always held of the American bishops, as Ryle does of the English, that they have too much power; and when Bishop Chase claimed, as Bishop, a veto upon the acts of the college Faculty, it produced painful estrangement. Professor Sparrow was ready to grant to the bishop, for his own life, all that was demanded, if it could be arranged that his successor should not inherit the veto power; but the bishop was honest in his convictions, and the alienation continued.

"Bishop Chase had the valuable faculty of an unerring judgment as to whom he could use with the best effect, in laying the foundations of the Church and promoting her healthful growth; and when he commenced his school and college at Worthington, Mr. Sparrow had to yield to his urgency, and accept the Head Mastership of the whole Institution. He had spent some time," at an earlier period, "at Cincinnati College, during the presidency of Bishop Chase; was a communicant of the Protestant Episcopal Church, and looking forward to the ministry. He was," when appointed to the mastership at Worthington, "Professor of Latin and Greek in Miami University, admired and beloved by all his associates, a great favorite—as I subsequently learned from the President, the late Dr. Bishop—with the students and the inhabitants of the village, and had a very competent salary. Bishop Chase could offer him but little pecuniary inducement, but insisted that it was his duty to the Church that he should resign his Professorship at Miami, and join him. Mr. Sparrow yielded, and never, so far as I know, regretted the financial sacrifice which, in the interests of the Church, he thus made. The community at Worthington was originally an Episcopal colony from Connecticut. They had erected a spacious church, of brick, and an academy, two stories high, of the same material, and endowed it with one hundred and fifty or two hundred acres of good land, conveniently and very favorably situated. The situation was pleasant, but the bishop changed his views of the desirableness of the locality for the college and theological seminary, and, with the advice of the Convention, purchased a large tract of wild lands; and on a bold promontory, jutting into the narrow and picturesque valley of the Kokosing, within five miles of Mount Vernon, the capital of Knox county, decided to build Kenyon College. He erected temporary buildings for his family, teachers, and scholars, and moved all to the new site, three or four months before I joined them. I found the bishop and Professor Sparrow, with their families, occupying a double one-story log cabin, and the appearance of everything as simple and primitive as can well be imagined.

"The bishop," says Dr. Fitch, speaking of a period only a few months later, "confined himself to the financial interests of the college, soliciting funds, clearing grounds, and putting up buildings. Mrs. Chase kept the books, and attended to the college commons, and the personal wants and comforts of the younger students. Dr. Sparrow had been Professor of languages, the Rev. William Preston tutor of mathematics. When I came I took the department of languages, and Dr. Sparrow devoted himself assiduously to the duties of the theological seminary. His great mind was devoted to the intellectual and moral culture of the young men. In this he was so successful that he won the hearts and the admiration of all; not only of the students but of multitudes who visited the college and heard him preach. His preaching was not limited to the college but was extended to Mount Vernon, Newark, Zanesville, and the wide circle around. Till Bishop McIlvaine came, no one could hold the breathless attention of an audience for a whole hour or more, but Dr. Sparrow. By the students he was held in the same estimation at Kenyon as he has been since at Alexandria. All who came under his training believed him the most competent of professors, having a giant intellect, and richly stored mind, and a pure heart. Bishop Chase," while at Gambier, "was absolutely head, but took no part nor seeming interest in the college as an institution of learning, did not know what students were taught, nor definitely who taught them. He presided at commencements. Dr. Sparrow, as senior professor, presided in Faculty meetings, and was to the students what they looked for in the head of the college. They had confidence in him and revered him."

These brief quotations give some idea of the nature of Mr. Sparrow's work, and of the peculiarity of his relations to the seminary and college during the period of his connection with them, under the Episcopate of Bishop Chase. This was from June, 1825, until September, 1831, when the bishop resigned, left the diocese, and transferred his labors to what was then the missionary territory of Illinois. That resignation grew out of certain issues connected with the management and government of the college and seminary. Deferring all notice of these for the present, we would desire to gather up everything of interest connected with the subject of our memoir during this time, and in this his first position of importance. That position, as we have seen, was one of great labor and responsibility; and in self-defence, on one occasion, he mentions the inducements urged to enter upon it in the beginning. The mere labor of teaching, at first, was very heavy, and the sort of material with which the work began was anything but attractive, that of youths to be prepared for the classes of the, as yet prospective, college. As the mere drudgery, in this respect, was lessened by the addition of other teachers, and the college began to assume shape and proportion, so the additional responsibility of administration and government went on to increase. He had to do the actual work, and assume the responsibilities of the head of an Institution, whose nominal head was elsewhere and otherwise employed--making Episcopal visitations, building saw-mills, putting up college buildings, or soliciting funds for these and similar purposes. The peculiarity of this arrangement, in its very nature, risked complication and collision from the beginning; conflict of authority between the actual and the universal governing power. There were other difficulties, also, connected with the position, as mediate between the bishop and the other professors, and the students of the Institution. These difficulties, in the course of time, made their actual appearance; and were, no doubt, eventually, a source of great regret to all the parties concerned. But prior to any such difficulty of a serious character, there was an important work, in which Bishop Chase and Mr. Sparrow cordially and harmoniously co-operated. That work was the foundation of Kenyon college, and the theological seminary. These Institutions, if they have not fulfilled the promise of their incipiency, say from 1825 to 1841, the first sixteen years of their existence, under the administration of their first vice president, certainly had such promise then, to a degree most flattering. The manner and full explanation of failure in the fulfillment of that promise do not lie within the track of our undertaking. We may, however, express the hope in passing, of a brighter and more successful future, upon the efforts and labors of their present guardians. Our object now, is to look at the undertaking as it was, during those earlier years of which we have been speaking, and with which our task is now occupied, when the old bishop, and his youthful colleague, in their respective spheres, wrought together for the great common object which they had before them—the building up of an Institution of theological and secular learning, under a strong religious influence, in the newly opening territory of the West, and for the benefit of Western population. "Our design," says Bishop Chase, in 1829, "is to cherish an Institution of Christian education, at a rate of unexampled cheapness, bringing science, with all its blessings, within the reach of thousands and tens of thousands of persons who, by reason of their straightened circumstances, must forever remain in comparative ignorance. It is to teach the children of the poor to become *school masters*, to instruct our common schools throughout the vast valley of the Mississippi. It is to teach the children of the poor to rise, by their wisdom, and to merit the stations hitherto occupied by the rich; to fill our pulpits, to sit in our Senate chambers, and in our seats of justice, and to secure, in the best possible way, the liberties of our country. This is the object of the institution of Kenyon college. This is the reason of our unremitting exertions to make our plan as extensive and permanent in its operation, as it is pure in its design."

To these common objects, in the establishment of the seminary and college, the energies of these two chief laborers were devoted; and to no small degree, with marked success, during the period with which we are now engaged. At the close of this period, 1831, the school at Worthington, changed, both as to locality and character, had become the college at Gambier. A college Faculty, with classes in college studies, and a grammar school, were organized and in full operation, with provision, at the same time, for theological education to any candidate applying. Bishop Chase, in his report to the Convention, from which the above quotation is made, speaks of "the number of students as ninety, six of whom, at the Commencement ensuing, would receive their degrees of A. B., besides several who, in the intermediate time, have been qualified as teachers, now so much wanted in our common schools."

Of Mr. Sparrow's particular part of this work, brief intimations, in the extracts of Messrs. Preston, Fitch and McElroy, have already been afforded. His work of teaching and government, as thus intimated, was connected with that of preaching, and to these were added, after a few years, the labor of editing a diocesan weekly, "The Gambier Observer." During this same period, we find his name among the members of the Standing Committee, as delegate to the General Convention, and as secretary to the Convention of the diocese. His relations to Bishop Chase, as also, doubtless, his recognized practical wisdom and integrity, made him, in many cases, the bishop's confidential adviser. And, in after life, he would sometimes speak of the peculiar cases which thus came under his observation. Some of his pupils of those later years will, perhaps, remember his account of a theological examination at which he was present, and of the mode in which a candidate was relieved of his difficulty. "Mr.," was the question of the bishop, "by what are we justified; by works or by faith?" The poor man hesitated, but at last ventured to say, "by faith," but, as he looked at the bishop, and looked at me, his heart misgave him, and he corrected himself, and said "by works." "By neither," thundered the bishop, "but by both!" The Doctor's account of the peculiar episode, at this time, of a certain George Montgomery West, who, as we shall see further on, gained the bishop's confidence, and was sent to England to make collections, and came back claiming the right to succeed the bishop as diocesan of Ohio, was no less amusing. "He was," said he, speaking of West, "a man of the most consummate vanity, as to his pulpit performances. 'That passage, sir,' he would say, 'that passage in my sermon, when I delivered it, the whole congregation were melted to tears—they could not help it, sir; they could not help it.'" Not unfrequently, also, in alluding to this period, was he in the habit of speaking of the impression made upon persons by the appearance of Bishop Chase. He, himself, in his first introduction to the bishop, had been greatly impressed by this appearance. "He was not in at the time of my arrival; and as, waiting for him in his study, I turned, hearing his approach, I thought, as my eye fell upon him, he was the most majestic looking man I had ever seen. He filled the whole door!" In connection with this, he mentioned a little incident which took place during one of the bishop's visits to England. It seems that in making collections for the seminary and college, the bishop had received a donation from a noble lady, who, in some manner, had received the impression that Bishop Chase was a person of very diminutive proportions. Not very long after, as it happened to be made convenient to do so, the bishop, in person, made his acknowledgments of the donation. So favorable was the impression, both of presence and manner, and, perhaps, of a fuller presentation of the object, that the donation was very largely increased.

Something has been said, already, in regard to Mr. Sparrow's work, in the way of preaching, during this time, and a report given of his efforts, in this respect, during the first year of his ministry. Similar reports are made to the Conventions of 1829, '30, and '31. These labors, missionary in their character, extended over a large surface, but seem mainly to have been within one or two days' ride of the college. The places specified in the report following include most of those to which he ministered, although others, Berkshire, Chillicothe, and Perry, in earlier reports, are mentioned. This, of 1831, the last made under the administration of Bishop Chase, is of interest. It contains, also, an intimation that these labors, in at least one locality, had not been in vain.

"Rev. William Sparrow reports to the bishop, that since the last Convention, he has preached in Gambier thirteen times, in Mount Vernon eight times, in Newark, nine times, in Delaware six times, in Worthington thrice, in Hanover, Licking county, and Boardman, twice each, in Zanesville and Canfield once each. He has administered the communion once, attended two funerals, and baptized thirteen children.

"The Parish of St. Paul's Church, Mount Vernon, has gone on most vigorously, in the erection of their Church, since last Convention. The building, which is forty-five by sixty-five feet, with a tower ten by eighteen feet, and a basement story, is expected to be ready for consecration by Sunday next. Considering the peculiar situation of this parish, that their number is so small, that they have been so recently organized, and that the members have had the privilege of attending the services of our Church but once a fortnight, and then at a very unseasonable hour of the day, the erection of a church like this is to them a most creditable circumstance, and must be to Episcopalians generally a source of gratification."

It was in meeting these engagements that the long horseback rides were taken, of which he often spoke in after life. He was thus, too, brought in contact with the people, and came to understand their character. One of the greatest charms of intercourse with Dr. Sparrow, was his rare colloquial power, the variety of illustrative incident always at his command, and this very largely drawn from his own experience or observation. Much, doubtless, of this was gathered during these preaching tours in Ohio. One of those rides, for a whole day, was with the author of a work which has had a large circulation, "The Philosophy of the Plan of Salvation." During this ride the argument was stated, and portions of it discussed and criticised. Years after, when objection was taken, in his presence, against a certain part of the argument, "that objection," says he, "I made to it, before the book was written." Whether it was a mere roadside acquaintanceship which elicited this discussion, or one of longer standing, we are unable to say; more probably, however, the latter. The incident is not without its interest, both literary and personal.

Two or three other little incidents of this period, pleasantly related by himself, will not be without their interest. "I was traveling to one of my appointments, when I came, about sunrise, on a cool, frosty morning, to quite a considerable stream, where I found a man waiting for an opportunity of crossing. He begged to be allowed to get up behind on my horse, and I, after some hesitation, consented. On we started. But before we got over, he became alarmed, and in his fright and struggles, we were both pulled off into the water. The poor man was very penitent; but I had to go on in my wet clothing." "It was my lot," said he, on another occasion, "to be present at a wedding, where the parties were my personal friends, and would have preferred for me to perform the ceremony. The laws of Ohio, however, at that time, granted licenses to clergymen only for the counties in which they lived, not, as in Virginia, for the whole State. So a Methodist local preacher had to be sent for. He came; but knowing, as he did, why he was called in, seemed to feel that I ought not to be slighted, and, as he finished the ceremony, he added, turning to me, 'brother Sparrow, if you have any word of exhortation to say, say on!' On another occasion, I was requested by the bridegroom, before the performance of the ceremony, 'to say something that would touch the feelings.'"

"Brother Sparrow," says an old friend and brother in the ministry, speaking of this period, "came to see me, and preach for me. Sunday morning he had a chill, and could not go out. What should I do! So new in the ministry and no preparation. He said, 'take two of my sermons, and preach them; you are entirely justified, under the circumstances.' I did so. After church, a distinguished lawyer said to me, Mr. P., you never preached so good a sermon in your life! which was very true, for it was not mine; but I mention it to show what was then his standing as a preacher."

This portion of Mr. Sparrow's ministry is of interest, as that in which, perhaps, the largest number of his sermons were prepared.

His sermonizing, indeed, continued until the close of life. But it was very largely, in later years, in the way of reconstruction and re-writing of earlier sermons. The bulk of them seem to have been written in Ohio; and a very considerable part during the first four or five years of his ministry. His time for such preparation was on Saturday, after the labor of the week's teaching was finished; and it was not unfrequently that the manuscript, with the ink hardly dry, had to be taken to the place of preaching. There seems to be little doubt that the great body of his sermons, thoroughly elaborated as they are, in manner and matter, were prepared in this way. Under any circumstances prepared, they are, many of them, wonderful productions. Specially wonderful are they, in view of the facts of their actual preparation. They show marvelous capacity of intellectual concentration and continuity. But, with the labor of the week's teaching preceding, and the expenditure of nervous energy of the next day's delivery from the pulpit, there must have been a terrible strain upon his physical constitution. We are not surprised to be told that while he was at Gambier he was in such delicate health that he never came to the door without a red bandana handkerchief on his head; "that his nervous sensibility," at one time, "was so great, that he could not trust himself with the government of the students." "He was," says one of his friends of that period, "so genial, so interesting, so perfect in mind and in heart—all but his poor, suffering body; that was never well." "Not lazy, but constitutionally tired," as he himself, once playfully quoted a friend's description of his physical condition. In some respects, there was an improvement of health after his removal to Virginia, his nervous headaches, from which he had been a great sufferer, almost entirely disappearing. But it is not at all improbable that the delicate health of after life finds a great deal of its explanation in the overwork of the first ten years of his ministry. His power and popularity as a preacher, at this time, are largely attested by his Ohio contemporaries, Drs. Fitch, McElroy, Preston, Allen, and Dyer. The sketch quoted from Dr. McElroy, would very well describe him, after he came to Virginia. The extemporaneous power which he increased greatly after leaving Ohio, gave him advantages not then possessed. But with this exception, an exception rarely exhibited anywhere but in the Seminary chapel and prayer hall, there was but little change. It is remarkable, that a capacity so thoroughly acquired and mastered in the lecture room—that of exact extemporaneous expression—should have been so little used in the pulpit. When thus used, however, it was always to the delight and gratification of his hearers. Weary listeners, especially uncultivated ones, were sometimes to be found under the delivery of his manuscript sermons. But rarely, if ever, was this the case with any class, under his extemporaneous addresses.

During the year 1829 his duties were varied by a visit to the North, probably, from a hint in one of his letters, with reference to the interests of the College and Seminary. This seems to have been a pleasant episode, and successful, to a certain degree, in the attainment of the object had in view. It was not to him wholly satisfactory, and he speaks of a plan of his own, rather than that of the bishop which was actually tried, and the preference of which to his own he regrets. The allusion to this visit is contained in a letter to his beloved friend, and for many years intimate associate and colleague, Dr. Wing. This constitutes the beginning, so far as remains, of a long correspondence, upon which we shall draw for important material in our undertaking. This, written very soon after reaching home, December 8th, 1829, is here inserted. Three others, written to the same correspondent, and within the next six months, are added. They help to throw light upon the period with which we are now occupied, as also they help to exhibit the spirit and work of the writer.

"GAMBIER, December 8th, 1829.

"DEAR BROTHER—

"So, then, you felt just as I did. I don't know when my heart was filled with such mingled feelings of surprise, and joy, and regret, as at the moment I grasped your hand between this and Wooster. The sight of you was cheering to my heart; but then the sight of my eyes was so soon taken from me! I can assure you we spent the remainder of our way home in idle regrets that we had met only to part. We blamed *you*, we blamed *ourselves*, and we blamed every one who had any control over our movements after we had started from New York, when, in truth and reason, perhaps, nobody was to blame. But all the blame I may have heaped upon you did not prevent my heart from yearning over you, and my spirit from going with you, and my thoughts from often, since, turning to the dearest friend I have ever made in Christ. Here let me assure you, dear brother, we have remembered you at the throne of grace, and expect, in time to come, that you will often be in our hearts and tongues, when kneeling before our little family altar. And having said this, may I ask that you will remember us, especially that you will pray the Lord in my behalf, that I may be made equal to the *new* and momentous duties now devolving on me. Yesterday morning, for the first time, I fully realized the awful responsibility of my station; and when I compared the duties to be performed, with my feebleness as a Christian, my deficiencies as a scholar, my inferiority in point of talent, the corruptions of my own heart, the wiles of Satan (a subject I have lately preached upon), and the sophistries of talented but irreligious men to be unraveled, my soul seemed sick for very fear. You, I doubt not, can judge pretty correctly of the state of my mind. You have your own overwhelming cares and anxieties, and like Moses when sent to warn Pharaoh, and to deliver God's people from bondage, you are ready to say, who am I that I should go? Perhaps you are ready to adopt these words of his, especially, "O my Lord, I am not eloquent, neither heretofore *nor since thou hast spoken unto thy servant*, but I am slow of speech and of a slow tongue." But you remember the answer also. God grant you may be enabled to exercise faith upon it; and what I ask for you I would entreat for myself. One thing is certain to my mind, faith is needed more than anything else; not faith in this particular promise merely, but *universal* faith, which will bring the realities of eternity close to our minds, and make us duly feel the preciousness of immortal souls. Of this truth I have been more fully convinced than ever. Oh, let us pray, dearest brother, each for the other, that we may have faith, and every other grace sufficient to our day and duties.

"I doubt not you have many here to remember you. On my arrival, I heard much said about your departure, indicative of no ordinary feeling. My father, amongst the rest, though you did not bid him good bye, joined in the general expression of regret that you had left us. And none, I believe, have such selfish regrets as myself, for amongst other things, I have to lament that I have now no friend at hand to whom I may run when my head or heart is full, and pour out their contents, trifling or otherwise, with confiding frankness. But I must stop this. I did not mean to waste my paper thus. Immediately after my arrival here, I wrote the Bishop, proposing that Mr. Kendrick should fill my place, and that I should employ the year to come in preparation to teach theology, the first half of the time to be spent here, and the second wherever I please; and that while here, I should give religious instruction to the college classes and Grammar school students. He has acceded to the plan, and yesterday I sat myself down to study, grappling mightily with Hebrew grammar. Oh that you were here to hear me recite!

"Mrs. Chase has just had letters from England. Mr. West is coming out in April, with Mr. Bates, the giver of the £100 per annum, for ten years. Until April he preaches in a parish in England. Lord Kenyon also thinks of coming soon. His trip to France, to see, I suppose, how he would like the Catholics *there*, has put him in a traveling mood. Mr. Bates is going to purchase the north section, and, oh sad! to fetch out settlers with him. Our wandering star, S., has just paid us a visit, through the mud, for the purpose of—seeing and being seen. Several students have come on since my arrival, and all things seem to be going on well.

"About my trip I have many things to say, and if you were here, I think I could keep you awake with talk—noise I mean—till twelve o'clock to-night. I labored under many disadvantages while in New York, yet, on the whole, the trip was very pleasant, and, I hope, profitable. Oh, that the bishop had acceded to my first plan—but 'what is said can't be mended.'

"The Bishop has had an interview with Bishop Brownell, at Cincinnati. From Cincinnati he was to visit Piqua, and then take his shortest route to Washington. From Chillicothe to Portsmouth, guess how he traveled—in *a skiff!* a new Episcopal conveyance; but I am mistaken, perhaps. If the apostles were bishops, don't you think Episcopal visitation has often been performed in a similar way? By the way, S. has written and published two verses of bad poetry, on a card, with the author's name attached, to be used at 'week-day service,' in the Episcopal Church, at ———. There is no choice to the worshipers, though the General Convention *has* furnished new hymns; they must use *these* eight lines, if for no other reason, out of compliment to their pastor! 'Oh my country,' said the despairing patriot! Mrs. S. joins me in hearty remembrances.

"Your affectionate friend and brother,

"W. SPARROW.

"P. S.—You see I have written a large sheet full; do you the same, and tell me everything about yourself. You know me too well to expect I would correct my letters. In place of wrong words you must substitute right ones. "W. S."

"GAMBIER, March 12th, 1830.

"DEAR BROTHER—

"As my paper is short, I will hurry 'in medias res.' A fortnight after I received yours, I was induced to take an excursion, and set out in company with D., intending to visit Chillicothe, but owing to frequent dyspeptic headaches, we got no further than Columbus. P., whom I saw in my journey, seems to be getting on well in his parish. He is raising up a few of like mind with himself, who afford him some comfort, and refresh his spirit when dejected at the character and disposition of the *old stock*. If he were not a diligent man and good preacher, and if, withal, gospel truth had not a power, which, even while repelling to a certain distance the formal and irreligious, at the same time attracts them, and, like the centripetal force in astronomy, keeps them from going off in a tangent, he could not maintain himself in his position. They hate his Low-Churchmanship, though they respect the man.

"But I must be more brief, or I cannot give you the items of news. Brannan and Samuel Chase have undertaken to teach a *High School* at Newark. The people in Mount Vernon are about building a church. I am to preach upon the *duty* of so doing next Sunday week; and then the subscription is to be circulated. They are also going to build in Columbus. Lyster is to leave Cleveland in May, and visit Ireland, to return, however, to Ohio. Potter, Caswell, and Tillotson Bronson propose to go as missionaries to the heathen, if any society will send them. By their request, I have been corresponding with B. B. Smith, Dr. Milnor and the Bishop, on the subject. Dr. Milnor is going to England, to attend the British and Foreign Bible Society. Since I wrote the last sentence, a Mr. M., a Scotch clergyman, has arrived, with letters to the Bishop. He has been a Presbyterian minister, and wants to enter the Church. I will, perhaps, have more to say of him in the next letter. Just now I have to take him over the college, to introduce him.

"I lately preached a sermon on Luke ix, 49, 50, a copy of which the students requested for publication; of course, I declined. From the text* you may judge of the subject, and, from my principles,

* "But John answered and said, Master, we saw one casting out devils in thy name; and we forbade him, because he followeth not with us. And Jesus said unto him, forbid him not; for he that is not against us is for us."

you may guess how I handled it. I go to Chillicothe on the 25th, to attend an association. If I should feel like traveling, on my return, I may visit Boardman. But whether so or no, I shall not cease to remember and pray for my dear brother who lives there.

"W. SPARROW."

"GAMBIER, May 14th, 1830.

"REV. AND VERY DEAR BROTHER—

"To be sure, my last letter was written on half a sheet, but if I recollect aright, the characters were small and the lines close; you had *multum in parvo.* However, I believe I should have sent another after it very soon, had I not set out, about that time, to attend Bausman's association. Brother Preston and I were the only clergymen there; we had quite an interesting time, and some good was done, I trust. Since that time I have attended another, in Delaware, more interesting yet. The weather being much better, the congregations were very large. We had service on Friday evening; on Saturday, at ten o'clock, a meeting of the communicants in the church; at two o'clock in the afternoon, an anniversary meeting of the Sunday school. Service again in the evening. Sunday morning a meeting of the communicants at Mr. L.'s house, and then the regular forenoon and afternoon services, with communion and baptisms. On Monday evening we had service in Berkshire, and on Tuesday, Preston, Hein, Dennison, and myself, returned to Gambier.

"The Bishop, you know, has returned, and is up to his eyes in business, as usual. His health, however, is still poor; I am afraid will long continue so. He cannot rest at night. He brought along with him a physician, Dr. Farnum, who is also to act as Professor of Chemistry. He is highly recommended, and is, no doubt, very able in the branches he professes. We have now 120 students, and they are coming in every day. Two of the houses in Gambier have been remodeled and finished for their accommodation, and the carpenters and plasterers are about to take hold of a third. A large addition has also been made to the store, and the frame next your old abode has been finished off for a hotel; for you must know we have a daily mail stage running to and from Mount Vernon, *William Sparrow, Stage Proprietor!* Our periodical will, probably, be issued in two weeks. Could you not send us something local to insert in the first number; something, I mean, connected with your parish. Anything relating to this diocese will be peculiarly acceptable at all times. Sanford has got us a good many subscribers. You must increase your list by and by.

"I was pleased and thankful you had a refreshing time at Easter. If you could muster courage, I should think it would be a most judicious plan to call the communicants together, as was done at Delaware, the morning of communion day, and pray and sing with them, and give them an exhortation. It would, undoubtedly, be most edifying to them, and refreshing to yourself.

"I have lately had a letter from E. He is in Natchez, earning ninety dollars per month, as clerk to a court. How great must be the risk of life, where he could promptly procure such a lucrative situation. He says that in the sickly months clerks are often found dead in the stores in the morning, having been seized so violently during the night as not to be able to call for help. This surely must be the plague.

"I would be glad to know how your folks like the 'Gambier Observer,' and much more, how you like it yourself. Any suggestion you may make upon the subject of our paper will be most thankfully received and maturely weighed. But will you not send us some communications. Oh, do send us short articles, or anything you please, especially local matter. I know your excuses; but they will not be taken.

"Poor Keene, who had been sick so long, died Saturday. My belief is, he is gone to heaven. The Providence will, I trust, be blessed to some of the students. Mr. Taylor, on Sunday evening, at their prayer meeting, spoke with great effect upon the subject. At our last communion two of them joined the church, and two others were put upon probation till another season. We have now about one hundred and thirty in good health, and, I think, doing well. The bishop is very feeble. He was not able to fulfill the appointments made in the 'Observer,' owing to another injury received in his leg from a fall. Though he is going about continually, it is still in a bad state.

"The corner-stone of a church was laid in Mount Vernon last Thursday week. They have raised twenty-five hundred dollars, and have contracted with Mr. A. to build it for $3650, he having a lien upon the unsold pews for the surplus of the latter over the former sum. Bronson laid the corner-stone. None of us attended. S. is getting up very fast. He preached a sermon on Episcopacy the other day, which, however, Judge P. thought exceptionable. But it is no more than I long ago anticipated. In the present state of the Church, with all the influence on one side, it requires both a spiritual mind and a sound judgment to persevere in a steady course. Mrs. S. is not very well. She is now sitting at my elbow, and desires, in all sincerity of Christian friendship, to be remembered to you. I must be excused for this scrawl. I write in haste, in languor and in fever.

"Your brother in Christ,

"W. SPARROW."

Within the next few months, there came up two disturbing issues, which, for a time, were productive, to Professor Sparrow, of great anxiety and trial, ending in a controversy with the bishop, of a most painful character. The first of these was the West difficulty. This individual has already been alluded to, in his exhibitions of inordinate vanity. It would seem, however, that the bishop regarded him more favorably than did his youthful colleague; and was eventually induced, upon his representations of his influence and associations on the other side of the Atlantic, to send him, as a special agent, to obtain contributions for the College and Seminary. What the transaction definitively meant to the bishop, was never very clear, as the subsequent career of his protégé rendered it a subject upon which he was indisposed to enlarge. But so it was. When West started, it was with the episcopal blessing, received in the last interview, and with the laying on of hands. The bishop, like Mr. Wesley, when he parted from Dr. Coke, in all probability, only meant to commend his agent in his work, and in the most solemn manner possible, to the Divine blessing. But to West, as to Coke, it meant, or it was construed to mean, a great deal more—even the assured succession to the episcopate of Ohio. That made him the King of the Romans; and in due time, if he lived long enough, he would be Emperor! Big with these hopes, West took his departure, and, for some time after his arrival in England, most cheering accounts were received of his success. At one time there came a report of £50,000 secured for the two Institutions, from English noblemen contributors, who were coming over to visit Gambier. Some of these, after a while, were found to need modification; and when he actually returned, it was ascertained that the proceeds of his three years' mission, so far from reaching fifty, did not exceed one thousand pounds. This, however, in his own estimation, did not invalidate his semi-consecration to the episcopate, and this, his expectation, in due time, he took occasion to make known. The allusion, in one of the letters which we give, to the scene following, of which the writer seems to have been a witness, is irresistibly amusing; although the consequences to the writer, as to the Institution, for some time following, were anything but amusing—were exceedingly serious and annoying. West, after remaining for a few days, posted back to New York and Philadelphia, and so succeeded, in the former place, in exciting suspicion and prejudice against the bishop and his management of the Institutions, that some of his best friends became alienated, and the fund of the Milnor professorship, that of Professor Sparrow, was temporarily endangered. The noble promptness of Dr. Milnor in this emergency, and the gradual revelation of the real character of West to those whom he had led astray, eventually obviated these difficulties. But they were very serious, as they were experienced, and the whole episode is a most singular one. West afterward attempted to start a church of his own, perhaps, to enable him to exercise the episcopal gifts which had once seemed to be within his reach; and one of the curiosities of liturgical literature is a Prayer-book prepared for its use.

The other issues of this period, complicated, for a while, with this of West, was that of the prerogatives of the bishop, in the government of the College. Postponing the fuller notice of the difficulties in this, and their results, we give the two letters more particularly connected with the case of West. The characteristics of the writer, as familiar to his friends in later years, will be immediately recognized.

"GAMBIER, Aug. 3d, 1830.

"DEAR BROTHER—

"According to your request I write you promptly, and having thus complied with yours, I hope you will comply with mine, which, following the advice of Horace, "in medias res," I make without further preface. When I was far away last fall, and it was out of my power to say yea or nay, the bishop, I find, appointed you and me to preach the Convention sermon. When I saw it I was startled and grieved. Having been appointed not very long before, and living here on the spot, and the appointment coming from my own connection, I had and have insuperable objections against discharging the duty. I write to let you know it will devolve upon you alone, so without any demurring, set yourself patiently down to do your *duty*. Give us a close, spiritual sermon, and let us see that 'the Kingdom of God consisteth not in meats and drinks, but in righteousness, and peace, and joy in the Holy Ghost.'

"And now for other subjects. As to Mr. West's £50,000 it is all a farce. The bishop says he has not collected, during his three years' mission, exclusive of the £500 given as a legacy, from Lord Kenyon's daughter, and a few other sums given while he was in England, but not through his agency, over, I think it is, $4000!! How, then, is this report to be accounted for? Why, thus. He professes to have, from a gentleman in England, a promise of a legacy to that amount, but he says the laws of Great Britain preclude his giving the individual's name to those concerned, as by so doing they would forfeit the legacy. All this and much more you can see in a printed pamphlet which he published and brought with him, scattering some copies on the way. But this is not all—tell it not in Gath, publish it not in the streets of Askelon—he modestly asked the bishop if he might hope to succeed him in the episcopate, and whether he would have his influence to that effect! You may judge of the scene; my pen fails me. '*Steterunt comæ, vox faucibus haesit.*' The conclusion is, Mr. West is gone, most probably, never to return. He stayed here but three or four days, but in that short time, gave pretty good evidence that he is a Universalist in doctrine, and anything but a Christian in practice. His vanity, self-conceit and ambition, have disgusted every one of any discernment. The poor bishop often thinks, no doubt, of the Apostolic precept, 'lay hands suddenly on no man.'

"The 'Observer' will be out to-morrow. Oh, do write for it—articles I mean. As to the signatures I cannot give you any certain guide. They are changed, and most probably will be, every week. When they become fixed I will let you know.

"The bishop and Mr. McElroy went to Berkshire, and had Confirmation there last Saturday, and in Delaware on Sunday, and were back by one o'clock yesterday, Monday. Was not that an episcopal visit?

"S. has recently been thrown from his horse as he was riding him, without saddle or bridle, round an orchard, for amusement, and had his shoulder injured. Mrs. Sparrow desires, as always, to be affectionately remembered to you.

"I am, dear brother, yours most sincerely,

"WM. SPARROW.

"P. S.—If you cannot read this, why, I cannot help it. I cannot read it over and correct it."

"GAMBIER, Nov. 26th, 1830.

"REV. AND DEAR BROTHER—

"I supposed you would have written me long ago, without waiting for a letter to answer; for, however busy you may be, I am confident you have not half as much to do as I have. Never was I so burdened as I now am. Between my new duties in the way of instruction, and the care of the paper, I have not a moment left me to breathe. I had, yesterday, to tell C., the Irish gentleman you saw here last Convention, that I really had no time to converse with any one, except when walking out or at my meals. The Irish require broad hints. Since my return home the bishop has brought up the old question between him and the teachers; and notwithstanding the vote of the trustees, insisted on having an absolute negative upon all our proceedings. We have conceded it, till the trustees meet and settle it finally, it being understood as a *concession*. For the part I have taken in the business, he is so offended, that he avoids all communication with me, except by letter, through the post-office! I never was more cut down by the way he acted, and the way I have been treated, especially as I have no direct interest in the question. I have the satisfaction, however, of knowing that I have endeavored, in this business, to do my duty. The bishop sets off, in January, for the Mississippi country, a begging.

"In consequence of my trip North I did not go to the Chillicothe Association, and Bausman is anything but pleased. What made it worse, Preston, who set out to go, was driven back by the rain and rheumatism. So Stem formed the Association.

"Our number of students is 150. There has been some considerable seriousness among them, and a few have come out decidedly pious.

"Mr. ———, remaining on the hill for some time longer, died lately, from mania-a-potu. I was called to preach the funeral sermon, and never discharged a more unpleasant duty. B. has purchased the 'Western Aurora,' and is about commencing the printing and bookbinding business. My theological students are C., who, you know, is married, also S. and H. The last has been told that we all think he has mistaken his calling. He took it very kindly and said he had long suspected it himself; that his preference and tastes were decidedly for the law, and that if he could get rid of the sense of duty which has been urging him on he would give up the idea altogether! Curious man. He now studies merely for the sake of information. His classes are engaged in Hebrew and Homer. Do you prosecute your Hebrew? Have you commenced a system of study? Let me know. Dear brother, I can't help thinking God has a good portion in store for you somewhere. In this I am joined by my dear wife, who often talks with me about you, and who desires to be remembered to you. Write me soon.

"Your affectionate brother in Christ, W. SPARROW."

In one of these letters the nature of the difficulty with the Bishop is foreshadowed. This went on for some time, and it was finally terminated by the resignation of the Bishop of the Episcopate of Ohio, and his departure to Illinois. The peculiarity of this movement gave rise to a great many new questions, to much exciting discussion; and in the General Convention following, which had to act with reference to the resignation of the Bishop, and the consecration of his successor, serious doubts were entertained as to the consequences of failure in making a satisfactory adjustment. In the judgment of one who was largely in the Bishop's confidence at the time, and not implicated with any of the controversies preceding, this determination was very sudden, and in its final result, a surprise, perhaps, to all. It had been preceded by difficulties in the conduct and government of the Institutions, of a varied character. Some of these originated with the pupils, in the form of complaints as to the fare, and their mode of treatment. Others, from the professors and faculty, in the form of complaints against indefinite episcopal interference, to the weakening of all proper collegiate discipline and authority. And, others, again, from the Bishop, in the form of complaints against plots and schemes that were going on, as he believed, to deprive him of his proper influence. It would be worse than useless, at this time, to be reviving the particulars of this extinct controversy. One feature in it, however, is of permanent interest, and this is one which may be discussed without personal bearing in any direction, that is, the question which was practically at issue when Bishop Chase resigned the episcopate of Ohio, which was again raised under the episcopate of Bishop McIlvaine, and which, in some form or other, will be apt to present itself in every Diocesan Institution. That question is, what are the relations of the episcopate to any such Institution? Are they academical or episcopal, created and regulated by academical law, or inherent in the episcopal office? In Ohio, the charter of the Institutions really seems to have given the power to the bishop, of indefinite interference. And, so far, Bishop Chase had the law on his side. But it was found to be a power which, in its exercise, proved intolerable. Of course, upon the theory that it is inherent, back of law and above law, its exercise became still more intolerable. Underneath all the other difficulties and troubles at Gambier, at this time, this, doubtless, was the fundamental one, and it amounted to this: shall the Faculty have the whole duty and responsibility of their position, but divide its powers? Shall they so divide those powers that what duty and responsibility indicate may immediately be reversed by some one else? Mr. Sparrow, as the head of the Faculty, had to bear the brunt of this conflict. His original position was that of mediator, especially in the matter of difficulties of the boarding and management. His relations to the Bishop in one direction, and those to the pupils and other members of the Faculty, in another, placed him in this position; and, for some time, he was enabled to relieve many of the troubles and sources of complaint. "At one time," says Dr. Preston, "Professor W., the most amiable of men, and myself, and the students, were on the point of rebellion, when Mr. Sparrow calmed the troubled waters, by saying we must bear all things, for the sake of the Bishop and the noble Institution." It was impossible, however, under these and similar circumstances, to avoid having an opinion of his own in regard to the matters of issue. And the Bishop reached the conclusion that he was working against him, an impression which it was found impossible to remove. "I once told him," says Dr. Preston, "that Mr. Sparrow was one of his best friends, and that his influence was all for good." "I know," the Bishop answered, "you cannot tell me anything about William Sparrow. Why sir, he has such an influence that he could at any time raise a mob of students, who would drive the old Bishop off the hill, only they know they could not get their dinner the next day." From Mr. Sparrow's own subsequently published statements, and references to rebutting facts and circumstances, as from the testimony of common friends, who were in communication with both parties, it is manifest that the Bishop was entirely mistaken in this impression; that he was opposed not personally, but as a matter of principle, and as one of policy, for the object of common interest to both—the benefit of the college. But, with this impression, right or wrong, it was impossible for matters to go on comfortably. And when the distinct issue was made, of a claim, by the Bishop, of a veto upon the action of the Faculty, the matter came to a head, in the Diocesan Convention. Here effort was made to settle, by compromise, some of the difficulties, but without success; and the final result was the Bishop's resignation. During the progress of these troubles, or rather, as they were drawing to a close, Mr. Sparrow, in personal vindication, made a reply to certain publications by the Bishop, of an earlier date. Without going into the particulars, we give the close, as indicative of the spirit in which it was prepared. "What I have written has been written in self-defence, and with a view to the interests of the Diocese. If the call had not been imperative, I never should have put pen to paper. Unwillingly did I commence this answer; at every step I have proceeded with reluctance, and now rejoice that the task is ended. It is the first controversy I have ever been engaged in; it is my sincere prayer that it may be the last." It is a grateful fact that this prayer was answered. With the exception of a brief reply to a most unwarrantable attack made on the character of his teaching, and admitted into the diocesan paper (during the last ten years of his life), he was spared from this form of trial, the work of controversy.*

During this contest we have two letters to the same correspondent, Professor Wing, which enable us to see some of the difficulties and perplexities with which the writer was struggling. The West affair, it will be seen, very much complicated these others; and at one time, it seemed as if they would compel him to seek a field of labor, and support for his family elsewhere. The trial of spirit involved, under these experiences, may well be imagined. The system of non-intercourse, except through the post office, odd and whimsical

* Rev. Mr. Syle mentions as a fact, characteristic of its author, that this pamphlet, after being prepared and published, was very partially distributed, that the larger portion of the edition was held back, and eventually used as waste paper.

as it appears, must have been very embarrassing. But the letters best tell their own story.

"GAMBIER, January 20th, 1831.

"REV. AND DEAR BROTHER—

"I have been confined to the house the last few days, by a violent influenza, the same disease which has carried off one of our students, and, therefore, have a little time to spare. If you should not be able to understand the improvement which I make of this leisure, in the following epistle, you need not wonder. My head is so full of disease that there is no room for ideas. I go to work, however. A., about whom you inquire, is settled at Dayton, they say with good prospects of success. The people in Piqua want to have F. He spent the vacation with them, and *took* mightily. He tells comical stories of M.; as for instance, that after his dismission from the charge of the parish, Mr. J. having been invited to preach and administer the communion, when the time came to ascend the pulpit, M., being present, he stepped up and did the duty himself, leaving J. and his manuscript to enjoy their leisure. You may well suppose that J., and also the congregation, were somewhat confounded.

"You have heard of the revival in brother Bausman's Church. K. and S. have made a profession of religion. Is not this marvelous? It is, it must be the Lord's doing. Brother B. and brother S. were to be in Columbus last Sunday, I presume, holding an Association. When I returned, last fall, from Boardman, I found it impossible to go, according to promise, to Chillicothe; and as brother P. also was prevented, no Association was held. Great censure has fallen upon me for this. I spent Christmas in Newark; I hope not in vain. B. has made dreadful havoc there. It is not too much to say that, although he may not have intended it, he has, in effect, been as a wolf in sheep's clothing, and he has sucked the life-blood of almost the whole flock. However, it is but right to say, that he seems to have been, at first, eminently successful.

"Affairs with me are in rather a critical situation. I know not but I shall be in a parish very soon. T., and the rest of them, in New York, have been all set on fire by West, and, as would seem, cannot easily be quenched. The Bishop is about to publish a series of pamphlets, giving a full history of the college, and an explanation of all difficulties. This I have indirectly. I have had no intercourse with him for several months. The last time we met in private, when I begged him to agree to differ, in order that we might live in peace and Christian love: his reply was "peace, but no intimacy, no intimacy." He has kept his word. He has been lately circulating on the hill a certificate contradicting West's slanders. When it was presented to me, I declined, on the ground of my connection with him. This has led him to demand explanations, till I am wearied with the system of diplomacy, which, considering that we are but a few rods apart, is perfectly ridiculous. I ought to tell you, I had other reasons besides the one mentioned above, one of which I gave Mr. P. when he handed me the paper, and these additional reasons I gave to the Bishop when required, but in a manner which he could not well find fault with. They related to the things asserted in the certificate; some of them I could not, in conscience, subscribe.

"Now, the difficulties which this certificate is intended to remove threaten the overthrow of the Milnor Professorship fund, and if that goes, I go with it. After the stand I have been constrained to take, the Bishop would not likely give me employment in the college. While I was in Boardman, P. went on, for goods, to New York, and T. then told him no more money should be paid till everything was cleared up, and they have been as good as his word. I have received nothing, and so far as I see, am likely to be left in the lurch long enough yet, if not altogether. I begin, *inter nos*, to think of Zanesville and Newark. There is field enough there to cultivate, though it would require more muscular arms than mine to do the work thoroughly.

"You may well suppose, from the above incoherent statement, that I am not very comfortably situated, and but ill at ease. It is even so. The Bishop is dealing strangely with me, and in a manner that I neither deserve nor expected. May Heaven direct me, and at all events, keep me from everything unworthy of a Christian. I find myself exposed continually to the same errors into which I conceive him falling. Even since I commenced this, something most trying to patience, has occurred. The worst of it is, for me, that it breaks down my spirits. I have no courage to go about my work. Mrs. S. desires to be kindly remembered to you. She wishes you were President of Kenyon College, and thinks I would then have peace.

"Pray for your affectionate brother, in Christ our Lord.

"WILLIAM SPARROW."

"GAMBIER, April 13th, 1831.

"DEAR BROTHER—

"I returned a few days ago, from an excursion to Worthington and Columbus, and found your letter waiting for me. I should like right well to purchase the 'Observer;' but if I can get bread for my children these times, it is as much as I can do. I never was so situated as I am at present. Unless I leave the college I can do nothing but live in hope till the trustees meet, when something may be done for me. To leave the college would, undoubtedly, humanly speaking, benefit my health, and, I have reason to believe, not circumscribe my means of living. But who comes into my place? This is the question. And where could I do as much good as here? this is another. The last session, I have reason to believe, I have been more blessed in my endeavors than ever before. And though the infirmities of my flesh were peculiarly painful at the time, I look back upon them now with thankfulness, and shall commence the next session with some little encouragement. This, together with the advice of a few friends, is what keeps me here now. My wife is sick of war, and so am I, most heartily. But if I go, there is good reason to fear that a man of different views may be brought into my place; and then all the glorious prospects with which we have comforted ourselves will be at once blasted; the Institution, as it regards religion, losing all its life and feeling.

"I went down to Columbus, to try and find out what was best to be done. Everything that occurred there was consoling; as also what I learned from Chillicothe, from brother P., who went down there for me, I tarrying in his parishes. A proposition was made to me in Columbus, which would have relieved me if acceded to; to go as a missionary through the State, till Convention. I thought strongly of the scheme for a time, but have pretty much given it up. One motive for wishing to go, though subordinate, of course, was that I might pay you a visit. I should long to have a long tete-a-tete with you; and while I derived benefit from your counsel, and comfort, and sympathy, in return astonish you not a little. I could assure you, and so could P., that strange things have befallen me. I desire to have your prayers, that I may do my duty, and leave events to God. Oh, what would I not give to be able to say, as some have said, 'the Lord reigneth, let the earth rejoice'! It is something, however, to know that the feeling which it expresses is proper and desirable. This conviction has, of late, been forced upon my mind with more than common power. I wish to leave all things in God's hands, believing that He does all things well; but oh, my unbelief! I catch myself continuously laying plans and supposing cases which are, in fact, an impeachment of Divine Providence. Pray for me, I repeat, dear brother, that I may have the path of duty made plain before me, and may have grace and strength to walk therein. If I leave the college I shall seek some large town. I know I could do nothing in the country. Most probably I shall leave the State, the causes which drive me from the college naturally driving me further. But I must stop. Mrs. S. desires her Christian regards and hearty wishes for you, that you may find a bird for your cage. As ever,

"Your brother in Christ, WILLIAM SPARROW."

In a fragment of a diary, the two following brief records have their interest in connection with this subject. The first is December 20th, soon after the bishop's resignation; the second, May 6th, of the year following.

"Since my last record strange and unexpected events have taken place, in which I have taken part. Though I have great reason to be humbled before God, for the feelings which, at different times, have arisen in my heart, and been allowed to harbor there, yet I can say, thank God, 'I have wronged no man' in this thing. I pray God overrule all for the good of His Church."

"I have just sent forth my reply. In writing it I have been unhappy. Thank God, it has afforded me no delight to engage in this controversy; but the reverse. Lord, overrule all for good, and in all my trials be my stronghold and consolation. Help me to withdraw myself from dependence upon any creature, even my dearest friends. In this thing Thou knowest I have erred. Help me, also, to banish from my heart everything of hatred and malice. O Lord, give me the spirit of Him who prayed for His enemies, even upon the cross. Grant that I may abide in love, avoiding every expression and thought which may spring from bad feeling, or have a tendency to excite it. Help me to conduct myself as becomes thy servant, in my intercourse with the world, especially my associates. Lord, pity my weakness, and give me wisdom and strength."

The alienation of this controversy, to Mr. Sparrow, was, in many respects, exceedingly painful, deepened, in view of the disruption it involved of old friendship and long confidential intimacy. It did not, however, prove irreconcilable. The old bishop, some years after, whether recognizing his mistake, or waiving the question altogether, of the merits of the controversy, determined to have a reconciliation. And his movement met with a prompt and cordial response. The manner of that movement was characteristic. Passing along the street, in Cincinnati, with one or two in company, he recognized his old friend on the other side. Calling him over to him, they met as Christian brethren, and the controversy and its painful alienation were terminated. Whether any of their unpleasantness remained with one of the parties, we have no means of knowing. But with the other there seems to have been a complete obliteration. The writer of this memoir was not aware of the particulars of this controversy, or that reconciliation had been effected, until after the death of Dr. Sparrow. That there had been some conflict, he knew; but supposing that the subject would be a painful one, no inquiries, nor direct allusions were ever made, which would have elicited an explanation. At the same time he is persuaded that Dr. Sparrow supposed that he knew all about it. But the point of special interest just here is, the mode in which he always spoke of Bishop Chase, the kindly and pleasant feelings with which he recurred to their early intimacy and labors together, and the large allowance with which he spoke of the bishop's mistakes and errors, as he regarded them, both of doctrine and administration. No one could have known, from these allusions, or would have suspected, that the parties had ever been in conflict. The fact is one that is honorable to both. We can now gratefully think of them in that higher sphere of effort and of service for a common Master to which they have been exalted, where all misapprehension and alienation are impossible—are at an end forever.

We close this chapter with extracts from the fragment of diary already mentioned. Some of these come earlier than the two already given. They all occur within the last two years of the period included by this chapter.

"January 1st, 1830. Another year is commenced. God grant that it may end well! Oh how much have I to do, and how little ability of body, mind, or spirit. Lord, be thou my helper! Make my purposes pure and single, that I may be enabled to go on with good courage, hoping for thy favor and assistance.

"2d. Indulged in too much levity. Lord, help me to set a watch over my lips and thoughts.

"4th. Purpose not to talk, hereafter, so much and frequently about the parties in our Church. Many lose their religion in arguing and disputing about it.

"12th. Buried Mrs. F. to-day. May the prayer of my heart be granted and fulfilled in my case: 'Teach me to number my days, that I may apply my heart unto wisdom.'

"15th. Read Watson's answer to Paine. No Christian disputant should content himself with standing upon the defensive and answering impertinent cavils; he should draw forth the powers of his religion, and make a direct attack, not only upon the false theory of Deists, but also upon the evil heart of unbelief which has led them astray.

"March 2d. Finished Miller, on the Sonship of Christ. Plain, conclusive, conciliating.

"May 10th. My visit to Delaware has been instructive and agreeable. Meetings of professors on Sabbath morning, before communion, must be very beneficial. They make professors feel themselves a 'separate and peculiar people;' unite them more closely in the bonds of love; and afford the pastor opportunity for esoteric instruction and strong appeals founded on the nature of a religious profession.

"September 12th. Convention is over. I hope I have learned something.

29th. My trip to Boardman has been pleasant and profitable in some degree. But, oh, how unlike a true missionary do I feel, in these little excursions.

"October 2d. It is my purpose, from this day forward, to read nothing but what relates directly to a knowledge of the Bible and ecclesiastical history, except what may be necessary in editing the 'Observer,' or in preparing to preach.

"April 30th, 1831. Since my last record was made, some few pleasant things, and very many unpleasant things have taken place. May all work together for good. My recent trips to Delaware and Columbus ought to make me wise; but how am I to learn! One thing is very clear, that if do not take care, life will have slipped away while I am preparing to live. Lord help me to do what *thou* hast given me to do, and to lay all else aside. Pity my weakness, and help me in the discharge of my duty."

The forty-two years of successful labors that followed this petition—of influence as teacher, as preacher, and as a personal example—constitute its abundant answer. It was under peculiar pressure that it was offered; and we are now enabled to recognize in what manner it was heard and answered.

With the departure of Bishop Chase, and the changes therein involved, new questions, of course, as to the seminary and college, and diocese, naturally came up for decision; new modifications as to duty and responsibility were rendered necessary. With these we shall be occupied in the next chapter.

CHAPTER IV.

LAST YEARS IN OHIO.

The next eight or nine years were spent, in many respects, very much as those of the four or five preceding. The Institutions, both literary and theological, after their recovery from the temporary shock of the difficulties to which allusion has already been made, were increased as to their numbers, and enjoyed a good degree of prosperity. The College gave promise of meeting the expectation of its founders, and the Seminary had its distinct organization, with a respectable number of candidates preparing for the work of the ministry. The position of Mr. Sparrow was that of Vice-President, as under Bishop Chase, but as then, and from the nature of the case, with almost the full responsibility of the head of the Institutions. This relation was sustained alike to the college students, and to those in the theological seminary. At the same time, he gave instructions, as Milnor Professor, in the seminary, first in ecclesiastical history, subsequently in systematic divinity, also as Professor of moral philosophy in the college. In addition to these duties, were his editorial labors of conducting the diocesan paper, the "Gambier Observer." From reports made to Convention, we find that his practice of preaching in the neighboring parishes, was kept up, taking his part also in the chapel of the Institution. As delegate to the General Convention, he was absent from these duties once or twice for brief intervals. Similar absences are occasionally alluded to, as rendered necessary, on the score of physical debility. But with such brief exceptions, the time seems to have been spent in the routine of duty thus indicated. These duties were brought to a close by his resignation, in the close of the year 1840, and his removal to Virginia. This change constitutes a definite point of transition; and we, therefore, with the interval which it includes, occupy the present chapter—his connection with Kenyon College and the Theological Seminary at Gambier, under the episcopate of Bishop McIlvaine.

During the interval between the departure of Bishop Chase, and the coming in of his successor, from September, 1831, until October, 1832, the government and conduct of the seminary and college were, of course, with the Trustees and the Faculty. Soon after the consecration of Bishop McIlvaine, he paid them a visit, staying a few days, this being followed by a longer one, just before the close of the session. "I arrived," says he, in his first report to the Convention, "in Gambier, November 28th, where I remained till December 4th, inspecting the condition of the college. During this time, I held a private meeting of such students as were professors of religion, for the purpose of prayer and exhortation; preached thrice in the college chapel, and ordained Rev. C. W. Fitch, Professor of Greek, to the order of the priesthood. On Sunday night, preached in St. Paul's Church, Mount Vernon, a new Church recently finished at the cost of no little sacrifice and effort, and in which a congregation is fast rising to such a measure of strength as, it is hoped, will enable them before long to support their minister. On the following Tuesday, left Gambier, accompanied by the Rev. Mr. Sparrow and the Rev. Mr. McElroy, and rode to Berkshire. Next day arrived at Delaware, and preached at night at St. Peter's Church. I was particularly pleased with the appearance of the congregations last named. I have seldom seen a more animated and unanimous participation in public worship, or a more earnest attention to the preaching of the word."

This extract has been given, not only for its bearing upon the condition of the college, but as incidentally containing an exhibition of some of the results of Mr. Sparrow's preaching during the seven or eight years preceding. Two of the congregations mentioned, those of Mount Vernon and Delaware, and one in the next paragraph, that of Worthington, one of these with a rector, and the others almost ready to receive and support one, had been the object of his exertions. To those exertions, under God, were they indebted for much of their subsequent prosperity.

"I arrived at Gambier," is another and later statement in this same report of the Bishop, "on Wednesday, June 24th, and took up my residence here, having experienced the kind care of Divine Providence over my family and self during a very fatiguing and trying journey. My time since my arrival here has been principally devoted to such changes in the organization and discipline of the college as would naturally be required, after its having been so long without a head, and almost without hope. I am happy to state, that I found its internal condition more healthy and efficient than could reasonably be expected from the trying circumstances it had had to contend with, and that its present prospects are such as to inspire the most confident belief that, with the Divine blessing, it will soon exert a most salutary influence on the cause of sound learning and enlightened piety in the West."

Prior, however, to this, there had been events of deep interest, both to the college and the diocese, transpiring elsewhere. The resignation of Bishop Chase took the diocese and the whole Church by surprise. A minority of the Convention made another effort to bring about a settlement of the difficulties, so as to have the resignation withdrawn. And when this failed, it was doubtful whether the coming General Convention, that of 1832, would consent to the severance of the bishop and his diocese in this way, and sanction the action of the Convention in its choice of a successor. Mr. Sparrow was one of the delegates to the General Convention, and in view of his relations to the diocese and college, felt the deepest interest in the success of their application. During the last few months of his life he was led to allude to this Convention, and to speak of the anxiety and uncertainty of the earlier part of it, especially of their obligations to Dr. Wainwright, for his unanticipated but powerful advocacy of their cause, and of the gratification with which the result was hailed, both as settling diocesan difficulties and giving an impulse to the Evangelical interest, with which Dr. McIlvaine was so thoroughly identified. In this connection, Dr. Sparrow mentioned an incident, not without its interest, taking place during this Convention. On the day of the consecration of Bishop McIlvaine, there was quite a number of the clergy — perhaps all, for all were not many — of those sympathizing with the bishop elect, to dine at Dr. Milnor's. After dinner, at the suggestion of some one present, the company became an impromptu prayer meeting, for a Divine blessing upon the events transpiring. While upon their knees, some one was heard to enter, and, when the prayer was ended, it was found that the unanticipated visitor was the distinguished advocate just mentioned, who had rendered such essential aid in the discussion of the Convention. His presence just then seems to have been purely accidental, but it was none the less a grateful surprise to those who composed the meeting.

During the same year, 1832, we find in the diary one or two entries of importance; one of these immediately precedes his departure from home to the Convention. The others are upon points then of peculiar interest.

"June 29th. Every day brings news of the nearer approach of the dread cholera. Lord, enable me to leave myself, and wife, and little ones, in thy hands, to spare or not to spare, as in thine infinite wisdom and mercy shall seem best. If any of us perish, Lord, into thy hands I would commend our spirits. If we are spared, let us hereafter be wholly thine, and let this brief note stand as a memento of my obligations and my duty."*

"August 2. To-day I went to church, as a hearer and an invalid. Through the mercy of God, raised up from a fever, after an absence of four weeks, I have gone once again to the house of prayer. I might now be mouldering in the grave, yet it is not so, and why? O, my God, I would adore Thy goodness.

"By my sickness I trust I have learned some things which I really needed to be taught. One is, that during sickness is not the time to attend to religion, for the purpose of acquiring a knowledge of the truth; but rather a season for falling back upon and using religion acquired before. In many forms of disease the mind is unfitted to do anything but feed upon the promises. God grant that when my last sickness comes I may be enabled and entitled to appropriate them all, so that, casting myself entirely on the Divine mercy, I may fall asleep in Jesus.

"A second particular I have learned is, that attention to health is, especially in my present condition, a bounden duty. O, may I be enabled to perform it.

"A third, that I ought to provide, in some way, for my family,

* The present generation, even those who are old enough to know of the apprehensions connected with the progress of this disease in its subsequent visitations, can have no conception of the feelings, on this side of the Atlantic, with which, in 1832, its first approach was contemplated. Its progress from Asia to Europe, from interior Europe to the sea coast, until it reached France and England, had been watched with curiosity, not altogether unmixed with anxiety. As its fearful ravages in those last named countries went on, the question was anxiously asked, will it cross the Atlantic? And when the answer came, with its appearance in Quebec and Montreal, and soon after in New York, communities and individuals were made to feel, as they had never felt before, that there was but a step between them and death, that they must set their houses in order, as the destroyer at any moment might be at hand. The above extract was written while the pestilence was prevailing in the two chief cities of Canada, and only two or three days before it made its appearance in the city of New York. This was the most painfully exciting period of popular apprehension. Reaction, after a time, came on, and men passed through the storm with more composure than they had contemplated it in the distance.

so that, should I be taken off before them, they may not be entirely destitute.

"A fourth, that as a preacher, I have not been sufficiently practical. I have indulged too much in metaphysical refinement.

"A fifth—the root of the preceding—that I have not lived near enough to God. A feeble Christian makes a feeble preacher, and I am both. O God, help me to study Thy Word devotionally, to think of Thee and Thy ways and works, devotionally, that I may grow in grace as well as in knowledge, so that my knowledge may be sanctified, and made instrumental to holy ends. Lord, Thou knowest my weakness, and that I feel it in part. For Jesus' sake pity and lend me the assistance of Thy Almighty Spirit.

"Sunday, Sept. 23d. In two days I purpose setting out for New York; a long, and, at the present time, a somewhat dangerous journey. O, my God, I desire to commit myself, my wife and little ones, to Thy covenant care. Let Thy hand be extended over me, and Thy grace accompany me. O, Thou merciful God, whatever betide me, let me have the consolations of Thy grace. If it be Thy righteous will restore me to my family, and let me find them in health and happiness. If my days are drawing to a close, and my next parting is destined to be the last parting with them, Thou, O God of Abraham, Isaac, and Jacob, watch over, protect, sustain, and save them. Be the friend of my widow, and of my orphan children. They are in Thy hand. For Christ's sake preserve them and me, that, however our external lot may be cast, we may all rejoice, 'no wanderers lost, a family in heaven.' Amen.

"Dec. 20. Restored to my family and home, Lord what do I not owe Thee. Thy dealings toward me have been faithfulness, and truth, and much mercy. Thou hast saved me from sickness and harm; Thou hast crowned mine errand with success; Thou hast relieved me of long-standing trials, and hast brought me back to my wife and children with improved prospect of happiness. Lord teach me gratitude for Thy great and unnumbered mercies."

One or two more extracts will bring us to the close of the session 1832–3, contemporaneous with the date of the last extract given from Bishop McIlvaine's report to the Convention. They are, as those already given, of special interest, as showing the peculiar spirit with which Mr. Sparrow entered upon the responsibilities of his work under the new state of things. That spirit was one of profound gratitude for Divine mercies and blessings of the past, deep humility in view of imperfection, and failure of improvement; earnest resolve to be more in earnest and faithful for the future. The first of these extracts is with the opening of the year.

"January 1st, 1833. Another year has begun. Through God's mercy I am still in the land of the living. May I feel that the lengthening of my days is the enlarging of my obligations; and may this year be the most profitable to myself, my family, and the Church of God, of any that I have lived.

"January 3d. As I seem to make little progress in my studies, I shall, hereafter, note frequently what I read, that I may see the exact amount. I will also try and observe the following division of time and labor, except when preparation is to be made for the pulpit. The forenoon shall be devoted to Hebrew, French, Greek, and Latin; the afternoon to Theology; and the evening to miscellaneous reading. I shall, also, when I begin a work, endeavor to persevere to the end without engaging in any other, if it is worthy of a complete perusal, and when the task is done, record my feelings and thoughts in relation to it."

The next extract, some two or three weeks afterward, contains a fulfillment of one of the resolutions here recorded. But with a brief notation of two other books read at a later date, this is the only criticism of the nature indicated.

"January 22d. Since my last record I have read, 'Stuart on Romans,' but I must read it again. The writer judges according to evidence, and without regard to system, as much as any that I have ever met. I pray God to give me the same spirit of independence of mind; and while I allow no human authority to interfere with my conscience, may I feel my own great liability to err, and ever submit myself to the Divine authority.

"July 8. To-morrow, I again leave my dear family, in pursuit of health, and again would I commend them to the care of my covenant God. Lord, Thou knowest all my wants and weaknesses, and all my desires. I leave them before Thy mercy seat. Should I be taken from my family soon, and never permitted to see them again this side of eternity, Father of mercies, let me, for Jesus' sake, see them—see them in eternity, and before Thy throne, praising redeeming love. Should it be Thy good and indulgent pleasure that I be restored to my wife and babes, O Lord, make me thankful. Whatever be Thy will, take them and Thy servant under Thy care, for time and for eternity. Thou knowest, O Lord, I look only to Thee for real happiness, through Jesus Christ our Lord.

"February, 1833. Read the introduction to 'Edwards on the Will.' The writer, Isaac Taylor, is a man of great power, capable of close analysis and extensive generalization, and endowed, withal, with an imagination capable of illustrating every subject, possessed of a range of knowledge, affording his imagination abundance of material. He is so splendid one fears to trust him. This work goes to confirm an old opinion, that man is to grow in wisdom by receding from positions occupied rather than in taking new ones. I have long thought that man regards himself as capable of much more than he is, and that as he advances in true knowledge he will relinquish many things which he now holds as undoubted truths. Man is yet very ignorant of the real length of his plummet. The work of this writer clears the way for the free interpretation of the Scriptures, by showing the small practical importance of those principles according to which men have hitherto endeavored to square them. The author, therefore, will undoubtedly aid to prepare men's minds for the more unbiased study of the sacred volume. He is evidently a candid man, and cannot fail to influence the candid.

"'Tittman, on Greek Prepositions in Composition,' is an interesting article. It is a pity he has not given us more examples.

"'Life of Robert Hall,' contains many valuable hints, but does not afford much spiritual improvement. The reader is too much taken up with the gigantic intellect. 'Foster's View' contains some important suggestions.

"'Clement's Epistle to the Corinthians.' Is it prejudice that blinds me, that I cannot see the much talked-of excellence of the apostolical fathers? This Epistle is considered the best of their production; deutero-canonical, if not absolutely canonical in the opinion of some; yet what excellence has it, beyond simplicity? The writer was a simple and sincere Christian; having said this you say all. He displays no depth, either of intellect or piety, and he betrays a credulous spirit, and a want of soundness in Scripture interpretation. The story of the phœnix of Arabia is told as undoubted truth, and he finds bishops and deacons in Isaiah, lx, 17. It is its date which gives this work its value. In section 47, it is intimated that the dissensions at Corinth, in the Apostle Paul's time, originated mainly from one man. The fifty-fourth chapter was adduced in our General Convention of 1832, in New York, on the subject of episcopal resignations."

During the year in which this last extract was written, he took advantage of the leisure afforded by the vacation, to visit the Atlantic coast, being, for a time, in New York, but for a longer interval in New England. The main object of this trip, as appears from his correspondence, was the benefit to his health from the change and relaxation. He speaks, indeed, of the question of his remaining in Ohio being doubtful, on this score, as to its answer. And he felicitates himself with the assurance that, if he should find it impossible to retain his position, facilities have been opened for a change. The tour, in its effect upon his health, seems to have rendered the raising of such questions unnecessary. Certain changes in the college were taking place, as it appears, during his absence; some also preceding his departure. By one of these he was relieved from connection with the college, and the responsibility therein involved. This, however, was only for a short time; as we find him, later, in his old position, which he retained until just before his removal to Virginia. A couple of letters to his friend and colleague, Professor Wing, written during this Northern tour, may, at this point, be properly inserted.

NEW BEDFORD, MASS., September 3d, 1833.

"REV. AND DEAR BROTHER:—

"I have not received any letter from you yet, except that which contained Mr. Otey's testimonials, but I have just learned by a letter of Mrs. S.'s that you have written two others, and I, therefore, sit down to answer them, by way of anticipation. If they were directed to Saratoga, they probably arrived after I left it, and will be found forwarded to New York by the time I reach that city.

"My last letter to Mrs. S. was from Boston. The day after I wrote, I returned with C. to Andover, and tarried till Saturday, hearing Dr. Woods lecture once in the meantime. On Saturday I went over to Lowell, and spent the Sunday with brother Edson, preaching for him, sorely against my will, but he was so hospitable and kind, and withal, so urgent, that I held forth morning and afternoon. The only ill effect was the usual languor on Monday, and an increase of the pain in my side. In the evening of Sunday, a black brother preached in the same pulpit, wearing a pair of silver spectacles, and a gown and bands like myself; indeed, the likeness was very complete, except the color of the skin, which, you know, is nothing, and the circumstance that, whereas, I have a superabundance of nose, he has a remarkable deficiency. His name is L., from Baltimore. He was begging for means to pay off a debt hanging over his church, and an African school which he teaches. He got between forty and fifty dollars. His sermon was sound, being strictly scriptural, that is to say, composed almost entirely of Scripture. On Monday I returned to Boston, and saw S.; also attended a monthly missionary meeting which he conducted, assisted by Rev. Mr. M., from Virginia. Yesterday morning (Tuesday) I started for this place. Tell Mrs. S. I have, as yet, seen only Mrs. P. and family. They have sent the chaise for Mrs. P., and before I finish, she may be here. I expect to leave this on Friday, for New York, whence I shall write again.

"I suppose you would like to hear something of my travels, and the persons and incidents I met with, but my budget is so large, that I have not a tithe of the room, in this small sheet, to display my wares on. When we meet, and I get into a story-telling vein, I shall be able to do something towards gratifying your Yankee curiosity. The time I spent in Andover, was not unprofitably spent, only it was too short. In some things I was disappointed, and in some pleased. C. is preparing himself to go as a *translator*, to some foreign missionary station, thinking that his deafness, which appears to have increased, will stand in his way in other respects.

"The day after to-morrow, there is to be a convocation of the clergy of Massachusetts in Lowell. You have seen the notice of it in the 'Churchman.' The Bishop is to attend it, and it is to be continued monthly, from parish to parish, where the ministers and people are in favor of it. Fourteen or fifteen parishes have given in their adhesion to the plan, but several of the High-Church clergy and congregations stand aloof. Brother Wing, this Socinianism is a fearful thing. Where it does not corrupt the theory, it eats out the spirit of religion, and worse than all the rest, many who hold it in theory and practice, continue in our congregations. It is said that * * * Church contains a great many *Unitarians*. Does not this show that it is not the doctrine of the Trinity which gives offence; that this is only the pretext—that they are offended mainly by the everlasting cry of the Evangelical orthodox, 'ye must be born again.' But I must break off this strain till we meet, if God should so far bless me. You are now in the midst of Convention business; O how my heart aches that I cannot be with you; but I have done right. My only chance of a permanent abode in Ohio is in a complete restoration this fall. So fully am I persuaded of this, that much as I long to see home again, I would tarry till November, if means permitted. Should it please God that my health be not restored in Ohio, this journey has, at least, prepared the way for my settlement elsewhere. I suppose that you are putting up the front of my house and building the new one. As to this new building, my views have been often expressed before. I do not wish it to fall below the average of things in Gambier, as I perceive that the standard in such matters is likely to be much raised. You are, by this time, in my study. I pray you may find it a place of pleasanter toil and better health, than I have found it.

I trust in God you are all still preserved from the cholera. My mind grows easier on this head than it was. At first it made me wretched, and with difficulty could I restrain myself from an immediate return; but the silence of the papers, and Mrs. S.'s letter to Mrs. P., have set me at rest, comparatively. My kind regards to all friends.

"Your friend and brother, W. SPARROW."

"NEW YORK, September 10, 1833.

"DEAR BROTHER—

"I arrived here this morning, in the steamboat from Newport, and found two letters from you awaiting my arrival, and three from Mrs. S. Of course I have been much comforted on the whole, though they contain some things not very pleasant. I hope that you are not suffering from the fever. I understand it has appeared among you, and a stranger told me in the boat, yesterday, that the fall fevers had begun, in the western part of New York, with considerable severity.

"I wish I could have received your letters, to answer them in time, before the meeting of Convention. If you wished for my mind I also would wish to give it, on one or two points. Cheapness has always appeared a most important feature in the college; and no slang of 'cheap shop,' or anything else of the kind, can make me waver on the point. Why increase the expenses, and put the benefits of a collegiate education beyond the reach of our farmers' sons? Surely, it is desirable that the thing be as common as possible. Are we about to increase our style of living, so as to make an increase of revenue necessary! Then the glory is departed from us. Once the pride of life gets in, Kenyon becomes like any other Institution. Its irreligious tendency may be abated and checked, for a time, by the faithful ministrations of our President. But when we substitute style for simplicity, we introduce a system of means hostile to the influences of the pulpit and the prayer meeting, and subversive of their effect. I have been in New England, and am more and more enamored of simplicity and godly sincerity, and hope that we have men among us ready to exert themselves in pursuing the course recommended by Bishop Meade. I presume you will remember it. But the die is now cast, and I can only hope all has been directed and overruled by infinite wisdom.

"Tell Mrs. S. that I shall write to-morrow or next day, and will say something about my health. It would not be wise to touch that subject now, as I slept, or rather lay, on a narrow settee, with a sheet and a blanket, and no pillow, and in the midst of two hundred people, in the steamboat, last night. You may judge I do not feel over well. Remember me affectionately to all friends, and believe me, under every change, in truth and feeling,

"Your brother in Christ, W. Sparrow.

Records in the fragment of diary already quoted from, at long intervals, continue during the next three years. It will be seen, as they proceed, that the writer does not spare himself, or take self-complacent views, either of his intellectual or spiritual progress. At times, indeed, there is a tone of despondency that is almost morbid; not improbably connected with the infirm condition of health to which he was liable. They afford illustrations of a statement, already quoted from one of his friends, when he speaks of a "habit of self-depreciation, to which he gave way," and of his "always putting too low a price upon himself and his work."

"January 28, 1834. It is surely time to make some note. How much has God blessed me since the period of my last record! I have been brought home again in safety and in improved health, and up to this time have not, materially, failed; but have been able to accomplish more than usual. Lord, I thank Thee for Thy mercy, and pray Thee to give me strength to prove my gratitude by a life of more engagedness in Thy service.

"I have entered upon the important duty of teaching a theological class. How unequal am I to the task! How imperfect my furniture of talent, strength, knowledge, heart, and spirit. Lord, pity and guide, enlighten and direct me, for the sake of Christianity, and of those committed to my care, and of those who shall be committed to their care. My station is at the fountain of truth, whence flow streams watering many a distant region. May these waters never be adulterated, or in any way polluted by my means."

This last record will be better understood, in the light of an extract from the bishop's report, for this year, to the Convention. It will thus be seen to have reference, not so much to instruction given by Mr. Sparrow, as theological professor, as to the more systematic arrangement of the classes, in a regular course, with a theological faculty. "During the last year," says this report, "a regular course of study under three professors, one of church government, and the duties of the pastoral office; a second, of systematic theology and church history; and a third, of the literature and interpretation of the sacred Scriptures, has been diligently pursued; and a number of students, quite as great as could be expected in the first year of the arrangement of a theological course, have been in attendance." The number of candidates for the ministry, in the diocese, mentioned in the same report, is fifteen. In view of these encouraging prospects of increased influence and usefulness, the above record seems to have been made.

"March 12. Another birthday has come, but there is little to cheer me in the recurrence. My whole life seems to be nothing more than a blot. Nothing has been done for Christ, or His Church, or the world. Time has been frittered away in idle purposes. I have planned badly and executed worse; and the great source of the evil is not my want of health, however great, or anything of an external nature, but my want of a right spirit. I read President Edwards' Resolves last night; how exactly are my deficiencies in many cases there pointed out! Lord pardon and help me. I would cast out of my mind extraneous things, and do my proper work. I would cease to be troubled about many things, attending to the one thing needful. I would repress that impatience which, because it cannot effect everything, does nothing. When my next birthday comes, if it ever comes to me, may I be enabled to look back and see that the year has accomplished something. The past has accomplished nothing. May God pardon and help, for Jesus' sake."

"May 25, Sunday. Have I any reason to believe that I am advancing in the Divine life, if indeed I live in the Lord? When I look back upon seasons past, when I was young in the profession of religion, I seem like one in the infirmities and pains of age looking back upon the vigor and happiness of youth. My religion is seated too much in my head, too little in my heart. Now and again I attain very imperfect glimpses of what my affections and habit of mind ought to be, but that is all. The causes and occasions of my present coldness are various. One is, I study religion too much as a science, and having to do this in poor health, with little vigor of mind and body, it leaves me little time or ability for private religious exercises. It is very doubtful if I am justified in retaining my present position, in which professional duties so much interfere with private and personal. The world engrosses too much of my heart. I see its vanity. I have no schemes reaching far into the future. I am sometimes most deeply impressed with the truth that few and evil are the days of my life, and yet I seem to be engrossed with little matters more than is justifiable. And, again, I have got my mind into a trifling unsteady state, so that I read and think to little effect. I have a greedy and abortive kind of curiosity, which must be corrected for the sake of my mind and heart. It is utterly opposed to that calm and self-collected spirit which religion produces. I am, also, infirm of purpose, so that if, in the midst of this mental dissipation, I see and resolve upon the right, it is of no avail; my memory loses sight of the vow, or my will is too weak to put it in execution. Moreover, I allow unimportant matters to take the place of duty. I have no ardor in the discharge of my proper duties. My ardor is spent on trifles, and duty is a task. The main reason seems to be that duty is *continuous*, and requires perseverance, whereas I am desultory and unsteady. I drift a little into this and that, get here half an idea, and there a quarter, without reflection and the exercise of judgment, and this is easy and pleasant, requiring no effort and indulging sloth. Impatience seems, in a measure, at the bottom of all this, but be that as it may, I am in a wretched state. I 'am ever learning and never issuing to a knowledge of the truth.' Seeking to know all things, I really know nothing. I have dealt most unwisely and unfaithfully with the endowments, both of body and of mind, which I have received at God's hand, and with the advantages which, in His providence, I have enjoyed. God, in mercy, forgive me."

Over against these bitter things, thus written against himself, there follows, a few months afterward, but manifestly with no extenuating object, a record of work and duty which shows that his time, with their performance, must have been very largely filled; that, perhaps, what he really needed was not additional and more faithful work, but relaxation—physical and mental. This would have enabled him to work with more satisfaction, and to have looked back upon the results with less self-accusation.

"October 4. If I am ever going to improve, the time seems fairly to have arrived. I am comfortably settled in my dwelling, I have a competence, and my daily duty is plainly set before me. God grant me both will and ability to discharge my stewardship."

"My duties are those of the Vice Presidency, those of the Milnor professorship, those of the editorship, and those of the moral philosophy professorship. But am I to do nothing in preaching the gospel—the gospel of my Lord and Saviour? What is my excuse? How can I answer for this neglect? I excuse myself, I hope God excuses me, on the ground of my feeble health, and small talents, and my doing something in that way through the lecture room and the Gambier "Observer." But I must take heed that my heart does not grow cold, in this long absence from the pulpit."

The closing sentences of this extract have their natural connection with a fact occurring within the few months preceding that of Mr. Sparrow's resignation from his charge of the congregation of Mount Vernon. This charge had been in connection with his duties in the college and seminary, but, in view of his delicate health, had been discontinued.

"1835. Christmas Day. Another of these memorial days has rolled around, and what has it brought? The recollections of the year are full of interest; but so many are those of regret and self-reproach, that I can take little pleasure in them. I have received many lessons, and have learned little from them. Still I trust I have learned something. God forbid that it should be altogether in vain that I have been warned so often by my own sickness, and above all, that death should be allowed to take away my precious little Maria. Lord, give me entire resignation to Thy will, by convincing me more and more of Thy wisdom and mercy, and enabling me to realize that my deceased babe will live again, nay, does already live, through atoning blood, in the fullness of joy at Thy right hand; and that I also, and my dear partner, and my other precious children, may, after being scattered from their earthly home, be gathered again into a heavenly one. O Lord our God, prepare our hearts for this, and give us assurance of it. Then shall every tear be dried, and every sigh be hushed."

The event thus alluded to, the first death in his household, that of a darling child, is thus described by an intimate friend, who aided in nursing during its sickness. The whole account, with the statements following, bring out the peculiar features of Mrs. Sparrow's character already mentioned.

"I think the little child was about two years old. The night she died I wished to sit up with Mrs. Sparrow. But when she saw, what I did not, that the child was dying, she insisted so strongly that I should leave her, that I did; and when she came to my room, and I asked her how she was, 'she is at rest,' was the answer. They were both, the Doctor and Mrs. Sparrow, very submissive to the trial, which to them was very great."

"1836. Sunday, January 24. Life will have soon slipped through my hands, if I do not take heed; and what account shall I have to give? 'I have resolved, and re-resolved, and die the same.' This will be my whole history. Lord pity, and forgive, and help.

"I have recently read Todd's 'Student' and Edwards' 'Resolves,' but how little am I of what the one describes or the other practiced? Wherein am I wrong? 1. I do not value and improve time. 2. What I do I do slothfully, and not with all my might. 3. I indulge in reverie to no profit. 4. I dissipate my attention upon a variety of objects. 5. I want perseverance in everything. 6. I am governed by impulse, not regulated by a sense of duty. 7. I do not control my appetite so as will best promote sana mens in sano corpore. 8. I am not sufficiently studious of the original Scriptures. 9. I do not pray without ceasing. 10. I procrastinate irksome duties. 11. I am perplexed and cast down from not laying more steady hold of divine comforts. 12. I do not exercise sufficiently for health. 13. I do not devote time enough to my children.

"But, alas, there is no end to the catalogue. Can I not amend, even for the week to come, or must I give up in despair? Great things must not be attempted; what little things can I do? With God's grace I will do this much.

"1. Read twelve verses of Hebrew and review, per diem.

"2. Ride to town and back at noon.

"3. Deny myself at table. My allowance such as will leave me with an appetite.

"4. I will get my recitations ready, and write all my letters."

Here the record closes, probably, from its abruptness, by an interruption, and there is no resumption.

Returning from these extracts, we are reminded of a particular work, to which allusion, more than once, has already been made, that of the editorship of the diocesan paper, the Gambier 'Observer.' This paper was started in 1830, under the editorship of Professor Sparrow, and we find his name connected with it in 1834, in company with that of Professor Wing. In 1831, 2 and 3, Professor Wing appears as sole editor. It appears that during this whole time Professor Sparrow was working, to the extent of his power, and even after the last of these dates, for the benefit of this publication. The object in view was not so much controversy as that of giving religious information, of advancing practical Christianity. "The articles," says the opening prospectus, "which may be expected to occupy the columns of this work, will be of the following kind: — Essays on the doctrines and duties of religion; sketches from ecclesiastical history; religious biography; correspondence of persons eminent for their piety and talents; missionary intelligence; proceedings of Bible, tract, Sunday-school, and temperance societies, and other moral and benevolent institutions; notices and reviews of new publications; poetry, selected and original; summaries of news, literary, political, and miscellaneous." "It is with unfeigned diffidence," says the opening editorial, "the present publication is commenced. Entire inexperience in matters of this kind, and the heavy pressure of other duties, prior in obligation, and paramount in importance, make us feel a real distrust of our competency to the undertaking. Why, then, it may be asked, is the thing attempted? In answering the question we can truly say it is not with the expectation of personal emolument; for should any profits arise from the work, they are pledged to charitable purposes. Nothing can accrue to us but trouble and expense. We engage in this enterprise only with the hope of promoting, in some small degree, with the blessing of the Spirit, the reign of righteousness and peace in the earth. The 'set time to favor Zion' seems to have arrived; and we, amid the crowd of His more efficient servants, would offer ourselves as feeble but willing instruments in accomplishing God's purposes of mercy."

It is, of course, impossible, now, to identify contributions, except those which are strictly editorial. The reference of these latter were generally to passing events and circumstances, and do not, therefore, afford material for extracts bearing upon our specific object. Professor Sparrow's connection with the paper is mainly of interest, as showing one of the many modes in which, at this time, he made his influence felt, and exerted it for good. It also constitutes an indication as to the amount and variety of labor which was actually going on while he was charging himself, in his diary, with failure and inefficiency. These self-condemning accusations show that his standard of excellence was high. But the estimate of those with whom and upon whom he was working shows that this work was not only effective and abundant, but fully appreciated. Such was the case with his students, whether those in the seminary or under his government in the college. It was no less the case with his associates and fellow-professors. The real wonder is that in such condition of health he should have been able to attend to so great a variety of duty and employment.

In the year 1838 he received the honorary degree of Doctor of Divinity. His estimate of such titles is given in a very amusing letter, written some thirty years later, to a pupil who had just been doctored. In one written only a year or two after his reception of the title, it will be seen that he was rather embarrassed by it than otherwise. This last has its interest with regard to other points, especially as throwing light upon his feelings and state of mind as a seeker of truth and knowledge, and as endeavoring, by his sermons, to bring it to bear upon the minds of others. How strangely different his own opinion and that of his hearers as to the merits of his sermons. One who did not know him thoroughly, would hardly know how to take such language. Undoubtedly it came from the very bottom of his heart.

"GAMBIER, March 28th, 1838.

"REV. AND DEAR BROTHER:—

"Your letter arrived last night, and was most welcome to both myself and Mrs. Sparrow. I had long been wishing to hear from you, as I am endeavoring to prove by a prompt reply.

"I am much pleased to hear that you are so delightfully situated.

The scenery with which you are surrounded must be to you an exhaustless source of pleasure, and the society of the family in which you live a continual feast. There seems nothing in your account of yourself which does not cheer your old friend, except your despondency in regard to your performances and prospects of usefulness. With such feelings I can deeply sympathize, for though, on account of my Irish peculiarities, of an external kind, it might seem as if I had a very comfortable opinion of myself and my doings, my poor fagged and jaded heart knows full well all about the depression which you now experience. If I am ever sanguine or self-confident, it is only for a moment; the settled habit of my mind is a deep consciousness of my own deficiencies of mind and heart—a consciousness that they are infinitely greater than any creature besides myself is at all aware of, and which is, therefore, accompanied with a feeling that I am *acting a part*, appearing, if not professing to be, what in truth I am not. My office as professor and vice president, let me say, and my very title of D.D., ever since I have borne them, have in this way been sources of permanent annoyance. The fable of the ass in the lion's skin is constantly before me. What you say about your possessing 'little talent,' or even 'no talent,' my own feelings tell me I ought to take and apply to myself. Think not, therefore, that 'some strange thing hath happened unto you;' your lot, in this respect, is not peculiar.

"But you will tell me, though 'misery loves company,' it is not much alleviated thereby. Well, then, let us both remember that the Creator and Ruler of the world has ordained that there should be men of all grades of talent in the world and in the Church, and that he can find work for all, and that all may be happy in his employment. This is my chief consolation; let it be yours also. One of the evils incident to a desire for improvement, is that it may be carried so far as to issue in discontentedness with what we are and have, in an intellectual way. This is a 'sore evil,' as Solomon would say. It is a great source of present uneasiness, and, as I know by sad experience, it actually stands in the way of future progress. Let us, then, try to unite contented acquiescence in the measure of attainment allowed us now, with a steady and moderate effort after excellence in the time to come.

"A word on sermonizing. Who that ever wrote a sermon did not loathe it after it was finished? Certainly I never did. To say nothing of more substantial reasons, does it not naturally arise from the close scrutiny with which, in the course of composition, we have examined all its parts? A plate of polished steel, seen through a microscope, is like a plowed field: how much more will this apply, even in the case of a good sermon! Another point. I have spoken above of an incidental evil; another such evil connected with such study as you have gone through, however imperfect, is a straining after new ideas. An uneducated man is content with common-places; an educated man looks for something more; and let him look; but let him also remember that nineteen-twentieths of the staple instruction of a people, from the pulpit, must be 'things old.' The body is fed and nourished by substantially the same food throughout the year, and it is only now and then that a new dish is or can be indulged in. Only let the *cooking* and *serving up* be our own, and let that be done carefully and neatly, and our chief duty is performed. That you can do all this, I believe, in spite of your desponding fears.

"But I see that I am wasting my paper in prosing, when I ought to be about other matters. Do you know I am going to be absent from the Institution all the summer? I have got a furlough from the Trustees till November 1st. At present I think of going to Europe, and am trying to raise funds, but I fear it will prove one of the impossible things. If I should not go to Europe, I shall travel across the mountains, and perhaps, in my wanderings, stop to see you in Honeywood. Would you not be surprised to learn that Mr. Sparrow was at the door, inquiring for his old pupil? If I go to Europe, I leave home soon, say in a fortnight; if not, I shall remain here until the summer is pretty well advanced. You understand that the furlough was asked and obtained on account of my health, which has been miserable the past winter.

"And now, my dear Mr. B., I must close. Mrs. S. desires to be remembered to you. Please present my best respects to Col. C. Write when you can, and believe me, whether at home or abroad, at sea or on land, sick or well,

"I am your sincere friend and brother,

Rev. Alfred Blake. "WM. SPARROW."

During the fall and winter following this letter, that of 1838–9, Dr. Sparrow made a visit to Europe. This was twenty-one years from the time of his departure, in 1817, for America, and we may easily imagine the feelings with which he revisited the home and scenes of his boyhood. Twenty-one years had doubtless wrought great changes, but many of the old friends, and acquaintances, and relatives whom he had known in early life still remained, and he was fond of telling, in years afterwards, of the mode in which one of his aunts received him—very much as in his boyhood, by asking him what she should prepare to gratify his appetite. At the same time there were associations and changes that would naturally be productive of mournful feeling. This, probably, was the time of his day's travel in the vale of Avoca, with its remembrances and anticipations, so many of the latter to be clouded with sadness, when he found, at its close, his old teacher and so many of his fellow-pupils no longer in place to welcome him.

None of his correspondence during this visit remains, and we are unable, consequently, to trace his course. He was undoubtedly on the continent, and during this visit, or that of 1848, ten years later, visited Geneva. But what other portions of the continent were visited we have no means of ascertaining. He returned in the spring of 1839, and resumed his duties at the College. We there meet him, by means of a communication from one of his pupils, at that time in the College, and as it gives definiteness to certain impressions of his work, we here present it to our readers.

"I formed my acquaintance with our dear old Professor, to whom we owe so much, and whose memory we shall always love and cherish, during my college life in 1839, when I was a boy of fifteen, and he in the full prime of life. My impressions of him, therefore, at that time, must be taken for what they are worth, as those of a mere youth.

"There is an incident connected with my introduction to him, which I may mention at my own expense, and which may serve to illustrate, as well as anything that I can remember, the difficult position which the Doctor then occupied, the wrong impressions which young men often associated with such positions, and the ready way in which he disabused the minds of all who had an opportunity of knowing him in his true character. When I went to Kenyon, the college and seminary were united under one administration, having the same board of trustees, and the same Faculty of instructors. This had been the case, I believe, from the commencement of the Institution, when Bishop Chase had charge of it, and Dr. Sparrow, who was nearly connected with him by marriage, was associated with him as one of the earliest professors. At that early period in the history of the college, no doubt the students had quite a rough time, and were kept under a more rigid discipline than generally prevailed in such institutions. The traditions which had come down to the students of my day, through much less than a score of years, gave very exaggerated ideas of the tyranny and oppression that had prevailed under the regime of the old pioneer bishop and his coadjutors at Gambier. These ideas were duly instilled into the minds of most of the new comers, from session to session, and as a matter of course when I entered college, I fell heir to my full share of these traditional impressions. During the winter of 1838–9 Dr. Sparrow was absent in Europe, and I had no opportunity of knowing him until the following spring. My first interview with him was brought about in the following manner: I was then a thoughtless youth, not much inclined to stand in awe of those in authority over me, and very jealous of certain imaginary rights. Among other things, I had heard that Dr. Sparrow required every student, on meeting him or coming into his presence, to take off his hat, and assume a very humble and obsequious manner, and I had been told how he had dealt roughly with some offenders in these particulars. I had remarked, in a rather boasting or defiant spirit, that I could not yield to such a requirement, and would only return such tokens of politeness as were shown by the other party. One morning the tutor came to my room, and informed me that Dr. Sparrow wished to see me in a certain lecture room. I was somewhat startled by the announcement, for I took it for granted that he could only wish to see me to remind me of some misdemeanor, or to enforce some necessary discipline. So I left my room in a high state of excitement, declaring in strong terms, greatly to the amusement of my room-mate, how I intended to resist aggression, and to maintain my own dignity and rights. With this very erroneous and absurd state of feeling, I tapped at the Doctor's door. Opening the door, I saw, for the first time, that delicate but majestic form, sitting in his Professor's chair behind the table, leaning back in an almost reclining attitude, to rest after dismissing his class, with his gold spectacles upon his brow. As soon as his eye met mine, he asked if I were M———? And being answered in the affirmative, he arose and approached me in the kindest and most agreeable manner, and before his hand had time to reach mine, my hat was off, and I felt that I could not make any suitable acknowledgment of such kindness and courtesy from a man in his position toward a schoolboy. He asked me to have a seat near him, and then opened the conversation, as he only could do, with words of wise counsel and tender interest, such as I can never forget. He told me that on his return from Europe, to his duties of Vice President of the college, he had inquired in regard to the students, and had learned of me as an only son, and that my father's letter evinced so much interest and anxiety on my account, that his own sympathies were touched; that he was glad to hear of improvement in my department, and he wished to do what he could to encourage me. His words and manner were so kind and fatherly, that when I left the room I felt that it had been good for me to be there. Never were false impressions and wrong resolutions more speedily reversed. From that moment I entertained the greatest love and reverence for Doctor Sparrow, which grew the more I knew of him, in our subsequent relations of teacher and pupil, both at Kenyon, and at the Virginia Seminary.*

"Within three months of the above date I was a candidate for confirmation, and, of course, sought advice and instruction from Doctor Sparrow, in my preparation for that step. It was cheerfully and faithfully given, and was such as might have been expected from one of his character and attainments. It was a rare privilege, at that important crisis of one's life, to have received counsel from such a source. It pleased God, just at that time, to vouchsafe such blessings to the members of that Institution as have not been often realized. It was not like what is generally known as a 'revival,' and yet it *was* a revival, of the true Scriptural type—a season of heartfelt interest in spiritual things—pervading the very atmosphere, and communicating itself from one to another, until every one seemed to be under its influence, and to

* As illustrative of the sort of influence exerted by Dr. Sparrow in this way, while in charge of the college, was the case of an eminent public man, who, many years afterward, while upon his deathbed, received baptism at his hands. The account may be given as derived from himself. "As I was passing," said he, "along Pennsylvania avenue, I was stopped by a gentleman calling to me by name, and who to me was a perfect stranger. When he came up he introduced himself, and reminded me that he had been a student at Kenyon, and that I had once sent for him to my study (an incident which the Doctor did not recall), to remonstrate with him in regard to his course. He regarded that remonstrance as the turning point in his life, and thus took the opportunity of making it known, as also of offering his grateful acknowledgments."

be in sympathy with the surrounding scene. Doctor Sparrow rejoiced in this season, and entered into it with intense interest. His sermons, which always abounded with rich views of religious thought, such as few minds could either discover or pursue, were at that time surpassingly fine. He was then in the very vigor of manhood, and in the maturity of his mental development. In a diary kept at that time, I have a memorandum of his texts, together with a brief outline of his sermons, which show how wisely they were selected, and with what masterly power the subjects were handled. In the course of the session a large number of the students devoted themselves to the service of Christ, and many of them became useful and prominent men in the Church, both as clergymen and laymen. This result was due, in a great measure, to the influence of Dr. Sparrow, although he modestly disclaimed it, with many earnest regrets that he could not do more to promote the spiritual welfare of the students.

"Within a year from this time he received the appointment of professor in the Theological Seminary of Virginia. It so happened that I then had an opportunity of seeing Dr. Sparrow, and talking with him frequently while he was preparing to take this important step. The idea of making that change was a great trial to him, for up to that time all the tenderest associations of his life were clustered around that spot. He came there in his youth; and for many years had presided over that institution, and had conducted its affairs with marked ability and success. His name was identified with its entire history—the bishop of the diocese being the President ex-officio, while he was the Vice President and acting President of the college Faculty. The grave of his father was there, and everything combined to make the spot very dear to his heart. On one occasion he said, 'It is very easy to take up a young scion and transplant it in another place, but if you dig up a full grown tree, and try to remove it, there will be so many roots broken and so many bruises inflicted, that the chances are against its taking root and flourishing in a new soil.' At length, when he had decided to go, the members of the two literary societies appointed a committee to invite him to deliver a valedictory address at the close of the session. Being a member of the committee, I well remember how gratified he was to receive that expression of regard on the part of the students. The request was communicated to him, not as a piece of ceremony or token of respect due to his official position, but as a mark of true appreciation and deep regret at parting with such a valuable member of the Faculty. After some hesitation, he consented to the request, and at the appointed time delivered an address on 'Truth,' which was, as might have been expected, a masterly production. Some years afterward, while a member of the seminary at Alexandria, I was permitted to read that manuscript, and often regretted that it was never published."

The closing address thus alluded to is one well worthy of perusal, and in any future publication of the doctor's addresses may properly find its place. Its conclusion is here inserted.

"And now, young gentlemen, let me speak a parting word to you, and through you to all the students of the Institution. It is a matter of no little gratification to my feelings that you should take so much interest in my removal from this place, as unanimously to request me to address you on this occasion. But if it is a matter of interest to you, how much more to me! My local attachments are, constitutionally, of the very strongest kind; and they have here had long time and much seclusion to give them permanence and strength. But they must now be broken up, and I must enter, by personal experience, into the meaning of that expression which I have often used, but never so fully realized before, 'the place that now knows me shall know me no more.' And if, in such an hour, the very stones in the street and the trees in the wood around, and the most familiar and common objects, the moment the thought of separation comes up, seem to speak mournfully of years of intercourse which never can return, how much more painful to think of parting from persons who have known and held communion with me since the days of my manhood. Attachments, moreover, partly professional and partly personal, have bound me to the students of Kenyon College, by association with them from the time it was a grammar school in the lowest forms to the close of the last college year. Standing before you, therefore, as one formerly an officer of the college, I see represented in you the classes I have been connected with some fifteen years, and bidding farewell to you, I seem to bid farewell to all. In thinking over the anxiety and comfort, the joys and the sorrows which I have experienced, during so large a portion of my life, it would be strange indeed, if my heart did not go forth in all those feelings, one-half parental, which a professional teacher seeks to exercise and cherish toward those committed to his care. Amidst much infirmity of every kind, which no man knows so well by observation of me, as I do myself, by painful consciousness, I hope I can say, my first desire has not been to earn a morsel of bread, but rather to be useful to you and to those who have gone before you. It would, perhaps, be unreasonable to expect that students generally should make allowance for the difficulties, and fully appreciate the true desires and endeavors of those who conduct their government and discipline. But it soothes and delights my heart to say that I have nothing to complain of in this regard; quite the reverse; I have almost uniformly met as much good will on their part as I could possibly desire. In the few cases in which it has been withheld by single individuals, it has been only for a time; in after life, out in the broad world, it has been fully repaid. While, therefore, as in every situation in life I have had my trials, in this respect I have been spared; and I can look back upon my years of labor, in connection with the students of Kenyon College, with but one feeling of regret—that they are ended. But their memory need not end. And when, in a few days, I remove from the objects all around so familiar that they seem parts of myself; when I part from friends even longer acquainted and dear to me as brothers; when I separate from the ashes of my children and my father slumbering in this graveyard; and break up the associations of a life never again to take root so deeply, I will carry with me and cherish throughout my days the pleasing reflection that I have a place in the heart of the earlier students of Kenyon College.

"But there is and shall be no selfishness in the feeling. My removal does not destroy my interest in the Institution, or any of its branches. My desire and prayer shall be, as for years they daily have been, that it may more and more promote those great interests of the human kind which are paramount to all considerations of persons and places, and of personal and local feelings. May the smiles of Heaven rest upon it! May the officers and students be a mutual blessing and satisfaction! And, when I meet any who have gone forth from these walls, may I hear of tenfold more prosperity than it has been my lot to witness. Kenyon College is, and ever shall be to me—not my alma mater, but something far, far more dear. Gentlemen, farewell."

But this address, as indicated in these extracts, and in the letter preceding them, was called forth in view of a matter of much deeper interest, that of a change in his residence and sphere of operation. The determination had been reached to leave Gambier and to remove to Alexandria. The causes of this determination it would be difficult, in all respects, fully to explain. Without undertaking to do this, it may be said that there were several which made the position of Dr. Sparrow an embarrassing one. The old difficulty as to the limits of prerogative between the nominal, that is the Episcopal, and the actual, that is the Academical, head, had not been perfectly adjusted. The action of the Diocesan Convention of 1839 was rather in favor of the former. Its further, and specific action, by which the President and Professors were deprived of the power of holding trusteeships in the institution, had its bearing in the same direction. And when, still further, the election of a President to fill the vacancy created by the resignation of the Bishop took place, the acting President, who, for twelve or fifteen years had been performing its duties, was passed over, and the office given to another. This, in view of the relations of Dr. Sparrow to the College, could scarcely be agreeable. The question, moreover, of salary, with his large, dependent family, was one which he was obliged to consider. Some of the reminiscences of Mr. Syle, towards the close of this volume, bear upon this subject, and are of value as showing Dr. Sparrow's feelings under the circumstances. The invitation, within the next twelve months, to Virginia, relieved him from an embarrassing position. That a very great mistake had been made in letting him leave Ohio, that a still greater mistake had been made in putting him in a position in which the invitation so to do would be favorably considered, very soon, but too late, became manifest. The repeated and flattering invitations to return were alike honorable to him and to those by whom they were given. Some of these will be noticed in their proper place. It was no doubt a severe trial to make up his mind to leave this work, to which he had grown, this his peculiar field of ministerial and professional duty and labor, the Institutions which he had so largely contributed to found, and to which nearly fifteen of the most laborious years of his life had been devoted. He seemed, indeed, almost to feel as if the main part of his work of life had been accomplished; that it would be difficult if not impossible elsewhere to occupy a sphere of influence and usefulness equal to that which he had been filling. These feelings doubtless took their hue from what then seems to have been a very strong conviction, that, from the state of his general health, his term of usefulness or of labor would be but a short one. In reality, however, it was only to transfer himself to a new field of usefulness. And the fifteen years of influence and work in Ohio were to be followed by thirty-three more, no less beneficial and gratifying, in these respects, in Virginia. The change, moreover, had one most desirable effect. It relieved him from one class of duties, those connected with college work and administration, and thus enabled him to devote himself entirely to the more congenial work of the Theological Professorship. This, indeed, constitutes one great difference between Dr. Sparrow's recognized position and influence in Ohio and in Virginia. In Ohio he was known as a preacher and theological professor, but mainly and more prominently as at the head of Kenyon College, as the successful governor of a literary institution. In Virginia, on the other hand, while known by his previous reputation in these other positions and spheres of influence, he was peculiarly known as the Theological Professor, as having concentrated his energies upon the work of teaching and training men for the ministry. During this latter period he occupied other positions of great importance; was member of Standing Committee for many years, delegate to the General Convention; confidential adviser of clerical pupils and brethren in all directions. But these were incidental. His main and special work, as already indicated, was Theological teaching, the preparation and training of Theological candidates for the great work to which they were looking forward. In this, as we have seen, he was permitted for a third of a century longer to be engaged, and with him in this peculiar sphere of effort, saving a brief interruption during the war, will the remainder of our narrative be occupied.

The full determination to make the change from Ohio to Virginia was reached towards the close of the year 1840. The following letter to Dr. Milnor, in reference to the Milnor Professorship, vacated by this change, brings the account of this period to its termination.

"GAMBIER, December 17, 1840.

"REV. AND DEAR SIR:—

"Having concluded to remove from this diocese to that of Virginia, and accept a situation offered me in their Seminary, it seems proper that I should apprise you of my intention.

"Years ago, when I was much younger in age, and much younger still in health and strength, you, very unexpectedly, nominated me to the Milnor Professorship. That so much confidence should be reposed in one so young, and so little known, was a wonder to me; and I can truly say, helped, with higher considerations, to make me solicitous to discharge my duty faithfully. The value of truth, pure truth, 'the truth, the whole truth, and nothing but the truth,' in matters of religion, even more than in the affairs of the judgment hall, I have always felt to be important; and the incident referred to was a stimulus additional to every other, to 'give heed to my doctrine.' How far I have succeeded is certainly known to none but the infallible Judge in Heaven. This, however, I think I may say to you, that during eleven years in this station I have never seen occasion to depart, in the least, from the spirit of those instructions which, when a lonely student in New York, I used to seek in the lecture-room of St. George's, on week-day evenings. May they as certainly carry me, through infinite grace and mercy, to the inheritance which I seek above, as I have endeavored to inculcate them on the minds committed to my care.

"I regret exceedingly, that when I was last in New York I was not able to enjoy more of your society, and have some free conversation with you about the state of religion in our Church. Your long and careful study of events as they have arisen among us, would naturally give weight to your judgment upon such matters, and not least with me. How you interpret some of the signs of the times I cannot conjecture. In reference to some things, there is more obscurity, vacillancy, and ambiguity, about the doings of some portions of our Church, than I like to see. I think the declaration of the ———, whose ability and honesty I respect, that the only difference between the High and Low Church portion of our Communion is one of feeling—a question simply of more or less zeal—one of the severest satires ever inflicted on a respected and *intelligent* body of ecclesiastics. Were I near you, I should like to canvass with you in person, the truth of this assertion. But you will excuse all this irrelevancy. My only object in writing, was to announce to you, as the person who nominated me, and will have the nomination of my successor to the Milnor professorship, that I expect to retire from my present position about the end of next spring vacation; that is, about the first of

May. Present my respects to Mrs. Milnor, and believe me to be, reverend and dear sir, most truly

"Your obliged friend and servant, WILLIAM SPARROW.

"*The Rev. James Milnor*, D. D., *New York*."

Within the next four months the movement was accomplished, and Dr. Sparrow and his family reached Alexandria in April, 1841, just in time to enable him to be present at the diocesan Convention held in that place, and to meet there with his subsequent colleague, Dr. May, with whom, for eighteen years and more, he was afterwards affectionately associated, Dr. May being a visitor to the Convention.

CHAPTER V.

FIRST SEVEN YEARS IN VIRGINIA.

Dr. Sparrow's resignation at Gambier took effect with the close of the half session, in the spring of 1841. He removed to Virginia very soon afterward, arriving there, as we have seen, in the month of April of the same year. The Faculty of the Virginia Seminary then consisted of Rev. Dr. Keith, and Professors Lippitt and Packard. During the remainder of this session, that of '40 and '41, Dr. Sparrow gave instruction to the classes in Church History. At the same time, he had classes in Mental and Moral Science, and Political Economy, in the neighboring Institution, the Episcopal High School. The death of Mrs. Keith had taken place not long before Dr. Sparrow's arrival, in December, 1840; and before the close of the next session Dr. Keith's health became so seriously impaired, that he was obliged to give up his work, so as to seek, by change and travel, a restoration, and Dr. Sparrow took his position, the Professorship of Systematic Divinity and Christian Evidences. This position he occupied to the close of his life; most of that time, also, as Chairman, or Dean, of the Faculty, and the Head of the Institution. The classes at the High-school were given up before, or, at the furthest, by the end of the second session, and his whole time devoted to his theological classes. We thus enter upon the work of the last thirty-three years of his life. That third of a century, in its even tenor of ordinary duty, presents very little of striking incident for biographical narration. While full of interest to the successive generations of students brought in contact with him, and coming under his quickening influence, it is difficult to specialize that interest in tangible form, and present it to the minds of others. The whole period, indeed, in certain respects, is so much alike in its parts, that there seems to be a difficulty in breaking it up into shorter intervals. There are, however, certain points of time which may be made use of for this purpose; and for the sake of clearness, four are here indicated. The first, from his entrance upon his duties at the Virginia Seminary, to the time of his visit to Europe, from 1841 to 1848. The second, from this latter date to the breaking out of the war, and the closing of the Seminary, 1848 to 1861. The third, from this closing of the Seminary to its reopening, 1861 to 1865; and the last, his work from this time until his death, from July, 1865, to January, 1874. In the present chapter we are occupied with the period, between 1841 and 1848, his first seven years' work in Virginia. This was between the fortieth and forty-seventh year of his age, the very prime of his intellectual power, as of his vigor in his pulpit ministrations. At the time of his arrival, April, 1841, no residence had been provided, and he, therefore, with his family, for a few months, remained in Alexandria, and subsequently, during vacation, occupied a portion of the Seminary. The journey, as was necessary in those days, had been in stages, over the Alleghany, from Wheeling to Cumberland, and for the rest of the way by rail, to Washington. Coming up King street, Alexandria, for the first time, Dr. Sparrow met his future colleague, Dr. Keith, whose place he would be so soon called to supply, and received his welcome. Dr. Keith, it seems, at the moment was depressed and abstracted; and the effect of this upon the new comer, as described by him years after, was to depress him also. In a very little time, however, he was made to feel that he was at home, in the cordial welcome of his Virginia friends; and in a letter to his old friend and colleague, as also to one of his former pupils at Gambier, we have his first impressions.

"ALEXANDRIA, April 19th, 1841.

"REV. AND DEAR BROTHER:—

"You were the man, of all those in Gambier, whom it was most painful for me to part with, and to you, therefore, I write my first letter. It is the request of Mrs. Sparrow, also, that I should lose no time in communicating with you.

"We arrived here on Saturday last, sick and sore beyond description; and we have by no means yet recovered. Mrs. Sparrow has a violent cold, and all the children are still sick. As to myself, I am no better. Per contra, however, we have been received with inexpressible cordiality. We stopped at the house of Mr. L., and remained there till Wednesday, when we moved into lodgings. A kinder couple we have never met than our entertainers. They both have all the cordiality and hospitality of Virginia, purified and regulated by Christian principle. We have already been overwhelmed with more visits than we shall be able to return in a long time. I am pleased with the society, so far as I have met it. Last night Mr. L. gave a party, out of compliment to us. I went; Mrs. Sparrow was unable. I do not know when I saw so large a party so perfectly free. From beginning to end, it was one perpetual clatter of conversation, in which form was as much cast aside, and there was as much real enjoyment, as one would see among so many children. The gentlemen seemed very intelligent, and the ladies were, of course.

"I have been twice out to the Seminary, and there, also, have been received with open arms. Their kindness, I confess, is a trouble to me, as it indicates that they expect much of me. I have done nothing, as yet, in the way of teaching, and, I presume, will not do much this term. Three times a week are all I shall be under the necessity of going out to the Seminary; and a lesson each of these days in the Seminary and High-school will be all my duty.

"Bishop Meade called to see me yesterday morning, having arrived the night before. He went on immediately to attend to the publication of his consecration sermon,* which, after the fashion of the times, is to have notes appended, on Tradition, and other points connected with Oxford Tractism.

"I have been visited by the Rev. Messrs. Dana and Johnston (the resident rectors of the churches in Alexandria), and am to preach for them both on Sunday. The latter is very polished, and the former very affectionate, especially for an old bachelor. Dr. Keith I heard preach last Sunday, in Mr. Dana's church, with great effect. He is a very holy man, and very solemn in the pulpit. I suspect he brings the strong meat of Calvinism, in huge joints and sirloins, on the table. It is not with him, as at Gambier, employed as sugar, to sweeten the tea.

"I have allowed my thoughts to wander back to Gambier as little as possible. Ever since I left there I have found it my wisdom to keep them directed forward as exclusively as possible, though my prospects of happiness are very good, indeed, if Heaven should bless me in my family, and enable me to do my duty as Professor adequately; yet one thing is manifest—I cannot spend here, as I have there, the prime of my life, or form the same strong attachments. I thank God that I was able to leave Gambier with such kind feelings towards *all* there, and possessing such a large and

* At the consecration of Bishop Elliott, of Georgia.

undeserved portion of their good will. Especially am I thankful that the Bishop felt so kindly towards me. When I went to bid him farewell, his affection was evinced in the most unequivocal manner, and I can truly say that every such feeling was more than reciprocated. Do not fail, on the receipt of this, to present to him my most respectful and affectionate regards. I shall write him before long. I wish you, also, to say to Major Douglass that I regret I did not see him at the time of parting. I went to see him and the Bishop; but, in truth, the Bishop so occupied my thoughts that I forgot to inquire for the Major.

"Remember me most kindly to all my friends; the officers of the Institution, including my old friends, Blake and Badger, the students who were especially intimate with me, and those outside of the Institution. To many of them I shall write, though I cannot say how soon. It will be a considerable time before I have settled down into that quiet frame of mind which is most favorable to writing letters of friendship. To you I shall write, in season and out of season; and shall hope that you will prove as good a correspondent as in days of yore. I have just had a letter from H. He saw his mother, and so satisfied, as she said, her last earthly wish. She died the Monday after his arrival at home. Amongst the persons I shall write to is Mr. S. Tell him, however, that I shall be glad to hear from him in the meantime. In his bachelor loneliness he may, perhaps, feel disposed to write me first.

"My best regards and good wishes to Mrs. Wing. We are anxious to hear about her health. On this head, therefore, you will be particular when you write. I need not say Mrs. Sparrow joins with me in best regards and heartiest good wishes.

"Your old friend and brother,

"W. SPARROW.

"P. S. In excuse for this scrawl, I plead my confined condition, a bad cold, and part of the time Thomas on my lap, a la mode Hooker. W. S."

"THEOLOGICAL SEMINARY, FAIRFAX COUNTY, VA.

"MY DEAR MR. SYLE:—

"I have written Mr. M. and Mr. W., and the bishop being now absent from Gambier, I feel as if I ought to write to you next. It is fairly a duty, and my duty here is my pleasure. My family also urge it. They all agree with me that your claim is one of the first. They often speak of you, and, I doubt not, think oftener than they speak.

"Through great mercy we got here (I mean Alexandria, though I date my letter from the Seminary, and wish all letters for us directed thither), without any serious accident, but perfectly worn out. We have not yet recovered, by any means. Cold and bruises still continue. I am very thankful, however, that my little Elizabeth has begun to walk again, and I trust will soon be restored to health.

"We are boarding, but shall get out of it as soon as possible. It is not the thing for children. After so much latitude and range as my little ones have enjoyed, their life will soon appear to them as that of prisoners; as yet they are pleased with the novelty of the sights which the city and river present.

"We have found the people here exceedingly attentive, and I think we shall like them much. Amongst the better class of people there seems a good share of religious feeling.

"In the Seminary, things are in better condition than I expected to find them. I should think the students are contented and happy, and doing well; the spirit which prevails amongst them is good, whilst there is no irregularity that I can see; their main attention is directed, not to the external, but the internal. I have done one week's duty amongst them, and could I feel myself qualified for the office which I fill, I should be satisfied with the result. If they will have patience with me, however, and not seize me by the throat prematurely, in due time I hope I shall be able to teach the dry details of Mosheim's chaff, and mingle a little of Milner's farina, putting the whole through the bolting cloth of Christian philosophy (am I not quite imaginary in my comparison?). The study of abstract subjects so long, has unfitted me for the concrete, but if I can recover an ordinary ability to handle the latter class of ideas, to remember and recall with facility, incidents, persons and dates, the possession of the former will prove in the end helpful to me, and especially, serve me when I attempt written lectures.

"I have walked out to the Seminary four days this week, and back again. The distance is about two miles and a half, by the foot path. It agrees with me right well. How I can bear it in the hot weather is to be tried, but I hope by that time to be residing 'on the hill.' My house is begun; they waited for me to fix the site, which has thrown the work back, though it was very kind in them. Before it is done, I hope to move to another house, near the Seminary, for two or three months. The walk out is all up hill, but it is rendered less laborious by the beautiful prospect all the way.

"The season here is very backward—six weeks or more behind time. It has rained much since we arrived, and the children have been the more like caged birds.

"Thus far I see no cause to regret the move I have made, if I could only abate my strong personal and local attachments. I love Ohio much, and Gambier more; and I thank God I can look back and think of all my acquaintances there with unmingled feelings of affection. I never have been retentive of unkind feelings. The least exhibition of regard on the part of others has always drowned them, and I am sure there was quite enough of such feeling manifested at my departure. The bishop parted with me in the most affectionate and brotherly manner.

"Your friend and brother in Christ, W. SPARROW."

The two following letters, to the same correspondent, the one on his departure for England, and the other soon after hearing of his arrival, have their place at this point. The latter of the two touches upon certain questions of controversy at that time under discussion.

"THEOLOGICAL SEMINARY, NEAR ALEXANDRIA, VA.,
"September 17th, 1842.

"MY DEAR MR. SYLE:—

"I have been prevented from answering you sooner, partly by absence from home, and partly by a painful reluctance which I have felt and now feel to sit down to write you a final letter before your departure. It is truly painful to me to bid you farewell, never expecting to see you again this side of eternity. At the same time, I am free to say that if you think a longer residence in this country would interfere with the main object of your life, I would not throw the smallest obstacle in your way. God forbid I should. Were you my brother, with a heart set on a foreign mission, I would cheerfully part with you, however trying to flesh and blood. If, then, you think duty calls, Heaven speed you. My prayers accompany you, and shall follow you to my latest breath.

"Have I told you how I was pleased with my visit to the interior of Virginia? But I cannot tell you. The hospitality of the people surpassed anything I had ever seen. I was at two associations, with four other clergymen, and the attendance upon the meetings was most excellent. I trust good was done. One of the associations was held at a church in the woods. There were fifty carriages, and I can't tell how many horses fastened under the trees all around.

"After morning service, they all went to their carriages, as to their homes, let down the steps, brought forth their cold dinners, put one dish on one step and another on another, took their food in their fingers, sitting in the carriages or standing about them, and so 'eat bread,' with as much of an accustomed air as if they had been seated at their tables. These were the first people in the land. After refreshment they went back to the church, quietly took their seats, and without any ringing of bells, were ready to hear as soon as the pastors were ready to speak. Virginia Christians are much more in earnest than any we have in the West. The line between them and the world is more distinctly drawn. You will be surprised to find me saying, that I have known but one man in the West who comes near my idea of a thorough Christian (I speak of the laity), and that is W. I wish I could show you two letters he has recently written me, spontaneously. He tells me, by the way, that T. is married to a lady of decided piety, in Columbus, who is likely to exert a salutary influence over him. But let me draw to a close.

"Am I, then, to see you no more in this world! The Lord's will be done. But let me hear from you. You have promised to remember me, and I have no doubt you will, but also write to me. A letter from you will always be deemed a privilege by me and mine. As long as I live I shall take a deep interest in you, and not least when you get into your missionary field. When there, remember that a letter from you will not only be a refreshment to Mrs. S. and myself, in the weary pilgrimage of life, but also may be made a blessing to the young men here preparing for the ministry. Above all, let me have your prayers, as you shall have mine. Lastly, should anything unforeseen prevent your sailing this autumn, fail not to remember that there are here persons ready to receive you with open arms, and to make your situation as comfortable as their power will permit. Of course I will expect to hear from you again. Mrs. S. and all the children send their love.

That the presence and blessing of a covenant God may be with you, by land and by sea, now and forever, is the prayer of your friend and brother, WILLIAM SPARROW.

"*Rev. E. W. Syle.*"

"THEOLOGICAL SEMINARY, NEAR ALEXANDRIA, D. C.,
"December, 1842.

"MY DEAR MR. SYLE:—

"Your letter caused us heartfelt joy and gratitude to God, that he had brought you in safety to your native land, that 'glory of all lands,' and it proved also an occasion of pleasure, as an evidence that you had thoughts of us, even amid the chaos of delightful associations which an arrival at home after so long and distant an absence must necessarily occasion.

"The account you gave of your voyage was quite interesting to us all. Your story, under the head of 'unprovableness,' went to prove what I have long been persuaded of, that in reference to the low, the outcast and neglected portions of society, we are too apt to say, with the Pharisees, 'this people, who knoweth not the law, are cursed.' Our Saviour has not been sufficiently imitated in his hopefulness, in regard to the most vile, and especially in His direct efforts to restore them to virtue and happiness.

"I should have written upon the very heels of your letter's reception, but that we were then expecting, in a few days, a visit from your friend, Mr. H——. He came, in due time, and stopped with his old West Point friend, Mr. P——, but was several times at my house. He preached for us, at night, on the subject of his agency. I liked the man, more for your sake, than on any other account. His sermon, though good as a composition, and full of statistics, seemed more stiff and straight-laced than my notions of the Gospel could approve. In conversation, I found that, on many points of great moment, I could not accord with him. One topic of conversation was the Christian priesthood (*sacerdotium*, not *presbyterium*), which is now in everybody's mouth, in consequence of a couple of sermons of the Bishop of Maryland, just published. The Bishop's notion is, that we have a priesthood as much under the New as under the Old Dispensation, and as really a sacrifice and altar (the bread and wine, and the Lord's table). The fundamental idea of the priesthood he defines to be ministerial intervention for the forgiveness of sins. Now this may be readily admitted, on the principle of 'how shall they believe in Him of whom they have not heard,' etc. (understanding 'such' as referring to the tidings furnished, rather than the authority to carry them); but if it is carried so far as to suppose that justification is tied to the sacraments, and that they are anything more than generally necessary to salvation, I think Scripture and reason violated thereby, and the door opened for some of the worst errors of Popery. Talking with Mr. H——, I told him that it was enough for me that I was, by my ministerial office, made a preacher of the 'good tidings of great joy,' and also a ruler in the house of God. Snapping his fingers, he said, 'if *that* was all that was in the Christian ministry, he would not give a fig for it; desiring us to look at the different sects around. When Mr. P—— told him to look at the consequences of the opposite doctrines, and see how much more pernicious they were, 'he did not think so.' That Mr. H—— is a good and laborious man, and that in private life he is very agreeable, I doubt not; but I see that though he aims to be a 'tertium quid' man, he is all on one side. These remarks I would not make upon your friend, if I thought you would misunderstand me. The occasion of speaking, is the excitement caused by the publication of the sermons just mentioned, and the *motive* is to let you know where I stand in relation to such points. The time has come when every man in public must take his stand somewhere; and I, after many an hour's, many a year's anxious thought, have taken mine; it is natural that we speak freely to particular friends about what most interests us.

"I believe there is nothing new in Alexandria to communicate. Neither is there much here. You learned, I believe, before you left, that we had a junior class of twenty. Dr. May is here, and exceedingly acceptable. I think you would like him *very much*, if you were acquainted with him. He is a sweet man, of good sense, of Evangelical principles, and moderate in his church views. He is very successful on Thursday nights, and is much liked as a preacher. He is a little more Calvinistic than you or I would like, perhaps, but it is not brought out offensively. Mr. Lippitt will be glad to hear from you. Your other friends in Alexandria speak of you in the kindest terms. I believe all there, as well as here, were sad at parting with you, except ———, and he only because of your most unchristian enthusiasm!! You know Dr. Eastburn is going to be consecrated Bishop of Massachusetts, assistant to

Bishop Griswold. This is an acquisition to our Church. He is a man of right views, and one-half a countryman of yours.

"I ought to have mentioned that one of Bishop Whittingham's sermons was preached at the institution of H. V. D. Johns, as Bishop Johns' successor. As it contradicted some views which Bishop Johns had exhibited in his farewell discourse, and as it professed to teach the people in what light they should regard their new pastor, Henry Johns thought that this placed him in a false attitude and character before his charge, and he thus felt constrained to define his own position at night. The discourse was, consequently, extemporaneous, for the most part, but he afterward wrote it down, and published it. To a person who merely knew that he preached, at night, against what the bishop had preached in the morning, it might seem as if he had been rash. But when we consider that the bishop had *expressly* contradicted Bishop Johns' exposition of his preaching in that Church for years, that this contradiction was made as the *connection was forming* between the new rector and the parish, and that Henry Johns is of a mild, not a harsh, a cautious, not a hasty temper, it will appear, I think, that he was actuated by a constraining sense of duty. His sermon I have read, and like it much, making allowance for its extemporaneous character.

"In regard to the subject* on which you ask for 'hints,' I can say nothing. You may judge, from the previous scribbling, that I am not in a condition to touch a theological question. Indeed, I am only fit to do just what I am doing—pouring out thoughts, as they arise, to a friend who will not ask what their value, but whence they come. Order and system are important, there can be no doubt; and the benefits of concentrated action, by the way, have been exhibited, not only by Episcopalians, but by the Methodists, Presbyterians, and Baptists; witness their missionary feats. The only question is, whether we shall leave this *concert* and *co-operation* to be sustained by 'the elective affinities,' and voluntary energies of vital Christianity, or force them into existence, and maintain them by principles which trench on individual rights, and, in their final result, on the spirit and power of religion. Order, consolidation, and strength, are easily secured, for they have been secured under all systems, political and religious. Christianity

* This subject appears to have been that of the organization of the Foreign and Domestic Missionary Boards, under the General Convention.

consents to seek them only in one way—that which leaves individual responsibility untouched, and spiritual religion paramount. Luther, you remember, was not hasty to remove the symbols of superstition; he would first remove the *spirit* of it from the minds of the people. So, in reverse order, the *spirit* of *unity*, in the love of Evangelical truths, it seems to me, ought to precede the outward *form* of it. To press the latter unduly, is not only to prevent the introduction of the former, but *positively to depreciate it.* Much is said in the New Testament about the one; very little about the other. The greatest feats of Christian enterprise were done, when, in the nature of things, much external unity was impossible, in Apostolic times. Authority and order may be carried to the degree of destroying that individuality which is specially fostered by Christianity.

"Mrs. Sparrow and the children unite with me in sincerest love. A standing petition at our daily devotions, is 'for friends, far and near;' you are very often distinctly included. I am kept very busy. I have not yet got release from my entire duties, and go every Sunday to Georgetown, to preach for Mr. Hoff. This will probably continue a month or two longer. I am hardly able to bear the labor and exposure, but circumstances make it expedient. Do write me soon. I prescribe two topics—first, of yourself, secondly, of the state and prospects of true religion.

"Your brother in Christ, WILLIAM SPARROW.

"P. S. I have not strength to read this over."

In the course of the next six or eight months a residence was erected for him on the Seminary grounds. Into this he was able to move at the beginning of the session 1841–42, and he continued to occupy it until after the resignation of Dr. Keith. This last event left a dwelling unoccupied, more commodious and nearer to the Seminary; and into this Dr. Sparrow moved, and, with his family, found their home, until the day of his death. His family at this time was quite large, two sons and five daughters. And we find, during the period with which we are now engaged, that the solicitudes of a parent, realizing that he might be taken from them at any moment, entered largely into his experiences and feelings. No man, perhaps, ever more thoroughly appreciated or gratefully enjoyed the blessings of domestic and social life. The dependence, both of the individual and of the community, for moral health and safety upon the family, was a truth of which he was never forgetful, and, as his ideal of the family was that of the well regulated Christian household—the best type on earth of heaven, the elevating and purifying power to individuals, the conserving and restraining influence upon communities—so his effort was to secure these highest benefits to his own family, the objects of his warmest affection. Extracts, already given, from his diary, of an earlier date, when about to leave home, contain indications of his feelings in this respect—his thorough appreciation of his home blessings, his deep affection and interest for the dependent members of that home, his parental solicitude and anxiety for their comfort and welfare.

As already remarked, Dr. Sparrow's work, as Professor at the Seminary, began with the classes in Church History. Distinct from this, for two sessions, were his classes at the High-school, in Mental Philosophy. In these latter recitations the writer first made his acquaintance. Very distinct are the recollections of the first one of those recitations, of the anxiety preceding it, of its almost immediate removal as the kindly, genial questioning and explanation went on, of the pleasurable conviction following, "he knows all about it, and yet he is not out of sympathy with those who are still ignorant, but who are trying to know." For weeks, and even months before, Dr. Sparrow's arrival had been anticipated. His great reputation as a Teacher and Preacher, his former position as President of Kenyon College and head of the Theological Seminary, had produced the impression that there would be great difficulty in meeting his requisitions. With the studious the first trial was sufficient to dissipate all such unpleasant impressions. The assurance was almost immediate, that the Instructor was not only capable himself, but appreciative of a pupil's difficulties; that while rigidly exacting in his demands as to what was attainable, he was ever ready with such assistance as was really needed. Four of the class on that occasion, Bishop Whittle, Dr. Perkins, of Louisville, Rev. Wm. M. Nelson, of Kentucky, and the writer, are now among our clergy*—most, if not all, of them, coming subsequently under his instructions at the Seminary.

The course of this instruction at the Seminary has already been briefly indicated. The change from Dr. Sparrow's work

*** Rev. John A. Harrison, Rev. A. F. Freeman and Rev. E. B. Jones were probably members of the same class. But there is not distinct remembrance to justify a positive statement to that effect.**

as Professor of Ecclesiastical History began during Dr. Keith's sickness, and was fully made when it became manifest that the latter would be unable to resume his duties. Dr. Sparrow was then appointed to the Professorship of Systematic Divinity and Evidences. About the same time, or a little later, Professor Lippitt resigned the Professorship of Church History, taking charge of the diocesan paper, the "Southern Churchman," and Dr. May was appointed to supply his place. The Faculty thus constituted continued together until the breaking out of the war, in 1861, Dr. Sparrow, for the larger portion of the time, occupying the position of Dean. Among his papers is one which seems to have been prepared at this time, having in view the more effective working of the Institution, and, as most of the particulars there mentioned have been adopted, the paper itself will not be without interest. It is entitled, "Suggestions in relation to the Theological Seminary of the Protestant Episcopal Church in the Diocese of Virginia."

1. The literary qualifications for entering the Seminary ought, perhaps, to be made more definite. The catalogue speaks only of "literary and scientific attainments." With the High-school at hand, to furnish education in all the preparatory studies, something more specific might be required. Candidates, on their entrance, should *be examined.*

2. The Senior Class, like any other, ought to be examined at the end of the year. The final examination, before the Bishop, by no means renders the Seminary examination superfluous.

3. Those who take a regular three years' course ought to have a certificate or diploma, as evidence of the same, from the Trustees or Faculty—none others to receive it.

4. No one ought to be advanced to a higher class without a regular examination on the studies of the lower. Their proficiency should not be presumed.

5. Whatever a class studies, in conformity with the course laid down in the catalogue, ought to be a matter of public examination at the end of the year; otherwise there will be remissness on the part of the students or teachers, or both.

6. The Faculty should keep a full and faithful record of all their official proceedings. Its influence is salutary, alike on the governors and the governed.

7. As there is a strong inclination amongst students to leave the Seminary at the end of the second year, could not something be

done to counteract it—if not by the Trustees, yet by the Education Society?

8. So much attention is necessarily bestowed on the Greek and Hebrew Scriptures, that the English Bible is liable to be neglected; to obviate this evil, and secure such familiarity with its language as will make quotation easy, ought not the Trustees require that portions of it be weekly committed to memory?

Most of these suggestions seem to have been adopted. The last one of them, that of committing portions of the English version, was acted upon by himself, with some of his classes, for several years, though it is believed that he eventually discontinued it. The portions selected were usually the Apostolical Epistles. There was some little fear, for a while, with some of the old friends and Alumni, that the Seminary might become too predominantly collegiate in its character—a place for the enlightening of the head at the expense of the warmth of the heart. These dangers it was found, however, were imaginary. The very effort to encourage study, to make it more extensive, and thorough, and systematic, was so conducted as at the same time to encourage and to aid a more thorough cultivation of the religious affections.

With reference to the latter of these objects, the proper cultivation of the heart, the moral and spiritual preparation for efficient work, for spiritual influence and results in the ministry, Dr. Sparrow recognized not only its transcending importance, but the accountability of himself and his colleagues to encourage and further it in every manner possible. One form of instrumentality to the attainment of this desired result he found in operation, the Faculty meeting, the weekly prayer meeting, on Thursday evening, of the professors and students. Into the spirit and purpose of this he immediately entered, and largely used it during his whole subsequent career. It may, indeed, be said that this constituted his favorite and most effective mode of impressing himself upon the minds and hearts of his pupils; of impressing upon them the spirituality of their work, the need of personal spirituality to give them efficiency and success in its performance. While in his personal intercourse, as in his sermons delivered on Sundays in the chapel, this matter occupied its full place, and, indeed, was never entirely out of sight, yet it was in these informal weekly meetings that it received its most specific consideration. These meetings, beginning under the administration of Dr. Keith, and tested as to their beneficial influence by him and his colleagues, at once commended themselves to the regard of his successor. He was in the habit of making thorough preparation for them, as was, indeed, necessary, at first, through his want of experience in extemporaneous speaking, such experience, prior to his residence in Virginia, being largely confined to the recitation room. This specific preparation continued, however, even after the sort of necessity just alluded to had ceased to exist, when it had become as natural to him to clothe his thoughts in words in the Faculty meeting, as at recitation. He expected and prayed for fruit, results of spiritual benefit, from these occasions, and he conscientiously used the means, and made the effort to obtain them. Some of the subjects we subjoin in the Appendix, with a sketch of their treatment. His colleague, Dr. May, who became a member of the Faculty within the first eighteen months after his arrival, September, 1842, like himself, took the deepest interest in these occasions, and was peculiarly happy in his presentation of topics of an edifying character. But there was a great difference, at that time, between the two, in one respect—the comfort with which the duty was performed. With Dr. May it seemed to involve as little of effort to extemporize as it did to converse; and whatever his preparation, in specific cases, he could, upon very brief notice, and without appearance of anxiety, be exceedingly profitable. It had, indeed, been with great effort, as his pupils afterwards ascertained from him, that he had attained this freedom; in such freedom having greatly the advantage of Dr. Sparrow. To the latter, while the Faculty meeting was a recognized means of grace to himself and his pupils, and therefore conscientiously used, it was yet, for a very considerable time, a severe task and duty; one looked forward to, week after week, with anxious solicitude, and to which he had to nerve himself up for its performance. There was, to the hearer, very little indication of anything of the sort, saving the fact of a little more excitement of manner in the beginning—very little difference between the exhortations and addresses of 1842 and those of 1872. In fact, one of the happiest efforts that he ever made, to be spoken of further on, was the year after the earliest of these dates. And others of the same period might be specified. But, for all, there was the difficulty and reluctance, never entirely overcome, to trust himself, beyond the recitation room, and, later, the Faculty meeting, in this manner of speaking. "It was," said he, alluding to it subsequently, and after the trial in these respects had passed away, "it was to me a source of anxious anticipation and solicitude for a good part of the week before, especially when I had to open the meeting. On Thursday night, after it was over, I would feel relieved. But it was not long before I began to dread the next one." His earlier pupils may thus more gratefully estimate the instructions and suggestions of those meetings; not only in view of their intrinsic value, but of their cost—the expenditure of heart involved in their preparation and delivery. No less may those of a later date, who received similar pleasure and benefit, gratefully congratulate themselves that he thus persevered, in spite of his reluctance and his difficulties, until what had been irksome became pleasurable; and he thus became ready to pour out, week after week, those counsels of wisdom, of love, of warning, and of encouragement, by which so many were incited and strengthened to the work of ministerial duty. This result proved, moreover, what he might have done, had he undertaken to preach his more elaborate discourses with the same kind of preparation, that is, the material thoroughly mastered, as to its digestion and arrangement, and the language extemporaneous. But, however it may have been with such undertaking, or with efforts of similar kind elsewhere, certainly there was no doubt as to his success and efficiency in the Faculty meeting. Here, during the later years of his life, he was perfectly at home, as much so as in the recitation room. And there are few of the listeners during those last years, say, after the restoration of the Seminary in 1865, who will not bear them in grateful remembrance. It was pre-eminently "the old man eloquent," especially when the topic, started by some other member of the Faculty, would strike upon some great truth in which he was particularly interested. The last one of those addresses—who that heard it can ever forget it, so suggestive to the hearers, so full of wisdom and of love, unconsciously yet so beautifully descriptive of his own career, just about to close!

Perhaps, as illustrative of the character of these addresses as any other, was one delivered in the spring of 1846, under circumstances peculiarly solemn, both to himself and his hearers: that on the Thursday night following the reception of intelligence of the death of a member of the class graduating the year before, and, therefore, personally known to most of the hearers. There were, moreover, additional features in the case which made the event specially impressive. The death had been very sudden. This sudden death was that of one who had enjoyed unbroken vigorous health; who was looking forward to a career of activity; and who was expected, by his teachers, and his fellow-students, to take a commanding position, and to wield a mighty influence. The language said to have been used by Sir Isaac Newton in regard to one who was taken in the dew of his youth, perhaps expressed the feelings of Dr. Sparrow in thinking of the death of Albert Duy, "if that young man had lived, we should have known something." As late as 1870 or 1871, he gave a striking expression to these feelings. Some of the students of this later period will remember his allusion to one who, in his expectations, would prove a "*malleus hereticorum*," but whose sudden and early departure showed the vanity of all earthly expectations. It was, therefore, with deeply solemnized feeling that he first heard of this event, and endeavored to make use of it for practical improvement. The sketch which follows is, of course, only an outline. It will, however, afford some exhibition of his own feelings, as also of the mode in which he endeavored to render similar feelings in others productive of profitable reflection.

"A Departed Friend.

"A few words appropriate to the topic of the moment: but that topic itself needs no interpreter. It needs none to the stranger who reads the fact in the newspaper. It is more than an ordinary passing bell, announcing the general fact of mortality. Especially is it more to us. Next to his family we stand. The intimacy of three years and the same calling constituted a bond of communion. After his departure he kept up, by correspondence, his connection with this place. On Saturday last, perhaps the last letter he wrote reached here. Death was standing by, bidding him finish and prepare. The next morning he was gone!

"The result of all this intercourse has been to give us all a high opinion of our departed brother.

"He came to us with a high reputation for so young a man, was possessed of natural talent, had enjoyed opportunities of improvement, and was blessed with permanent health. To these, under a faithful pastor, Rev. Dr. Clark, he had added a Christian profession. The promises involved in these he had fulfilled. What pleased us most, and the value of the consideration now plainly occurs, was his growth in Christian character. The ripening of his mind was apparent; so was that of his graces. When he left us we had great hopes. He was found to be a useful man, and the people wished him to continue in his position. He visited his home, in Philadelphia, to consult, and wrote to me, in part, about that. This was on Wednesday. He was seized on Thursday, and died on Sunday; and now he is in the grave, and we are mourning his loss. Lord, what is man! Lord, what is human life—what human expectations!

"These lessons are apt to be forgotten. As the track of a ship in the waters, of a bird in the air, or as the changing of a summer's cloud, they leave no permanent impression. Let us not be 'forgetful hearers of the word' of such dispensations.

"1. It teaches us the sovereignty of God. We are apt to forget this, through our worldliness. If all things flowed on in an equable current, we should forget God. 'All things continue as they were from the beginning of creation,' is the language of mocking unbelief. God breaks in upon this equable course, plants seed, but lets not the harvest ripen; lays a foundation, but raises no superstructure. This He did with our friend. 'The Lord gave, the Lord hath taken away.'

"2. Again, we are taught the insignificance of man. O, that we should ever be proud or think highly of ourselves! What have we that we have not received? Every gift, every opportunity of cultivating them, every sphere for exercising them, every hour allowed us in the vineyard, is of the Lord. Last Sunday I had occasion to remark, 'how readily the Lord can dispense with us; and that He employs us not for His, but for our sakes. He has made us, and He would make us happy by employing our energies; and this can be done only in His service. Therefore it is that he uses us.' But little did I think what a sad verification my words were receiving; that he was refusing to employ an instrument that seemed eminently fit and meet for the Master's use. 'I have no *use* for thee, go at once to thy rest in Heaven!'

"3. It should repress ambition. How inconsistent in the followers of Jesus! He promises not crowns, but a cross. How absurd in itself! See where it must end. God only knows how soon.

"It should teach us to prepare and to be prepared for our great change. Youth and its anticipations, youth and its preparations, youth and its comparisons with old age, make us forget our mortality and sudden liability to death. Our friend being dead, in all these respects, speaketh. We should, also, love to weep with them that weep; as we feel our need of sympathy, should extend it to others."

Connected with these two forms of effort and of influence, was another, already alluded to, which just here may receive more specific notice, that of his Sunday's work in the chapel. The professors, in turn, officiated on these occasions, each thus becoming due on one Sunday in three. Dr. Sparrow was, perhaps, at his highest capacity, as a preacher, at this time. His reputation had preceded him, but it was soon recognized to be fully deserved. The most striking characteristic of his sermons was that of systematic thoroughness. The subject, whatever it might be, was carefully and naturally approached, very frequently through an elaborate introduction, which, however, was often made use of to tell in the subsequent discussion, or to dispose of subordinate issues. When thus reached, the subject, or truth, or principle to be enforced, was fairly and vigorously grasped, analytically extricated from all irrelevancy and sources of confusion in thought or in language, put in its relations to other and corroborative truths, and pressed, with these its accumulations, to his anticipated result. Along with this argumentative power, was that of a chastened yet vigorous imagination, peculiar felicity of illustration, especially of Scriptural quotation, whether as sustaining the point at issue, or as more clearly exhibiting its meaning. The language and style of discussion were simple and unpretentious, always dignified and earnest, often exceedingly impressive, sometimes startlingly so, at times rising to the highest degree of impassioned earnestness. The description of Dr. McElroy, as he heard him twelve or fourteen years before, in Ohio, already given, brings to view the main characteristics of delivery which continued during his whole course. The felicity of the expression used by Dr. McElroy, that of "his whole countenance as a blaze of light," will be recognized by some of his hearers of this period. There were, of course, at different stages of his ministry, different degrees of physical power, of nervous energy, having their natural influence upon his effectiveness in delivery. This was more sensibly felt by his old pupils, who heard him after a long interval. There were times, indeed, happy moments, even to the last, occasionally through the whole sermon, and during passages in almost every sermon, when he was all in delivery that he had ever been. The closing address of the session of 1869, and that of 1872, will occur to some of our readers as illustrations of this remark. So far as regarded capacity and vigor of thought, there was, to the close, no trace of abatement. His intellect was untouched. There was no manifestation of failure or decay, not even in what is usually their first intimation, that of a failing and defective memory. The changes alluded to, of effectiveness in delivery, were owing mainly to physical causes, the approach of age, diminished capacity of sustained exertion, and the interest corresponding. They were partly due, also, in certain cases, to causes of a different character. The impossibility of entirely reproducing the freshness of feeling and of interest with which sermons of an earlier date had been prepared and preached, when they were subsequently repeated, was one of these. The habit, again, of later years, of omitting parts of the discourse, particularly of leaving out the introduction, for the purpose of shortening, was another. This latter practice always had the manifest effect, and one easily recognized by the watchful hearer, of dampening the interest of the speaker, disturbing his flow of feeling, and interfering with his thorough absorption in the subject matter of discussion. These omissions were more connected with his later years. When he first came to Virginia, they were much less frequent. The introduction enabled him to approach his subject in such a manner as to put himself in thorough sympathy with its material as it was reached; to give him impetus and increase of interest, so as to carry his hearers with him, successfully, to the close; the peculiar charm, indeed, of his preaching, consisted very largely in this last peculiarity—thorough identification of intellect and of feeling, alike with the truths and ideas presented, the emotion, the voice, and the whole personality so kindling with the thought, and expressing it, that its full power was conveyed to the hearer. No reproduction of these sermons upon the printed page can give any conception of their power as preached, say, during the first half of his ministry in Virginia. The same remark may be made as to many portions of those discourses as delivered from the pulpit during the later years of his life. It was a rich treat to his pupils to hear him at the Diocesan Convention, where he usually preached during some part of the services; no less so in the meetings of associations and convocations, which, during the vacations, he was sometimes in the habit of attending.

As already intimated, these discourses were delivered, or rather read from the manuscript, the reading bringing out the feeling and thought, sometimes in a very impassioned manner; but still it was reading, no attempt at anything else. As to extemporaneous preaching, the difficulties already alluded to, in connection with the Thursday night services, were felt in connection with the pulpit, and with increased force. Occasionally, however, at this time, during the Lent services particularly, he would make short addresses from the chancel. One, of a very striking character, the writer remembers, made to the pupils of the High-school, soon after the death of one of their number, and another to the students, during the first visit of Dr., afterward Bishop Boone, to the Seminary, in 1843. But with these exceptions, his sermons were delivered from the manuscript. At the same time, while there was such distrust and low estimate of his own extemporaneous powers, he had great admiration of it as exhibited by others. Indeed, it was almost amusing, sometimes, to hear his expressions of admiration for what was very little more than the power of verbal continuance. The wonderful thing to him was, that a man, without flurry or discomposure, could stand before an audience, and discourse with the same ease and connection as under ordinary circumstances. Especially was this feeling expressed in connection with the power of amplification. "When," said he, speaking of his own difficulties, "when I state my proposition, I have nothing more to say. How to expand, to enlarge, to amplify, this is my trouble;" and yet, in the recitation room, he was doing it daily, without embarrassment or hesitation. As some of these difficulties diminished, by practicing in the Faculty meetings, and otherwise, there was a corresponding diminution of his admiration of mere fluency. But he never lost his estimate—indeed, it was rather increased and heightened—of the importance of the extemporaneous capacity.

One of the efforts of that kind, already alluded to, will be recalled by this allusion to the sermons of that period; that which took place at the closing meeting, in the old prayer hall, of the professors and students, with Bishop Boone, towards the close of the session of 1842–3. During the week previous, Bishop, then Dr. Boone, in his first visit to this country, after the opening of the four Chinese ports, and with all the expectations suggested by that event, had been holding a series of meetings with the students, and conferences with individuals, in reference to the great work opening in that country to successful missionary exertion. A most remarkable degree of interest had been called forth, and a large number of the students were occupied with the inquiry as to their own course of duty. The day of his departure, July 4th, there being no regular exercises on that day, there was a closing meeting of final appeal and reiteration, in reference to the topics of previous occasions. Dr. Packard and Dr. May followed Dr. Boone, with remarks corroborative of what had been urged, and expressive of their interest in the subject of which they had been specially reminded; and, for the first time during the series of services, they were followed by Dr. Sparrow. His object, as he remarked, in his opening sentences, was "to remove any wrong impression that might be created by his silence, as to his want of sympathy in what had been said, or of interest in the great work of which his brethren had been speaking. Such impression he could not consent should exist. No language could fully describe his interest in this great work of extending to the heathen the blessings of the Gospel. That work in itself, in its results to the missionary, to his pupils, and to the world, when successful, passed all possibility of human estimation. It was one, moreover, which, entered upon in a proper spirit, could not know of utter failure, would be productive of beneficial consequences. Even supposing what, in the world's view, would be regarded as failure—that any such effort to carry the Gospel to the heathen should end in catastrophe; that the little band of missionaries, after having bidden farewell to Christian friends and relatives, should never reach their point of destination; that 'He who has gathered the winds in His fists' should send after them the overwhelming tempest, and that, with all their sanctified aspirations and plans, they should go down in mid-ocean! even in such case, the example and self-sacrifice would not be lost. This sacrifice and effort would be endless blessing to those making it. Even as undertaken, although the undertaking should be a failure, it would incite others to similar exertions to take up the work which had fallen from their hands, and carry it on to a successful conclusion!" The brief indication thus given of the line of thought in the address can, of course, afford no adequate conception of those thoughts as clothed in words at the time, and finding their highest expression in the fervid emotion of the speaker. Taken altogether, it was one of the most stirring and eloquent appeals to which the writer has ever listened, paralleled, perhaps, by expository discourses on the Temptation, and one on 1 John, i, 9, during the Lent services of 1871–2, but not exceeded by these or any others of later periods.

During this earlier portion of his residence in Virginia, also, when there was greater capacity of meeting it, there was very considerable demand for his services in the neighborhood. He preached very frequently in Alexandria, Georgetown, Washington, and Baltimore. But it was with more special enjoyment, that he attended and took part in the associations for preaching, held in the country parishes. The convocational system, at that time, was unknown in Virginia. But a great deal of the work which is now done through the convocations, was then done through the associations, so far as the matter of preaching was concerned, perhaps more effectively.

It now remains that we speak more particularly of his work in the department of instruction, his special duties as Professor. During the first year, as we have seen, he taught Church History; and this again was added to his duties at a subsequent period, during the partial disorganization occasioned by the war, from 1861 to 1866. His notes and questions show a very pains-taking and thorough mastery of the materials. It was a part of the course, however, for which he had no special inclination; and he speaks, in a letter of 1841, of the effort with which he entered upon his duties. The work by which he was better known to the ten or eleven generations of students who were with him in Virginia, was that in the departments of Christian Evidences, and Systematic Divinity. And of these it will be proper to give more specific notice. The former of these, Christian Evidences, including Butler's "Analogy," occupied the latter part of the junior and the earlier portion of the middle year. During the first ten years, perhaps, in Virginia, the Evidence course was one which he himself had worked out. It consisted of written questions, with references. The recitation was accompanied by a full discussion and exposition of the topics presented; and there was opportunity afforded to the student to correct or fill out imperfect answers. Opportunity was thus given of thorough preparation for review. At a later period this was changed, and text-books were used. At the time spoken of the practice was as described. The peculiar interest was in the exposition and the discussion. And the effort of looking up the material for the answers, as also the previous study of the questions, constituted an admirable preparation for these, and enabled the student fully to understand and appreciate them. But for Dr. Sparrow's habitual self-depreciation, he would probably have continued this mode of instruction. Such course, from year to year, with additions, bringing up the arguments and replies to new objections and difficulties from time to time urged, would have been a valuable contribution to the department of Apologetics. The hope, indeed, was indulged, even to the last, by some of his friends and pupils, that among his papers something like this would have been found. His high standard, and his sense of deficiency, constituted to such effort an insuperable difficulty. Whether, on the whole, with his physique, and daily duties, demanding a certain amount of daily exertion, he did not accomplish more, going on as he did, and refusing to be implicated in the labors and vexations of literary life, is a question not easily answered. But without deciding this point, there need to be no hesitation in saying that such self-depreciation was carried too far; and that inferior men, as they always will, if superior ones stand aside, or are backward, had to do work that he might and could have done very much better. This was particularly felt during the existence of the "Evangelical Quarterly," from 1852–61; when effort was frequently made, but in vain, to enlist him among the contributors. One of the most admirable articles of that Review was written by a clergyman, not one of his pupils, who, after drawing him out conversationally, on a certain subject, and getting him to state his views, put them upon paper, and thus brought them before the world. Not less was it a source of regret, with reference to works of a more permanent character. "Doctor," said one of his pupils to him, in 1844, in reply to a remark which he had made, in regard to Burnet's exposition, "Doctor, why do not you prepare a book on the Articles? You have the material, why not write it down." "Bishop McIlvaine," was the reply, "urged me to do so ten years ago." But the wish of bishop and student alike failed to bring the desired result. One of Dr. Sparrow's pupils particularly, the early-called and lamented Henry Dennison, was especially pertinacious with reference to this matter, and from year to year recurred to it. But the objections and difficulties were always insuperable. Apart from sermons and addresses, published by special request, his nearest approaches to authorship were in this system of questions on Evidences, as also in a similar one on Systematic Divinity.

Following his course on specific evidence, was his instruction based upon Butler's "Analogy." Dr. Sparrow made a great deal of this part of his course. It was not only an exposition and development of the great argument of that work, but also of its principles, in their manifold application. The work itself he had thoroughly mastered. With its line of thought, as its details and illustrations, he was perfectly familiar. His own thinking was greatly in accordance with its principles, and his effort was to imbue with it the minds of his pupils: to teach them, with Butler, to assert and positively decide no further than real knowledge would justify; to discriminate carefully between what was really known and what was not known; and in all doubtful cases to judge of the unknown by the known, so far as they had anything in common, and not to judge of the known by the unknown. It may be said of him, that he Butlerized in all his teaching, as in all his thinking and argumentation. The "Analogy" stood in about the same relation to his theological course as Hooker seems to have intended that the first book on law should stand to his subsequent argument on polity. What, however, Hooker failed to do with the principles of the book on law, Dr. Sparrow succeeded in doing with those of the Analogy. He consistently applied them, and never seemed to lose sight of them. And it was usually in this part of his course that the question with any particular pupil was decided, whether or not he would diverge from, or travel on, sympathizingly and lovingly, with his instructor. This decision was, no doubt, in many cases unconsciously made. The beginning of the divergence was not at the time, perhaps, suspected. But events made it manifest, as the application of Butler's principles, at a later period, came in conflict with some cherished opinion. Apart, moreover, from such application of these principles, or their controlling influence in his subsequent teaching, the intellectual training involved in his mode of mastering and applying the argument to the specific purpose of Butler, was highly quickening and beneficial. In this, as with the Evidences, there were written questions. But these were used only in review. The work was first gone over, studied, recited, and its principles fully discussed, the questions coming in and giving distinctness and form to the whole preceding process. These recitations on Butler were sometimes anticipated with special anxiety. But they were rarely remembered with any other feelings than those of gratification. In more cases than one, his pupils at the Seminary had studied and graduated upon the book elsewhere. But never in such manner, or to such degree of perfection, as to prevent their finding new light in it from their new teacher—applications and meanings hitherto unrecognized and even unsuspected.

The study of this work was followed by that of Systematic Divinity. Prior to his residence in Virginia, Dr. Sparrow seems to have used other works, at the same time very largely a system of his own, like that on Evidences, with questions and references. He found in use a text-book, Knapp's Theology, introduced by Dr. Keith, and adopting this, continued to use it until the close of his life. A large portion of the Middle year was occupied with this work, in the examination and discussion of topics of General Theology, while the Senior year following was more particularly given to the theological standards of the Church of England, the Articles, and Homilies, and Prayer-book. The characteristics of teaching already alluded to, in connection with Butler, were exhibited in these later portions of the course. The object in Systematic Divinity was to settle it upon a Scriptural basis, to establish correct principles of interpretation, throwing out everything irrelevant and doubtful, and thus giving prominence to what was clear—the meaning of which was undoubted. With this there was the constant recurrence to certain great established principles, the truth and the light, wherever clear, being fearlessly followed. At the same time, while indicating the region of doubtful speculation, there was a refusal, while within that region, to indulge in anything like dogmatism. Among his qualifications as a theological teacher this was not the least important—the capacity of ascertain-in gand distinctly recognizing the real limits of human knowledge in historical fact and statement, as of human attainment in theological and philosophical speculation. He recognized and presented to his pupils, in these latter departments, the real nature of the issues involved in certain problems of speculation; and thus showed the incapacity of finite powers to comprehend, much less to solve them. His constant effort was to quicken thought, to stimulate a spirit of investigation, not only as to facts, but their causes and relations; and in such effort he was pre-eminently successful. But, in thought which was not definite, and in investigation which had no practically specific object, he had little interest or sympathy. Consciously living himself in a world of realities, he impressed his pupils with the same conviction—a conviction transforming alike the highest results of legitimate speculation and the simplest materials of revealed precept into those of practical affection and personal action.

Nor was it merely in the recitation room, in the Thursday night meeting, or in the chapel, that his peculiar gift of impartation was exercised. He was a teacher everywhere, without intending it, unconsciously fulfilling his vocation. Men who met with him in social life found that they were learning from him, that his conversation was bringing to them new ideas, new facts altogether, or old facts under new aspects and in new relations. This was peculiarly the case in his intercourse with his pupils. His study was always accessible, visits from students were always cordially welcomed, and he was ever ready for conversation. Especially did he seem to welcome and enjoy such visits when not well enough, from his headaches, to study, but able to enjoy conversation, and even partially to forget his discomfort. Never was the power of mind over matter more clearly exhibited than on some of these occasions, in the change from languor and weakness to apparent strength and health, as his countenance would lighten and glow with the interest of conversation and discussion. A visit and a talk, in many cases, seemed to act as a restorative.

Of course, there were some students who enjoyed such opportunities more largely than others. But it was simply because they more sought and appreciated them. And some, perhaps, of the most pleasant reminiscences of students of those days have their connection with such occasions in the Doctor's study, or as they might fall in with him in his walks to Alexandria. The account of one of these latter, from the recollections of a pupil, will not be, just here, without its interest. "It was my first talk with the dear old Doctor, and it comes back to me with a freshness and feeling of pleasure which it is impossible for me to describe. I was in the early part of the Junior year, and had not as yet met him in recitation, when I overtook him, one afternoon, about half way between the Seminary and Alexandria. I had one or two bundles, and my wood saw, which I was taking to town to have sharpened." The students of the present generation may here be reminded, that in those days of primitive simplicity wood was the only fuel known on the Hill,* and, with a few rare exceptions, the students, each one, did his own sawing. Cumberland had not, as yet, appeared. The Post-office for the Seminary was in Alexandria, the students taking it by turns, alphabetically, to go in, each afternoon, for the mail; and bundles of all kinds, to and fro, came and went in the hands of their owners. But, leaving this digression, we resume the account. "The Doctor, as I came up, noticed the number of my bundles, and insisted upon relieving me, which he did, by taking the saw, and carrying it to the edge of town, where the sharpener lived. We were soon in conversation, the most interesting part of it started by a question about the Oxford Tracts, but going on from this to other topics. Especially do I remember an opinion about Coleridge, expressive of a high appreciation of his genius, but at the same time objecting to some of his principles, as transcending those of the Baconian and Butlerian systems. How the conversation passed from these topics to that of poetry, I have no recollection. But I well remember that portion of it; and his expressions of admiration in regard to some of the lyrics of Thomas Moore, as also the manner in which he repeated a couple of stanzas from one of them. Certainly the lines were very beautiful, especially as he repeated them. But there can be, I think, as little doubt that their association with Ireland, and the circumstances under which they were first heard, in early youth or childhood, added to his impression of their beauty. The pleasure of that afternoon's walk and conversation I shall never cease to remember. And I hope its imperfect reproduction may recall as pleasant ones to others of his pupils who have enjoyed the same opportunities."

It will thus be seen that Dr. Sparrow was finding his full sphere of influence, as of grateful occupation, in his new field of duty. It was not very long, however, before there was presented a disturbing question, inducements to a change, which required deliberation and a struggle, enabling him to decide as to what constituted his course of duty. In the year 1844 there came an invitation and earnest request that he would return to Gambier, and resume the duties of his old position. Subsequent invitations, of a most flattering character, as we shall see, were given him to the same position. But this first one came so soon, and it brought back so

* Dr. May, who had lived in the coal region, first introduced Anthracite to the community on the Hill, and soft coal followed, a few years later, when the canal from Cumberland reached Alexandria.

many of the associations and schemes of usefulness in his early field of labor, recalling as it did his deep interest and early efforts for the success of the College and Seminary, that he was greatly moved by it, and found some difficulty in reaching his decision. As will be seen from his correspondence, his work in Virginia, and his official connections, were all agreeable. The only difficulty which had its weight, was that connected with the use of slave labor, in the domestics of his household, to which he had not been accustomed, and to which he felt reluctance. His general views of that subject will come out incidentally, in the course of our narrative. It is here alluded to simply as indicating one of the elements to be regarded in reaching his conclusion. This, however, and all others, were fully and carefully considered, and the result of that consideration was that he ought not to make the proposed change. The following letter to his old friend, Dr. Wing, written immediately after reaching the conclusion thus indicated, will have its interest in connection with this subject:—

"THEOLOGICAL SEMINARY, FAIRFAX COUNTY, VA.,
"September 26th, 1844.

"DEAR BROTHER :—

"I write with a heavy heart, in part because I know my letter will give heaviness to yours. After a most painful and protracted consideration of the question of removal to Ohio, I am brought to the conclusion that I *ought not* to leave my present post. I have weighed the matter, day and night, ever since it has been placed before me. Whether reading, or talking, or dreaming I might almost say, there has been an under current of thought upon this subject, which has never for a moment ceased to flow. The various considerations that have presented themselves, it would be impossible for me to give or even hint at. Indeed, it would answer no purpose. I may say, however, that amongst the influences which have swayed me, has not been anything like indifference toward the persons who have been any way connected with the giving of the call. The bishop's happiness I should deem it my happiness to promote, to the utmost of my ability; and you know that in the welfare of the college I take the deepest interest. For the Faculty, also, I have great personal regard. As to yourself, I feel constrained to say, the occasion is so very special, that there is not a man of all my acquaintance in close neighborhood to whom I would rather live and die; and my family partakes fully of the same feeling toward yourself and Mrs. Wing. But after a careful and prayerful consideration of what my friends on both sides of the Alleghanies have said, I cannot see it my duty to leave this Institution.

"I can scarcely refrain from going into the reasons of my determination; but I feel it would be an unsatisfactory and abortive attempt, in the narrow space of a letter, and, therefore, I forbear. I wish, however, that it may be distinctly understood that I consider the post so unanimously offered me by Bishop McIlvaine and the Trustees as one highly honorable, responsible and important, and requiring to fill it adequately, a man of higher attainments and greater ability than I pretend to possess.

"I rejoice that you did not come to see me, under the circumstances. Under any others, it would rejoice my heart to see you. I go next Monday to the General Convention at Philadelphia. I wish you were a delegate, that I might talk over old times with you.

"I have written to Mr. Bronson, as Chairman of the Committee. The bishop I shall see in Philadelphia. I wish he could know of my determination before we meet.

"This is the seventh letter I have written, 'hand running,' and I am tired. Mrs. Sparrow and the children join in affectionate remembrances to Mrs. Wing. Your affectionate brother,

"WILLIAM SPARROW."

The General Convention thus alluded to was the first in which Dr. Sparrow appeared as a delegate from Virginia. For many succeeding sessions he occupied a similar position. From his repugnance to the effort of extemporaneous speaking, as from all want of practice in parliamentary discussion, he was one of the silent members of the body. One, however, of the most effective of his fellow delegates, in debate, as in all other respects, Mr. Philip Williams, always spoke of him as pre-eminently wise in council, and, therefore, a most valuable member of the delegation.

It will be remembered that this earlier portion of Dr. Sparrow's labors in Virginia, from 1841 to 1848, was contemporaneous with the most earnest part of the Oxford Tract controversy. The first Diocesan Convention which he attended, soon after his arrival, in May, 1841, in Alexandria, witnessed a struggle in reference to that subject. The chairman of the Committee on the State of the Church, Dr. Empie, having, in his report, alluded to the Tracts, and warned against them, objection was offered, and the effort made to prevent its acceptance, and, of course, endorsement by the Convention. One of the objections, most pertinaciously urged, was that of the incompetency of the Convention to an opinion upon the merits of certain publications which the majority had not read. This objection was neutralized, to a great degree, by the closing speech of the author of the report, in the shape of abundant quotations, the meaning and drift of which could scarcely be misunderstood; and the report was accepted. It was a gratifying indication to Dr. Sparrow, as to the nature of his new ecclesiastical associations, and of the sympathy and assistance upon which he might depend, in the performance of his official duties. His own position, as to the leaders and principles of this movement, was clearly defined and distinctly understood. From the first, to his mind, their real character and tendency were manifest. He, therefore, made it his special work, recognized it as the work to which, in his peculiar position, he had been providentially called, to counteract and neutralize their influence. It was, in his estimation, an effort, under the forms of sacerdotalism and sacramentalism, to materialize Christianity, to pervert it as a religion of inward spirit and life, to one of outward form and ceremony. The excuse itself, which was made for this movement, and which doubtless actuated some of its leaders, that of expelling the demon of German Rationalism by Patristic authority, was, in his view, a dishonor done to God's word, and only calculated to increase the evil which it undertook to remedy. With these views, there could be little doubt or hesitation as to the character of his teaching. As the questions specifically raised in this controversy came up, they were subjected to thorough examination, and this with reference to a twofold object. First, to show that the novelties with which so many were fascinated, and which, from this feature of their novelty, had a charm to a certain class of mind among his students, were old errors. Secondly, that they were not only errors tested in the light of Scripture, but distinctly repudiated by the English and Continental Reformers; not capable of adjustment to the system of those Reformers, but belonging, in logic and in spirit alike, to the system from which they had separated. The trumpet, upon these points, gave no uncertain sound. His own convictions were clear, as to the nature of the issues involved, as to their fundamental character, as to the impossibility of compromise, especially of the favorite one of that period, the via media, except by a betrayal of essential Christian doctrine. As these convictions were clear to his own mind, he attempted to place them clearly before the minds of others. His pupils, whether they adopted his views or not, were in no doubt as to his meaning. When failing to produce conviction, he never failed in the impression of thorough earnestness and truthfulness of intent, as of transcendent ability. This impression, that of the sacredness of truth, and of all convictions attained in its reception, reached all classes of his pupils, even those who differed from him most widely. While to a special class, those who were in sympathy, or who, in the attitude of learners, were seeking to know the truth, to clear and systematize their views, to be able to see and to give a reason for the hope that was in them, these instructions were recognized as of the highest interest and importance. The effective Teacher, of course, who forms the sound and spiritual theologian, is the Holy Ghost. Where His teaching has not preceded, and does not accompany that of the theological professor, the result must and will be a failure. It is not, therefore, properly a matter of surprise, that a portion of the pupils of Dr. Sparrow, or of any other teacher, should eventually be enlisted among his opponents. Even with these, however, a powerfully modifying influence is often exerted. Their sacerdotalism, or sacramentalism, or ecclesiasticism, is of a very different character from what it would have been, formed under other influences. These elements, in many cases, precede the teacher's instructions, survive, in spite of them, but are greatly modified by them. At the same time, there is a different class; and Dr. Sparrow had the joy of knowing that there was a good proportion of it among his pupils; those who thoroughly sympathized with and appreciated their teacher, fully received his instructions and principles, and then carried them out in lives of ministerial activity and usefulness. The great contest to which allusion has been made, and to which his teaching of that period necessarily had large reference, was reaching its climax at the time of the General Convention in which Dr. Sparrow first appeared as a Delegate from Virginia. The fullest discussion of its merits, of any in that body, took place on that occasion. This discussion only preceded, by a few months, the first decided exode of the leaders of that movement from the Church of England to that of Rome. One prominent individual took part in this discussion, scouting all notion of Romeward tendencies in the Oxford leaders or their objects, who, in a very short time, followed them. These latter developments, perhaps, had more effect than any discussion, in arresting this movement, and bringing discredit upon its advocates. But its elements remained, as the seed of a later harvest of error and annoyance; elements of unscriptural error, palliated and toyed with on one side, and resisted on the other, until they reached their development in full-blown Ritualism. Dr. Sparrow's work, therefore, all along, during the lull between, as during the hottest contest of the Tractarian and Ritualistic controversies, was to expose and to refute error as it appeared, and to guard his pupils against the reception of germinal principles in which the worst errors of these movements found their origin. In this respect, his whole professorial career was a contest; a contest in which many who agreed with him doctrinally did not sympathize, and, indeed, regarded as unnecessary. But "wisdom is justified of her children." Certainly, the evolution of the last ten or fifteen years justifies every effort in the way of Scriptural teaching to anticipate and prevent it. Had no such effort been made, no warning preceded, how much more hopeless would have been the present effort and prospect of resistance.*

The following communication, from one of the Virginia clergy, Dr. Slaughter, who, during this period, was brought into association with Dr. Sparrow, will be read with interest, not only in view of the criticism expressed, but as exhibiting the views of the Doctor himself upon a topic, at that time, of exciting interest and importance. As already mentioned, Dr. Sparrow found great pleasure in attending the religious meetings carried on for several days by associated clergymen from neighboring parishes. We find, from his correspondence, that such was his habit in Ohio; and when he came to his new home, in Virginia, this habit was continued. His part of the work, however, owing to the peculiarity alluded to already, and by this correspondent, was that of preaching from the pulpit. The

* "For forty years—ever since the first Oxford Tract was issued—Dr. Sparrow has stemmed this current of error which has been coming in like a flood upon our Church. To him, under God, we owe it, more than to any other man, living or dead, that we still have a body of Evangelical clergy, or that there is still hope that Achan shall be cast out as one that troubleth Israel."—*Dr. McKim's Sermon on the Sunday after Dr. Sparrow's Funeral.*

exhortations following the sermons, or of the informal prayer meetings, he left for others. In some few exceptional cases, under pressure, he departed from his usual rule, but always at the sacrifice of feeling preceding, and with annoyance following. The criticism, therefore, is very largely correct, as to the Doctor's peculiarities, of that time. But, it will read very strangely to some of his pupils of later years. These will remember not so much the intellectual power, wonderful as that sometimes was, but the close, searching, startling, practical appeals to the heart and conscience. But we let the writer speak for himself.

"I cannot lay a just claim to any special intimacy with Dr. Sparrow. He always seemed to be 'so above me,' that I was content to look up to him with admiration, as we do at the stars, and silently rejoice in the light which he shed all around him—a light which will long stream above the horizon which hides him from our view, as does that of the sun after he has gone down to our eyes. I have never come in contact with the man who combined the like breadth of comprehension and luminous insight into the heart of a subject, and who marshaled his thoughts in such logical phalanx, and made them march in such lucid order, as this great master of sentences. It was one of the purest joys I have ever known, to have him, in private converse or in public discourse, unfold a dark, intricate topic, until it was transfigured into an illuminated transparency.

"And yet, with all his wondrous powers, our friend had a serious defect as a preacher; a defect of which he was painfully conscious, and which I have heard him bitterly lament. I mean in practical, in moral capacity, to come down from the purely intellectual sphere in which he habitually moved, and adapt himself to the average hearer. He had power to convince the understanding, and that was the objective point at which he aimed. He had less skill in awakening the conscience and moving the heart. What are called thinking men, moving in literary circles, and, necessarily, educated hearers, too often forget that it is not by pure reason that people in general are made better—not by any rational process, so much as by the magnetism which streams from highly charged emotional natures, and by 'those touches of nature which make the whole world kin.' Dr. Sparrow saw this truth clearly; and he has often come unexpectedly to associations where he heard there was an awakening, declining to preach, and averring that he came to try and detect the secret of other men's success on such occasions, and endeavor to go and do likewise. I remember that he spent a week or more with me when I was pastor in Petersburg, and holding daily services for many weeks continuously. He professed the greatest longing for the gift of successful preaching; and often said he would sacrifice all he possessed for the power of adaptation—the wisdom to win souls.

"This defect was not of the intelligence, for all things to him, humanly speaking, were possible in that sphere. It was probably the result of his life in the chair of the professor, making it incumbent upon him to be armed at all points, and equipped for all emergencies—in a high and peculiar sense, a defender of the faith. Hence the habit of sounding everything to the bottom, measuring its length and breadth, weighing it in the balances, and finding precisely what it was worth. This habit of treating every subject thoroughly, and guarding his front, flanks and rear, like a trained tactician, made it morally impossible for him to condescend to that guerrilla warfare, in which a sharp eye, and a ready hand, and celerity of movement will often be more effective than the heaviest artillery wielded according to the art of war.

"To change the figure, if he saw a man struggling in the water, while he would sympathize as tenderly and heartily with him as others, perhaps more so, the habit of his mind would be to call for a life-boat and save him according to the rules of art, rather than instinctively plunge and swim for his life, dragging the drowning man, by his locks, to the land.

"There was one subject on which Dr. Sparrow and I were in perfect accord—the subject of African colonization. He believed that America in Africa was the true solution of Africa in America. Knowing his interest in this question, I always nominated him as a delegate to the annual meeting in Washington, and he always attended punctually. In handling this subject, I always felt the need of a satisfactory basis for the institution of slavery, as it existed among us; and I sought it from Dr. Sparrow. This led to frequent conversations between us, and to a correspondence, of which I have preserved one of his letters. Although he was born in the North, and educated in Ireland, he had no sympathy with immediate abolitionists. The following extract from his letter will, I think, be of interest. It seems to me 'like apples of gold in pictures of silver.'

"'When Christ came into the world it was full of kingdoms. That these should be held together was indispensable to the existence and progress of society. Society cannot advance *per saltum;* it must advance by degrees. So also it must be improved, for the most part, from within. External ameliorations, which outrun the internal, do no good; witness the South American Republics and the history of France. To improve society, we must implant the principle *within* it, and let it leisurely and without violence work itself out to the surface, amending, last of all, the municipal arrangements. This is the general rule. Now Christ came to set up a kingdom not of this world. It was not of the same class with existing kingdoms; it was not to be their rival nor their fellow. It was to be comprehensive of them all, taking possession of them, and having them use their external features and peculiarities, except as these might be gradually and silently modified by its permeating and all pervading influence. Among these external relations, I set down war, the political relations of men, domestic slavery, and, in a certain sense, divorce. Now, in regard to these, there is a certain *ideal state* which all would call perfection, and which may be realized, perhaps, in the Millennial times, and in the meantime to be approximated. This state we would call *absolute right,* and it consists in the total removal of some of the things named, and in the modification of others. To bring about this state of things, so far as the present time is concerned, was the object of setting up Christ's kingdom. And that object will not fail. It may tarry, but it will come at last. But how is Christianity to realize in the *actual* this beautiful and infinitely desirable *ideal?* It must not precipitate matters; that would prove disastrous. It would be like plucking up the tares before the proper time. As the defects and abuses of society referred to are *governmental,* to assail them directly would bring the kingdom of Christ in direct collision with the kingdoms of this world; which would be most pernicious several ways. Humanly speaking, it would exterminate the Church of Christ; for men would fight against it without restraint of conscience, looking at it as a mere earthly interest. Aside from this, the effect upon the world itself would be most blinding. Christ's kingdom is not wealth, nor political sagacity, nor military prowess; 'but righteousness, peace and joy in the Holy Ghost.' Above all, it would set aside those positive precepts which Christ has given in regard to the powers that may be over us. In all this Christianity is regarding the *expedient.* Just as divorce was allowed to the Jews, though the true idea, the *right* in regard to marriage, was otherwise; so Christianity forbears to press things which it hopes to see realized hereafter in the world. In fixing her eye upon the right, she makes provision for progress. In regulating the pursuit of that object by the expedient, she has a wise reference to the nature of man, and the condition of the world as fallen, and takes care that the progress shall not be checked. Right gives an onward motion to the car, expediency keeps it from running off the track. Each is indispensable in its place; neither can be omitted, nor can their order and mutual relations be interfered with, without consequences which self love, benevolence and conscience must recoil from. To present the subject properly, would require much expansion and explanation; and if I was writing to one who would read what I have written in a captious spirit, I would add many limitations, checks and illustrations.'

"The last sentence is a good example of what I said above, of the Doctor's aversion to touch a subject which he could not exhaust and put beyond all cavil and misconstruction."

In reference to the closing topic alluded to in this communication, a remark was once made in Dr. Sparrow's presence, as to the mode of teaching and action pursued toward it by the Apostles and inspired writers of the New Testament. His reply, in substance, was, that the way in which the New Testament writers dealt with it, in the light of what was going on around him, constituted, to his mind, high evidence of their inspiration. It was not, under their outward circumstances, the wisdom of man.

The following reminiscences of a student of the latter portion of this period, Rev. Charles E. Ambler, while referring to one or two points already mentioned, contain others, which will have their interest in this connection. Of special interest is the last incident related, illustrative of Dr. Sparrow's feelings in regard to everything which would bring reproach upon the Seminary, or suspicion upon the Christian character and consistency of his pupils. He had a high standard of ministerial and lay consistency. With this, he had a clear perception of the opinions and judgments of worldly men, in reference to open improprieties of Christian professors. And thus, in view both of their spiritual benefit, as for the avoidance of reproach upon their Christian and ministerial calling, he endeavored to impress his convictions upon those under his instruction. Herein, too, he was eminently successful. There were pupils, as already mentioned, who did not adopt his theological system. But rarely, if ever, was it the case that one could be found who did not bow in reverence to his high demand for Christ-like excellence and holiness; for single-hearted devotion, in a life unspotted from the world, to the Master's service.

"It was in the year 1842 that I saw Dr. Sparrow for the first time. He had then but recently come from Gambier, in Ohio, to take the chair of Systematic Divinity in the Virginia Seminary, and was attending the Virginia Convention, which that year met in the town of Staunton. His reputation as a learned man and profound theologian was already very great; and, though but a boy at the time, I can well remember how, as he sat in the Convention, with folded arms and down-turned countenance, saying nothing, but apparently noting everything said by others, he seemed to come up fully to my ideal of a great divine.

"When, a year or two after this, I went to the High-school, near the Seminary, in the chapel of the latter, for the first time, I heard the Doctor preach. I had been told by my schoolmates that, though no doubt a great preacher, he was quite too deep to be understood by boys; and that, therefore, there was no use to listen to him. So fully did I become impressed with this idea, that, for several times when he preached, I would not pretend to follow his train of thought, but would sit, enduring as patiently as possible what I believed it impossible for me to enjoy. But, even then, while taking little account of what he said, I remember watching, with delight, the play of his fine countenance, reflecting, as it did, with the most pleasing variety, the sentiments he was uttering. His high, expansive forehead, his mild, yet piercing eyes, so radiant with thought, as he looked up from his manuscript; the smile that would play on his countenance, as some truth of the Gospel would come up before him with new fullness and beauty—all these seem still before me, as I recall the image which he left upon my mind in those early days.

"At length, becoming more and more dissatisfied with being a mere looker-on at the Doctor's preaching, I determined, at least, to make an effort to understand him, and so, if possible, get some of that pleasure and profit which others seemed to draw so largely from his discourses. Accordingly, one Sunday, as I seated myself, after the Morning Service, I made up my mind that I would give him all the attention of which I was capable, from the beginning of his sermon to its close, and thus fairly test the question whether I could understand him or not. To my great surprise and delight, he opened his subject in a manner perfectly clear and simple, and and at the same time highly interesting, riveting my attention from the start, and carrying me along with him, with increasing interest, to the close of his argument. As he concluded, with some practical lessons from the subject, my mind seemed to be left in a state of perfect satisfaction and acquiescence in what he had said. And such was ever afterwards the effect of his preaching upon me when I was privileged to hear him.

"In the year 1845 I became a student of the Seminary, entering the junior class, which, at that time, was taught by Dr. Sparrow, as well as my memory serves me, only in the Evidences of Christianity. The subject, in itself one of deep and absorbing interest to every intelligent and earnest-minded Christian, seemed peculiarly adapted to bring into play the finest powers of Dr. Sparrow's mind. While his questions stimulated to the utmost the spirit of inquiry as to the foundations of our faith, his lucid expositions left no room for doubt as to the broad and solid basis of historical evidence on which it rests. No difficulty was blinked, no objection left unanswered, while the positive evidences of our holy religion were set forth with a clearness and force of logic perfectly overwhelming, the whole effect being incalculably heightened by the enthusiasm of personal conviction with which all his arguments seemed to glow.

"Having referred to Dr. Sparrow as a teacher, it would be improper to leave the subject without mention of that trait which, more than any other, characterized him as such—his absolute deference to the Bible, and the Bible alone, as the infallible authority on religious questions. He fully appreciated the value of the ancient creeds and modern confessions of faith, and of much that has come down to us from the fathers and reformers, as valuable testimonies to the fundamental truths of our religion, and gave them, as such, a prominent place in his teaching. But he ever taught that our faith does not rest in these as ultimate authorities, but only as they are supported by the Word. The creed of the Church, according to a favorite illustration of his, is a convenience, like the weights and measures used in commerce, and like them, in its proper place, is indispensable. Yet like them, also, it is not an ultimate authority, but in case of any dispute, is itself to be referred to an ulterior standard, fixed by law. It is, he would say, not a *mensura mensurans* but a *mensura mensurata.* His very distinct views on this subject, leading him, as they did, to question and reject certain so-called Church doctrines, which rest, as he conceived, rather on ecclesiastical tradition than on Scripture, and which are not in the creeds, gave occasion to some, to whom these things seem to be of the very essence of the faith, to call him a rationalist. But no charge could be more unjust and misplaced. A rationalist, in the proper sense of the word, is one who subjects Scripture to the test of his own reason, rejecting freely its acknowledged teachings when not in accordance with what he calls the light that is in him. But while Dr. Sparrow recognized it as within the province of reason, enlightened by the grace of God, to determine what is, and what is not the teaching of Scripture; this once ascertained, no one bowed with more absolute submission to its deepest mysteries than he. And such was the childlike spirit of his faith in the pure word of God, that I do not believe he would have hesitated to have abandoned the most cherished convictions of his life, had their incompatibility with the word of God been made to appear to him. Surely there was nothing in common with the rationalism of the day in such a spirit as this.

"Shortly after I entered the Seminary, there occurred an incident which may be worth mentioning, as illustrating a point in the Doctor's character, and the type of personal religion which he exemplified.

"A number of the students of the Seminary were invited to an evening entertainment, given by a family in the neighborhood, well reported of for religious consistency. Quite unexpectedly, so far as the students were concerned, shortly after the assembling of the company, music struck up, and the young people began to dance. The dancing did not last very long, and none of the students took part in it. But the incident was the subject of deep regret to Dr. Sparrow. Possibly, he did not know how entirely innocent these young men were of the intention of being at a dancing party. But whether he knew this or not, it pained him to think what might be the effect of the reports going abroad, probably without explanation, that these young candidates for sacred orders had mingled in the frivolous scenes of the ball room. He made the incident the occasion for preaching a sermon on Christian consistency, appealing especially to those who were to be standard bearers in the Lord's host to keep themselves pure, and without reproach, as regards such things, which, if not sinful, were at least doubtful in their character.

"To some, this incident may seem to imply a narrowness of mind, quite out of keeping with his reputation as a great theologian. It may be said, however, in defence of him on this point, if he needs any, that at that time the Church had not come to so entire an agreement with the world as to the innocence of such amusements, as it seems to have done in these days, and even a great man may be excused for taking up, to some extent, with the prejudices of his day. And then, perhaps, after all, there is room to doubt whether the ideas which rule on these points in modern days are truer and better than the old; whether those who look with jealousy upon the influence of fashionable amusements upon the young, or those who take it for a settled maxim that the amusements of young people must needs be innocent, or at any rate, are not the proper subject for the interference of the Church, take the broader view—the view which, in the long run, will prove the truer—the one most for the glory of God, and the good of men. At all events, it is certain, that if this jealousy of the influence of such amusements is narrowness, it is a narrowness fully shared in by the primitive Church, as shown by the numerous and stringent canons enacted in those days against dancing, theatrical shows, and the like. But whatever may be thought of the judgment displayed by Dr. Sparrow in this incident, there can be no doubt that the spirit by which he was actuated was that of Elijah, when it was said of him that he was very jealous for the Lord God of Hosts.

"And I may here remark, as a suitable close to this sketch that, after all, the crowning glory of Dr. Sparrow's character was his deep and ardent piety. Those who only saw him at a distance, and only knew him in his public character, may have been most impressed by his intellectual power; but what most impressed those who came in close contact with him, was the deep-toned spirituality of his mind. This was the secret of the almost magic power by which he used to hold us all spell-bound, in his Thursday night talks at the Faculty meetings. These were the simple outpourings of his heart before his fellow Christians of the Seminary, in personal religion. Without reserve, and without egotism, the rich results of the Lord's dealings with his own soul would be laid before us, for our profit, and his must indeed have been a cold nature whose heart would not often burn within him, while he talked of these things. Many would retire after these wonderful discourses to their rooms, to meditate and pray, and to form new purposes to live more for the glory of God, and the good of men, and eternity alone will disclose the full results of the good impulses, by God's grace imparted to so many candidates for the ministry, on these blessed occasions."

The correspondence following, included in this period, will throw light upon parts of it not brought out in the narrative. The larger portion consists of letters to Dr. Wing. The rest are to other friends, and with one exception, to pupils in the ministry. It is to be regretted that more of these could not be obtained. His correspondence with Bishop Meade, for instance, would have been specially valuable, but was, in all probability, destroyed during the war. As illustrative of many features of his character, both as to mind and heart, those here given will well repay perusal. That peculiar charm of his intercourse in social life, which lighted up everything by his presence, his geniality, ever full of cheerful suggestion, but never giving pain or producing bitterness, will be recognized on every page. His deep interest in certain great issues in the Church then pending, as also in the ministerial success of his pupils, will be no less clearly manifest. These letters also contain an indication as to the mode in which influence exerted upon his pupils during their Theological course, was perpetuated in their subsequent career of ministerial exertion.

"Theological Seminary, Fairfax County, Va.,
"July 15th, 1841.

"Dear Brother:—

"I should have written you by Mr. E., but that you possess the privilege of a Congressman, and it was, withal, very inconvenient to me at the time of his departure. Examination was coming on, and my heart was in my mouth; it is now over, however, and my heart has got back to its proper place, and, therefore, as a matter of course, I write to you. But I am urged, also, by Mrs. Sparrow, who wishes the enclosed letter sent to Mrs. Wing. She would have sent it directly had she known where to direct it. That Mrs. Sparrow should write her at all, these times, I regard pretty good evidence of a strong friendship. She suffers excessively from the heat here, and that, together with her domestic cares and other things, makes it hard for her to get through her necessary duties. She talks much of Mrs. Wing, and will be much disappointed if she does not see her here.

"We have just got through the examination, and though Dr. Keith was absent, on account of health, and it, therefore, lost much of its interest, so far as it went, it passed off very well. As to your humble servant's part of the performance, I can't say much. I hated Mosheim and all his tribe, at the outset, and do not love him now. But after a severe struggle against it, my mind has consented to try and master him. I began modestly, when I took charge of the class, confessing my sins of omission and disqualification, and that made them moderate their expectations. The consequence has been, I hope, that when the session closed they were not dissatisfied. I say this to you, because I know (as I suppose), that you sympathized with me in my anxieties on this head. Altogether, I think I have been appreciated far above my deserts since I came here. I think it does not puff me up. I hope it will make me thankful to God that He has turned away my fears in some measure. My duties thus far have been very light—but four recitations per week, two in the Seminary and two in the High-school. I shall propose to do more, even if they do not put more on me, the next term.

"The Convention in Alexandria was a glorious thing. Although not as much religious feeling as usual, there was a good deal of seriousness, and the very best spirit prevailed. It detracted, however, very much from our examination. Having been here so recently, the clergy and laity, who usually attend the Convention in great numbers, were unwilling to come again.

"We have now at the Seminary two foreign missionaries, Hill and Payne. Mr. Payne delivered an address yesterday. Mr. Hill will do the same this afternoon. To-morrow I go on to Fredericksburg, to preach on next Sunday at the ordination of several deacons and some priests. I regret my consenting to go, but it is now too late. My regret is chiefly that I have not been able to write for the occasion.

"While I am away, Mrs. Sparrow and the children are going to take charge of the Seminary buildings, for the vacation. This is a delightful arrangement. There will be no limit, of course, to our room, or rather our rooms; and we shall board at the Seminary table, the trustees and the matron, a most excellent lady, consenting to the arrangement. Our house is now plastering, and will be finished in a few weeks; but we think it safest not to go into it till October. In truth, I should be perfectly willing to remain an indefinite time at the Seminary, if we could have it all to ourselves, and Miss M. to superintend for us, or her servants to take care of us. They have adopted my plan of the house, or rather yours, just as it was furnished. My only regret is that we did not furnish a larger plan. They were quite ready to make it larger; have already taken down the end of the kitchen, and enlarged it several feet. In short, they have done all, and more than all, I expected. I mention these things to you, because, if you were in my situation, and I in yours, I should be glad to hear them.

"I was rather thrown aback by your declaration of readiness to receive, and reluctance to answer my letters. If you have a disinclination for such work, I hope you will overcome it in the present instance, and especially while Mrs. W. is absent. It will beguile a lonely hour. But however remiss you are determined to be in time to come, write me on the receipt of this, and let me know all about yourself, your family, and Gambier. Remember me kindly to old friends. Often do I think of them, and always with affection and sadness. I shall write several of them on my return from Fredericksburg. Mrs. S. joins me in best wishes.

"Your true friend and brother, WILLIAM SPARROW.

"THEOLOGICAL SEMINARY, FAIRFAX COUNTY, VA.
"September 1st, 1841.

"REV. AND DEAR SIR:—

"Last evening I went into Alexandria, spent the night at a friend's house, went thence by the nine o'clock boat to Washington, and spent the day in the Senate chamber, listening to Berrien, Rives, Clay, etc., till about three. By the four o'clock boat I returned to Alexandria, came out in Mr. L.'s carriage to the Seminary, about seven—and what then? Why, to my surprise and delight, I found Mrs. W. had been here nearly all day. She had had rather a troublesome time in getting here, and is rather tired to-night; not so much, however, as to prevent her sitting and talking with Mrs. S. But about her health she will write you in a few days. In the meanwhile, I write to let you know she is here, and that we mean to keep her here over next week.

"I thank you for your last letter, though rather too brief. It seems to me you make too much of a business of writing a letter. If you would scribble anything that comes uppermost, it would be very acceptable to your old, and now distant, friend, and far better than your hypercritical and over nice taste would suppose. Don't expect of me, I pray you, nicely rounded periods and terse and pregnant thoughts (though I do listen, now and again, to the magnates of the land, in high debate), and do not suppose, therefore, that I expect them of you. But I do expect that, with all your cares, you will not forget your old, and one of your truest and most cordial, friends, almost a brother.

"I have had a letter from P., full of tenderness and Christian submission. He says, in his strong way, that 'he is crushed like a worm'—strong, yet no stronger, I am persuaded, than he feels. Every time his eyes rest upon his children, I have no doubt, he feels an anguish which tries both his Christian fortitude and resignation. Since I heard from him I have had a letter from A. *He* says P. is doing exceedingly well, and that his labors are much blessed. From A. I have not heard. Have you? I hope he is doing well. He is a true man. The news here I shall not attempt to give you; the papers will do it much better. There are great searchings of heart, and many surmises what the President will do with this second bill. Should it be vetoed, it is confidently asserted the Cabinet will resign, and Rives and Cushing, etc., be appointed in their places. So much for politics, and that *quantum suff.*

"Our vacation will close this week, and then I begin again, after a long respite. I have been very busy preaching, however; this whole vacation not a Sunday has passed that I have not been in the pulpit, at least once—quite enough for health, this warm weather, I assure you.

"My house is now painting. They have been quite expeditious. I have but one regret—that I was so modest in my demands. I have always regretted that there was not more brass in my constitution. As to you, your regret should be that there is none at all in yours. No bell ever sounded well, and afar off, without it.

"Write me soon, and tell me all the news. Do you know anything of T., and his prospects? I have just had a very good letter from him, but he has none of my egotism, and, therefore, tells me but little. My best regards to all my Gambier friends. My friend

B. I must especially name at this time. Wish him much joy for me, and, what in this world is more stable, much happiness.

"Hoping this will find you and your little ones in good health, I remain, dear sir,

"Most truly, your friend and brother,

"WILLIAM SPARROW."

"THEOLOGICAL SEMINARY, FAIRFAX CO., VA.

"REV. AND DEAR BROTHER:—

"Most welcome was your letter by Mr. E., and most pleasing the intelligence of your marriage. Conscious that in a single life I would have been most miserable, I have always been a strong advocate of matrimony, and consequently rejoice when my friends are found entering into that state; especially when there is such a good prospect of happiness as in your case. I have little personal knowledge, indeed, of Mrs. ——, but I know under what training and maternal influence she was brought up, and I have heard others speak of her, who do know her; and I feel myself authorized to wish you much joy, as I do, with all my heart.

"It must have been exceedingly pleasant to you to have the presence of Mrs. F. on the occasion of your marriage. I wish I had been there to see her, as well as on many other accounts. I hope that she and her husband enjoy good health. How does Bishop McCoskry come on in Detroit. I have heard some say that he is not so acceptable as he used to be, but I can hardly think it. His open, cordial manner cannot fail to please the people of the West.

"Your account of the improvements in Milnor Hall, and elsewhere on the Hill, is quite pleasing. I doubt not, if I should ever see the place again, it will be so improved I shall hardly know it. Nature, at the deluge, if not at the foundation of the world, did her part toward making it a beautiful place; art must now do its part; and Major Douglass, every one knows, is just the man to execute her will.

"What news from Cincinnati? How come on our common friends there, and the city mission? How, also, is friend G.? I have often thought it had been well for him, if not for the Church in Cincinnati, that he had been continued in the office of city missionary. If I had my will, and could bring it about, every student, after going through a regular course in a theological seminary, should go, first of all, and preach to the poor, and preach, not only from his pulpit, but from house to house. Thus only can the unpractical and abstract habits of a theological seminary be broken up, and the best style of preaching the Gospel be learned. But I forget myself.

"I have seen but very few of your Virginia friends here, and those few in such a transient way, at the Convention, that I do not remember their names. All that I can recollect is, that one or two inquired most kindly about you. Col. C. was not at the Convention, or I presume I should have more to say to you about such matters.

"As to my position here, it is much more agreeable, in every respect, than I anticipated; though that is not saying much. I left Ohio with a heavy heart. I pray God never to put me, unless He sees it necessary to paramount interest, to such a trial again. From the earthquake of feeling in my heart—I know not what else to call it—which my removal occasioned, I never expect to recover; as long as I live, there will be deep and ruinous traces of the convulsion in my nature. It was impossible, therefore, to have bright anticipations in removing to this place. I left Ohio because I thought I must. To say, therefore, that my lot exceeds my expectations, would be to say but little. Thank God I can say more. If my health, and that of my family, is preserved, and I find myself useful and acceptable, I think I shall have no reason to regret the change, so far as external things are concerned. But though I have been overwhelmed with kindness on every hand here, I cannot forget the old and true maxim about old books, old wine, and old friends, and shall be anxious to cultivate the kind remembrance of Ohio friends, among whom you are reckoned, let me say, one of the oldest and dearest. The thought of being forgotten by them would be most painful, for they can never be forgotten by me.

"Present me kindly to Mrs. ———. You must not fail to write me occasionally, and when your cares will not allow it, ask Mr. B. to be your substitute. Most gladly would I hear from him at any time. How is our common friend O. coming on; a good man, and true.

"With earnest prayers for a blessing on you and yours, and on all your undertakings, I remain, most truly,

"Your friend and brother, WILLIAM SPARROW."

"THEOLOGICAL SEMINARY, FAIRFAX CO., VA.,
"March 5, 1842.

"REV. AND DEAR BROTHER:—

"Knowing that I might as well wait for the Mississippi to run by, in order to cross over, as to wait for an unprovoked epistle from you, though you have the franking privilege, and plenty of time to spare, I have concluded to try if even a challenge will draw a letter from you. Pray, how are you? Much more, how is Mrs. Wing, and the little ones? Mrs. S. is constantly saying 'I wish I knew how is Mrs. W.' From the fact that none of our recent letters from Ohio say anything unfavorable about her health, we have been led to hope that it is good. As to my family, they are, just now, better than they have been since our arrival here; though we have had a great deal of sickness during the winter. M., F., and E., have all been quite unwell. The boys are all well and hearty, especially the youngest. My own health has been as good as usual—that is not saying much, you will think—and I have, though under many disadvantages, enjoyed myself better than for many winters past.

"Dr. Keith, you are aware, is in very bad health! so that there is much reason to fear he will never return to duty here again. I have, therefore, to do his duty and my own, for the present. This has, necessarily, brought with it much labor and more anxiety. I have been in continual apprehension that the students would be dissatisfied; but thus far, thank God, my fears have been turned away from me; and though they are fully conscious that Dr. Keith was a man not to be matched in his peculiar department, they have borne with me, and shown a kindness, and forbearance, and confidence, which I did not expect. The Seminary here seems to be in a prosperous condition, and if we only had a proper man in Dr. Keith's place, or the Lord would restore him to us, I think it would grow and prosper much more. Personally, I think they are a fine body of young men who make up our classes. Their talents, and attainments, and manners, and spirit, are, for the most part, very good. Some of them are very superior young men. The notions which have prevailed about the *irregularity* of things here, is certainly a mistake. If there was want of order in times past, there is not now. The true want, according to the feelings of those who complain, is want of Oxford-Tractism in doctrine and discipline, against both of which Bishop Meade sets his face, and is not ashamed to avow it. His trip to England, of the effects of which I was fearful, has only confirmed him more fully in his old opinions of Evangelical doctrine, and moderate, or Low-Churchmanship. But I must stop this, before my paper is used up.

"The winter here has been very delightful, and the spring is very forward. We have put out all fires, except in the kitchen, man being, at all seasons, a cooking animal. Do write me soon, and fully. If you knew as much of this place, in common with me, as I do of Ohio, in common with you, I should fill my paper with gossip. Tell me all about Gambier, Mount Vernon, Columbus, etc., etc. Especially about you and yours. What are you at! How do you fill up your time! Ah, I wish you were here. This is the place to keep a man alive. Since I began this letter I have been visited by Mr. S., from Washington, and he has been telling me of the Temperance doings, till my blood has fairly coursed through my veins for joy and sympathy. The reformation of the drunkards, and the influence upon the whole of society there, is very great indeed. Remember me, affectionately, to your family, to the Bishop, and Messrs. Blake, Badger, and Sandels. Also to other friends.

"Truly, your friend and brother, WM. SPARROW."

"THEOLOGICAL SEMINARY, NEAR ALEXANDRIA, D. C.,
"September 7, 1842.

"REV. AND DEAR SIR:—

"It is customary with those who leave their creditors unsatisfied, when compelled, by the force of circumstances, to pay their debts, to carry a high head, as though they had done some great thing; they mistake a discharge of obligation for a pure gratuity. In this way I explain the loftiness of the beginning and ending of your last epistle. Perhaps, however, it may be accounted for, in part, by that paternal pride which is so very natural and excusable, on announcing the birth of a little daughter. Be that as it may, and whatever we may think of the weakness of the father, we cannot but rejoice at the arrival of the new comer and the health of the mother.

"In regard to the farm, I confess I know not what to say. I am sorely perplexed, and all my faith is put to the trial, when I think of the situation of my family, and my precarious health. My hope had been, that T. and Mr. M. would have so arranged matters that the lot on which my father lived would have been mine, and formed an asylum for my wife and children, at my death. However, as this plan seems to be frustrated, I can only say, for the present, I will consider the matter. Your letter has been lying on my table, you must know, for a couple of weeks, during my absence at two Virginia associations. This fact, with the deep feeling of responsibility to my family which presses upon me, will account for the postponement of a categorical answer. I feel verily guilty in relation to my family. I have allowed the business of my personal life, teaching and preaching, so to engross my thoughts, that I have not been provident for them. Whether the evil can be in any measure repaired, God only knows; but when I reflect how destitute they must be, if I should be this moment taken from them, a perfect horror comes over my mind, not only at the idea of their sinking into poverty, but also, because I cannot acquit myself of being, in some measure, passively, if not actively, the cause of their misfortune. Had I bestowed upon them some of the thoughts which my classes have occupied, it would have been better for me and mine. But enough of this.

"I have seen Mr. B. Mr. U. is teaching in this neighborhood. M. dined with me yesterday. Yes, even our friend! He is to be married on Saturday, to a Miss ——, the sister of his first wife, I suppose. I did not like to ask the question, having the fear of the General Assembly before my eyes. I see, from the papers, the Bishop is going to Cincinnati; and I perceive the Doctor has resumed the 'Observer,' and 'fears no man.' In regard to Andrews, his letters from Europe pleased me better than any I have read from clerical pens. He is a sound theologian. All the family join with me in kind remembrance to yours.

"Yours most truly, W. SPARROW."

"THEOLOGICAL SEMINARY, January 25, 1843.

"REV. AND DEAR SIR:—

"I have been diligently seeking a moment of leisure from pressing duties, to write you. I do not know that I ever was more occupied than at the present time. I am acting as temporary supply at Christ Church, Georgetown, and that occupies a part of Saturday and Monday, as well as Sunday; and the rest of the week I am kept in the full jump, to fulfill all my duties to my family, the Seminary, and myself. I know not that I should be writing you just now, but I am impelled by the sad news which I have just heard, of the burning of your house; and also, by a desire to make an inquiry of you. I hope it is true, as I hear, that your house is insured, and that to the full value of it. Should such be the case, the affliction, I should suppose, will rather fall upon the company than upon yourself. Is it true that Mr. L. has lost all his furniture? Were they keeping a boarding house? How did it happen?

"It seems the Bishop is sent a begging. I think it the wisest course they could possibly pursue, not only because I trust he will succeed, but because, even if he do not, it will take away objections that were made against him at his election. Will he come this way? If he should, how ought I to carry myself? I am disposed to meet him with all cordiality. Certainly, I feel most kindly towards him; and had I been left under the impression produced by our parting, I should never have had one more unpleasant thought in regard to him. But several little matters have reached here since, which make me doubt whether he would not repulse me, in a manner which I would neither like nor deserve. As to his object, I feel truly interested in it. Neither toward him nor Kenyon can I ever have a cold heart.

"As to yourself, I trust that the gloom under which you last wrote was only temporary, and that by this time you see things in a more cheerful light. Alas, dear brother, how vain are the expectations of youth! How certain that man is born to trouble! May the Lord sanctify to us every sad feeling, and prepare us for our change. O, what a glorious thought is that, there is, indeed, a land where there is no more sorrow, or sickness, or death. O that we could have a full assurance of our inheritance therein!

"As to myself, I am as happy as I ever expect to be in this world. There is, indeed, nothing very special to trouble me, but the largeness and helplessness of my family. When seated at our large family table, with four children on each side, and Mrs. Sparrow at the end, and I think that my death must plunge them into poverty, I feel a pang which nothing but the promises of God can, in the smallest degree, abate; and these are comparatively ineffectual, by reason of my little faith. With this exception (enough of itself, you will think), my situation is pleasant. There has been no change for the worse since I came. More than all my expectations have been realized. Friends continue friends, and as yet, I believe, I have no enemies, except the enemy to my peace, which haunted me in Gambier, and everywhere else where I have been, and will, doubtless, follow me to the grave. If I could see a prospect of the continuance of their present lot to my wife and children, I should have so many blessings, that it would almost be wicked to ask for more.

"What do you think, and what does the Bishop think of the signs of the times in the Ecclesiastical world? I am charmed with Bishop ———'s last movement. He goes so beautifully 'in a gang by himself,' with so much Low-Church facing to his coat lappels, collar, and cuffs! What sort is your Chillicothe editor? Remember me most affectionately to Gambier friends.

"Your old, true friend, WILLIAM SPARROW."

"THEOLOGICAL SEMINARY, FAIRFAX COUNTY, VA.,
"July 14, 1843.

"REV. AND DEAR BROTHER:—

"I received your letter the day before yesterday, when hard at work at our examination; yesterday I was occupied every moment, with sundry urgent matters, among the rest, delivering an address, of an hour and a quarter in length, before two Bishops, one Bishop elect, and I do not know how many clergy and laity; of course, I could not condescend to think of a far-off Ohio friend; to-day, however, as the bells are ringing half-past six, A.M., at the Seminary and High-School, I sit down to answer you.

"I was right glad to hear from you, though it was after your own brief fashion. It really does seem to me that you forget that I know all the persons and things about Gambier, and therefore must needs expect you to enter into particulars, which I, when addressing you, cannot. If you were acquainted here, as I am there, I think I should write to you, not only as I think, but as I talk, too—freely, minutely, and frequently.

"As to your paper, if the effect of it is to keep out the 'Banner,' I wish it God-speed. That paper is doing the good cause much harm, especially in driving out the 'Episcopal Recorder.' The 'Recorder,' it is, that has fought the battle; and however it may fare with other papers, that ought to be sustained. As to your's, I wish to be put down as a subscriber, and, if you desire it, as an agent at this place. Lathbury's 'Episcopacy' I have not read, and, therefore, can give no advice. I will ask Dr. May if he has read it, and if I have anything, will add it before I send this letter. I hope it is not High-Church. I think Evangelical men must see, from the experience of the last ten years, that Evangelical and High-Church principles do not agree; and that, though 'paired,' sometimes, they are never 'matched.'

"Bishop McIlvaine is expected to be here to-day. I have twice asked you what kind of greeting I might expect of him, but you have never answered me; and, therefore, I infer it will be exceedingly cold and icy. However, I shall meet him in another spirit, and if he does not reciprocate, I cannot help it. I wish he had been here yesterday, at the delivery of my address, that I might have his judgment upon it. Immediately after I delivered it, they had a meeting, subscribed and paid down the money to print, and requested of me a copy. What to do I know not, and my perplexity is most painful. You know my repugnance to publishing; and there is the additional consideration, that the New York 'Churchman,' the 'Banner,' and our neighbor, the 'True Catholic,' will come upon me, like the Harpies on the Trojan viands, and that is something which I have not nerves to endure. On the other hand, the Bishop and other friends here say, it is out of the question, I must print; and, besides, the money has been paid down for the expense, and the givers are all dispersed. It is, of course, gratifying to my self-love, and tempting to my vanity, to be thus solicited; all the circumstances, indeed, were most gratifying; but, after all, my heart falters, as if I were going to the stake. The pleasure is so balanced by the pain, that I think if I could know really what is my duty in reference to myself, and the cause of truth, I would be able to decide; but there I am perplexed. I do not feel that the production has the strength necessary in one which would promote the cause of truth, in these troublous times.

"To Ohio I cannot go at this time, or I should, with great pleasure. Where are you going to visit this vacation? S., it is said, may be here with Bishop McIlvaine. You have heard that his pocket was robbed of a hundred dollars, received for his Church, as he was witnessing the great doings in Boston.

"Doctor is a queer man; that is all, just now. I hope F. will prove a thorough, Evangelical, Low-Churchman. As to yourself, pray, where do you stand now? How many rounds of the ladder? At the top, and feeling out for more? These inquiries should recur often in these days of change. If you are in statu quo ante bellum, I hope you will not fail to exert your influence in the Seminary. Do speak out. You need not involve yourself in controversy, but do speak out, clearly and plainly. See how things are going in New York.

"We have all enjoyed usual health this summer, thank God, not excepting myself. I suffer much, as usual, in my head; less, indeed, in the way of pain, but a good deal in the way of pressure on the brain, and, of course, great stupor. If you knew how I feel at this moment, you would give me credit for writing you. Since Monday morning we have been busy at examination, and the doings were wound up by my long-winded speech yesterday; and this morning, Friday, I am utterly collapsed. In such a state you cannot possibly expect me to promise a contribution for your paper. What, indeed, could I write about, and if I did, where would you find room for it? Lathbury's 'Episcopacy,' and Episcopal appointments and acts, will leave no room for even a Tom Thumb essay. All my family join in affectionate regards to Mrs. W., and your family. Do not let my god-son forget me.

"Your friend and brother, most truly,

"WILLIAM SPARROW."

"THEOLOGICAL SEMINARY, FAIRFAX CO., VA.,
"December 4, 1843.

"REV. AND DEAR BROTHER:—

"I have just received your letter, and as it is more like a friendly communication than any I have been favored with for a long while, I will overlook the severe reproof with which it begins, and in the spirit of charity, answer you at once.

"In regard to your paper, let me say, I am glad to hear so much of the editorial has been written by yourself; for, to speak the truth, without fear or favor, I have been, generally, very much pleased. I did not give you credit for so much. I knew, from old experience, that nothing you wrote would be worthless or commonplace, but I did not suppose that you could muster resolution to be so busy in such work; your old dislike to writing, I supposed, you could not so far overcome. I say this in truth; and in the same spirit, let me express the hope that you will not be swift to speak to others for help in the editorial columns. Unless driven by the heavy pressure of other duties, you had better stand in your lot, and play the editor all out. These are times when the helm should be only in the safest hands. Let me add, that one principal object of an editor, these times, should be to recognize—silently, and by implication, is the best way, perhaps, in most cases—the existence of the Protestant churches besides our own, and so habituate the minds of readers to liberal views. The prevailing attraction for Rome, and repulsion from Protestants who are non-episcopal, needs to be checked, and as Providence has put it into your hands to do something in that way, do not let the opportunity slip.

"I take it for granted that you stand where you did when we used to hold daily converse upon Church matters. As to myself, I have not varied a hair's breadth, that I am aware of, except it be that I am more 'established, strengthened, and settled,' in the godly ways of Low-Churchism. On the subject of the Apostolical Succession I am clearer than ever; and I do not think that a man can, logically, and consistently, hold to that as an essential of a valid ministry, and maintain true Protestant principles. That was the που στω on which the Tractarians planted their lever, in the first numbers of their series, and by which they have been enabled to move the Church, as with an earthquake. And so long as a man, or a Church, holds to it, he is liable, or it is liable, to go off in a Romish tangent, further and further, till met by the secant of Romish infallibility.

"What you tell me of the college and its affairs is no news. I have heard from several of its dwindled condition, of the unpopularity of its president, of his opposition to the Bishop, and his leanings toward Tractarianism. These things have surprised me much, for I did not see how, under the new order of things, any other than personal difficulties could arise. I believe it will be found, that the less bishops have to do with any other than purely *ministerial, or purely Episcopal matters,* the better for the Church. Bishop White seems to have seen this. The truth is, the bishops are so peerless in the Church, that when they pass over into the world for the transactions of business, they, from mere habit, if from nothing else, are disposed to carry this characteristic with them, and some are disposed, from feelings correlate, to accede to them at once, and without the exercise of judgment; but though some, not all, and these last create the difficulty, often with reason, often without it. Had my situation been that of the present incumbent, I should have been there still.

"I have but one great anxiety about Gambier, and that centres in my theological successor. I have no doubt that he is a good man, and orthodox. Is he so decidedly Evangelical, and Low-Church—you see I do not mince matters—that the clergy he will send forth from the Seminary will choose a worthy successor to Bishop McIlvaine? That is the question. When you can assure me of that, you will relieve me much. The other side of our Church direct all their energies toward providing for the succession. The Bishop is de facto, the Church; for he can make it what he pleases, always excepting what the world, the flesh, and the Devil may do to prevent it. In some cases, I fear, these conspiring principles are not called upon to prevent; all they have to do is to aid. Witness much in the history of our Church during the last few years.

"You ask my opinion about Ohio affairs. But the subject is long, and my paper is short; and I really am not sure whether or not I have a matured opinion upon the subject.

"We are here getting along, through the Divine blessing, pretty well. My labor is lighter than it ever has been elsewhere. I have but seven recitations a week. But they are enough for my feebleness, especially as a class of twenty, some of them quondam lawyers, doctors, merchants, etc., tax a man much more severely, than our little Gambier tete-a-tetes. For a nervous man, it is pretty hard to sit up in a chair and be shot at by such marksmen, for an hour or so. Besides teaching, I preach about once a Sunday, in the Seminary chapel, or elsewhere. These things, with my correspondence, and study, and sermon writing, and the care of my family, occupy my whole time. These last, thank God, are now pretty well. While I was North last summer, Mrs. Sparrow was dangerously ill, but I did not know of it till the danger was over. Mr. Syle, who has returned from England, is teaching the three oldest children, and Miss S., who lives in the family, the rest. They are all growing up so fast, that I feel myself an old man. I am glad to hear that C. is coming on with his studies, and hope that my namesake, when he recovers from his sore eyes, will follow his example. Mrs. W. has made our girls quite happy by her epistle. Give my very best regards to her and the children, and remember me to all my Gambier friends.

"Most truly, your affectionate friend, WM. SPARROW."

"THEOLOGICAL SEMINARY, FAIRFAX CO., VA.,
"April 5, 1844.

"REV. AND DEAR BROTHER:—

"It is rather hard that such changes should be taking place in Kenyon, and that the man who first taught in it should not hear from the second employed, though friendly relations subsist between, so much as a hint upon the subject, not even a petty catalogue. Do tell me something about matters and things, the doings of the board, the resignation of the president, and the plans for the future.

"I have just received a letter from brother Dennison, saying that Bishop Chase, being about to publish the Kenyon College part of his reminiscences, has addressed him an epistle, to know if he repents of the part he took with Sparrow, etc., and is willing, by acknowledgment of his sin, to save himself from disgrace in this world, and from punishment in the world to come. So, you see, I have to be put through another ordeal. I have made up my mind what to do, namely, either to observe a profound silence, or just to say, in some public print, that I have seen his publication, but that, as the subject was thoroughly discussed at the time, and in one way or another acted on and decided by the Trustees, by the Ohio Convention, and afterward by the General Convention; and, as many years have since passed away, and with them all the controversial feeling which the difficulty occasioned, I shall let the matter rest, being willing to abide the judgment of the world and the Church, and the final Arbiter of all things. This, it strikes me, will be the most Christian and expedient mode of dealing; and certainly, it is the course which my feelings would dictate. The older I grow the less I love controversy, and I never loved it much.

"I saw Judge M. a few weeks ago, for a few minutes, in Washington. It was most pleasing to me to see the face of an old Ohio man. I could have wished to know more of Ohio affairs. When are you coming this way? At the next General Convention? O, do come, and let us see one another's faces in the flesh once more. Mine—my face I mean—you will find care-worn, and marked with the multiplying hieroglyphics of age. As to your's, I suppose it is smooth, and sleek, and plump, an index of the equability of your temper and of your life. Mrs. Sparrow, also, would be right glad to see you, though, I suppose I may say, without offence, not so glad as to see your better half. As to my seeing you in Ohio, there is nothing in the way but the expense, but that is a serious obstacle.

"How is your family? How are my god-sons, especially my namesake? As to mine, thank God, we are all alive, but have a great deal of sickness, chiefly occasioned by cold, during the last three months. My own health has been, during the winter, quite as good as usual, and, perhaps, better, until within a fortnight or three weeks since, when I have been suffering from such an influenza as I have never had before.

"Of our Seminary, you have learned something from our catalogue. We are prospered more than I expected, but our prosperity gives great uneasiness to some. I really believe they would think it well if we could be all sunk in the Potomac. But that matters little, if we are only found faithful before God.

"Do tell me something about your Seminary and professors. My family send true love to yours.

"Ever yours, WM. SPARROW."

"THEOLOGICAL SEMINARY, FAIRFAX CO., VA.,
"January 2, 1845.

"REV. AND DEAR SIR:—

"I am truly pleased to have heard from you, and especially to have received from you such a well-filled letter. I should have answered it ere this, if I had not been prevented by an unusual amount of work and headache.

"When I talk of the amount of my work, I do not judge by your standard. What would be a grasshopper to you, would be a burden, a mountain to me. The man that can prepare three written sermons a week, and two Christmas sermons, as extras, attending, at the same time, to the sundries of parochial duty, can hardly understand what work is. He may do it, as the man who talked prose, but like him, be as ignorant all the time what it is; the word might as well be stricken out of his vocabulary, at least when he is talking of himself.

"One pleasing feature of your letter was the mention in it of so many old friends. In Delaware, as you know, I preached my second and third sermon, and many more afterward, and as I always met kindness from the inhabitants, of course I feel no slight attachment to them.

"So you are going to have a $12,000 church! The Lord enable you to pay for it, and fill it with spiritual worshipers. I sympathize with you most fully in your feeling in your new position, and your anxiety to see fruit from your labors. What is life worth to a minister of Christ, unless he is enabled to be useful, and is made the instrument of saving souls alive? To the worldling it has another value. We profess to see no utility in it except as a means of saving ourselves, and those who hear us. Dear brother, let me urge one thing upon you. I do it with a deep consciousness of my own deficiency therein, but it is multum in parvo, and when faithfully attended to brings every other good with it—'all other things are added unto it.' I refer to private prayer for blessing on your labors. The man that does good, and will appear at the last day with a great company saved through his instrumentality, is the man of prayer. The philosophy of the thing, as theologians would say, is familiar to you; but there is a Divine philosophy applicable to this matter which it is far better to rely on. I mean the philosophy of faith. God has said that He Himself gives the increase, and that he gives it in answer to prayer. That is enough. If more were needed, without going into deeper speculation, induction proves the same; all eminent ministers of Christ have been earnest in private prayer. These remarks are no novelty to you, or me, or any other Christian, yet I make them. It is by such obvious truths, coming from every quarter, and through every medium, that we daily live and grow as ministers of Christ.

"We are pretty prosperous here. I believe there are fifty-two students on the ground. Satan, and Alexander the Coppersmith, and Demas, are to be looked for everywhere; but, perhaps, we are as little troubled by such visitors as any community to be found.

"You have not yet heard of the regular conspiracy in the General Seminary to Romanize the Church. The students had formed a society, secret, with the watchword 'C. U.,' Catholic Unity, and have been in communication with the Romish Bishop. They meant to colonize here, that the work might go on simultaneously everywhere. I wonder whether there be now any of the revolutionists among us already!! The subject is now before the Faculty in New York, and a committee of three Bishops, Lee, Henshaw, and DeLancy, have been appointed to investigate the matter. It is curious enough that this should come out after they had, by resolution, just whitewashed the Seminary.

"Bishop Onderdonk is probably pronounced upon this day. The whole will be published, testimony and all. One of the female witnesses was under examination six hours! It was designed, they say, to intimidate others by the rough handling given her, and it had, in part, its effect. But she and some others carried themselves well through it all. If the man is guilty, may the Lord, for the Church's sake, reward him according to his deeds, so far as human censure is concerned; and may it have the effect of leading him to true repentance. O, what mischief he must have done to true religion! How many serious thoughts, in young and old, must have been dissipated; how many infidel and blasphemous remarks must his known misconduct have occasioned.

"My family, thank God, are all well. The two oldest children went, yesterday, with Dr. May and Miss S., the Doctor's niece, to the Levee. The day was most lovely, as is this. So was Christmas Day, and so was our chapel, being decorated with evergreens. Remember me to all my friends, and believe me,

"Most truly, your friend, WM. SPARROW.

"*Rev. E. H. Canfield.*"

"THEOLOGICAL SEMINARY, FAIRFAX CO., VA.,
"January, 3, 1846.

"REV. AND DEAR BROTHER:—

"You have, doubtless, wondered that I have not written before this; but you know my 'often infirmities,' both of body and of mind, and will bear with my neglect.

"I returned, a few days ago, from Baltimore, where I spent two Sundays with my daughter Mary. Had I not been unwell, the visit would have been an exceedingly pleasant one. Mr. Thompson went on the day after me, and spent the first Sunday there, on his way to Philadelphia. I preached in the morning, and he at night. He was taken (so much honor do gray hairs secure), for old Dr. Sparrow, and I for young Mr. T. He preached with as much ease and freedom as if he had been in the pulpit for the last twenty-five years. His elocution was very fine, and pleased the people very much. He has been offered the assistantship at Christ Church. Whether he will accept is not yet known. W. had been in the post for some time, but had just resigned it, with Dr. J.'s approbation, for a country parish. The Doctor, of course, was willing to see another parish under good influence. W., who always promised well, has come out a very sound man, and I rejoice to add his health is most wonderfully improved. It gave me great pleasure to see him recovered in spirits from his heavy affliction, and restored to soundness of body.

"Of course, I saw Mr. P. Mary stopped at his house, and is there yet. He is doing well. His school is prosperous. He is most fiercely set against the new-fangled Protestant notions of the day. You know how I love P., and this last intercourse with him has only enhanced my esteem for him. He is one of Nature's noblemen.

"Dr. J. is very prosperous. He, of course, stands in the fore-front of the battle, and has, therefore, to endure a great many hard knocks; but he bears up manfully against it, and the Lord seems to be blessing him in his Church. I preached there twice last Sunday, and never saw nobler congregations.

"Newman, you know, has gone the way of all consistent Puseyites, and has published a book. It is called 'An Essay on the Development of Christian Doctrine.' I am now reading it, the first work of his which I have read, except a few of the Tracts. It shows great ingenuity and learning. Certainly he must be a powerful man. Pusey, by his side, is a driveler. The book, I would think, must bring many halting minds in England to a decision. As for American Puseyites, they are not sufficiently in earnest to cut off the right hand, and pluck out the right eye, in the service of what they deem the truth. Would that they were. It would be better for them as men, and it would be better for us as a Church. Our being able to slough off this dead matter of our system will depend, I think, much on this. If those who are not of us go not out from us, the leaven will still be left at work in our midst. People will not believe that it exists, or else they will fancy it is innocuous. As, therefore, the American Puseyites are not so self-sacrificing as the British, I expect to find our Church laboring under this disease, long after that of England has been restored to health.

"Things are getting on here about as usual. The High-school has fifteen pupils for the start. Mr. D. has taken hold with prodigious energy, and is getting his school into perfect discipline. West Point cannot surpass it. I have no doubt that if he perseveres in his present course, in one year he will have as many pupils as is expedient.

"I was much interested in your account of yourself. You seem, indeed, to have taken charge of an unpromising field; but I trust things begin to look more cheerful. Though I have been so dilatory in writing, I am unreasonable enough to wish to hear from you again soon, that I may know how the Lord prospers you in the good work. I have had letters from Dr. R., Dr. B., and D., of your class. Dr. R. has been over-persuaded to settle in his native county, where the field is very unpromising. Dr. B. was hardly under way yet. D. is well, and pleased with his post.

"Thus I have given you all the items of news I could think of. I am a poor hand at such work, but you will be glad of anything in your out of the world condition.

"The prospect of war has saddened me much, but thank God, the clouds are breaking away. 'The Lord reigneth,' in Church and State; that is our security and comfort. Remember me in your prayers, especially the Seminary. My family desire their kind regards.

"Your friend and brother in Christ, WM. SPARROW.

"*Rev. C. Walker.*"

"THEOLOGICAL SEMINARY, FAIRFAX CO., VA.,
"July 16, 1846.

"REV. AND DEAR BROTHER:—

"As to your examination for Priest's orders, you need have no apprehension. Bishop Meade will take no exception to your views. Though the Bishop eschews everything that sounds or looks metaphysical, he would, I am persuaded, practically approve your position.

"I wish you had been with me at the examination. We had Bishop Lee, and Dr. Tyng, and sundry others, especially Mr. Fowle. He is famous, perhaps, as you already know, as a Calvinist. He is much more systematic and open than any of his brethren. He is not content, as John Newton said, that Calvinism should be like sugar in his tea—dissolved and diffused through it; he will have it in lump. I had a little talk with him on these nice points, but though I thought him exceedingly extravagant in some of his positions, I was much pleased with the man. He has a pretty strong, plain mind, and of a sweet disposition, I should judge. Dr. Tyng preached the Alumni sermon (though not an Alumnus), and the ordination sermon. He is a wonderful man. As a preacher, especially in the extemporaneous way, I know no man like him. Bishop Lee preached, they say, an excellent sermon for the Missionary Society. His recent charge on the Rule of Faith is as 'sound as a bell.'

"Our classes did so-so. They went off in good spirits, and purposing all to return again, except the graduating class, which seemed to leave with true regret. Norton preached for Mr. Johnston, Dr. Stearns for Mr. Dana, Weed for Mr. Bean, Tyng for Mr. Shiras, and Woodward at Falls Church last Sunday. The people were, in general, highly pleased with the performances of these young men. The class contains a fair share of piety and talent. May the Lord increase them tenfold, and bless them in the conversion of souls.

"I do not wonder you feel as you express yourself about Duy. I never felt, from a death out of my own family, such a blow. I had flattered myself that he was destined to great usefulness; but God's thoughts are not as ours. I hoped to see him an able advocate of the truth with his pen; and the rather, as he seemed to be maturing and settling down, every day, more firmly on what I deem the true foundation. The last letter I received from him, written four days before his death, was, in this view, most charming in its character. But regrets are vain; nay, they are wrong, when the object is an ordering of the all-wise providence of God.

"Our Hill is nearly deserted. Dr. Bache, Superintendent of the Coast Survey, has made the Seminary Cupola one of his 'stations,' and will soon be here with his family, mathematical and otherwise. This may give a little variety to our life. Hoping you may be able to visit us at the time you speak of, I remain,

"Very truly, your friend and brother, W. S.

"*Rev. C. Walker.*"

"THEOLOGICAL SEMINARY, FAIRFAX CO., VA.,
"December 12, 1846.

"DEAR BROTHER:—

"It pains me to think that I should be left so long in profound ignorance about the health and happiness of my most intimate, and almost, my oldest Ohio friend; and what my feelings are toward you, are Mrs. Sparrow's toward you and your wife. Often, during the last months, have we talked together about you both, and felt a true desire to know how you and your family are. I have written you, and she has written Mrs. Wing, but neither of us has yet got an answer. I write this to see if I cannot elicit something. I know you may be pressed hard with duty, and especially, perhaps, have much writing to do. In that line I have much experience myself, as much, perhaps, as has ever fallen to my lot before. But still, I think, we both ought to continue, by an occasional letter, to keep the chain of an old friendship bright, or, at least, not to let it be eaten up of rust.

"I was sorry to hear, through Canfield, that you had been sick in Delaware, during the Convention, and that fact has disposed me not to judge you too hastily for your silence. I trust, however, that sickness did not last long. We have all enjoyed tolerable health, during the past summer and fall, except that about one-half of our number have had slight attacks of what troubled you, chills and fever. I was confined to my bed for a week, and thought it was going to be a severe attack, such as I once had in Ohio. But it passed away, through the goodness of God, and did not return. The children and Mrs. S. had slight attacks, but in the case of the children they returned frequently. We are all well now, thank God. There has been much sickness of that kind, all through this country, the past summer, even in the most unlikely localities.

"Do tell me, also, about the College. Truly, I long to hear of its prosperity. If it had been at all possible, I would have gone on when so kindly invited by the Bishop, especially to attend the Commencement and the Convention. My hope now is that I may be able to do so next summer; though all such hopes are, with me, much more languid than they used to be, partly because I am older, and have a deeper feeling of the uncertainty of life, and partly because I find it not so easy now to bear the expenses of traveling. Remember me kindly to President B., and any other of the Professors who would be pleased to hear from me.

"Do you often see brother D. now? Remember me affectionately to him when you have an opportunity. Many years ago I selected, in my mind, yourself, and Dennison and Preston, as a trio of peculiar friends. And though, owing to peculiar circumstances, I have never troubled D. with my letters, I have ever held him in the same estimation I did, especially, as I see that, in religious and ecclesiastical matters, he has, in this changing age, remained unchanged.

"Speaking of Preston, I have, through him and otherwise, received some private overtures about Trinity Church, Columbus, but have not felt at liberty to give them any encouragement. If I ever go into a parish, it must be one where things are settled and fixed on the firmest foundation. I might preach, and do pastoral duty in an established congregation, with, perhaps, some little efficiency, but trouble would break me down at once. I had my share of that in former years, and I do not mean to seek any more, though it may be the Lord's will to send it to me.

"What is the condition of Ohio ecclesiastically? I am often asked this question. Help me to answer it. How does the Bishop like his new residence? What use do you make of his old house? When I think what a nice place it is, I almost wish you could provide some sinecure in connection with the College or Seminary, and give me that house to live in. What are your duties now in connection with the Institution? Are you secularized in any way besides, as I am in the Post-office? By the way, I give the perquisites of my office to my assistant, and during the past year have had even to pay him for my letters, though I shall do so no more. How is Mr. W. and family? Remember us all to them. And now, what shall I say more, except it be that Mrs. S. and myself will grieve much if we do not soon get an answer to this, and to assure you that, in silence on your part or otherwise, I am ever, still,

"Your friend and brother, WM. SPARROW."

"THEOLOGICAL SEMINARY, November 20, 1847.

"REV. AND DEAR BROTHER:—

"It would be hard to say how often the thought of writing you has come into my mind without attaining to objective reality. That the thought should come is proof of my friendship; that the letter did not go was proof of my laziness, procrastination, and general inefficiency. There are some extenuating circumstances, partly permanent, and partly accidental. Of the first is my often infirmities; of the second, my absence during the summer, and unusual press of business since I got home. Immediately after vacation I went up into the Valley with two of my children, and spent five weeks most agreeably. I was at home but a few days, when I set off again for Pittsburg and Ohio. I attended the Ohio Convention, and saw many friends. I also visited my old residence, and went up to Lake Erie, and wet my hand once more in its waters. It was very grateful to my feelings to see old and kind friends, and to visit the scene of former years' labor, and pleasure, and pain. I did not get back till the second week of the term.

"Soon after my return your letter was handed me by Mr. R., but I have not seen him since, except *en passant*, though I formally invited him to tea on one occasion. He seems a fine young man, and I shall endeavor to get acquainted with him. My reputation is so bad, for my Low-Churchmanship, that, perhaps, he is afraid of me.

"I am pleased to hear that you are getting along so well; though that phrase is so indefinite that any sense may be put upon it. It may or may not have a spiritual reference; it may include only popularity, and not, also, usefulness to the souls of men. Of this, dear brother, I doubt not that you are aware; and that you look for fruit as well as blossoms, though the people generally do not. I often think how different the estimate the world (and the Church) makes of clergymen, and that which Paul, or our Divine Master would make. By the way, this has been very much pressed upon my mind of late, by reading the life of Simeon. Though not a well compiled work, it is most instructive in a spiritual way. Simeon was a man of no extraordinary abilities, by any means, and yet, by rightly understanding his proper work, and devoting himself singly and unreservedly to that, he did more good, as I believe, than any of his contemporaries. His operations were, to a great extent, silent and secret, but they were very effective, and extended far and wide. Another book of a similar character I am now reading, which has pleased me much, 'The Life and Remains of McCheyne,' a young, Scotch Presbyterian Minister. And, since I am talking of books, let me mention Mrs. Nicholson's 'Stranger's Welcome to Ireland,' the only book that contains a true idea of the poor, potato-eating Irish. She is a perfect original of a traveler, a female Borrow, and though there are several things about her I do not like, she is a perfect heroine, and deserves well for her benevolence to a most afflicted people. Unlike most travelers, she sought out the poor, not the rich, and so cast in her lot with them during her sojourn, in a village or a cabin, so as to have a full view of their lives and characters.

"Of Hill's 'Divinity,' I think as you do. It is many years since I read it in the English edition, but I thought its author the most philosophical divine in the language who had attempted a system of Theology.

"By this time, I suppose you have been called to fill R.'s place, and I surmise you will accept. Notwithstanding your acceptability in your present position, I cannot say I wish to see you continue there. I feel persuaded that for your ultimate ministerial character and usefulness, a place of different cast, for a few years, is desirable. When you have made up your mind, do write and let me know. My interest in your welfare is the only cause of my request. At the same time, do let me know of B. and his family. Pray visit them, and present them my best respects. I saw them all last summer, at the Springs, but have heard nothing since. I know not when I have been more struck than by the prudence, firmness, and Christian resignation of Mrs. B., in her great afflictive trial.

"As you failed, last examination, to be with me, I hope you will not fail the next. It is a great encouragement to us to have the countenance of old friends on these occasions. As to my address, I have not been able to satisfy myself about the expediency of publication, though I have been pressed beyond measure by Bishop Meade. You might like it, but others would not. With sincere prayers for your personal and ministerial welfare, I am, most truly,

"Your friend and brother, W. S.

"*Rev. C. Walker.*"

"THEOLOGICAL SEMINARY, FAIRFAX CO., VA.,
"January 4, 1848.

"REV. AND DEAR SIR:—

"The arrival of your letter, a few days ago, afforded me much pleasure. Why apologize for what you call your egotism! If you were writing to a stranger, or an acquaintance who was indifferent to you and yours, such thoughts would not be unnatural, but they are quite out of place in the present instance. Notwithstanding the marvelous powers of the telegraph, it does not inform us about absent friends, neither do the newspapers, and I suppose, as long as the world stands, we shall have to depend on the letters we receive for such information.

"The account you give me of sickness and death is very saddening to the flesh, though the spirit may rejoice in the reflection that 'the Lord reigneth,' and doeth all things well. In Mrs. L.'s affliction I most tenderly sympathize. In Delaware, I was for a long while received as a guest of Mr. L. He and Mrs. L. had then been married about two or three years. It is a long time now since I became acquainted with them, and how intimate, in that space of time, the union that has subsisted between them, and how necessary they must have become to each other. After an affectionate union of twenty-five or thirty years, man and wife grow almost into one personality; and how bitter, therefore, must be the separation. No doubt this cementing of unions and dissolving of unions is designed of God, to prepare us for our great change, by making us see the vanity of all earthly things, even the tenderest and most beloved. I hope Mrs. L. has been enabled to go to the true source of all consolation in this great emergency, and has found peace in the assurance that it is designed for good, and is in the experience of the peaceable fruits of righteousness which it is already producing. Please remember me most affectionately to her, and assure her she has the feeble prayers of myself and Mrs. S. Remember me, also, to her children, and tell the boys, especially my namesake, that I hope they feel the importance of the position in which Providence has placed them, by calling them to stand in their father's place, and be the stay and comfort of their mother.

"The account you give of Mr. F. is truly painful. How sad to see a man resort to broken cisterns, when he might go to an exhaustless fountain. In his case it is the more sad, as I believe that in early life he had the best instruction. Please remember me to him, as an old friend, and say that my hope is that all the vicissitudes of life to which he and I may be subjected may have the happy effect of drawing us to that Divine Saviour who can alone comfort and sanctify.

"All here are as usual. The number of students is small; smaller than ever since I have been in the Institution, but the prevailing spirit is good. My own family, thank God, has enjoyed usual health. They are all hard at their studies, Latin, German, French, and English. With God's help, I mean to make them scholars. An education is all a poor parson can usually leave his children, especially one so little endowed with Yankee thrift as I. Of my voyage to Europe I say nothing, for manifest reasons.

"If we are spared to next fall twelve months, and you are still in Delaware, I may visit you with some of my children.

"Truly yours, W. S.

"*Rev. E. H. Canfield.*"

The publications of Dr. Sparrow during this interval were, the commencement address, of 1843, on the right conduct of Theological Seminaries; a sermon, preached at the Convention, at Fredericksburg, entitled, "Love among Christians Urged," and the annual sermon in 1844, before the Board of Missions. The former was an elaborate exposition of the subject which it proposes, with its special bearing upon the controversies at that time pending. Assuming that there must and will be such Institutions, the question is proposed, how they can be conducted so as to escape their perversions, and secure their highest benefits. To secure this, it is insisted that *knowledge* shall be imparted, that this shall be knowledge of *God's truth*, God's *revealed truth* being the ultimate and only standard. For this it is further insisted there must be right principles—hermeneutical, logical, practical, and moral; and for the consistent Episcopalian, a certain system—that in the Articles, Prayer-book, and Homilies; and that the effect desired, a successful Gospel ministry, can only be reasonably anticipated when, with all these other qualifications, is combined that of spiritual character, personal piety, personal experience of the reality and power of the truths studied and to be preached to others. The most striking portion of the address, perhaps, is that which exhibits the great cardinal doctrine of the Reformation, its position in the system of the Gospel, as of our standards, and its relations in these systems to other doctrines.

The second of these publications was a sermon, first preached in the ordinary course of chapel ministry, and mainly of interest as an appeal for the cultivation of a spirit of love, of positive Christian affection for all true followers of the Lord Jesus, whether found in our own or in other Christian Churches. The text, "Grace be with all them that love our Lord Jesus Christ in sincerity," was shown to have its application to all such, and wherever found; and the failure cordially to recognize such application was traced to a defect or an absence of that love in which so largely consists the Christian character. Objection was made at the time, not to the doctrine of the sermon, but to its illustrations. Sad it is, now as then, that those illustrations are to be found in such abundance.

This brings us to the close of our chapter. In the Spring of 1848, the offer of a trip across the Atlantic, free of expense, was made to Dr. Sparrow, and accepted. With the close of the session he began his preparations, and starting from Savannah, spent the summer in Europe. It was during this journey, while outward bound, that the autobiographical fragment, as to his childhood, already given, was composed.

The following letters, all to the same correspondent, were written during the interval with which this chapter is occupied. They will help to throw light upon some of the facts and incidents to which allusion is made in the narrative. At the same time they bring to view others of no little importance. To use an expression of the correspondent to whom these letters were written, we have in them "material for that unconscious autobiography which is to be found in the correspondence of one who writes as Dr. Sparrow did, fully, and correctly, and ingenuously. Indeed, it is this gift or habit—with him it was both—of conscientious letter writing, as a part of his ministry, which may be fixed upon as one of his valuable characteristics." The feelings and views, moreover, here and further on expressed, as to the great work in which his correspondent was engaged, and the spirit in which it should go on, are peculiarly valuable.

"THEOLOGICAL SEMINARY, FAIRFAX CO., VA.,
"May 14, 1841.

"MY VERY DEAR MR. SYLE:—

"I received your letter this morning, by a student from the Seminary, as I was stepping out of the house to go and preach a Fast sermon in Christ Church, in this place (Alexandria), and though, of course, my head was full of other matters, I could not resist the temptation of reading it as I walked through the streets, and by the time I reached the vestry room I felt disappointed and sad. Why did you not come? I was not only willing to do all that I said, but desirous to do it. I wanted to see you here on many accounts, some of them selfish, if, in strictness, I could be selfish where you are concerned. I would have valued the instructions you would have given the children much more than the trifling expense, which so frightens you. On a mere quid pro quo principle I wished you here, and that without taking up one moment more of your time than you spent with them in Gambier. Rev. Mr. S. would have been glad to have his little daughter recite along with them, to your profit.

"May 24, 1841.

"I was interrupted by a visitor when I had written the above, and not being allowed soon to return to the pleasant work of writing you, I concluded to wait till after our Convention. I now write in a state of collapse, almost. During the last eight or nine days our town has been crowded with people—clergymen, laymen, and laywomen, from all parts of the State, and from other States. Doctor Milnor, from New York, Doctors May and Clarke, from Philadelphia, and Drs. Johns and Henshaw, from Baltimore, with sundry others who are not Doctors, and, therefore, not to be particularly named! Bishop Meade, and, above all, Bishop Moore, was here. The latter is a most venerable old man, and though, of course, very infirm, being upward of eighty, preaches with considerable spirit, and no little pathos. The preaching throughout was excellent. I had the privilege of hearing Johns, Clarke, May, and my old friend and pastor, Doctor Milnor. I cannot say that much good was done in the way of serious impression on individual minds, but time, I trust, will bring such cases to light. Some have already appeared. We had a Missionary meeting on Sunday afternoon, with addresses from Doctor Vaughan, Doctor May, Doctor Milnor, and Bishop Meade. Seven hundred and forty dollars were collected for foreign missions. Between three and four hundred had been collected before, for another purpose. The scene presented by the whole Convention meeting was enlivening in the extreme. The cordial recognitions and greetings on every hand were truly pleasing. Virginia cordiality and hospitality were exhibited to great advantage. The Convention business was quite a subordinate matter, with one exception. Prayer, and the hearing of the Word, occupied nearly all the time. Our six o'clock morning meetings were well attended. The body of the Church was always full. The exception I referred to, was the discussion on the Oxford Tracts. The Convention passed a strong vote of censure upon them. Doctor Campbell, the future Missionary to Mesopotamia, was here, with Doctor Vaughan, but he did not speak. He is, as yet, a layman.

"Remember me most kindly to all my Gambier friends, and tell Mr. Keller I shall be most happy to hear from him. Fail not, at least, to write me soon.

"With best wishes and prayers for your happiness, in every way, I remain, dear Mr. Syle,

"Your friend, WILLIAM SPARROW.

"*Mr. E. W. Syle, Gambier, O.*"

"THEOLOGICAL SEMINARY, FAIRFAX CO., VA.,
"September 16, 1841.

"MY DEAR SIR:—

"On Saturday night I got your very acceptable letter; L. having gone to Alexandria, and brought out the mail, which would otherwise have been there till this morning. I was glad to learn that you are so pleasantly situated; but Philadelphia is not a place to be despised.

"The freshest news is that E. has got back, and that Mrs. Wing is with us, and will probably remain over this week. She has been quite disappointed in not seeing you. Her health is but little improved. Nothing from Dr. Keith, and little from Bishop Meade, except that when last heard from he was in Inverness, in Scotland. E. was some weeks on his way home, so that his news had grown stale. He brought me a note from B., on the eve of his marriage.

"The bell is now ringing for morning prayers, and I must stop for awhile. Up from breakfast again, with a letter from Bishop Meade. He writes from London; had been in Ireland and Scotland, and was on the wing for Paris. He hopes to sail from Liverpool on the 19th inst. He has everywhere met with the greatest kindness. The Irish clergy are the least infected with Oxfordism of any that he met. In Scotland, as we might expect, from their history, and as I know from observation, so far as that could extend, they have their faces more set toward Rome. Much of the same evil the Bishop met in England, but he says, with the exception of the Tractarians, the Establishment is much improved.

"I have, with the Bishop's, got a sweet letter from a sweet cousin in Ireland. It is odorous with the grace of the Gospel. Written by a superior mind, highly cultivated, and under the pressure of a heavy affliction, though sustained by the promises of Christ, it goes at once to my heart. What a comforting reflection that the presence of our covenant God is all pervading, when we find ourselves unable to go and minister consolation, personally, to those we love.

"Most truly, your friend and brother in Christ,

"William Sparrow.

"*Mr. Edward W. Syle.*"

"Theological Seminary, near Alexandria, D. C.,
"May 28, 1842.

"My Dear Sir:—

"I returned last night from Staunton, and feeling fit for nothing else (how complimentary), I purpose writing you a few lines. I went to the Convention with Mr. Cassius Lee, in a private carriage, and spent the previous Sunday in Winchester. I was unwell when I left home, and though we had a pleasant drive, and through a delightful country, I was not better when I reached Winchester. Thence we proceeded on Monday, and by Tuesday night, when I got to Staunton, I was as sick a man as could well travel. I went to bed immediately, at the hotel, but next morning was removed to private quarters, and there, by advice of two physicians, I was bled, and blistered, and so forth, and confined to the house during the whole Convention term. On the last day, for an hour, I was taken to the house, that I might give in my vote for an Assistant Bishop, but immediately returned, no better for the trip. Such is the history of my visit to Staunton, to attend the Convention. I ought to say, however, that I went to church, and preached my ordination sermon on Sunday. I regretted my inability to attend the Convention, and the religious exercises connected with it, for it was the unanimous opinion that it was altogether more profitable and pleasant than the one held in Alexandria. The religious exercises were everything, and gave tone and character to the occasion. The preaching was spoken of as very good, and the spirit of brotherly love that prevailed was highly gratifying. Bishop Meade shone.

"He certainly is no common man. He possesses wonderful influence over others, and has great control over himself. There is a mixture of moderation and firmness in him that is very unusual. His confirmation and farewell addresses were excellent. The Trustees have authorized me to offer the Professorship to Doctor May. I shall not write him for a few days yet, and if you should learn anything, or know anything, which it would be well to communicate, pray write me promptly.

"My family, from the greatest to the least, even Leonard, by sympathetic imitation, desire to be most kindly remembered to you. They all look with strong desire for your return. In regard to a governess, the great obstacle is the expense. Anything you might learn, without official inquiry, I would be glad to hear.

"Ever truly, your friend, WILLIAM SPARROW.

"*Mr. E. W. Syle.*"

"THEOLOGICAL SEMINARY, July 2, 1842.

"MY DEAR MR. SYLE:—

"I have just learned, from the 'Episcopal Recorder,' that Mr. H. has been elected Secretary of the Missionary Society; and as a king may arise that may not know Joseph, I have thought it expedient to take up my pen, and suggest that there is no necessity of tarrying longer in Egypt, that the way is clear, back to Canaan, and that many are there to receive, with all gladness of heart, 'him that was separated from his brethren.' This unexpected election will cause us to expect you much sooner.

"For your letters I am under many obligations to you. Some of them have given me a hearty laugh, especially that about Thomas Jefferson, and the one that speaks of Mar Yohannan; and all have pleased and cheered me. Since I have got back from Convention, I have scarce had a headache till to-day; so you may judge I have enjoyed myself not a little, corporally. In other respects, also, I have had, perhaps, more than my usual share of comfort, far more, at all events, than I had reason to expect. The only anxiety I have just now is, that Dr. May should not accept. We have offered him the department of Ecclesiastical History; he balks at it, though he has not given a final negative. If the offer had been Systematic Theology, I doubt not he would have accepted at once. Ought I to give that up, and let him take what he desires? (I say desires, though he has not expressed any such wish.) The settling of this question gives me trouble. I hardly know what is duty. Mrs. Sparrow says no. She thinks I ought to retain what I like best, and incur no burdens by trying to qualify myself for my new office. The Lord direct me.

"They think of starting a theological seminary in Massachusetts, in the neighborhood of Boston, and overtures have been made to me on the subject, but I do not think seriously of the matter. The plan is peculiar, and has some plausibilities in theory, but in practice will not be found, I think, to work well.

"The prospect here, if we can only get the right kind of a man, is improving, I think. They say we shall have a large class next year. The revivals in Virginia are likely to turn out many candidates for holy orders. Our students seem to feel that they have done a good year's work, and some of them certainly have, in the middle class. Had White, Hiester, and Richmond, been able to stay with us, I should have made a decent exhibition on Mosheim and Knapp. Even as it is, I hope they will do well at the approaching examination. The seniors, I fear, will not appear, by any means, so well. There are but four to stand examination. In all this, about the students and Dr. May, I am thinking (not audibly), but legibly, and for your eye only.

"Supposing Dr. May should not accept, have you anything to suggest? Do you suppose Dr. Clarke could be induced to come here.

"A piece has lately appeared in the 'Witness and Advocate,' against our retention of an Assistant Bishop, maintaining that Bishop Meade is not as infirm as the case requires to entitle him to an assistant. I have attempted to answer him, in the 'Southern Churchman.' If you should find that the piece referred to is published in the City of Brotherly Love, and is thought to have any weight, I wish, without revealing the authorship, you would have the reply published, first correcting the tremendous mistakes of the printer, who talks of the 'permanent *instability*' of Bishop Meade (*inability*); of our Standing Committees as 'influential *people*,' instead of 'bodies,' and of my disposition to *argue* with my opponent, when I said *agree*. Above all, correct a sentence thus: 'Canons may be violated as well by interpreting them too strictly, as too laxly. In the matter of the Assistant Bishop, the latter course would multiply them when they were not needed; the former would preclude them where the Church was suffering for want of their services.' All this trouble is imposed upon you only if you find that the subject is brought into the Philadelphia papers. The Standing Committee of New York has signed the testimonials of our Assistant Bishop. Do you know what they are doing in Philadelphia?

"Ever yours, most truly, W. SPARROW."

"THEOLOGICAL SEMINARY, FAIRFAX CO., VA.,
"July 25, 1842.

"MY DEAR MR. S.:—

"I should have written to you long ago, but that I have been borne down, crushed into the dust, crushed like the moth, by my Seminary duties. For some weeks before examination I was at the top of my speed all the time, and, of course, when I got to the goal, I was completely out of wind, and exhausted of my strength. Ever since then I have been in a state of collapse; and when the reaction will take place I do not know. It is a labor to me now to hold the pen. Yesterday I could not crawl to church.

"My chief comfort under all this exhaustion, occasioned by Seminary labors, is that they have not been quite in vain. I have heard little or nothing, but I judge, from looks, that the examination was satisfactory. The middle class, I thought myself, did well. I ought to say there is another thing to cheer me: Dr. May has accepted. I cannot tell how much I was relieved by this intelligence, received last Friday. I have no doubt it will prove a great blessing to the Institution. And then, again, it will be the means, I trust, of securing your return to us.

"Considerable seriousness prevails in Alexandria. Mr. Dana baptized four young ladies, Friends, a fortnight ago, and for some time before, and ever since then, there has been a deep attention to religion. While the Bishop was here he held several morning prayer meetings, one at five o'clock, and the attendance was very good. Last Friday I went in and took part at the evening lecture. The house was crowded.

"But I must stop. I am really weary of writing, just as though it were hoeing corn or chopping logs. My family all desire to be affectionately remembered to you.

"As ever, your affectionate friend, WILLIAM SPARROW."

"THEOLOGICAL SEMINARY P. O., FAIRFAX CO., VA.,
"March 24, 1843.

"MY DEAR MR. SYLE:—

"I have just received your welcome letter, in a sick room, and begin in the same place to answer it; you may expect, therefore, that the reply will have many ailments, and hobble feebly along. But what of that: a friend on crutches is still a friend.

"Let me see if there is not some news. Rev. Mr. Johnston has been elected Bishop of Alabama, and declined! Dr. Fairfax told him his health would not endure the climate. You will have heard of the death of Bishop Griswold. He went out to visit his Assistant Bishop, Dr. Eastburn, fell at the door, as was supposed, from an affection of the heart, and died in a few minutes. He had just finished a series of papers on the Reformation, adapted to the times. They constitute his dying testimony, which, by the by, is becoming every day more and more needed.

"I should judge, also, from what I learn, that Bishop McIlvaine is not up on matters of discipline; not going up the ladder, but rather coming down. The world has yet to learn that doctrine and discipline are not mechanically, but chemically combined, and that to be truly sound on the one, a man must be sound on the other also.

"The Oxford men are making prodigious efforts. Newman's sermons are publishing, recommended by Bishops Onderdonk, of New York; Doane, of New Jersey; Whittingham, of Maryland; Ives, of North Carolina; and Dr. Seabury. Bishop Whittingham is about to publish a monthly theological.

"Your statement about the Church of Scotland interested me. If the Scotch Establishment goes the English will soon follow. But you know it is my opinion that the knell of all establishments is rung, though if I were to consult mere flesh and blood, I would rather have a rectory in a rural district in England, than be Archbishop of Canterbury, or Bishop of the Protestant Episcopal Church in the United States. Should you return, I wish you would bring me some three or four pounds' (sterling) worth of pamphlets on the Oxford movement, especially those touching fundamental points of Church government, and of such points, especially the 'Apostolical Succession,' excepting 'Palmer' and 'Percival,' which I have. Even if you should remain, and visit London, I will contrive to send you some money for this purpose. Pamphlets from first-rate men usually contain the cream of long controversies. Among the many publications commenced in this country I have often wondered a 'pamphleteer' has not been one of them.

"But I must draw to a close. My family, thank God, have enjoyed pretty good health this winter (the latter part of which, to the present time, has been very severe). I write this, Richard Hooker fashion, in the midst of them. I hope, dear man, that his temperament was not as nervous as mine. If it was he never could have written the 'Ecclesiastical Polity' in the nursery, at all events. My health has suffered by my exertions in going to Georgetown, but I faintly hope it will improve as warm weather comes on. The sight of you would do as much to renew it as any medical prescription, and I think rather more; for, in truth, I have pretty much given up the physicians, in my case. Time is my only physician, which will kill, and, as I hope, in infinite mercy, cure at the same moment. Our Seminary seems to be doing well. Dr. May is a man you would like, whatever you might think of him as a theologian. His wife is to come on after Easter. I hope for some improvement to our society therefrom. The Doctor has read portions of her letters to me, and I should judge her to be a most intelligent and Christian woman. I hope you will have written again before this reaches you; if not, that you will immediately after. In the meantime accept the regards of my most affectionate family, and let us have your remembrance in your prayers, as you always have in those of your ever faithful friend and brother,

"W. Sparrow."

"Theological Seminary, Fairfax Co., Va.,
"April 27th, 1846.

"Rev. and very Dear Brother:

"On the receipt of your welcome and long looked for letter, my first impulse was to sit down immediately, and pour out my heart on paper, thanking God for His preserving care of you and yours, congratulating you on your arrival in the scene of your labors, and telling you everything which I supposed would be interesting to you or Mrs. Syle. But I was checked by the reflection that for this latter work there would be no place—that your relations and our common friends in Alexandria would tell you all, and more than I could possibly communicate, in the way of news. Added to this, Dr. May's letter from you promised me a second one speedily, and so I have been induced to postpone writing until the present moment. I trust that, coming after the flood of friendly communications which your first letters to this country must have brought upon you, it will not be the less acceptable.

"But, with what, in the way of news, shall I begin? I begin with the last, and the most painful I have to communicate, and that which furnished me a subject in the pulpit yesterday, and in the Faculty meeting Thursday night—I mean the death of my dear young friend, Albert Duy. He was ordained, you know, last summer, and then, on my representation, called as assistant to Dr. Cutler. All the expectations of the Brooklyn Church were more than realized, and they were about to give him a permanent call as Assistant Rector, when he visited Philadelphia, to consult with his friends upon the matter, at the same time writing to me on the subject. He wrote from Philadelphia to me on Wednesday; I got the letter on Saturday; I wanted to consult with Bishop Meade, who came here on Monday, for his lectures; next morning, as I was drawing up to the table to take my pen to give him the result of my conference, in walked the Bishop, with the startling intelligence, 'Duy is dead.' He had been taken sick the Friday previous, and died on Sunday morning, at six o'clock, at his father's house, where you have often been. I cannot express my own grief at the event, for I had a high opinion of the talents and general character of Mr. Duy, and looked forward to his great usefulness in the Church, especially as an able advocate of sound views of doctrine and of discipline. But the Lord had need of him elsewhere, where it is better, far better for him to be; and we should, therefore, meekly acquiesce. I hope his death will be blessed to us here.

"As to Church affairs in general, the newspapers will tell you more than I can communicate. The perversions of Hewitt and Hoyt to Rome have made quite a noise. O, that a few more who are Romanists in heart would follow them. This would be a blessed thing for them and us. We shall never be at peace till we have gotten rid of this popish leaven. There are very many now, in our Church, who, though they may approve of the effects of the Reformation in curtailing priestly tyranny, checking open traffic in souls, putting down gross superstitions, etc., do not cordially receive the fundamental principles of the Reformation. The supremacy of the Scriptures, the unfettered right of private judgment, the powers of the Church, as distinguished from the Clergy—these are things which their souls hate, though some of them do not know it. But never will the inherent power of Christianity, as the power of God, appear, till these principles are acknowledged and men are ready to meet their consequences. Troublesome consequences follow, you know, from all principles. We cannot even go to Heaven without 'much tribulation.'

"Things in New York are very quiet, and likely to be, till the next General Convention. In the meantime Bishop O. will probably have been abandoned by his partisans. Though the man be abandoned, not so his principles. Dr. Seabury has come out openly in favor of the principles of Tract No. 90, as those on which alone the Church can stand. Bishop Hopkins has, in consequence, published an address to the Bishops and other members of the Church, in the United States, warning them of the danger. I have not yet seen the work. Happy the man who has not, in these days, yet to make up his opinions, and who knows, and feels the power of first principles, else he must be driven fearfully about by the varying winds of doctrine. My conviction is that the instability which our Church has displayed in these latter days has arisen from a want of moral and intellectual courage, which would lead, directly, to a trust in God, and His word and government, and from a consequent leaning on human authority and human expedients. 'But the Lord reigneth,' and he who is established in grace need not be anxious about the result.

"I have had great apprehensions of a war with England. Our Western members of Congress are desirous of war, and many others, under party influence, join with them in the clamor. They believe that they can 'whip England,' and they would love to do it. As to title, I believe our pretensions are quite as good as those of England, and that, of course, is enough for the Hotspurs. But what a calamity to the world a war would be. The Lord in mercy avert it. I believe that if our Union held together, England would be eventually worried out, but, in the meantime, what havoc of life, property, morals, religion, and everything which we call good. Last summer I stayed at home, except a trip to Norfolk, and I am going to do the same thing this year. My health has been quite as good as it has ever been since you and I met—rather better. My duty in the Seminary is not so irksome, in consequence. I have reason to thank God, also, that my family have enjoyed pretty good health. I teach Bessie and William German, orally. I find I take more and more pleasure in intercourse with the children, as they grow up and I grow older. On my last birthday I was saluted with three rhyming epistles from the children, and others in prose. One of them was from Kate, written, of course, by the mother, and if I had room, I believe I would transcribe it, for the amusement of yourself and Mrs. Syle. Perhaps I may do it in my answer to her letter, with the understanding that no allusion be made to it afterward. Of course, it is a *trifle*, but it is *domestic*, and that gives it value in my eyes, and, perhaps, will in yours also.

"Thus, my dear Brother, I have endeavored to fill my sheet with news. Such a gossiping epistle I have never written in my life before, but I have supposed it would be more acceptable than—what it would be easier to write—disquisitions on matters and things in general. This I reserve for a future communication. In the meantime, let me assure you that the arrival of your letters on this hill have given me and my family intense delight; and when we have gone to town, we have had another feast of friendship in mere sympathy with the joy of your friends there; I rejoice that you are now in the field of your life's labor. Though I shall not give up the hope of seeing you again in this world, I shall look upon China as the scene of labors and usefulness for a much loved friend, to the end of his days; and often shall my prayers ascend to Heaven, that he and his precious wife may enjoy constant tokens of the Divine favor, and be eminently blessed in their work. That Heaven may bless and prosper you both, is *ever* the prayer of

"Your friend and brother in Christ, WILLIAM SPARROW."

"THEOLOGICAL SEMINARY, FAIRFAX CO., VA.,
"December 12, 1846.

"REV. AND DEAR BROTHER:—

"Yours of June 28 reached me a short time ago, and I sit down to answer it, regretting that you have *seemed* to be so much neglected by your friends, and hoping that this letter will reach its destination. I have written to Mr. Irving, on the subject of our letters, and will write again. But to business; and first, about the Mission. What are the feelings of our students in reference to China just now, I cannot say. I think, however, there are some searchings of heart amongst them. Last night we had a missionary address from one of the students, which was calculated to awaken the conscience. In our prayers we remembered all missionaries, and especially those who had gone from this institution, and entreated the Lord to send forth more from the same place. Experience has taught, I think, that we should leave the matter much in the Lord's hands. If the person is not self-moved, *i. e.* by the Spirit of God in the person, the soul's very centre, only evil can come of his mission. A question. I have a horrible idea of the

Chinese language, and your letters and your wife's, and all others, confirm the impression. Such being the case, can I urge those to follow you who have not more than an average gift in the linguistic line? Please tell me how those of small abilities in that way get along, and to what extent they are likely to be useful. I think the language is a serious objection in many minds. You speak of Drs. ——, and ——. If Dr. —— were not encumbered with a large family, I think he would go to China. I fear he is not doing well in his missionary church in Richmond. Suppose you write to him. R—— was supposed to have become disengaged a short time ago, but I understand the engagement has been renewed. If it had not been, I should have written to him. You cannot spend your spare time better than in writing to *individuals* who you think have qualifications for the work, taking good heed to set forth the hardships before them, as did the Saviour when he called his disciples, and emphasizing the proper missionary *Spirit.* Some may be touched by a direct appeal who would not feel if addressed as in a crowd. S—— would make a noble missionary, unless I'm much mistaken. I thank you for the extract from ——; but do tell me, how a people using an instrument calculated to make and keep them ignorant, should retain so much learning (such as it is), and such a fondness for it. The Arabs, having good horses, are famous equestrians; the French, having a light and tripping language, are conversational; the Germans, a deep and expressive one, are metaphysical; why, with a language which is a hindrance rather than a help, are the Chinese so learned? Was it that, being, by the force of accidental circumstances, started in that way, the language, by its fixedness, kept them to it? I hope your miscellaneous budget will enlighten me on this and many other topics. At all events, I shall look for it with extreme interest.

"As to the great controversy in our Church, I can't say much now. There is a lull of the storm, and will probably be until the meeting of the next General Convention, when Bishop Onderdonk's case, and that of the General Seminary, will come up for decision. In the meantime, some four of our clergy have gone to Rome, and some have published their reasons for so doing. In consequence, there is much condemnation of Puseyism in certain quarters, but alas, many that 'judge do the same things.' The leaven is working in the mass, and in my opinion there are to be yet great convulsions in our Church before it is eradicated. Dr. Seabury goes on as ever. He and his correspondents are rabid in their language, and yet men will have it so, as they show by the support of their subscriptions. Our troubles, of course, have their chief root in sin; but after that, in error and misapprehension. What *I* deem the master error, you well know; it is, in one word, *a sacerdotal character* in the clergy. Till we are rid of that we shall never have peace.

"Bessie and William are studying German with me. He is decidedly a bright boy, but, like myself, is indolent. Frances studies French with me, and has made considerable progress. I have never in my life done so much in my family. My labors in the Seminary are also more abundant, and thus far I have written a good deal, this term, for the pulpit. I was strongly tempted to answer Dr. M.'s review of my sermon, but did not.* Dear Brother, you wish to see me in the *press;* alas, you know not how I would be *oppressed.* With my poor health, it would be madness to assume the burden and responsibility of publication. Discouragement would absolutely paralyze my mind, and *that* I must expect if I step down into the arena of authorship. The most I ever expect to do is to write some lectures for my classes. They lately sent a deputation to me to that effect, and though it was meant to be complimentary, it has alarmed me, lest I may have been neglecting duty. I endeavor to make my sermons lectures; at least, 'sermons to the students.'

"Let me turn the tables. If you should have leisure, would it not be well to plan some publication about China, its language, institutions, etc. It would have a happy effect in calling attention to the mission, and literary men might be benefited and pleased. For the sake of this and every other good work in which you may be engaged, I rejoice that your sight is so much improved, and pray that it may continue to improve; and, now, a word to your better half. Tell her we are all delighted to learn that she has gone to housekeeping, and that I trust she has not a captious overseer to complain when the butter is not fresh, etc. Tell her, also, that I was gratified with the perusal of her letter to the bishop, and that there is a presbyter in Virginia, who, with his family, would be rejoiced to receive a letter whenever it might not interfere with important matters. I put this exception because I conceive

* That on "Love Among Christians," preached at the Convention, in Fredericksburg.

that she is already overburdened with letter writing. For this reason, though I might, I do not plead her promise to write me *once.* It was extorted at a moment when no promise but one could with propriety be considered binding, that one absorbing all the rest! I have been up stairs to announce that I am writing, and have come down loaded with messages to Mrs. S. and yourself. Truly our heart's desire and prayer is that grace, mercy and peace may ever rest upon you both.

"Ever your friend and brother in Christ,

"WILLIAM SPARROW."

"THEOLOGICAL SEMINARY, FAIRFAX COUNTY, VA.,
"August 31st, 1847.

"VERY DEAR BROTHER:—

"For your kind remembrances of us, and prompt correspondence, accept the hearty acknowledgments of a large and affectionate family. We never cease to think of you and Mrs. S., and since you have become parents, of your little one, and not only to think but also to pray that Heaven's choicest blessing may ever abundantly rest on you all. We have received not only your letters, but also your presents. They have been very highly prized, as a memorial of true friendship, and as a means of instruction. I have often exhibited them and talked about them, so that I could almost deliver a lecture on the Chinese language and customs.

"In regard to the mission, it does, indeed, seem to be sorely tried. About the bishop, we are all extremely anxious, and pray that it may be the Lord's will to spare him. Whatever be the result, it is delightful to know that, however weak in body, he is strong in spirit. I pray that Mr. S., of whom I know nothing, may be a man after the Bishop's own heart, and ready and able to co-operate with you in every good work. We have in the Seminary, of one year's standing, a son of Dr. Keith, his younger son, who proposes joining you when he has completed his studies. He has spoken of it only to me, I believe, and does not wish it to be generally known. He is a young man of real ability and great application in study. His forte is language. And should the Lord mature, sanctify, and consummate his present purpose, doubtless, he will be an able assistant, as a translator, at least. We have one young man in the Seminary, Hoffman, whom I should like to see go to China. Though not college bred, he has a good education, is a hard student, has good talents, is most systematic, energetic and persevering, and for sweetness of character and untiring beneficence surpasses anything I have ever known. He thinks of Africa. He will be in the senior class, coming term.

"The Seminary goes on about as usual. Last year I taught more than at any previous period, and perhaps with less deficiency. I teach in the family, and that consumes time and strength. In looking forward to the next year, my heart fails. The students, through a committee, not meaning it for a censure, just before our commencement, made a request that I would deliver some formal lectures. Though they did not intend it, it oppressed me much, as the same request was made the previous year. I have neither time, nor strength, nor confidence for the task.

"At our commencement I delivered an address on the difficult topic of subscription to the Thirty-nine Articles, and the trustees requested its publication, especially Bishop Meade. But I cannot be satisfied that it is wise to comply. Thus, you see, I am tortured, as of old.

"Dr. Brooke has left Cincinnati, and, in an informal way, I have been invited to his place, but shall not go. A year ago, when the Doctor threatened the same step, brother Wing gave me to understand that the Bishop and the Cincinnatians all wished it, and asked my assent to the proposition, but then, also, I declined. I begin to think I am too old to transplant, though I do long for a place which may be the home of my family when I am taken away.

"I have spent five weeks with W. and S., in the Valley of Virginia. It was a most delightful time. One half of it, we were under the direction of Bishop Meade, who laid himself out to make our trip agreeable. I attended three Associations, and in thirty-four days preached sixteen times. We saw a great many good people. I am thinking of starting off, in a few days, for Ohio, my first visit since my removal. Mrs. Sparrow is the mover, and what she sets herself to do with me she usually effects. I had not the most distant thought of it two days ago. If I go I shall hope to be at the Convention at Louisville. The General Convention will be an exciting scene; the Lord grant not a disgraceful one. Dr. Seabury and his men are bent on the restoration of Bishop Onderdonk. But they cannot succeed.

"This letter would have been addressed to Mrs. Syle, if your last had not stepped in between. Tell her how gratified I am that she did not forget her promise of writing, and that I shall not forget mine, of replying. You may, also, assure her that I shall not gibbet her letter before the public. At the same time it is well for the wife of a Missionary to be as callous in reference to all such matters as possible. When deep interest is taken in the Mission, and great pleasure felt in receiving communications from the Missionaries, persons will feel an instinctive temptation to let others participate in the joy. The judgment, also, may suggest that it may prove edifying as well as pleasant to others. I cannot but rejoice that you both are where you are. I feel great confidence that it is the Lord who sent you to China, and think He has a great work for you to do. May the Lord preserve your lives, and give you a hand and heart for all good enterprises and labors. All here, thank God, are in pretty good health, and join in earnest good wishes to you and Mrs. S. Your remembrance of me on my birthday touched my heart. May the Lord ever remember, for good, you and yours.

"Ever your friend and brother, W. SPARROW."

CHAPTER VI.

VISIT TO EUROPE, AND WORK OF NEXT TWELVE YEARS.

The period of the present chapter, from the close of session, June, 1848, till the beginning of the war, and the temporary suspension of the Seminary, May, 1861, is one but little diversified as to incident of special character. The previous seven years of residence in Virginia, and the intimate relations into which, during this time, Dr. Sparrow had been brought with the clergy and laity of the Diocese, had enabled him to identify himself with its interests and affairs, as he had formerly with those of Ohio. His pupils, year after year, were filling the parishes, and thus strengthening his connections, and increasing his influence in every movement of Diocesan effort and advancement. Most grateful were his reunions with those pupils, both to them and to himself, sometimes in his occasional coveted visits to their field of labor, but more ordinarily at the Annual Conventions, and at the Commencements at the Seminary. The position which he had occupied from Ohio, as delegate to the General Convention, was soon again assigned him by the Convention of Virginia, and retained until the General Convention of 1868. His affection for his old friends, and his interest in old associations, did not, indeed, pass away; and we find that there was a strong response of feeling, on his part, to another call, given during this period, to return to Gambier, and resume the duties of his former position. That question settled, he turned to his peculiar task, and session after session employed himself in training his pupils for their work. The vacation with which this period begins, 1848, was spent mostly in Europe. It had been ten years since he had last visited his friends and relatives in the localities of childhood and youth, on the other side of the Atlantic, and it would seem to have been to him an occasion of great enjoyment. As mentioned in the close of the last chapter, the brief autobiographical sketch given in the opening of our narrative was written at sea, during this trip, on his way to Europe, to the scenes of the events which he was describing. It was thirty-one years since his first departure, as a youth of sixteen, from Ireland, and we may easily understand the emotion which the changes of the present, and the remembered incidents and associations of the past, would naturally produce. It is greatly to be regretted that more of his correspondence during that journey, and of the one ten years before, has not been preserved. We are not able to read the account as he alone could have given it, and as he doubtless did give it, of those summers' tours of 1838 and 1848, especially the portions of them devoted to the scenes and associations of early boyhood. "I remember," says one of his children, "my extravagant joy at his return; my being allowed to sit up till eleven o'clock to see him (as he came from Washington in our carriage, which was sent for him). But I was too young for any definite memory of that period."

"I remember perfectly," is the communication from one who was then an inmate in the Doctor's family, Miss Smith, "his second visit to Europe, but nothing of the minutiæ of it. The greatest pleasure he seemed to have had was during the time passed in Ireland, among his relations. He spoke most enthusiastically of the cordial reception they gave him, particularly his three aunts, sisters to his mother. He appeared to think himself quite spoiled by them for ordinary civility; for they went back to his boyhood, appearing to forget the years that had intervened, and petted and caressed him as they had been used to do. It was in summer, and they were at their country home, where he had passed so many happy hours from his fifth to his sixteenth years. His whole face was lit up when he spoke of his rambles over familiar ground, and how, in memory, he lived his boyhood over again. Those who knew him but slightly would have been surprised to find the depth and warmth of feeling evinced in speaking of this visit to Ireland. He had the most tender regard for his mother, and being with her relatives seemed to have revived pleasant memories of her.

"He went to the Continent, but, as far as I can remember, did not go to Italy on that trip. He was in France, in Germany, and I think went to Switzerland. Want of time, I suppose, prevented a more protracted journey, as he went to be absent only the vacation. The larger part of the time was passed in Great Britain. He took letters from clergymen to prominent persons, many of whom were acquainted with his brother-in-law, Bishop Chase, who was favorably known in England. In this way he procured a ticket to the Queen's Chapel. Not very long after his return he attended a Convocation in one of the Counties near the Seminary, and in quite a large company spoke of this privilege, for such he considered it. There was quite a number of young ladies present, many of whom were very gaily attired. 'Young ladies,' said he, addressing himself to that part of the company, 'I was most favorably impressed with the Queen, who was seated beside her mother, the Duchess of Kent, and the contrast in their deportment was striking. The mother talked and behaved most irreverently, while Victoria's manner was most exemplary.' He then went on to say, that when the Queen came out and knelt on a cushion while the special prayer for herself was read, he was struck with the plain simplicity of her dress. Knowing him so well, I was amused at the way he brought this in; as usual, I was plainly attired, so did not take the reproof. 'The Queen had on a simple white muslin, without an ornament, except the crown, which she was called upon to wear on that occasion.' He made no remark on the preacher or his performance, that I remember."

Within the next four years there were several efforts made to induce him to change his field of labor. One of these was an invitation to the rectorship of St. Paul's, Richmond. "We were all alarmed," writes Dr. May, in February, 1850, "some time ago, at the prospect of Dr. Sparrow's going to Richmond, as successor to Mr. Norwood. He seemed much inclined to go; the question with him being narrowed down to one of justice to his family, and, indeed, as he said, to his creditors. But he yielded to the representations of his friends." "At one time," says Dr. May again, a year later, April 17, 1851, "we feared lest Dr. Sparrow might be taken from us. He was importuned to return to Kenyon. Mrs. Sparrow, who feared for his health, was on our side, and we prevailed. He ought never to think of leaving us." Not very long after, again, during the next year, 1852, the question of the Assistantship of Trinity Church, Boston, with Bishop Eastburn, was pressed upon his consideration. These propositions were made in the most flattering manner, and there were pressing reasons why they should be carefully considered. Some of those reasons will appear in the correspondence which follows. The invitation to return to Gambier seems to have been extended to him during a visit made by him to Ohio. During this visit, the second since he had left Gambier, in 1841, he was present at the Diocesan Convention, meeting there with many of his old friends, and visiting different localities, the scenes of his early Missionary labors. The General Convention, of which he was a member, met that year, 1850, in Cincinnati. After its adjournment, he made a visit to New Orleans, going from thence to Mobile, and taking the route by Charleston and Richmond home. This trip, particularly the portion of it on the Mississippi, was one of which he had vivid recollections, and in after life it was quite amusing to hear his descriptions of some of his fellow passengers. Once, during the trip, there was an alarm, in the middle of the night, of fire or collision, and he was roused by a fellow passenger rushing to the upper deck for safety, whom he speedily followed. His decided impression, more than once expressed, was, that the danger of crossing the Atlantic and that of going down the Mississippi were not to be thought of in comparison, so much greater were the risks of the latter. During a part of the journey, Dr. Sparrow was brought into closer acquaintanceship with Bishop Otey, of Tennessee, than at any former period. And he loved to speak of the conversations on subjects of practical religion which they held together, and from which he received edification and enjoyment. With some other members of the house of Bishops, as the letters following will show, he did not find the same enjoyment; especially with one whose peculiar gift seemed to be that of knowing, and expatiating upon, the ages, and varieties, and qualities, of the different kinds of wine imported into, and used in, this country! There were some others, also, whose views upon certain questions he found, upon comparison, to correspond with those of Romish Bishops, traveling with them on the same boat. The letters following, descriptive of this tour, and the events in Ohio preceding, are here given, with others, written before and after, to the same and other correspondents. Portions of this correspondence will throw light upon the biography of this period, not afforded by the narrative. Several will be recognized as to pupils of an earlier date. There is scarcely a page which does not exhibit the characteristics of the writer; especially that one which constituted the peculiar charm of his society, his geniality, the kindly spirit which ever delighted to make others cheerful and happy.

"THEOLOGICAL SEMINARY, FAIRFAX COUNTY, VA.,
"February 8, 1849.

"REV. AND DEAR BROTHER:—

"I am reminded of my duty to you and your letter, by the receipt of one by Dr. B. As I cannot, Cæsar or Napoleon-like, answer both together, I must take them on what Johnson or Parr would call, the 'molar principle,' of 'first come first served.'

"In regard to ——, I say this much. He is in an important position, to which he is admirably adapted, and it would be wrong to disturb him. His talents, though so admirably adapted to his present post, might not suit so well at the head of a college. He never took a regular degree, though he is worthy of one. Lastly, I am persuaded he would not, and could not, accept.

"To venture the suggestion of any other name, is almost too much for my nerves. So many, as Jefferson Davis said to Whiting, have been weighed in the balances of Kenyon College, and found wanting (myself almost included, for it would seem that I escaped only with the skin of my teeth), that I am afraid to risk a judgment, or jeopardize a friend. To lessen my risk by multiplying my number out of which you must select, let me name three, any one of whom, I do not say *would* but *may* succeed. Kenyon might prosper in the hands of either of these gentlemen. ——— is a man of very superior ability, of great self-control, of a warm heart, and a soul as big as the universe. ——— is a man of scholarship and tact, and an attractiveness that acts like a charm. ——— is a man of sense, a great deal of information, and great loveliness of character. Every one of them would strive for the spiritual as well as the intellectual improvement of the young men committed to their charge. The second, I suppose, would be the best preacher. Further your deponent saith not.

"The spirit which Mr. B. has manifested is truly admirable. If he leaves Kenyon, I hope he may find an agreeable position in its stead. Truly, it would be a windfall if you can get a gratuitous professor of languages. How my heart rejoices that brother Dennison is back again, and that he is giving so much satisfaction. Remember me most affectionately to him, and tell him, if Providence did not order it otherwise, it would afford me real delight to find myself once more planted between you and him, two of my oldest, truest, and most cherished friends. I often remember Kenyon in my prayers, on its own account; now I may do it 'for my brethren and companions' sake,' with new emphasis.

"So you are returned to town. Alas, it has always been my lot to live in the country, though vastly preferring the city. Happily, I have a city in view, or rather, two or three of them. I have the sight of them with my eyes every day; and what is a little better, any day, in two hours, I may tread their streets. But to me, at my stage of progress in life, after all, these things are small things, mere bagatelles. The great thing is, not to live here or there, but to have God's gracious presence, and so to be doing good, and getting good—good that will last forever.

"My family desire to be remembered to Mrs. W. Can't you bring her on to see us next summer? I have straitened myself by my trip to Europe, so that I shall have to stay at home for some time.

"Your friend and brother, WILLIAM SPARROW.

"*Rev. Mr. T. C. Wing.*"

TO THE SAME.

"THEOLOGICAL SEMINARY, FAIRFAX CO., VA.,
"June 2, 1849.

"REV. AND DEAR BROTHER:—

"I ought to have written you long ago, and therefore send an apology 'with these presents.' I was the less prompt to write because I supposed that my mere silence would show you how I stand in relation to the business part of your letter. In ordinary cases, silence is supposed to give consent; but in the present one, in which your old friendship and partiality shine out in such *persevering* lustre, and in which nothing could, with propriety, be done till I had spoken, it was enough for me simply to say nothing.

"There are many reasons why I should like to return to the West; but I cannot stir till it is made my *indubitable* duty so to do. 'Whatsoever is not of faith' with me, in this matter, would be emphatically sin. I have so many dependent on me, my health is so frail, and the experience of life has so much dampened my ardor, that I am afraid to stir an inch except at the *clear call* of *duty*, and I cannot perceive that I have *that* in the present instance.

"I hope that by this time you begin to see your way clearer in regard to Kenyon. I hope Alexander, the coppersmith, will do you no harm. If the College could get along without the sale of the lands, I should be sorry to see them sold. But when it is sale or ruin, I cannot see how any one can throw obstacles in the way. Who are the lawyers advising? Is their legal opinion respected by judges?

"Mrs. Sparrow is at this time enjoying herself much; Mrs. Kip is with her. Since I began this letter, I have thought that I should be exceedingly pleased to have two or three days' talk with you. But if we should meet, we could not talk as Mrs. Sparrow and her sister do, or as Mrs. Sparrow and Mrs. Wing would, if they should have an interview. The gift of speech is much more enjoyed by women than by men. Tell Mrs. W. this is not meant as a sarcasm, but as a compliment. We are all, thank God, in usual health, which, however, with some of us, is not very good. Mrs. S. and the children send love to Mrs. W. and her flock. We were remarking this morning, that *everybody* here sends *love* to *everybody;* and therefore, Mrs. S. has added to me in giving this commission: 'it is real love here.' Do be forgiving, and write me soon about your family and the College. Most truly,

"Your friend and brother in Christ, WILLIAM SPARROW."

"To REV. E. H. CANFIELD:—

"I suppose, in New York, you find your hands full of work. In your city, the great Babylon of the Western Hemisphere, there is enough to do, in all reason, for every one of God's people and ministers, and that right at the door. At first, I suppose you will be pretty much confined to your parish until it is well built up, and you have established yourself firmly in the confidence and affection of your people; and then you will have to lend a hand in more general operations, in committees, on platforms, etc. Wherever you labor, and whatever you undertake, may the Lord be with you and sustain you.

"As to matters here, I do not think of anything new to communicate. We are a *statu quo* people, anti-movement conservatives. The secular Alexandria is showing great signs of life, in consequence of the commencement of a railroad, and the prospect of the completion of the canal to Cumberland. But they have not yet paved King Street!

"We are expecting Bishop Meade here, to deliver his annual lectures, next Wednesday. What a useful man he is! If all our Bishops were like him, how would the Episcopal Church prosper. He will remain until next month, when the Convention meets in Alexandria.

"*April* 17, 1850."

TO THE SAME.

"I promised to write you during my journey. O, that I had your gift of gathering up the news. But we must be contented with our lot, and be thankful for what is given, and not envious for what is withheld.

"Delaware I have not been able to visit, though I have seen some Delaware friends, Mr. H. and Mrs. L., at Dayton; but I did little more than see them, because of an attack of sickness, which kept me most of the time in my room. In Springfield, however, I saw Mr. P., and had half an hour's talk with him, and told all about you, and learned what I could about him and his wife. Her, to my disappointment, I did not see. Many friends inquired about you and yours most kindly.

"The Convention was peaceful and pleasant. On Tuesday I returned to this place, not caring to be present at the rare show of the opening of the General Convention. Besides, I wanted to spend a little more time with my friends here. I return to-day, South, and hope to reach Cincinnati by nine o'clock to-night.

"When at Dayton, I received a formal invitation from the Trustees, by unanimous vote, to the Presidency of Kenyon College, $1200 per annum, and the expense of removal. Besides this, the clerical members of the association drew up a paper expressive of their feelings, and pledging themselves to support me in the position thus offered me. I have not yet responded, but soon shall. Never was I in greater perplexity, for everybody I meet, except my own kindred, expresses himself in the same way. The great argument is, that to secure my services, folk are ready to help the college, but of strangers they are distrustful. May the Lord in mercy guide to a right decision. Their conduct toward me is very flattering, and calculated to make me think of myself more highly than I ought to think; but, in truth, I am rather oppressed than elevated by it. It is a vital matter to me and to my family, if to nobody else.

"If you should feel at leisure to repay this meagre note with one of your robust epistles, telling me all about you and yours, and matters and things in general, New York ecclesiastical politics and measures, I will feel much obliged to you. I still think I shall go down the Mississippi.

"*Columbus, Oct.* 3, 1850."

To the Same.

"After the Convention adjourned, I went down the Ohio and Mississippi rivers to New Orleans, and thence to Mobile, Augusta,

Charleston, Wilmington, and Richmond, home. I spent one Sunday in Louisville, another on the river, a third at Natchez, a fourth at Vicksburg, a fifth at Memphis, a sixth at Oxford, a seventh at Natchez again, an eighth at New Orleans, a ninth in Augusta, and by Saturday, here. I have preached every Sunday since I left home, except one of the two Sundays at the General Convention, when I wished to be a hearer. I have mingled with all sorts, and sizes, and descriptions of men, clerical and lay, and that, too, not from our own Church only. Two days I spent on board a boat, with Archbishop Purcell, and Bishops Spaulding and Lanzy, of the Romish Church! I have had with them all much intercourse, and if I have learned nothing else, have learned something of that 'mystery of iniquity' which, in the Apostles' day, had begun already to work. The close blood relationship between Romanism and Puseyism, yes, and High-Churchism, too, was made manifest to my eyes. The doctrine of the Apostolical Succession, as commonly taught, is the back bone of both systems. Both alike resolve the being of a Church into it. Those that have it, no matter how heretical (I had the statement alike from a Catholic and a Protestant Bishop), are a Church; those who have it not, no matter how orthodox, and pious, and outwardly regular, are no Church. Good Lord deliver me from such a caricature of the simple and spiritual Gospel of Christ.

"You know of the action of the Ohio Convention at Dayton. There were so many peculiarities in the case, too tedious to mention, that I was afraid I should be neglecting a call of duty. However, here I am, and the Lord grant I may never repent of my determination.

"Ohio is wonderfully improved since I left it, and the next five years will improve it yet more. I think the set time for the prosperity of Kenyon College has come. Episcopalians are tired and ashamed of neglecting it, and they have grown strong enough to maintain it handsomely. If only sure of health, I feel that I could build it up; and it would be a good work, something to look back upon with pleasure! Then again, it would be a fine place for the education of my boys, and for settling them in business when their education was completed. The salary they offered me, too, was really better than I get here. But why do I speak thus? I had already quit the topic.

"I thank you for the information about your Convention. Truly, you are in a chaotic state. May the Spirit of God brood upon the face of the deep, and bring order out of it. I have been traveling so constantly, and so attracted by strange company and events, and sights, that I have not yet read the journal of your doings. Dr. Wainwright, I suppose, is of the Hobart School, but that school teaches Puseyism in the germ. However, I suppose you had a choice of two evils. The Pastoral Aid Society may help to turn the scale more decidedly. But, alas, where are the men? May the Lord send men into the harvest.

"I had a secret purpose, during my last visit to New York, of renewing it next Easter. But I have been traveling so much of late, that I shall have to stay at home for a year or two to make up leeway. When I can I will see the great City of Gotham again.

"W. S."

To E. W. Syle.

"I was in Ohio last fall. They made a great effort to bring me back to Kenyon, and I could hardly resist it. Even now I have my fears lest I should have gone. I was a delegate to the General Convention, and went thence down to New Orleans, stopping at all the chief towns. It was a most interesting though perilous trip. The danger of a trip down the Ohio and Mississippi rivers, to New Orleans, is greater than of one to Shanghai. Accidents were continually occurring before and behind me; and I had one most merciful escape.

"*April* 19, 1851."

A sentence in one of these letters indicates communication, at least, if not discussion, with some of the heterogeneous elements, ecclesiastical and theological, found among his fellow-travelers. It seems, however, that those already alluded to were not all. There were not only High and Low-Church Episcopalians and Romanists, but a Methodist, and perhaps a Presbyterian; all, in the eye of the captain, and in view of the payment of their fare, enjoying full toleration. As the time wore on, and the parties began to find each other out, a controversy sprang up between the Methodist preacher and one of the Romish priests, as to the great issues between Protestantism and Romanism.

The Doctor, of course, was greatly interested, and, doubtless, as the discussion went on, showed such interest, in the expression of his countenance. This led to rather an abrupt, if not rude remark, from one of the Priests, in the shape of a question, as to what he thought of it? His reply was a rebuke to the impertinence of the question, but, at the same time, an expression of opinion as to what had been urged, thus becoming one of the parties in the discussion. In a little while he found that he was bearing the brunt of it on the Protestant side; and that he must answer the two Bishops, and their Priests as he best could, as their arguments were presented. Eventually it was narrowed down to a discussion between him and Bishop Spaulding, who showed more ability and promptness than any of his party, and this, upon the issue of the dealing of the Church of Rome with the Scriptures. An assertion of the Doctor that they were not made accessible to the people, that they were practically withheld, was promptly denied. "This," said the Doctor, taking his Bible from his pocket, "this is my Bible, that I carry and read in my own language. In what language is yours? Let us see it?" Effort was made to evade this demand. But it was pressed, had to be yielded to, and as the Doctor anticipated, the Bible was a Latin one, not, of course, accessible to the masses.

Bishop Spaulding, in the Doctor's estimation, was the ablest member of his party, acute and clever, rather than profound. "His way," said the Doctor, "of putting things, was very telling; and he very often, to the lookers on and listeners, gave the impression that he had the best of the argument, when such was not really the case."

"Among our company," said he, once describing his companions, "we had a play actor, who, as the folk call it, was a star, on his way to New Orleans. I noticed him with a good deal of interest. He had a good many trunks and boxes, which I suppose contained his wardrobe, marked with his name and title, 'John Jones,' or whatever his name was, 'Tragedian!'

Another little incident of this tour he was accustomed to relate, as showing the extent, as well as the limit, of his deference to ecclesiastical authority. During a Sunday spent on shore, he was requested to take part in the services, to read service in the morning, and preach in the afternoon. There was no vestry-room to the Church, and the hotel was a half or three-quarters of a mile distant, most of the way being the street, or rather road, of a straggling village. When it was time to start, the Bishop put on his robes, and motioned to the Doctor to put on his surplice. After some hesitation it was donned, and the march was taken up to the place of worship; we walked back, of course, after the service was over. But," said he, "in the afternoon, when the Bishop robed himself, I refused, and preached in my citizens' dress. The Bishop, however, made his procession forth and back through the village, as in the morning. Poor man! he seemed to regard it as his cross, that ought to be borne."

The next year, in accordance with the determination expressed in one of these letters, seems to have been spent mostly at home. None of his correspondence for that year has been obtained, saving the following brief note in the possession of the writer.

"Rev. and Dear Brother:

"At the suggestion of Mr. L., now at my elbow, I write to inquire what will be the expense in the stage from Winchester to Staunton. We think of going up by private conveyance, and spending the Sabbath previous to convention with you. W. S."

This Convention, while an interesting one, as to the religious services, was not of special importance beyond the community in which it was held. Dr. Sparrow does not seem to have preached, as was usually the case. The writer recalls with pleasure a delightful stroll, and conversation with him, over the grounds of the Asylum for the Deaf and Dumb, and one or two of the topics incidentally coming up for discussion. One of these was in reference to preaching, and the mode in which truth could be commended to the minds of men. He had lately heard a young clergyman of much promise, in view both of his personal character and of his high cultivation. But it was with a feeling of disappointment at the bareness with which the material was presented, the want of illustrative exhibition, through which it would have been commended to the comprehension of ordinary hearers, and to the higher interest of the more cultivated. The other topic, upon which he seemed to feel more deeply, was the perverting influence of Episcopal expectations, both of a moral and theological character, and, in too many cases, upon men who all along previously had been in sympathy with Evangelical views and practice. The occasion of this expression of feeling was the substance of another sermon, to which he had lately listened, from a clergyman who had been spoken of for the Episcopate of a vacant Diocese. There was an elevation of ecclesiastical tone, corresponding to the new expectations, clearly apparent, to which he had listened with painful interest, as affording an intimation of what might be the speaker's future career. It is to be said, that the temptation to the person spoken of was never actually presented; and the theological and ecclesiastical change never went to the degree anticipated.

It was during this trip to or from Staunton, probably, that a little incident occurred, to which the Doctor made allusion, some years afterwards, as bearing upon the interpretation of the language in Genesis, in reference to the enmity between the literal seed of the woman and the seed of the serpent. Mention was made, to him, of one of his acquaintances who did not believe in the fact of any such antipathy, but who had clearly exhibited it on a certain occasion, by his eagerness to kill a snake which he had accidentally encountered. "I have no theory," said he, "but I know the fact. As Mr. L. and I were traveling along, a large snake bolted from under the carriage, and ran up into a tree, near the side of the road. Immediately we were seized with fury against the poor animal, and leaping from our vehicle, we pelted him with stones and clods, until, at last, one of them struck and killed him. It was strange how much we were excited. When it was over, and I thought of it, I felt quite condemned."

Since writing the above, remains of the correspondence of this year have been obtained, two of the letters, or portions of them, being of special interest. The first is one of a class, of which several will follow in the subsequent narrative, to a relative and younger brother in the ministry, replying to questions, and making suggestions in reference to preaching, pastoral intercourse, etc. The other portions of the letters, extracted from the Syle correspondence, refer to Mrs. Smith, his beloved daughter Susan, in her preparation for the work of love and self-sacrifice, to which her life was afterwards devoted. They are of deep interest as indications, not only of her spirit, but of her remarkable capacity for this great undertaking. And as we think of her brief career, in a field where so much was to be done, and in a work to which her heart was devoted, we can but remember the thought of her beloved father, in regard to the gifted but early taken Duy, a few years before. "The Lord had need of her elsewhere, where it is better, far better for her to be; and we should therefore meekly acquiesce."

"THEOLOGICAL SEMINARY, FAIRFAX COUNTY, VA.,
"June 25th, 1851.

"MY DEAR MR. JEROME:—

"Your letter, written about three weeks ago, was received in due time, and would have been answered before, but for the various impediments which hinder my progress from one day's duty to another, at all times, and not least just now. My Georgetown engagement takes me from home the large part of three days, and, of course, does not lessen the amount of headache at those times. These, with some other things, make me very good-for-nothing, and, of course, for correspondence. I am pleased with the account you have given of your examination. It illustrates the strong disposition there is, and has long been, in the minds of theologians, to be wise above what is written, and to rush in where angels dare not tread. I hold to development, but not in every direction, nor upon every topic. I believe it also a very slow process. It is slow in nature; it is much more slow in revelation. How long has it taken to build up science? how much longer ought it to take to build up theology beyond *ipsissima verba* of the divine Scriptures? The dogmatism of men upon the condition and necessities of infants, as such, has always amazed me in an especial manner. When we would build up an inductive, namely, a safe system of mental philosophy, where do we go? Of course to the adult mind. And why the *adult* mind? Because we there have phenomena. And why *not* to the infant mind? Because there we have only substance (which is a mystery and secret), and not phenomena. And yet, when the subject of theology is up, we presume to apply its every statement to the new-born babe, as to the man in the maturity of his powers, and to do so without regard to the laws of proportion, or the reservations which sound logic insists on, and uses, in such expressions as '*mutatis mutandis*.' And all this, too, with the utmost dogmatism and confidence. But why, why this confidence? Is the thing so clear in itself? No, not that, *per se*, it is certain; but because it is necessary to make some system '*totus teres atque rotundus;*'—which system itself, perhaps, began in the very same disposition to carry out human knowledge hastily, beyond the limits of the express inspired word. As to the question, what God can do or not do by his Spirit, without the truth, as in the case of infants, for the reasons just virtually mentioned, it may be equally presumptuous, *specifically* to decide either way. We may safely say, in general, that God can do, and will do, all that is necessary for it; but what he can actually do, according to his own laws, laid down to himself, and by himself, in the very creation of that being, we do not know, because we do not know that being. It is, as yet, in the thick darkness; it has not yet come out into the light. When it has, we may know and decide, but not till then. And while ignorant, specific dogmatism, as I have called it, is reprehensible on either side, God cannot treat brutes as men; this we know, because we are acquainted with both rational and irrational animals. But suppose we know only about men? What then? Or suppose we take brutes and angels; we, knowing all we do of the former, and of the latter only that they were a different order of creatures from brutes. What then? I need not, of course, reply to the cavil, that God is *omnipotent*, and can, therefore, treat brutes as men. What can *treat* mean in such a case? *Transubstantiate?* That sense would not answer the objector. A manifest absurdity! and, of course, if an absurdity, a contradiction, and if a contradiction, a nonentity; the impossibility of it derogates not from the Omnipotence of God.

"But I did not mean to indulge in such a metaphysical description. As regards the Sacraments, I rejoice you answered just as you did. You see the importance of maintaining that the officers of the Church only should administer them, or at least persons virtually authorized by the Church to do so. Whilst it is in manifest harmony with all the Scripture intimations on the subject, it is not in accordance with high and exclusive views of the ministry, or sacraments, or Church. I am glad to hear what you have said about Mr. S. It is only sad there should be a dead fly in such precious ointment.

"I can appreciate what you say about the little trials which beginning your ministry, '*a prophet* in your own country,' necessarily involved. Having been carried safely through them there, they will eventually, by God's blessing, result in good. It may be an advantage to you thus to have begun your ministry. There is nothing very new here, except it be what has just been brought to my ears —that *B.*, of the Junior Class, exhibits some signs of derangement. I hope it is not so, but very much fear it is too true. His derangement takes a religious turn, if indeed he is deranged, and this, to me, is a *pleasant* feature in an otherwise painful fact. One of the most impressive lessons I ever received, when a boy, was from observing the conduct of a pious clergyman *piously* deranged. The students have formed a society for improving the Seminary grounds. Nearly $300 have been subscribed; they expect to do much. The money is not to be touched until it amounts to $500. They have also collected a couple of hundred for the Shanghai Church. Morrison has contributed a hundred to each of these objects. Mr. Hubbard is to be ordained with his class. Mrs. May has been unwell, but is now recovered. The general health is good.

"All my household, if at my side, would unite with me in affectionate remembrances.

"Most truly yours, WILLIAM SPARROW.

"*Rev. J. A. Jerome.*"

TO REV. E. W. SYLE.

"April 19th, 1851.

"Susan (afterwards Mrs. D. D. Smith) is in the State of Mississippi, acting as governess to the children of our old friend Bledsoe, and Prof. Waddell, both professors in the University of that State. She is very much respected and beloved, to the great comfort, of course, of her parents. She has been studying mathematics with Prof. Bledsoe, and he solemnly declares to me *he never has taught any one,* with the same native talent for the subject! Allowing for the partiality of friendship, this is saying a great deal. I know that she has great powers of concentration. She once read Rauch's Psychology with me, and mastered it *far better* than any student in the Seminary; but I did not suppose her talent went as far as Bledsoe says.

"I have sometimes thought (this is entirely between us and not to be mentioned in any letter) that in the course of a few years Susan may turn her thoughts to China. She would make, I feel confident, a first-rate missionary. But I have never hinted it to her, and wish to have her mind entirely self-moved in the matter, if things should take that turn."

TO THE SAME.

"July 4th, 1852.

"This letter will be carried by Miss Jones, who will be a great acquisition to your Mission. I shall send by her a few sermons from the pen of your humble servant. I send them not from a high sense of their worth, but from the hope that, as the production of an old friend, they may occupy a few moments not unpleasantly. I have one, preached at our last Convention, now in the press, and I hope I may be able to send a copy of that also. I have *ventured* somewhat in the expression of my opinions in it, and should like to know how they appear to you. Indeed, I have often thought I should like to have a free conversation with you (or a free letter from you) on many theological topics, with a view to learn how looking at them from the stand-point of a missionary among the heathen has affected them. Please bear this in mind.

"I have told you, I believe, of my call to Boston, and of my strong inclination to go. I yearn for pastoral duty. My heart has not room, in its present position. But the 'stars in their courses seem to fight against me,' and I am not likely to get away; except it be to Kenyon, where, I am told, they think again of calling me. I care not for myself. The Lord direct me in reference to my children's welfare.

"I do not think it unlikely she (Susan) will be a missionary yet. She certainly would make a good one, and neither father nor mother would say nay, if circumstances favored it.

"Mrs. Sparrow is now in Western New York, to see Mary. She will be absent a month or six weeks. It is the second time she has left home without me, since we were married. The house seems as though half the roof were off."

Towards the close of this year, in the month of November, 1851, the Doctor was absent from home, for a short time, in New York, where he preached the Annual Sermon before the Directors of the Evangelical Knowledge Society, entitled the "One Mediator;" being an exhibition of the peculiar character of Christ's mediatorship, and made to bear upon the Sacerdotalism against which the efforts of the Society were directed. This was published, contains the most elaborate exhibition, perhaps, of his views on the subject that he ever presented, and is well worthy of a place in the contemplated volume of his select sermons.

Soon after his return from New York, he was again for a little while absent from home, for a short visit to Charlestown, Jefferson County, Virginia, where the Valley Convocation at that time was holding its meeting. The occasion was one of peculiar interest. The old church, for many years occupied during the pastorate of the Rev. Dr. Jones, had been thoroughly repaired, enlarged and beautified, in the year 1848. In a very few weeks after its reoccupation it was destroyed by fire. A new building was immediately planned and commenced under Dr. Jones. But its completion was left to his successor, the lamented Dudley A. Tyng, who became pastor in the Spring of 1850. This was nearly accomplished in the fall of 1851, and the time of Convocation was selected as that for the consecration of the new building. Bishop Meade officiated, and Dr. Sparrow, by appointment, preached the Consecration Sermon. This, in some respects, was one of his most remarkable discourses. Its exhibition of the proper purposes of such a house was exceedingly clear, forcible, and thoroughly Protestant. While its pathos, in speaking of the hopes of those who had labored for that building, and who had been taken away before the work was successfully ended, and of the classes who, in after times, would come to it as a house of prayer, burdened with their various wants and necessities, was exceedingly touching. 'Doctor,' said a strange clergyman, who was present as a visitor, 'Doctor, you have made me do what I have never done before, shed tears under a sermon!' Nor was he alone in that respect. Few, perhaps, were altogether unmoved at certain portions of its delivery, and none could have failed in recognizing its peculiar appropriateness to the occasion.*

Not long after this visit to Charlestown, he was called upon to consider the question of a change of position, already mentioned. In this instance, moreover, as in that of 1850, the decision to be made was one with reference not only to a change of position, but to one of work, the assumption of parochial duty. Bishop Eastburn, at that time holding the Rectorship of Trinity Church, Boston, was exceedingly anxious to obtain Dr. Sparrow as his assistant, and made a special visit to the Seminary to urge upon him its acceptance. It was not deemed advisable that a call should be extended, or even his name proposed, until there was some probability that he would be induced to accept, and the matter, therefore, at the time was confined to the persons most concerned. The proposition took him by surprise, and his first impulse was to put it aside, or rather, to regard it as one not to be seriously considered. He consented, however, at the request of the Bishop, not to decide unfavorably until he should hear from him again. Some of the reasons for not deciding at once come to view in the correspondence of this period. It will be seen in this case, as in every

* This sermon was afterwards published in connection with the consecration of a Church in Smyrna, Delaware.

other in which he was urged to leave the Seminary, that it would have been to his pecuniary advantage to have made the change, and that this, in his circumstances, with his large family, and the necessity of providing for their education, made it a matter of duty to give this item its due and painful consideration.

It has been with a good deal of hesitation that the letter following, and one or two preceding, touching the same topic, have been inserted. But the story would not have been a true story without them. That which, like the atmosphere, constitutes the daily pressure of a man's life, which he is scarcely for a day allowed to forget, cannot be left out in any proper estimate of his character and work. The pressure under which the character is formed and fully matured, under which work is done, and influence is exerted, enhances their value in our estimation. The moral significance of action, in such cases, is often more clearly seen. Especially is this the case when a decision is made to remain in the clear line of duty rather than seek relief in a movement where the call of duty is less undoubted. Such was the decision in the instance before us. It will not be uninteresting to note the spirit in which the whole matter was considered.

To Rev. E. H. Canfield, D. D.

"January 23d, 1852.

"I suppose it is too late to wish you a Happy New Year, and to wish you a Happy Old Year is to wish the wheel of time to roll back again, which, I believe, never has been, and never will be; all I can do, therefore, is to wish you and yours a Happy New Year; and that, accordingly, I do with all my heart. I think it probable I should have been more in season, if I had not been unwell for the last three weeks, confined, indeed, to my house and to my room. However, thank God, I am now better, and I have some faint hope of riding to Alexandria to-morrow, if the weather will allow, which I have not done for nearly four weeks.

"Apropos of weather: Are you not frozen up in New York? The thermometer has stood, on this hill, within a week, 10° below zero; the mercury must have disappeared from the bulb altogether in your frigid zone. The Potomac has been long frozen over, and even the ice-boat has been driven off the mail route several times, and latterly, has taken nearly 24 hours to work its way to Acquia Creek. I do not know that it is running at all now. The ice is so much accumulated above Georgetown, that they are in great fear of the destruction of their shipping and mills when it breaks up. They are removing the machinery from the latter.

"I wonder whether the cold has had any influence on Kossuth's projects and prospects. It was not sufficiently cold when he was amongst you New Yorkers. However, I did not perceive my Brother C.'s name among the clergy, and conclude, from that, he did not catch the fever.

"I suppose, however, the Church Clergy were more moved by Dr. Creighton's letter than by Kossuth's speeches. So you are back again in limbo. The Lord grant you all a safe deliverance out of it. I was really desirous to have Dr. C. retain his appointment, lest a worse thing come upon you. I do not wish to see —— Bishop, much less ——, and yet I am afraid one of them will be. One of our students, who corresponds with one of those in the General Seminary, says that they are thinking of rallying on —— again. One of our High Church Bishops said to me, that —— could never be consecrated, that he had broached errors, and had not retracted them, and *that* the Bishops could not overlook.

"I had a letter from T., not a fortnight ago. He tells me that R. is going to join the Church of Rome, and perhaps its ministry. R. confesses that he has been a Papist for three years. T. thinks that he has been greatly wronged by him; for he has been defending his Protestantism for some long time back, whenever it was assailed, and R. never dropped a word till the other day, from which he could gather the true state of his mind. T. is indignant to have been thus left in a false position. I hope it will do him good, and the parish too.

"I had a letter from Dr. W., about the same time, and am glad to learn that Kenyon is beginning to look up. Dr. W., at the instance of an old, and ardent, and partial friendship, expresses the hope that I may, one day, yet return to my old beat. My heart often turns in that direction, but at this present time my thoughts, at least, are flying Northward; and as a friend to be trusted, I wish to ask your advice, in confidence, upon the subject. I do not wish a word to be said to anybody, till I bring it before the public by my own act, if ever I do. You know my circumstances here. Now, then, supposing I could get a situation in Boston, worth $3000 a year, with very *easy duty*, ought I not accept it? You probably know what I refer to, but I am bound to be reserved on the subject, and yet I feel I ought to have the advice of friends. Friends here I cannot advise with—above all, with the man to whom I *am* bound to defer most, and whom my heart inclines me to respect more than any other. In this emergency I turn to you, and would be thankful, with all your knowledge of me, and of the situation referred to, if you would honestly give me your opinion. Let me hear from you, if possible, by return of mail; and let me beg you not to mention the subject to any one, unless, as I said, I have the situation offered me and *I accept it.* I owe this privacy to another, of course, not to myself.

"Nothing new here, except old Robin's death. Since I saw you, I have been with Dudley Tyng, who is a growing and most successful minister, much valued by his people. I have also been in Leesburg. Dennison is here, on his Bible agency, in good health and spirits."

TO THE SAME.

"January 31st, 1852.

"The great motive I had for considering the proposition," that of a call from Boston, "was the increased salary which it seemed to hold out to me. Not that I would be considered, or I think I ought to be considered, grasping and avaricious. But I have been anxious for some change which would relieve me from embarrassments that have beset me most of the time that I have been residing at this place. These anxieties are mainly about the future. If I can keep my debts down to their present point, I shall not be apprehensive that my death will be a signal of distress to my family; and to make this sure was the only reason that the call from Boston had any special attractions for me. But like causes are apt to produce like effects; and it is not easy for a man of a large family, with little skill in management, and no ability to do anything to lessen expenses, to rub along and keep the accounts squared. And it is not debt that I wish to guard against, but that dependence which such embarrassment occasions.

"Again, let me say, that I have no fault to find with the Institution which I serve. They have dealt liberally by me, according to their standard and their means. I should be ungrateful in making any other statement. I have thought it proper to obtrude my affairs upon you in this way, to disabuse your mind in reference to the precise motives which have led me to entertain the proposition in question. The personal interest you have expressed in me has gone to my heart; and while I am thankful there is no occasion for my friends to tax themselves on my account, I can appreciate, to the utmost, the willing mind which you, as one of them, evince. If our relations were reversed, I hope I should feel as you do.

"Your statements about Drs. Wilson's, Turner's, and Tyng's opinion of my sermon are truly gratifying. It was a trial to preach it, but much more did I dread the ordeal of publication. When they come to read, thought I, they will change their opinions. In view of what has occurred, what can I say, but that even wise men can sometimes make mistakes.

"Do you think I could have some twenty of the remaining copies of the sermon kept for me till next Easter, when I shall send for them? W. S."

Other letters of this year, 1852, are interesting, as connected with one or two sermons prepared and preached on public occasions. Some of the discussions of theological and practical questions, moreover, contained in these letters, are of permanent value.

To the Same.

"Theological Seminary, May, 1852.

"Rev. and Dear Brother:—

"It seems high time that a messenger should pass between us. How are you, and how doth the Lord prosper you? Since I last wrote to you, we here have been visited from the North, but I could not gather anything particular—such particulars as friendship is ever curious about. Do write me soon, and let me know all about you.

"But what shall I say to you? Events come so quick that I cannot post them up, or even record them in my day-book. Of our Convention you have heard. It was a very pleasant one; nothing to mar our pleasant intercourse. I cannot say, from hearing or seeing, that much good was done; but we may hope there was. The religious services were very frequent and very well attended. I hope in a few weeks to send you a copy of my sermon preached at its opening, and hope you will approve it.

"I was in Baltimore the other day, just after the Diocesan Convention, and was pleased to learn that our friends came off quite as well as such an insignificant minority could expect, and better than they ever did before.

"While I was there, the Democratic Convention was in session, and I went to it with the chaplain, a clergyman of our Church, and so sat upon the platform, beside the 'wheel-horse of Democracy,' and so forth! While there, I thought of you, and remembered you once throwing by your text-books to see the Whigs at similar work in the same place! By the way, I see from the papers that my brother Edward has been appointed a delegate from Louisiana, to the Whig Convention in Baltimore, next week. Whether he is coming I know not. I only hope.

"Will you not be with us in July? We are improving our grounds so that you will hardly know them. Do get a substitute for a couple of Sundays, and revisit your old haunts. You know, I trust, what pleasure it would give me to entertain you. Where is W., and what is he doing? Do try and get him into a place. He is a man of too much talents and worth to be allowed to rust out. When you see him remember me to him. Tyng, Dudley, I mean, has been called to your city; but I think it must be a mistake. I thought he was going to Cincinnati. McElroy, you know, is back in Delaware. I have heard that they have telegraphed Mr. Hubbard to hasten North, and sail for China. I hope to hear more about it by mail this evening. I wish to write him a farewell line before he leaves. He is, to me, a dear friend. Should you see him, and I not be able to reach him by mail before he sails, please remember me affectionately to him.

"My family are about as well as usual, except S. Mrs. Sparrow is going, in a fortnight or so, to Western New York, to visit M., and will be absent for four or five weeks, the second time of her absence in eleven years! You have seen notice of the death of Mrs. H., and Mrs. T. These have been heavy blows to the family.

"Remember me most kindly to Mrs. C., also to Miss H.; also to your junior self, and believe me truly,

"Your friend and brother, WILLIAM SPARROW.

"*To Rev. E. H. Canfield.*"

"THEOLOGICAL SEMINARY, January, 19th, 1852.

"MY DEAR J.:—

"I have just received your letter, and before my class comes to recite in my study, for I am afraid to venture out yet, I am disposed to spend a few moments in replying to it.

"Do not trouble yourself about answering my letters. Your

silence will make no difference in my writing, and may make a difference in your sermons or your health. You should tell your friends generally to take the same view of the matter, at least while you are under the whip and spur of so much pulpit preparation, as at present.

"By the way, I am not sorry that you have been driven to extemporize a little before the great congregation. Let me make a suggestion in regard to any such efforts. *Try and get into a way of making short sentences.* The only time I heard you extemporize I thought your fault was that your 'train was too long.' (You may take it in the railroad or the wardrobe sense: it is all one!) It is the fault of those most conversant with books. It is my own fault, and was so much more than it is. The evil of the habit is that it interferes so much with amplification, which is the very life of all such efforts. With long sentences a man may repeat, but he cannot amplify; and repetition kills the patience of an audience; cutting such sentences up into several, the speaker will seem to be adding a new idea each time. The style, moreover, will be more lively and more agreeable to most persons. It will tax the attention less; and last, but not least, it will not burden the mind of the speaker too much. The construction of long sentences, the mere framing of them, and putting them together, and the retention of the beginning firmly in the mind until the end has been reached, of itself calls for a great expenditure of mental energy. This saved, the mind is more at liberty to attend to other matters.

"In regard to bowing, in the Creed, I do not advise it. Had the matter been suggested before you went to N. at all, I might have given other advice; but *now*, I think a change would be unwise. It would encourage the people in that regard for little things which is already a besetting sin among them; and it would give them more confidence in that system with which the usage is now unhappily connected in many minds. Besides, being 'much ado about nothing,' it would foster in some the notion that you are beginning to feel the pressure of their influence, and that having gained an inch they may go on and ask an ell. This I would not, on any account, have. I am a great stickler for deference to the wishes of the people, where they have, by canon, a right to interfere their authority; and in private life and personal matters, as I think a clergyman cannot be too kind and conciliating. But in matters of this nature, which have religious relations, and yet are not subject to canonical regulations, nor falling, in any sense, under congregational control, they should be taught that the minister has a path of his own, a conscience of his own, and a liberty of his own. Suppose that, through the grace of God, you should be able to walk before them, in all your private conversation, circumspect and unblamably; and, at the same time, to preach the Gospel of Christ substantially as Christ would have it preached; do you think that a matter of this kind is going to stand in the way of your spiritual usefulness? Nay, will not a steady, mild, and silent adherence to your own convictions, in this particular, be rather helpful to you, showing the people that you act on principle, that you have firmness as well as gentleness, and that they ought to know what this meaneth: 'let every man be fully persuaded in his own mind.'

"In your peculiar and rather trying situation, you may be tempted to some anxiety about the future, as regards your acceptability among the people. Do not, for a moment, yield to it. God forbid that you should be indifferent to their good will, or should cease to be deeply and constantly desirous to go in and out before them in such a manner, as shall make them honor and love the Master whom you serve. But beyond this, take no thought for the morrow. I am persuaded, if God has a work for you to do in N. He will give you favor in the eyes of the people; and if he has not, then, I trust, He has elsewhere; and there are plenty of openings everywhere, as I can see, where you may, with His blessing, be useful and happy. Be not, then, for a moment cast down by your labors, or by any want of strict agreement and sympathy between you and the people. You are the servant of a faithful and tender Master. 'Cast your care upon Him, for He *careth for you.*' Yes, my dear J., this is my exceeding joy, that I believe 'He careth for you.' Go on, then, in peace. 'Be strong in the Lord.' 'In everything, by prayer, and supplication, make your requests known unto Him,' and 'His peace will keep your heart and mind.'

"On Saturday evening I received a letter from Bishop Eastburn, saying that he was going to propose me to the vestry of Trinity Church, Boston, as the Assistant Minister, with every assurance that I would be unanimously elected. He says that I can do as much parochial visiting as I choose, and that I shall have $3000 per annum salary. He offers sundry other considerations, and seems very anxious that I should accept. If I could see that I would be in the way of duty in leaving my present position, I should accept it. The proposition has many features to recommend it.

"I have seen nothing yet about my sermon, except commendatory notices; no doubt, after the sweet will come the bitter, and plenty of it. But, for the truth's sake, I care but little. The critics are not likely to shake my faith in the sentiments of the discourse, and that is the main thing. I had a long letter from Bishop Meade about it, which was very comforting, although accompanied with some severe rebukes for not exercising my talents more. By the way, I have another sermon which may soon see the light, by the request of the students. Should it do so, I will, of course, send you a copy. I have sermonizing enough upon my hands. The Bishop has appointed me to preach our next Convention sermon, in May, in Richmond; and in July I have to deliver an address at Commencement. Besides this, I have promised to write a sermon on the American Sunday School Union, and preach it in the District Episcopal Church, next month. This, with my other sermonizing, my letter-writing, my daily duties in teaching, and my "often infirmities," which wine, much or little, will not cure, will keep me busy enough. Whatever I do, may the Lord, in mercy, turn it to account for the advancement of the truth.

"But I must close, else my writing to you will interfere with your pulpit preparations as much as your writing to me. Remember me very kindly to Judge E., to Mrs. A. My love and blessing to M. and yourself.

"Affectionately, WM. SPARROW."

"THEOLOGICAL SEMINARY, August 9, 1852.

"MY DEAR MR. JEROME:—

"About your parish affairs, I do not feel able to say more than I have said in my letters to Mrs. S. I would devoutly commit your ways to the Lord, and pray Him to do with you and your dear household, as may best conduce to His glory and the good of souls. As long as you can keep your eye single for these objects, I shall have no anxiety about you. I do most firmly believe that all things work together for good to them that thus love God. My trouble about you in your present situation has not been that you have been cramped in your support, though that is painful, but that you were working too hard, and have had too much writing to allow of regular study, of a fundamental kind. In writing an address for our Commencement, on "Post-Ordination Study," you were much in my thoughts in relation to the matter. I suppose nearly all your reading is with immediate reference to writing. This has its advantages, but it cannot supply the place of other study. Besides, I fear you may get into a careless way of writing. By long composition under the whip and spur of weekly study, a man may lose the ability of *elaborating* anything. Do the best you can to guard against this.

"Your affectionate father and friend, W. SPARROW."

The sermon thus alluded to as preached before the Diocesan Convention, was entitled the "First Council of Jerusalem," and was largely a discussion of the great question of the relations of human authority to Divine truth. Its topics were: First, the occasion of this Council—the difficulties and dissensions of Jewish and Gentile believers as to the principles of Gospel truth. This leads to the topic of its authority, which is recognized as Divine, in view of the presence of the inspired element, and of the specific assertion of such element in its final decision. Then, the material of the Council is noted—not simply the Apostles, not merely the ministry, but also the brethren, the laity. This leads to the inquiry as to its Ecumenical character, and the position argued is, that it was not; that strictly speaking, such Council never has been held, and never, in all probability, will be; that even the work of such councils as those which were called general is better done, in the present condition of the Church and the world, by other agencies; that if resorted to, under the present condition of things, as superfluous, they would probably be mischievous. The sermon closes with calling attention to features of this Conference to be noted and followed. First, its spirit of forbearing toleration in regard to existing differences—the spirit of Christian breadth and geniality, as opposed to that of Jewish bigotry and exclusiveness; secondly, its practicalness; thirdly, its missionary element; in these respects a model to the body before whom the sermon was delivered. The whole closing with the important suggestion that the main work of the Convention ought to have reference to that characteristic of the Church which is internal. At this same Convention, Dr. Sparrow, as Chairman of the Committee on the State of the Church, made the report, perhaps one of the most striking and interesting presented to that body.

Allusions in these letters, to Mr. Jerome, indicate a change which had taken place—one, to the Doctor, of deep and tender interest—the first break in his household circle, in the marriage of his eldest daughter to the Rev. J. A. Jerome, whose field of labor, in Western New York, of course, necessitated a distant separation. Dr. Sparrow lived to see his large family reduced to himself and Mrs. S. and one remaining child. "For long years," to use the language of one who for a considerable time was an inmate, "for long years his was an unbroken family. But, oh, how short a time it took to scatter it. Mrs. Sparrow once, and only once, referred to the sad change in this respect. Writing, a few days after Christmas, about two years before she was called away, she said, 'I felt as if I could not bear it; the absence of my children, with the stillness, was more than I could bear. But I hope that feeling has passed away, *never* to return again.'" The feelings of which this language is an expression were also fully shared by the father of this separated household, and with his large forethought and paternal tenderness, the first separation, in its deep significance, was fully recognized.

For the next year, 1853, we have a letter of April 9th, of some interest. At the Convention of the Diocese for that year, held at Wheeling, he was unexpectedly called upon to preach the opening sermon, the appointed preacher not being able to be present. The sermon was one of a simple, practical character, upon the text: "For me to live is Christ, to die is gain," exhibiting the spirit of Paul—desiring to be with Christ, and at the same time willing and desiring to remain on earth to do Christ's work; in other words, to glorify Christ, whether by life or by death—as peculiarly the spirit of the Christian believer and the Christian ministry. This same sermon was preached in the Seminary Chapel, only a few months before his death, and constitutes a beautiful delineation of the genuine Christian character; a remarkable contrast, as to its style of excellence, to that preached the year before, at the opening of the Convention at Richmond.

The letter to which allusion has been already made, written to one of his old pupils, and preceding the Convention in point of time a few weeks, comes in properly at this point. Portions of it are more severe than was his usual mode of expression. But it was with reference to points upon which he felt deeply, and to errors and assertions which he regarded as compromising alike the spirit and substance of Protestant Christianity. Men who feel, as Dr. Sparrow did, that the conflict between the two great parties in our Church was one, not of incidentals, but of essentials, going down to the very foundations of Christian life and Christian doctrine, will make allowance, if it be needed, for such language.

To Rev. E. H. Canfield.

"Theological Seminary, April 9, 1853.

"Rev. and Dear Brother:—

"I have long desired to drop you a line by way of remembrance, but have been prevented by various obstacles. I now write in the midst of a sick family, though, I trust in God, convalescent. You have learned from our friend, Dr. D., perhaps, of the condition in which he found us. But I would speak of him rather than ourselves. His kindness has at once been very great and very unexpected. It really seemed most providential that he should visit us when he did. He came on, in the abundance of his benevolence, to see B., and he found the whole family just taken down of the scarlet fever; at least, all but one were then, or have been since. His visit itself was better than medicine. Those for whom he prescribed in New York last summer, all, had learned to put unbounded confidence in his skill, and his coming so opportunely increased that confidence. His prescriptions, too, have all had, so far as we can see, a happy effect. From my observation of Dr. D. when here, I look upon him as destined to be one of the first men of his profession, and I have had some experience as well as observation to guide me. I have been much benefited by his advice, and you know *I am* 'a hard case.'

"But enough of domestic egotism. I received a pamphlet by 'one Veritas.' Don't be offended. An author of Charles the Second's day speaks of one John Milton, 'a writer of dull verse.' I expect I am indebted to you as the sender and the author? In any view, you have my thanks. The work is an effectual exposure of that movement which, in horticultural phrase, would raise public opinion in our Church, as a man raises in a hot-house exotics from a tropical region, and of those who now say, with all the ostentation and tyranny of Louis XIV, but without his reason and truth, 'I am the State, I am the Church.' My only regret, when I read such blistering and excoriating productions, is that those at whom they are directed have the hide of a rhinoceros; still, it is well to keep at work. Even the buffalo and the alligator, though well cased, are not invulnerable.

"Our friends in Baltimore realize this fact just now. The perversion of Baker must be producing a great sensation. He was the most popular man they ever had as assistant at St. Paul's. He was a pupil and favorite of the Bishop, and had been talked of by some as his assistant. Mr. H., an eminent merchant, who left Christ Church on account of Dr. John's dispute with the Bishop, used to go a long way, with his family, to Baker's church, thinking him the model minister of our communion, and has scouted all intimations made by a friend of mine that he was inclining Romeward. In addition to all this, he is a respectable man in character, above the common standard in talent. It cannot be said of him that he is weak or crazy. Yet he is gone! Will their eyes never be opened?

"I have lately been to Princeton, and wished that I could go on to New York, and see how you get along. From all I can learn, the transplantation has taken place without retarding the growth and flourishing condition of the tree and its capacity to bear fruit. But how comes on the old parish? Who is likely to get it? I see my friend —— is casting a wistful eye in that direction. They need a peculiar sort of man, on account of the contiguity of the Seminary. May the Lord send them such.

"You have seen what trouble R. has got up in his church in Louisville. Mr. Fowles, with great simplicity, remarked the other day, he did not know why it was that so many of the men who preach *the doctrines of grace* have bad tempers. He is, himself, although dogmatical, not ill-natured, far from it. All here is in statu quo. If you should not be in Europe, I hope to see you as I go to Boston this summer. Believe me, as ever,

"Your friend and brother, WM. SPARROW."

It was on his return from the Convention at Wheeling that the writer visited, with Dr. Sparrow and others, the church at Cumberland, where, for several hours, they were detained. It was just as the afternoon service was closing, the congregation being small, the choristers, in fact, constituting the main portion. Among other objects of interest, was a chancel window, with the figure of the Saviour, larger than life, with various subordinate scriptural accompaniments. "What do you think of it, Doctor?" was the question of one of the party. "It must tend," was the reply, in substance, "to a sensuous religion. If people, in worship, surround themselves with such objects, to aid devotional feeling, they will depend upon them. After a while, they cannot worship without them, and then worship, especially that of the masses, does not go beyond them."

TO A DAUGHTER.

"OAKWOOD, March 16, 1853.

"MY DEAR B.:—

"'Better late than never.' Your congratulations on my reaching another birthday, received four days ago, would have been responded to more promptly but for my great indisposition of body—of body, not of mind; for as it is pleasant to receive such communications, knowing, as I do, that they are not empty compliments, so is it pleasant to reply to them. I am pleased to find that you have got hold of a work in German at once pleasant and profitable to read. I have frequently thought of trying to find some one in New York who was acquainted with German literature, and to put a sum of money into his hands that he might select some suitable works for your study, but have been prevented by my straitened means. I rejoice that the Seminary library has furnished you a copy of Gellert, and I trust it contains other treasures of a similar sort. During the next vacation you might make search in person. It is hard to find exactly what you need. Since the last century, the second quarter of it, there has been a subtle poison diffused through nearly all the classical literature of that gifted land, which operates at once secretly and powerfully on the reader's mind. Schiller is far from being an exception; and, although I trust your mind and heart are too well grounded in the truth as it is in Jesus ever to be removed from that firm, that *only* foundation of human hope and comfort, yet we know that it is a universal maxim, 'Evil communications corrupt good manners,' in a greater or less degree, and that, unless on constant and prayerful guard, intercourse with dead authors of unsound sentiments, like intercourse with living persons of similar views, is liable to prove injurious, even to those of advanced years and mature minds. This is an evil, however, which we have to encounter everywhere, not excepting even our own language. In English literature you are continually met in your studies by things offensive to a Christian taste, and repugnant to a Christian judgment. In the literature of our own country, if it is not premature to use such an expression, there is less that is objectionable than in that of any other land, thanks to the strong religious influence which pervades society, handed down from the first settlers of these colonies, and kept alive by our free Bible and free political institutions. But even we have not a morally faultless literature, and I think there are some symptoms of the growth amongst us of a literature, not, indeed, positively irreligious—public opinion will not tolerate that—but at least negatively so. Perhaps, indeed, until Christianity leavens the whole mass of society, so long as there is leisure and education among us, we may look upon such a godless literature as one of the offences which must needs come, and which belongs to the evils of this probationary state.

"Perhaps our part is, while we deplore the evil and strive to abate it, not to flee from it altogether, but, in the strength of the Lord, meet it and vanquish it, and improve the victory to God's glory. Perhaps it belongs to us to borrow some of the riches of unsanctified talent, as the Israelites did of the wealth of Egypt, and so, spoiling the enemy, restore the perverted treasures to their proper use.

"In the spirit of these remarks, I would advise that, in connection with Milner, you read Gibbon. Civil history is, of course, the substratum of sacred and ecclesiastical history, as natural life is the basis of spiritual; and there are none of the older histories by Englishmen, perhaps, if any by other hands, comparable, in point of learning and ability, to that of Gibbon; nor do I think he is very dangerous to one at all grounded in the Christian faith. His spirit is so bad that it arouses the indignation of the Christian; and if he is only set right in regard to a few *facts*, on which by sophistry or misstatement Gibbon might mislead him, I should think he would be rather established than shaken in the faith by his sneers, and cynicism, and indelicacy. I did not know that Bowdler had published an expurgated edition of the Decline and Fall, as he published a Family Shakspeare. Be that as it may, Milman has published an edition in full, with corrective notes, partly original, and partly selected from Guizot, who did the same thing in French. A copy of this, I doubt not, could be borrowed of some one in the Seminary. When you come to the chapter where Gibbon attempts to account for the wonderful propagation of Christianity through moral means, against the physical force of the world, you ought to stop and read some one of the many triumphant answers to his miserable and transparent sophistries. It will form an agreeable episode. So, when you reach the frustrated attempt of Julian to rebuild the temple, you should pause and peruse what Warburton has written on the subject; though this last topic is not at all, like the former, a vital one. If, however, I ought to add, Bowdler has done as you say, I would prefer that you get that. It is not well, if it can be avoided, to bring the mind in contact with anything impure, even where there is an antidote at hand; a *cure* seldom restores the mind to the original *health.*

"You judge wisely in seeking to perfect your education in all substantial things. If I were present at the Woman's Rights Society meetings, there is one of their rights which I would be quite ready to advocate and support, and that is, the right of self-support. Until a young woman has the means of maintaining herself, by her property or industry, she cannot be independent, or be in a situation to preserve, under all circumstances, her self-respect and true dignity. I desire, more than I can express, that you and your sisters be qualified, by your heads or by your hands, to earn your own livelihood, no thanks to anybody or anything, except that constitution of society which gives rise to the wants by supplying which industry lives, and that Power above, which has established such a constitution. When taken away from you, if I should leave you all thus qualified, though penniless, I should feel that I left you rich. But there is an education more precious still than that of the head or hands, the education of the heart; let us take heed that that be not neglected, nay, that it have our paramount regard. This education is for eternity, and eternity is very near at hand.

"But I must close. The Lord bless you, my daughter, and give you health of body, mind and heart.

"Ever your affectionate father, WM. SPARROW.

"*Miss E. R. Sparrow, Oakwood.*"

From this time until the close of the period included in this chapter, there is little of a specific nature to fill up the interval. Those of the deepest interest to himself were, doubtless, the changes taking place in his family, the beginning of which, the marriage of his eldest daughter, has been already noticed. Three others, of the same character, the marriage of Mrs. Dashiel, Mrs. Grammer and Mrs. Smith, took place during this same interval. The absence of his sons at the University during the latter part of this time had also its effect in reducing the number of his household. After the departure of Mrs. Smith, in 1859, with the exception of vacation times, the large household of eleven or twelve was brought down to four. "He often," says a correspondent, alluding to this time, "spoke of this change, and it was evidently a painful one to him." After a time, doubtless, the visits of his children and grandchildren helped to alleviate the change, and to present new objects of interest and affection. It doubtless, too, had its compensating result, in its removal of the painful forebodings of anxiety in reference to the welfare of so many dependent ones in case of his own departure.

The correspondence of this interval at command is more full than that of any other; this, with the reminiscences of one or two of his pupils, will occupy most of the remaining portion of this chapter. The letters are, many of them, to former pupils in their various fields of labor.

"THEOLOGICAL SEMINARY, January, 16, 1854.

"DEAR BROTHER SYLE:—

"Your letter, with the parcels, was brought to me from town on Saturday, as I was lying sick in my bed. It was a cordial to me. I had been longing to hear from you, and had I not had, during the last two months, an unusual share of sickness, keeping me behindhand in my duties, I should have endeavored to find out your whereabouts, and write you. It was pleasant to be remembered by you, and to receive such a token of your friendship.

"I do not wonder that you have been 'sobered.' Wave has followed wave; 'the clouds have returned after the rain,' and you may be tempted sometimes, I can readily believe, to say, that 'All these things are against me.' But it is a *temptation*, indeed, and should be treated as such. The waves are controlled by our covenant God; the clouds are moved at his command; and He does nothing arbitrarily nor heedlessly. There is a reason, wise, and good, and gracious, for it all. Remember that the Lord has set you in a very important position in His Church. Every Christian is a city set upon a hill; every minister more so; and every missionary most of all. For great work, great preparation is necessary; and in all the trials to which you are subjected (and your friends, those under this roof at least, know and feel them to be great), you are only acquiring meetness for your work. That work—how great it is! Who can estimate it rightly? Who can adequately span it? The mission to Athens has its importance, and much more that to Africa, for it relates to this country as much as that; two continents are implicated in it. But the mission to China transcends them all. Providence says so; it is not the mere inference of man. All the indications seem to promise that Chinese idolatry, which in extent so far exceeds every other, is destined to fall as Jericho fell. There is not to be a mere breach in the wall, the whole circuit of that wall is to be prostrated at once. Now, then, the man that is vouchsafed a part in this, the most sudden and extensive moral revolution which ever took place in the world, should expect that the Lord would deal with him not exactly like other men, but in a manner corresponding with the magnitude and extent of the work to which he is called. Let this, then, be your consolation, and endeavor to learn from the providences to which you are subjected the lessons which it is God's design to teach you.

"You speak of the intercourse you have had in Hartford, New York, and elsewhere. Doubtless you have met many men, and many minds. After you have completed your tour, you will be able to give a tolerable idea of the state of the Church—if anybody can. I add this condition, for there is such an endless variety of sentiment, and doctrine, and character among us, that I am not certain any very important and clear general conclusion can be arrived at. We are in a very chaotic state.

"In regard to the 'Epistle Congratulatory,' I should think it might be well, if a second edition is contemplated, to wait till the following explanation, to which you refer, has appeared. It might then be well for the author to republish, with a preface, in plain, didactic language, explaining why he adopted the Socratic *Ειρωνεια* in the epistle; how such a style of composition should be interpreted; and that the whole transaction which gave occasion to it was of such a character as required to be deeply impressed on the mind of the Church, otherwise the same thing might be repeated again, to the great detriment of her character, and of the reputation of our holy religion. It might be shown that some very impressive method of instruction was needful, because the Bishops had proved themselves, in previous cases, by no means apt scholars. Bishop Smith's trial was a most bungled affair. Bishop B. T. Onderdonk's was decidedly worse; and Bishop Doane's first *non*-trial, though it had been so long discussed in the papers, in every Church coterie, and at every fireside, and though it had led to such discussion that one would think every Bishop was in full possession of all the facts and principles necessary to give steadiness to their action, and wisdom to their judgment, was more glaringly inconsistent than any that preceded. Now, if after all this training, if they could be trained by experience at all, the Bishops came to the last meeting at Camden no better prepared than the event showed, it was plain their conduct called for full and unsparing exposure. They needed to be taught a lesson which they could not soon forget. They needed to be shown that they were subject to the same rules of propriety, and judgment, and respect for the opinions of mankind, that other men are, and that no figment of 'inherent rights' was able to secure them impunity when they transgressed against them.

"I understood your letter was brought to Alexandria by Mr. D. Had I been able, I should have gone to see him. Please remember me to him most kindly. I pray the Lord to bless him, and make him eminently useful in His Church. The laity seem specially called on, in these times, to make themselves felt in ecclesiastical affairs. By keeping themselves so far in sympathy with the clergy that they shall be able to understand them, and know how they are affected by arguments presented, and by maintaining in their own hearts a lively sympathy with the holy themes, and the devotional spirit of the Gospel, they can, in my humble opinion, do more for the true furtherance of the truth as it is in Jesus, than many who are exclusively set apart for His work of the ministry. This holds especially of lawyers. Do you know W? He is one of those men; a lawyer of considerable standing, a man of fine education, and of most lovely character. I hope you will get acquainted with him. Hoping to hear from you soon again, I remain, my dear Mr. S.,

"Ever most truly yours, W. SPARROW."

"THEOLOGICAL SEMINARY, November 18, 1854.

"MY DEAR J:—

"Your account of your parish is very pleasing. I pray you may continue to be encouraged, and be given to see the Lord's work prosper in your hands. It must be unpleasant to have such an overseer; but, by decency and order in all things ecclesiastical, you can make the evil merely negative. Who is he that will harm you, if you be a follower of that which is good, especially canonical and rubrical? You ask in regard to certain Universalists, heads of families, in your congregation. So far as the pulpit is concerned, I would not *know* the fact that they are such, except carefully to avoid giving the impression that you are preaching at them. In my sermons I would imply the doctrine they reject, rather than formally discuss it. In most cases, indeed, this method is best everywhere. The doctrine is not systematically discussed anywhere in Scripture, though it is by implication taught everywhere. In my intercourse with them and their families, pretty much the same course should be pursued. Controversy should at least be avoided. You will remember that the family is more than the head of the family to a faithful pastor. What you want is to get a religious influence over the whole family, especially the young.

"I like your notion of studying some philosophy. Reid's 'Intellectual Powers,' the edition by Walker, would be a good book. Walker has also edited some of Stewart, which I have not seen, but which would be good, if you cannot get Reid. Walker's notes on Reid are chiefly taken from Sir William Hamilton, the most learned metaphysician that Great Britain has ever had.

"I am pleased, also, that you have taken hold of writing with vigor. Diligently and laboriously pursued, it is profitable every way. Extemporaneous writing is not of much benefit. But when we labor to have matter, suitable matter, to arrange it rightly, and to bring it forth with true art, which, of course, is art concealed, there is not only the immediate effect of profiting the hearer, but the further effect of disciplining one's own mind. Most of my education came in this way. I owed nothing to my teachers.

"Last Sunday I was with W. I preached once on Saturday, and twice on Sunday. They say that he has become a high Calvinist, and hardly thinks it right to exhort sinners! It may be he did not like my sermon. But he is to be pitied. His affliction has been great; and he always will have peculiarities of manner, not always perfectly agreeable. The Seminary has exactly forty students, promising young men. The utmost love to W. and W.

"Affectionately, WILLIAM SPARROW."

"October 6, 1854.

"Rev. E. W. Syle:—

"Much that you say about 'Evangelical party-men' sounds strange to me. They are but men, and no doubt very imperfect, and not exempt from party spirit. Of two things I cannot have a doubt: that Evangelical principles, so-called, are the principles of the Bible, and of the Church, mother and daughter; and that these principles have been the life-blood of the Missionary cause, both foreign and domestic, in this country, especially the foreign. I say this, for the fact is undoubted, that Evangelical principles do avowedly advocate the cultivation of the *whole* Missionary field, while the opposing principles are, to say the least, comparatively indifferent to a portion of it. Besides, however imperfectly Evangelical men have carried out their principles, they have done nearly all that has been done in that way; and if I know anything about the secret workings of their minds and hearts in this matter, the great absorbing motive with them, in what they do, is a regard to Christ's command, a love for His name, a jealousy for His honor, a desire to see all men blessed with the Gospel. I am persuaded the Searcher of hearts knows that, at least, it is not *party spirit* which elicits *money from their pockets.* But I feel myself at strange work in thus writing to you.

"As to avoiding a misconstruction of our conduct on the part of others, I regard it, within certain limits, as our interest and bounden duty. We owe it to the Master whom we serve, as well as our own family and friends. I am conscious of having erred, in that particular, in times past."

"Theological Seminary, September 13, 1855.

"Rev. and Dear Brother:—

"I have an itching curiosity, and I write to ease it. I am told that you are going to Kenyon; as you love me, tell me, is it so, and also, anything else in regard to yourself and the Church which you think proper, and can find leisure to communicate. Ohio seems to be feathering her nest from Virginia. I hope she will not reduce our nest to the bare sticks. I do not like the idea of your leaving us, but if Providence so directs, what am I, that I should object, especially as next to Virginia I love Ohio.

"I have not been able to make you a visit this vacation, partly because I have been engaged to fill the pulpit of St. Paul's, Alexandria. Perhaps I may be able to visit you if you remain with us during the term. By an arrangement with my brother Professors, I can make a short trip in term time as well as any other.

"With kind remembrances to Mrs. ——, I am, truly,

"Your friend and brother, WM. SPARROW.

"*Rev. C. Walker.*"

REV. E. W. SYLE.

"October 26, 1854.

"DEAR BROTHER:—

"I am most happy to answer your letter of the 20th thus promptly, if it can in the least cheer you and your dear wife, as you are about to set out on another stage in the pilgrimage of life. The roving state of life which belongs to a missionary, and the frequent breaking up of associations connected with it, have one great advantage; they leave fewer ties to be rent asunder by the last great separation. This, I have no doubt, is, in part, the secret of the peaceful, and even joyous, end which has closed the career of so many missionaries. Their previous discipline had weaned them well from all mere earthly attachments to persons, places and things."

TO THE SAME.

"February 18, 1855.

"Dr. Van Kleek was here about a fortnight ago. I was sick, and only saw him for a few moments. He addressed the students for a quarter of an hour, in an appeal in behalf of Oregon and Bishop Scott. It was the fittest possible way of spending the few moments he had to spare. No field of labor on which our Church has entered, not excepting China, Africa, Greece, or even California, can compete with it in some respects. It is the least attractive of all, and the least likely to be thought of. If any one happens to turn his thoughts to the Pacific board, before he can reach that sterner and colder region of the coast, he is attracted by 'the gold region,' a place harder for the navigator to pass than Circe in the days of Ulysses.

"I thank you for the two copies of the 'Oriental.' The editor of it (the Rev. Mr. Speer) is an old Kenyon student. When you see him, remember me to him. He seems to be setting himself for the defence of the Chinese against the power and oppression of the Anglo-American. We have dealt hardly with the poor Indian and

Negro; I hope we shall not push the poor Chinese to the wall in the same way. Some restrictions on their political, if not their civil and social interests, may, for aught I know, be indispensable for a little time, but I hope nothing of that kind will be permanent, or in the slightest degree interfere with the general progress and improvement of the race. A semi-civilized people ought to be so dealt with that they will soon become a wholly civilized people. But I may be talking in the dark, and at random.

"Pray, what is your decision in the present diversity of opinions about the movements of the 'rebels' in China? I cannot give up the idea that good is designed, in the providence of God, by this movement. The fact that the leader is said to claim divine honors, does not stumble me. Hero-worship is better than worship of wood and stone. Besides, it is a change, just what the immovable Chinese need. And again, the adoption of the Decalogue as their moral code must be a great moral advance with them; and, unless they deal with it as do the Romanists, must be a great check upon all forms of idolatry. But there, too, I may be groping in the dark.

"Mr. ——— told me, at dinner, that twenty years ago, when he took charge, the congregation was not one-half as large, nor one-quarter as rich as it is now, yet it then gave more, and more cheerfully, to religious objects than it does now! There was genuine *naivete* in that!"

TO THE SAME. "July 7, 1855.

"I have lately had an experience of the Alexandria people that has pleased me. I have collected $1200 there towards the enlargement of our chapel. I have found them very ready to give in most cases. Ten of the subscriptions were for $100 each. I am not yet done with them. Elsewhere, that is, in our neighborhood, I have got about as much more. The accommodation of the chapel is to be doubled, and its appearance improved, and comfort increased.

"Our examination passed off very well. There was a goodly attendance of the clergy. The alumni have been very successful in their efforts to endow the professorships. You know we are building a library, which is to cost $8000, all contributed from abroad, $4000 from one person in Philadelphia. Our neighborhood is building up quite fast. Twenty years from now it will probably be very thickly settled.

"Since I last wrote, there has been a most sad event among us. Dear little Blanche has been taken from us. I have not received such a wound for many long years. The recurrence of the subject is still a dagger to my heart. We had forgotten she was not of our own blood. Ma, the girls, the boys, all loved her as a child or sister. And she was a most lovely and promising child. Such a corpse I never beheld. No sculptor's chisel ever produced anything so lovely. The image will haunt my brain as long as I live. The death occurred while Mrs. Sparrow was away in New York. She got home before the funeral, but that was all. Mr. Henning, also, was absent, and we deeply deplored it, though he has since said he does not. Of course, the chief burden fell on Susan, and nobly she bore it. O, she is a heroine, a Christian heroine, strong, collected, tender, and quiet to the last degree. I love and admire her more than ever. You will forgive this."

The allusion here is to a motherless child of the Missionary to Africa, Rev. E. W. Henning. This little one, finding a home in the family of Doctor Sparrow, had become endeared to him as one of his own children; and when taken by an early death, her departure was thought of with feelings of peculiar tenderness. One of the students of that date mentions the expression of thankfulness to him by the Doctor for some little acts of attention in connection with her funeral. It was the first stroke of bereavement upon his household after a long interval, and it came in a form calling forth his tenderest sympathies.

"May 12, 1856.

"How unlike the common estimate of human life which we find in the world! How similar in spirit to that of Him who came not to be ministered unto, but to minister, and give his life a ransom for many—the *humbling honor* of living for the same general purpose with Christ Himself."

"May 29th.

"We returned on Monday, from the Fredericksburg Convention, one of the most delightful that I ever attended. Eighty clergy present.

"I thank you very sincerely for the papers you sent me from San Francisco. They disclosed a singular state of society. It is beautiful to see how rapidly such a turbid and fermenting liquid can clarify itself in a Protestant country. In a Romish country it could not. The cauldron has been seething and bubbling for a long time in South America, but the lees will not settle to the bottom.

"We are in great confusion, at this time, in Congress, and personal violence has been offered, in two or three cases. Slavery the cause. The Lord, in mercy, save the ship of state from that rock!"

"THEOLOGICAL SEMINARY, April 23, 1856.

"MY DEAR JOHN:—

"I am sick with a headache, and have been since Monday, but I must say a word in answer to your letter received that evening. I had just got home from St. Paul's, Culpeper, where I spent the Sunday, when it arrived. It afforded us all true pleasure to learn that your prospects are fair, and your spirit hopeful. The last is as important as the first; even more so, for it is our duty. I trust that, hoping in God, you will hope on, and hope ever. The Lord has put none of us in vain into this world; he has something for us to do; let us endeavor to do it, and be happy in it. I like your determination to visit every family in the parish or village. Done in a religious way, it cannot fail to result in good. Let me warn you against lengthening unduly any religious services you may hold in the village. It is the rock on which I have split. Where the exercise is extemporaneous, the danger is special. Were I in a parish, I should study that point. I would *write* prayers to exercise myself in the language of supplication, and strive to have them pointed, applicable and solemn; especially would I guard against long sentences, and many connective particles. Separate and brief petitions should abound in all addresses to the throne of Grace. Long and complex sentences do for addressing men, not God.

"St. George's Hall will not be acted on till Convention. I must stop. Much love to Mary, and a kiss and blessing for Willie and Carrie.

"Your affectionate father, WILLIAM SPARROW."

"THEOLOGICAL SEMINARY, September 2, 1856.

"REV. AND DEAR BROTHER:—

"In regard to the argument in Butler I can only say a word or two.

"First, he argues on the grounds of the Materialist.

"Secondly, in conformity with these views of the Materialist, he makes a hypothesis, *i. e.*, that the motion of a particle of matter is so indivisible that it involves a contradiction to suppose one part to exist, and another not; in which case the particle must be one.

"Thirdly, he then assumes that the motion of a particle of matter is, to that matter, analogously, as consciousness to the living being.

"Fourth, and lastly, assuming consciousness to be absolutely one, he thinks himself entitled thence to infer that the soul, or living being, is one also, and, like the supposed particle of matter, indiscerptible.

"The infinite divisibility of matter cannot be pleaded, because the hypothesis with which he starts precludes it; and he makes that hypothesis to furnish an analogy, or parallel case of the known and admitted fact of the unity of consciousness.

"The argument seems to me a fair and good one, as a probable argument, and to the Materialist very confounding. If he admits the soul to have bulk, and at the same time that consciousness is one and indiscerptible, he must admit, in every fair view, that, despite of infinite divisibility, the former is, somehow or other, indivisible, and therefore indiscerptible. If he admits it has not bulk, then he is not consistent; and, at all events, there is no ground, in reason, to suppose it will ever be destroyed; there is nothing to warrant the presumption, for Nature knows of no destruction but disintegration.

"I have tried to be brief, without time, and you will say of me, 'brevis esse laborat obscurus fit.' I have not a copy of Duke, and have not time to look into Dr. Hanna, if I could find Dr. C.'s view in his four volumes.

"If you understand me, and think me wrong, please let me know. In great haste, but

"Most truly yours, W. SPARROW.

"P. S. My daughter S. is compelled to take a voyage across the Atlantic, for her health. The doctor insists upon it. This, of course, fills my heart and head, just at this moment. W. S.

"*Rev. C. Walker.*"

"PHILADELPHIA, October 9, 1856.

"MY DEAR J.:—

"I cannot give you Convention news; the paper reports would put to shame my meagre statements. I may say, however, that an excellent temper prevails, and that thus far all things have gone on well. Do not be surprised if you should receive liberty to read Morning service *alone* in the morning, and in the afternoon the Litany, or ante-communion service; and at night, the Evening service; when there is Communion in the morning, the Communion service alone being used. What emancipation this will be! What relief to feeble throats! What an impediment out of the way of effective ministrations of the Gospel! The Bishops are less *conservative*, as the phrase is, than the lower house.

"Ever your affectionate father, WILLIAM SPARROW."

"THEOLOGICAL SEMINARY, November 13, 1856.

"REV. AND DEAR BROTHER:—

"We are much tormented in our chapel pulpit for want of a good light, and it has occurred to me you might be able and willing to help us. You may remember I was struck with the fixture in your pulpit. It seems to me just what we want. You have gas, and we have not; but I should think that would make no difference. The contrivance might be arranged so as to suit the use of etherial oil, or even common oil, if thought best. Now then, can we not get, through you, a similar fixture to yours, made, and forwarded by express to this place? If you can get any liberal friend of the Seminary to bear the expense, I will be thankful, but if not, I will pay the bill myself, as soon as it is forwarded. Some layman might be amused with the idea of illuminating 'theologicals,' and shedding light upon the pulpit of the Theological Seminary of Virginia. Even a High-Churchman might think it worth boasting of. One thing I must make a condition, that you do not ask good Mr. Dunham. I should feel ashamed that a favor should be asked of one to whom I am already so deeply indebted. No one shall ever cast up to me the proverb, 'Give an inch, and take an ell.'

"Mr. Wharton is here, delivering a course of three lectures, on the 'Religious Elements connected with the Colonization of the United States.' I have had a letter from Paris, from Mr. Morrison. The travelers were improving in health.

"Please act as decisively as possible in regard to the lamp business. For one does not like to dwell in darkness.

"Affectionately yours, WM. SPARROW.

"*Rev. E. H. Canfield.*"

TO THE SAME.

"THEOLOGICAL SEMINARY, February 11, 1857.

"REV. AND DEAR BROTHER:—

"You remember N. He was a Seminary man of your day, and he is no common man. I hardly know the clergyman in Virginia of longer head, or sounder mind. He is, also, though not remarkable for his manner, an earnest, impressive, and instructive preacher. As a pastor, he is judicious and kind. As a man, he is genial and polite. Now, this your old friend I want to see in a wider sphere than his present. Cannot you help to find one for him? His people love him dearly, and will be loth to part with him; lately, they increased his salary, to prevent him from accepting a call. But he is not in his place. He needs more room to develop in, and a better salary than such a fold can give him. I ask again, cannot you help him to such a place? I am exceedingly unwilling to see him leave Virginia, but I am more unwilling that such talents and traits of character should not have an adequate sphere. Do turn this matter over in your mind, and, if possible, act.

"I wish you could snatch a moment to write me a line. I know your many duties, but I know, also, your powers of despatch. If, besides touching the above matter, you could give me one of your old-fashioned budgets, with your views of men and things, it would, of course, be doubly welcome.

"There is no news here—there never was, you know. It all comes from the North, and there it is pretty much frozen up at this time. I hope your health is better than it was the last time I heard of you. It is natural that I should be feeble, confined to the house for three weeks, as I have been of late; but your time for infirmities has not yet come. However, it is something above time which regulates that matter. May we be submissive to the regulation, whatever it be.

"Your affectionate friend and brother,

"WILLIAM SPARROW."

"THEOLOGICAL SEMINARY, April 20, 1857.

"MY DEAR J.:—

"In regard to John xv, 2, I would say this much. The language of our Saviour and His Apostles is generally complex, concrete, and synthetical, because it is briefer, simpler, and better adapted to practical use. So here. We are not told whether real or professed Christians are meant, and there was no occasion for the distinction. The object of the Saviour was to intimate the necessity of bearing fruit, and that it could be borne only in connection with Him. I suppose He did not mean to give forth a decision on the defectibility or indefectibility of grace; and if any man attempts to connect such questions with this text, it is not because they belong there, but because he has brought them there. Our Lord could teach the two great practical truths referred to without touching these knotty points. As to the most natural of the meanings of 'in Christ,' or 'in me,' in this case, profession is so, because it is applicable, with equal ease, in both clauses you quote. In this sense a man may be 'in Christ' whether he bear fruit or not. This sense, therefore, does not do violence, in any way, to the passage. I have only dropped a hint or two. Your account of your parish is cheering. The Lord, in mercy, bless your labors. It is a great thing to be the instrument to a fellow-creature of a good which abides and increases in value, just at the time when all other good fades away and vanishes. Let me warn you, however, against excessive exertion. It is not pious, any more than laziness is. I have been afraid, ever since I knew of your visiting that Sunday-school house, that you might do work there which might interfere with permanent engagements elsewhere, subtracting from your study time, and impairing your health. It belongs to a good steward not only to lend, but to put out on usury. He must not throw away health, any more than life, or be a suicide, by degrees, any more than at once. I hope your neighbor, in Carbondale, will prove a pleasant one. If he is a true Moravian, he must. Moravians are the denomination which best exhibit the graces of love and self-denial. What are the characteristics of the other denominations? Let the question furnish an hour's talk to you and M.

"Have you come across Stevens' 'History of Methodism?' Borrow and read it if you can. I have been much refreshed by it this week. It is calculated to do great good among 'all classes and conditions of men' and Churches; it brings before us so distinctly the original design of the Wesleys and Whitefield, viz., not to erect a new Church, but to revive and spiritualize the old ones, eschewing all dogmatic questions, and ecclesiastical questions, and all other questions that might call attention from that one thing! O, for the concentration of our hearts, and all our powers, upon the conversion of sinners, and the sanctification of saints! Alas, also, how are our minds distracted with the lust of other things, and how are our energies exhausted on vastly inferior objects! If the Churches, and individual ministers, would lay aside their denominational rivalries and controversies, and pursue, simply and solely, this one end, how soon would the world be subdued to Christ, and the 'kingdom be established to God, even the Father!' And questions of abstract truth, and of ecclesiastical arrangement, and the relations of Church and State, so far from faring for the worse, would, as I believe, fare infinitely better, being left under the direction of the Word in its simplest meaning, and its leading principles to the instinctive impulses of the renewed and highly sanctified heart. But enough of this.

"Bishop Meade is here, lecturing, and seems in tolerable health. I think, however, that he declines in vigor. He is hard at work bringing out his 'Old Churches, Families, and Ministers of Virginia.' He says he sets them in the order of their work! the ministers last! The work will be in two volumes.

"Give my tenderest love to M. and the children. Be assured of our continual prayers for you all, and let us not fail to be remembered by you. Separated in body, we may meet there, and be comforted, and edified, and strengthened there. Mrs. S. desires me to say to M., that the letter sent was just the kind she likes to receive.

"Yours, ever affectionately, WM. SPARROW."

"THEOLOGICAL SEMINARY, December 23, 1857.

"DEAR BROTHER SYLE:—

"I cannot tell you how much pleasure your letter, received a few weeks ago, afforded me and my family. It 'carried me back,' not to 'Old Virginia,' but to old times, and revived many pleasant recollections. We rejoice that the vine branches are so thriving about you, and that those who have the charge of them are doing so well, though troubled that they cannot do better. It must, indeed, be a trial to an active, spirited man, to find that he can do so little of what needs to be done. But there are many apologues to comfort us, among the rest that of the mouse and the netted lion. Missionaries, who lay the foundations of the Gospel, can seldom or never appear to do much, but, in reality, they do most, as the unerring judgments of another world will show. We may apply to them the maxim, 'dimidium facti, *qui cœpit habet.*' Your statements about the new recruits surprised me. But I suspect you must have bound them too much to the letter. The spirit, the substance of the doctrine of human depravity, I am persuaded they hold. Their character as Missionaries is almost proof of that. I have never heard of but one man (a Unitarian) that ever went to the heathen to preach the Gospel to them who denied it, and he quickly repented of his enterprise. I am rather surprised, also, at their seclusive and monastic habits. I cannot but hope that when the work of the ship-house is done, and the launch takes place, they will prove themselves good sailors, Heaven granting propitious gales. You Missionaries in China are, indeed, in prominent positions. The East generally seems to be the part of the world to which the thoughts of the thoughtful are directed. Europe may well forget herself in the distraction of her attention both East and West. She is like Issachar, 'the strong ass crouching down between two burdens.' I have been deeply engrossed with the Indian insurrection. It haunted me for several weeks. I trust now that great good will grow out of it, though purchased at a fearful cost. As to your field, with its teeming population, for it, as for India, it seems evident that great things are in store and at hand. The time was when I felt bound to wait, and have long patience; but now we seem to be authorized to believe that Providence means to move more expeditiously than of old. If not, why so many new agencies, and why such a general making up of mind, and breaking up of organizations? The signs of the times, in themselves considered, and the language of prophecy, alike call upon us to look up with expectation. Not, as one says, that with Isaiah, David, and St. John before me, I would write the newspapers ten years in advance. But while I disclaim all thought of particular modes, I feel confident about the general result. And I do not confine my view to Asia; every Continent is implicated. Among ourselves, great and good things, I trust, are in speedy preparation. Also in Europe. California is not out of the pale of my cheerful anticipation. The condition there is bad enough; New

Orleans was once as bad, or nearly so, but it is improving every year."

To a Young Friend in Extreme Sickness.

"Richmond, July 19, 1858.

"My Dear Willie:—

"Ever since I parted with you on Friday, you have been much upon my mind. I was reluctant to leave home while you were in such feeble health; and I have ever since felt apprehensive that in my last interview I did not use that faithful explicitness, in regard to my view of your case, which was needed. One so young as you, and who suffers more from weakness than from positive pain, finds it hard to realize his situation, no matter how critical it may be. Being anxious to repair any neglect I may have been guilty of, and to apprise you fully of the general opinion in regard to your case, I write you these few lines by the way.

"My dear Willie, let me tell you plainly, that your condition, in the opinion of all your friends, professional and unprofessional, is such that you ought, without a moment's delay, address yourself to the work of preparing to meet the will of Providence, whatever it may be. The Lord gave, why should not the Lord take away? He causes many to die in the cradle; why should he not call away others in early manhood? His is the right, and His is the power. Shall He not do what He will with His own? It is plain that there is no peace, and no security for man, but in resigning himself into the hands of God; but how can that be done? God is holy, and we are sinful; God is good, and we have been ungrateful; God has been forbearing, and we have been presumptuous; under such circumstances, how can we appear before Him in peace? O, how guilty we are, after years of transgression and sin! How polluted in our nature, in our hearts, and our lives, after living estranged from Him so long! How can such creatures as we ever escape His wrath, or learn to love His holy presence? Dear Willie, I know but one way: God Himself declares there is but one way. That way is Christ crucified. Christ came by His atoning blood to reconcile God to us, and by His Spirit to reconcile us to God. Let me beseech you, then, in this your hour of greatest need, to lay hold of this provision of mercy, found in the Gospel of Christ, and nowhere else. Stir up your heart to believe that, as you are going into God's presence, so there is no way of access to Him which will not fill the soul with dismay, but the Gospel. Call on God to help you to realize that you are fast fading away; that you must soon appear before Him; that He is a holy God and just, a merciful God and truthful, and that His grace flows to us through but one channel: that blessed Saviour who died upon the cross for our sins. In Him is pardon for the guilty, and sanctification for the polluted. O, look to *Him*, call mightily on *Him*, cling to *Him*. He can save unto the uttermost. The chief of sinners is not beyond the compass of His mercy. Though our sins be as scarlet, they may be made white as snow. In conclusion, let me beseech you not to let the hope of a prolonged life prevent your immediate, and earnest, and persevering attention to this one thing. It is your salvation, your all! Dear Willie, your case is hopeless for this world, but Christ is more than sufficient for you. Farewell; the Lord in mercy keep you, through Jesus Christ.

"Your true friend, W. SPARROW."

"THEOLOGICAL SEMINARY, November 7, 1859.

"MY DEAR J.:—

"I went to the General Convention, and enjoyed it as long as health permitted. But I lost the last week from sickness, and all the session I was suffering from neuralgia in my face. I think the spirit of the Convention was, on the whole, an improved edition of what we have previously had; owing, I doubt not, to the religious interest which pervades the country. Last Thursday night I returned to address the students upon the subject, and, a strange thing for me, talked for an hour! I was always, as you know, *prolix on paper;* there is, you see, danger now of garrulity. So do extremes meet in the same person!

"I have not written you since my call to Baltimore. But that topic is worn out. Suffice it to say, that while it cost me a painful struggle for a fortnight, I am well content with my decision. My brother Edward was very anxious for me to go; but my brother Thomas was opposed. The only thing that prevented was the fear that I should have to reproach myself for leaving a manifest post of duty for an uncertain one.

"On my return from Convention I spent a Sunday with the boys at the University. I preached in the morning in Charlottesville, and at night at the University, which is a mile from Charlottesville, where I had a congregation of five hundred young men. The three boys are well, and doing, I trust, fairly. I wish you would write them occasionally. I believe family feeling and affection to be a great aid to everything that is good in youth, and a great preservative against evil. You have heard of our prosperity here in brick and mortar, and also in students. Things are, externally, looking up; the Lord grant that things spiritual may keep pace with them.

"I am glad to hear that your congregations grow. I wish I could pay you a visit. I am engaged to go to Wilmington next month, to preach an ordination sermon, and should like to extend my trip to P. The only objection is that the time would be so short, it would not be worth while, or, as it is expressed in Latin, 'operæ pretium.' However, if the Lord will, I shall make you a long visit next summer. When is the next Association?

"My dear J., I feel the time is short. The night is, indeed, far spent, and the day is at hand. O, let us be ready for the dawn! To this end let us labor, and watch, and pray, and let much of our own prayer be intercession for one another, that we may live usefully, and die in peace. With tenderest love to M. and the children,

"Ever affectionately yours, W. SPARROW."

It was not very long before the date of the last of these letters, that the Doctor was called on to pass through one of his severest trials of natural feeling, that of separation, with little hope of reunion, from his third daughter, for the missionary work in China. Her marriage took place in June, 1859, and in the course of the summer she set sail with her husband for her chosen field of duty. "This," said he, speaking of her going, "this was the hardest wrench yet." And yet, when the question of parting had become a settled one, his whole behavior, although, evidently, it was a great trial, was as cheerful and buoyant as though he was receiving, not giving away a daughter. He afterwards said in a letter, "When I parted from her I feared it was for life; and it came to pass."

What his feelings and convictions were, under the circumstances, are beautifully exhibited in an extract from his sermon delivered at St. George's, New York, a few weeks after his daughter's marriage, on the occasion of the ordination to Deacons' orders of her husband, and only a few days before their departure for China. "Have we children? I will not say we shall not withhold them; *that* would be a tame expression, indeed. How could a Christian parent assume such a perilous responsibility? We will rather, I should say, offer them freely, desiring only that the Lord would fit them for the work, and bless them in it. Patriotism has often made fathers and mothers, with their own hands, gird armor on their sons to go and do battle in their country's cause. Shall not the love of Christ, the love of souls, the love of truth, holiness, and heaven constrain Christian parents to do as much with their children, offering them willingly, and rejoicing that they themselves should be so connected, through their sons and daughters, with the cause of humanity, and the interests of that kingdom which shall have no end? Yes, I will hope and believe that, through the good Spirit of God moving in our hearts, such will be the effect of this day's doing in our future homes. When we return from the ship in which they sail to expatriate themselves for seven long years, unless some afflictive providence should shorten their term of exile, be our part, the Lord being our helper, to help them in our prayers, and to keep back nothing of those things by which this sacred and loving enterprise will be advanced."

This was not the language of stoicism, knowing nothing by personal experience of the nature of the sacrifice to which it made allusion. It was that of deep, loving, and painful appreciation of all that such sacrifice involved to natural affection, and yet freely making it, gratefully recognizing the privilege and honor of being allowed so to do. A brief note, very soon after, in reference to certain changes proposed in the Seminary course, has its connection with what has been mentioned.

"Rev. and Dear Brother:—

"Your letter would have been answered before, but that I returned from New York, last Monday week, to take to my bed. The excitement connected with the departure of the Missionaries, following so closely upon commencement and other events, was too much for me. Besides, I have been troubled with a local affection which has cost me much pain. This or yesterday was the first moment I could possibly have replied to you.

"First, let me say, I am ready for anything, within the limits of my strength, which the Trustees may think proper to determine. And when I cannot bear my burden, I shall quickly say No, and there leave it. I am too old, and have learned too much of myself and of the world, to pursue any other course.

"In the next place, let me say, I am not disposed to be very *active* in any changes. I prefer to be *passive*. The time was when it was otherwise. There are a great many points in which I believe important suggestions might be made, but I must wait till I see you. If able, I am bound to preach next Sunday in Baltimore. After my return from there, or in the week following, I may make you a visit. An hour's talk will be worth four hours' writing. Please let me know when the committee will meet, that I may arrange accordingly. With kindest regards to Mrs. ——, I am truly,

"Your friend and brother, WILLIAM SPARROW.

"*Rev. C. Walker.*"

The results of the meeting thus alluded to were not at all agreeable to Dr. Sparrow, and when, within the next few months, he was invited to the rectorship of Emanuel Church, Baltimore, it was feared, by some of his friends and pupils, that he would be lost to the Seminary. Had mere natural feeling been allowed to control his movements, he would undoubtedly have gone. But earnest persuasions, from different sources, were addressed to him not to make the proposed change. And these, with his own careful deliberation as to his course of duty, and what seemed his most effective work in the Church, caused him to decline the invitation. This was the last effort made to induce him to leave the Seminary during this period. What might have been the result of his acceptance of any of these invitations, especially those to assume the pastorate, can, of course, be only a matter of conjecture. The judgment of some of his friends and brethren at the time, that this result would not have been favorable or successful, that any such movement would undoubtedly have been a great mistake, tested in the light of his missionary work, and reputation as a preacher in Ohio, was, to say the least, rather premature. The greatest of all qualifications for the pastorate, practical judgment, sympathetic earnestness, faithfulness in reproof, etc., he pre-eminently possessed. The greatest difficulty would have been in his sermons. But the same capacity which adapted those sermons to the peculiar material to which they were addressed, might have been quite as successfully exerted in endeavoring to meet the wants of other and different material. The writer has no hesitation in the expression of the conviction that, had Dr. Sparrow's life been given to the pastoral, rather than the professorial work, his peculiar gift of teaching from the pulpit, and from house to house, would have rendered him as successful in one of these spheres as he undoubtedly was in the other. The expediency of turning from one of these spheres of labor to the other, or the prospect of so doing successfully, after a man has passed middle life, is another and very different question. For the sake of the Seminary, and his pupils, during the next fifteen years, we may well rejoice that the experiment was not made, and that he continued in his old position.

The only item of interest for the closing year of this period, 1860, the writer finds in a couple of notations of his own; one as to the Diocesan Convention, and the other as to a later date: "Heard Dr. Sparrow, on Sunday morning, preach a sermon in regard to the reign of the Saints on earth, and enjoyed it very much." "Was out at the Seminary, November 30th, at the Thanksgiving services, spending the day with Dr. Sparrow, and hearing him preach a sermon for the occasion." Both of these sermons, in their general subject, as in the specific material, stood in sad contrast with the experiences of trial and trouble so near at hand to himself and hearers.

The last one of these sermons, while it looked back, had doubtless, also, its forward glance; for the elements of coming trouble were beginning to make themselves manifest. In the meantime, however, everything seemed to be going in its usual course at the Seminary. The number of students was seventy; was as large, if not larger, than at any former period. And while the excited feelings outside, doubtless, had their influence with its members from different sections, it did not interfere with regular performances of duty. Northern and Southern students, while disputing, at times, in reference to the great questions at issue, were still co-operative in their studies, and in their practical Christian efforts for the welfare of the neighborhood. It was only as the prospect of actual military movements became probable, that any serious interference with Seminary work was experienced. The definite form in which disorganization began, and the evils to come were foreshadowed, was in that of the departure of the Northern students, early in the Spring of 1861. This, it is gratifying to record, took place in a spirit, on both sides, of regret and brotherly affection. It was a sad day to all; to one side, to feel that it seemed necessary to leave the sacred studies and associations in which they were occupied; to the other, to feel that such departure could not be avoided. Peculiarly was this a day of sadness to Dr. Sparrow, and recognized as an omen of others still more sad in the future. The earliest impressions of his childhood were connected with the evils of civil war. His father's house, during the rebellion in Ireland, was, at one time, occupied by the rebels, and subsequently by the royal troops. The enforced removal of the family took place while his mother was suffering from sickness, and the refugeeism which followed, and still later the exile to this country after the contest terminated, all these things together, as family traditions, impressed upon his mind in childhood, produced an effect which went with him through all his after-life. These facts of early impression were mentioned by him in conversation, about the time of which we are speaking; and they help to explain the clearness of anticipation with which he foresaw and described what so many, in a little time, knew by experience. This horror of what was coming seemed almost to absorb every other feeling. In addition, moreover, to these general anticipations of evil to the whole country, from a state of warfare, was there a clear perception of the immediate prospect of it in the locality of the Seminary, within a few miles of the Federal metropolis. "If," said he on one occasion, "if Washington were up in the mountains of Pennsylvania. But for us now there is no escape." He thus clearly foresaw that the work of the Seminary, the work of his life, could not continue to go on in that locality, if, indeed, anywhere. And this retirement of the Northern students became a sad premonition of what must soon follow.

For some weeks longer the exercises of the Seminary went on. The work, moreover, of completing the new buildings, a part of Meade Hall, went on very nearly to the close, to be resumed and finished years after, when the impending conflict had ended. It had become manifest, however, by the first of May, that it would be impossible to go on. The funds of the Institution upon which its support depended were invested in Virginia; and if it went on at all, it must be where material in the shape of students and funds for support were to be found. The locality, also, of the

Seminary, apart from these considerations, was just in the track of military movements, and no place for academic or theological study. Such movements were anticipated daily; and yielding to what seemed inevitable, it was decided to close the exercises. Very sad was the occasion, and, as an item in the history of the Institution, it has its peculiar interest. The exercises closed on the seventh of May, with the examination of two of the members of the senior class, and their ordination on the same day, in the chapel. The congregation was made up of the professors and remaining students, and a couple of clergymen from Alexandria. No sermon was preached. And before the afternoon was over the process of dispersion had begun. As it was doubtful whether any reorganization during hostilities would be possible, Dr. May, whose connections were north of the Potomac, returned to Philadelphia; the death of Mrs. May had taken place only a few months before. Dr. Packard and his family moved into the interior of Virginia, as did, also, the family of Dr. Sparrow. The Doctor himself, and seven or eight students, remained at the Seminary. And, with the exception of an absence of part of a week in Richmond, at the Diocesan Convention, he remained at the Seminary until military movements actually began with the occupation of Alexandria by the Federal forces. This event closed communications with the interior; and to avoid separation from his family he rejoined them a few days afterward. It would seem that he left the Seminary with the hope of being able to return. But this was soon recognized as impracticable.

These closing days, between the seventh of May and the military movements some three weeks later, constituted a very peculiar chapter in Dr. Sparrow's experience. He spoke of it afterward, as a period, perhaps, the most trying to him of any through which, during the war, he was called to pass. The strangeness of all the surroundings, the absence of his household, the stoppage in mid-session of all exercises, the empty buildings, the disturbed and anxious condition of all with whom he came in contact, the certainty of evils coming, and the uncertainty as to their degrees and forms, the rumors of movements, and sometimes, in the boom of distant artillery, the actual hearing of them—all these seem to have had their full influence upon his feelings and imagination. And this influence, however realized during the day, when there was some relief in communication with the students and neighbors remaining, was still more oppressive when daylight closed, at night, in the silence of his lonely dwelling, unoccupied except by himself.

Two letters to Rev. Mr. Syle properly come in at this point. The one is an extract written the year before, on reception of intelligence of the death of Mrs. Syle, and the other, during this stay of Dr. Sparrow at the Seminary, after the departure of the students, in May, 1861. It was from a real sympathy with sorrow in the one instance, and a heavy experience of trouble in the other, that he thus gave expression to his feelings.

"April 17, 1860.

"We both have run through the greater part of life, and I trust understand something of its nature and design, and are enabled through grace to interpret rightly the details of life in its trials and triumphs, its losses and crosses, its joys and sorrows, its temptations and escapes. Dear brother, how imperfectly do those understand the philosophy of life who have not learned it at the feet of Jesus; and to those who have, how vain and unsatisfactory it is, aside from the end thereof, which is everlasting life. This truth has been, of late, very much pressed upon my own heart. I feel eternity to be very near, so that I can see, whether I do it or not, that I ought to count all things but loss for the excellency of the knowledge of Christ Jesus my Lord, through whom alone I can be prepared to meet it joyously. While I pray the Lord to comfort you, therefore, let me ask, my dear brother, your prayers for me, that I may be ever ready for any affliction, especially the last."

"TUESDAY, May 14, 1861.

"REV. AND DEAR BROTHER:—

"I am all alone in my house, having sent off my family to Staunton ten days ago. I go to our Convention to-morrow, in Richmond, and return on Monday, to take charge of the premises, as I have been doing since the Seminary was prematurely closed.

"I had a letter last night from Susan. It seems that unless help is sent to them immediately, they will have to come home. The thought seems almost death to her and her husband. To be driven home for want of a bare support, just when ready to be useful, is dreadful to them. Cannot something be done? She says they are going to sell all that they have, and keep along till it is made evident that the Church will not sustain them. If I had the means, how happy should I be to sustain them myself in a work so good in itself, and so near their hearts. Cannot some good, generous person—lady, if you please—be found to furnish them a few hundred dollars, to live along there till better times. Had Sue's true spirit been known among the rich ladies of our communion, as it is known to you and me, I think there would not be any doubt of her finding prompt relief.

"But why do I write? All is known to you; and, doubtless, you have been contriving some relief. The mail that brought the letters to me brought them to you, also, and all concerned in the cause in New York. I leave the matter in God's hands. S. says that the first announcement that they would soon have to leave was a most astounding and stunning blow to her and D. But they soon felt more calm, and were able to leave the matter at the Divine disposal, determined to trust though He should slay them; for next to slaying would a return be before they had gathered in any harvest.

"I have no heart to speak about things here. I feel really broken-hearted. Is there on record the case of a nation holding to its lips a cup so full of blessing, and so wantonly and wickedly dashing it to the ground? My own individual trials in this matter are most peculiar and painful; but oh, my country, it is for thee I feel!

"Let me hear from you at your leisure, and believe me ever your friend and brother, W. SPARROW."

Dr. Sparrow rejoined his family about the first of June. A few lines will terminate the narrative in regard to the little community which he left behind, and of the Seminary until it came into military occupation. Six or seven students, most of them from localities not very remote, were placed in occupation and charge of the buildings, to save them and the property in them, as far as possible, from depredation and destruction.

Within a few weeks following the occupation of Alexandria, squads, sometimes of stragglers from the army, sometimes of vicious persons from the neighborhood, began to make depredations upon unprotected property. Particularly was this the case with unoccupied houses. One of the outer buildings of the Seminary had been broken open during the night, and a request was made to the officer commanding in the neighborhood to furnish a guard for the protection of the property and its inmates. The writer, as an eye witness, can describe the close.

I went out with Mr. Lee to the Seminary, to meet the guard that Col. Heintzelman had promised for its protection. It was a bright afternoon in June, and everything was looking very fresh and beautiful. But for the closed houses of the professors, it might have been taken for the time of vacation. We found the six or seven students in possession, apparently anxious in regard to the protection which had been requested, and we endeavored to reassure them. In less than twenty minutes the guard made its appearance, too large, as I thought, for the purpose—some twenty or twenty-five men, under the command of a lieutenant. We received them at the front door, and, after a few words, they marched into the prayer hall and stacked their muskets. I mentioned to the lieutenant that this was the place of prayer for the students, morning and evening, and that arrangements would be made for the accommodation of his command in other parts of the building, and we soon took our departure. We had hardly got back to Mr. Lee's house before we received a message from the students that a line of sentinels had been drawn around the buildings, and that no one was allowed to pass through it. On our return to remonstrate, we found that Dr. May's and Dr. Sparrow's residences had been broken open, so as to be searched, that the rooms of the Seminary not already opened had been subjected to the same operation, and that the guard, which had been asked for protection, had actually taken possession. The inmates, of course, got away as soon as they could; and within the next four months the buildings were appropriated to hospital purposes. Providentially for Dr. Sparrow, the Rev. Mr. Jerome was chaplain for a time at the station, and thus his papers, a considerable portion of his books, and some little of his furniture were saved.

These particulars are mentioned because there is a common impression that the Seminary was abandoned, and without inmates, or proper representatives of its owners. This is a mistake. The official guardian of the property at all other times was, at that time, at hand, and acting. It was a merciful overruling of Divine providence for the Institution that its buildings were eventually appropriated to hospital purposes; in all probability this was the means of saving them from complete destruction.

We may now return to the subject of this memoir—the refugee-life of the head of the Seminary, in his new and trying sphere of experience. This will form the subject of the next chapter.

CHAPTER VII.

REFUGEE LIFE IN STAUNTON AND HALIFAX.

Our last chapter closed, so far as Dr. Sparrow was personally concerned, with his departure from the Seminary, soon after the occupation by the Federal army of Alexandria and the adjacent neighborhood. The occupation, with the establishment of a line of pickets beyond the Seminary, closed communication with the interior, and thus presented the alternative of departure or of indefinite separation from his family. Other reasons for such departure, connected with the resources of the Institution, and the prospect, in any degree, of doing its work in such a time, have already been mentioned. He, therefore, during the last week in May, obtained a passport from the commanding officer, and rejoined his family at Staunton, where they remained for a short time. From thence, after a brief sojourn, they went to the Stribling Springs, a watering-place not far distant, and there spent a part of the summer. His family at this time with him consisted of Mrs. Sparrow and two of his daughters. From the other members of his household he was, by the events of the period, immediately and painfully separated. Two of his daughters, Mrs. Grammer and Mrs. Jerome, were north of the Potomac, with but little opportunity of communication, the difficulties, in this respect, being increased in the case of Mrs. Smith, who was in China. Two of his sons were in the Confederate army, a third in the Confederate service in another department; one of his brothers was in the Federal and the other in the Confederate Congress. These simple facts will be sufficient to show the painful interest with which, from the start, he could not but regard the whole struggle. And, just as all these elements of trial were making themselves manifest, there came another—a trial at all times, but as deeply and tenderly felt in seasons of general calamity and distress as at any other, perhaps by these latter increased and deepened—the loss of a beloved child, Mrs. Dashiell, who died very suddenly, in Richmond. When little Blanche Henning died, in 1853, the Doctor gratefully recognized the mercy of God which, for twenty years, had spared his household from bereavement. This bereavement, when it came in the death of the adopted one, like that of his own child twenty years before, was that which was involved in the loss of an infant. But this of 1861 was different and much severer, to be followed, at no long interval, by two others of the same nature.

A letter to his friend, Cassius F. Lee, Esq., written during the summer of this year, contains some of the facts above stated, and may properly come in at this point. It is to be borne in mind that this, like all the communications of that date passing through the lines, only went by private hands, and was, therefore, probably subject to long delay in its reception. It will be seen from it that, with the burden of his own troubles as a refugee, he had room for sympathy with the troubles of others.

"STRIBLING SPRINGS, AUGUSTA COUNTY, VA.,
"July 13, 1861.

"MY DEAR FRIEND:—

"I received your letter of the 4th last night, and hasten to answer it. It made me glad and made me sorry. It is ever a pleasure to hear from you; but it deeply saddens my heart that you are placed in such trying circumstances. But my faith is strong that our Lord will carry you safely through. In Him have you trusted, and He will deliver you. Would that I could be with you, to interchange thoughts and feelings, and, by mutual Christian communion, receive and impart comfort. When I left the Seminary, it was my intention to return, and, therefore, I took nothing with me, not even my manuscripts. But as soon as that affray at the Court-house occurred, I could not persuade my family to let me go. Indeed, it seemed to me that I had no right to subject their feelings, and especially F.'s health, to the trial of nerve which would be incident to a departure from them under the circumstances. But I have been restless and uncomfortable ever since, as though my proper place were at the Seminary, to do what in me lay to protect it, and my own property, and that of others.

"In regard to yourself, I can only say that I have written letters and held conversations, in several instances, all exhibiting the views of your letter just received. I thought I understood your sentiments on this greatest of calamities perfectly, and have not failed, where I could, to enforce them. My dear friend, the Lord is a strong tower to them that trust in Him; and I earnestly pray that you may abundantly realize the truth, not only in security to you and your dear family, but in the peace, quietness and assurance of your own mind. Myself and family daily remember you in our prayers. Do write me as often as you can, and let me know how things are getting on.

"I came here from Staunton a few days ago, and will remain a month. My situation in Staunton was not favorable, and Mrs. S.'s and my daughter's health suffered. The evil was, no doubt, aggravated by the sudden death of my daughter in Richmond. My son Leonard is in an artillery company on Aquia Creek, my son Thomas has gone to the West, as one of the University volunteers, and my son William is employed as an assistant engineer on the railroad west of Staunton. We have heard of Mrs. Grammer, in Columbus, Bishop McIlvaine having brought the letter to Washington, but not from Mrs. Jerome, in Pennsylvania, nor Mrs. Smith, in China. It is altogether probable, nay, certain, that there are letters for me at the Seminary, at Alexandria, or at Washington. I am told there is a way of having them forwarded, but I know not how it is. Should you know, you will render a great service by having it done, and any expense incurred will be cheerfully paid. I am told that it is through the *Express Company*, and that it pertains only to foreign letters—the most desirable to us.

"Mrs. S. and my daughters desire to be kindly remembered to Mrs. L. and family.

"Ever your affectionate friend, W. SPARROW."

Nothing, during the summer, was done, in the way of specific effort, toward reorganizing the Seminary. In the month of October, however, there was a meeting of the Bishops, and some of the Trustees and clergy, in Richmond, with reference to an effort for such purpose. Dr. Packard being kept away by sickness, Dr. Sparrow was the only one of the Faculty present, and took part in the deliberations. Various plans were proposed and considered, but there was great difficulty in deciding upon any. The difficulty of communication was so great, and so little was known, at the beginning of this conference, of the condition of the Seminary buildings and grounds, so much doubt was felt as to whether the buildings were not destroyed, or damaged irreparably, that with some there was a decided inclination to find a new locality more in the interior, and there organize for future operations. Information was communicated that the buildings and grounds of the Hugonot Springs, in Powhatan county, some sixteen miles above Richmond, could be obtained for a comparatively small sum, $10,000, and it was proposed that this should be the locality. A committee was appointed to visit the premises, examine them, and make a report. Some, indeed, were in favor of the purchase, only for temporary purposes, and having in view a return to the old locality, as it would be a desirable investment of funds which, in all probability, through the contingencies of war, would become worthless, a result which was actually realized. As, moreover, the buildings were extensive, the plan included the restoration of the High-School at the same locality, and a temporary continuation, so far as the boarding department was concerned, of the two Institutions. The complications of such arrangement, and the anticipation of financial and other difficulties in carrying it out, led to its abandonment. Just at this point, moreover, reliable intelligence, from one who had come through the lines, was received, that the Seminary and its buildings, as he had seen them within the few days previous, were uninjured, and presented very much their old appearance. The effect of this announcement was very cheering, and it was eventually decided to give up the effort in regard to the High-School, and to make trial of the Seminary at Staunton. It is a noticeable fact, that the proposed new locality, near as it was to Richmond, was one of the few in Virginia untouched by military movement or occupation, and that its purchase would probably have saved its value in funds of the Seminary, those especially in bank stock, which at the close of the war were of no value. Dr. Sparrow evidently regarded the proposed scheme of reorganization, particularly that feature combining the two Institutions, as visionary and impracticable; and in this opinion, Mr. McGuire, the Principal of the High-School, fully concurred. It is a leaf in the history of the Seminary, as in the biography of Dr. Sparrow, which will not be without its interest to some of our readers.

The actual carrying out of the plan thus decided upon was unavoidably postponed for a few months. It was entered upon by Dr. Sparrow and Dr. Packard in December. In the interval the former was called as a delegate from the Diocese of Virginia, to attend a special council of the Southern Dioceses, at Columbia, South Carolina, to consider the question and manner of distinct organization. The result of this meeting was the proposal of a constitution to be submitted to the dioceses, and, upon their acceptance, to be the basis of a general council of the dioceses consenting. On his way to this meeting, he spent several days in Richmond, where the writer met him, and was particularly struck, in conversation with him, by the absence of two states of feeling which, at that time, with others, seemed so prevalent, those of bitterness and despondency — wrath against men, and want of faith in God. His invariable tone was one of forbearance and cheerfulness. The latter was most remarkable. Indeed, with the exception of the season of perplexity incident to the condition of things during the spring of this year, and before hostilities actually commenced, this peculiarity of his disposition remained unaffected. It was encouraging to one's spirit to be with him, to witness his repose of spirit, his cheerful trust in the overruling wisdom and goodness of God, his ready sympathy and prompt aid wherever they could be afforded. One little incident remains, coming up in conversation, and bearing upon the conflict then going on. He was speaking of the facility with which efficient soldiers could be created out of our population. "When," said he, "I was at Stribling Springs, I was walking with one of the boys, some ten or twelve years of age, who had been out with his gun in search of game. 'Look there, Doctor,' said he, pointing to a small bird up a tree some distance off, 'look there, I am going to shoot that bird's head off.' And sure enough, the bird fell, and his head was gone. Small chance for an object the size of a man if that boy should ever be a soldier."

The conference at Columbia terminated toward the close of November, and soon after the Doctor returned to Staunton. In December the effort was made to resume, with such students as could be obtained, the exercises of the Seminary. The number was small, and this was made smaller by the conscription of the next spring. Dr. Packard, at this time, rejoined him, and for five months they gave instruction to the students under their charge. In the spring of 1862 it was thought advisable, in view of military movements feared or contemplated, to make a change of locality. Dr. Packard, therefore, returned to his family, in Fauquier, and was prevented by sickness and other providences from taking part in the effort to keep the Seminary going, until after the close of the war. Dr. Sparrow, at the same time, moved to Halifax county, in the southern interior of Virginia, where, after awhile, he was rejoined by the students, and for five months, that is, until the winter of 1862, gave them instruction. During this time he found a home at the house of the Rev. John T. Clark, and, as mentioned by his host, was not only engaged in his teaching during the week, but nearly every Sunday, at one point or another, preached for his brethren in the neighborhood. "He was about four miles from my house," says the Rev. Mr. Powers. "I had known him before, and he frequently visited us during his sojourn in Halifax, walking the four miles, and sometimes spending a day and night with us. His unfailing cheerfulness, the charm of his conversation, his familiarity with every topic, at home in the simplest as well as in the most abstruse, and enjoying the one as much as the other, his unostentatious simplicity, his power of adapting himself to every one, so that all, children as well as grown people, felt at home with him, and delighted to be in his company, were traits that made us look forward to his visits with delight and expectation that we shall never forget." "Our little band," says one of the students of that time, Rev. William H. Meade, "was scattered from Staunton, whence Dr. Sparrow proceeded with his family, to Rev. John T. Clark's, in Halifax. Late in the following summer, some five students, P. D. Thompson, Davies, N. H. Lewis, E. H. Ingle, and W. H. Meade, collected around the Doctor, all except E. H. Ingle boarding in Mr. Clark's family. We were thus thrown into very intimate relations with him. A little later, two others joined us, Burke, and J. A. Mitchell, of Maryland. In the following winter we went back to Staunton again.

"The general result of this intercourse, while I do not recall anything special to relate in connection with it, was to deepen in us love and admiration for the man. There could be no question as to the Christian and the scholar. We found him genial and gushing as a boy; ready to take part in the homely sports of our country home. In social intercourse he took strong hold of the hospitable community in which he was sojourning. He was virtually, so far as the pulpit was concerned, the minister of the parish, preaching, as he did, almost every Sunday while I stayed in Halifax. He seemed specially to delight in the religious exercises Mr. Clark was accustomed to hold upon his premises for colored folks; often would Dr. Sparrow conduct them himself, while he was largely influential in getting us at similar work about the neighborhood. In a word, we were all drawn to him as teacher, counsellor, friend—almost companion—and to me his memory is precious."

One little circumstance, mentioned by the doctor himself, in connection with his sojourn in Halifax, just here has its place: "I was," said he, "one afternoon standing on the porch, and saw a wretched-looking man—a soldier—approaching, who, I supposed, was seeking assistance, and it was only after he came up and spoke to me that I recognized him. I did not know," said he, his face flushing and his eyes filling, "I did not know my own son!"

It was just before the removal to Halifax that an event took place of mournful significance to Dr. Sparrow, to the Diocese of Virginia, and the whole Church—the death of Bishop Meade. The Bishop's relations to the Seminary, as one of its founders, if, indeed, he may not be regarded as its founder, and, as President of the Board of Trustees, had brought him into close relations with Dr. Sparrow in his work. Their thorough accord upon the great questions at issue in the Church brought them still more closely together. It is deeply to be regretted that their correspondence, which seems to have been full and frequent, should have entirely disappeared. And it was with no ordinary emotion that intelligence of this mournful event was received by the survivor. His feelings found expression in the sermon affixed to the biography of the Bishop, preached originally, and soon after the event, at Staunton, but afterwards incorporated by Bishop Johns in his volume.

But the sadness of this loss to himself, in common with the whole Church, was followed by another of a personal, private nature—that of another beloved child, Mrs. Smith, in her distant home of missionary labor. It will be remembered that in the spring of 1861 he was greatly perplexed and grieved at the prospect of the abandonment of the mission, and the return homeward of herself and husband. Arrangements, however, had been effected by which the mission could be sustained. Scarcely, however, had he received the announcement of this fact, before it was followed by that of her departure. The following letter of Bishop Boone tells the mournful story:—

"SHANGHAI, July 30, 1862.

"MY DEAR BROTHER:—

"It grieves me to communicate the melancholy tidings we have received from the North. Your precious daughter Susan, our beloved sister, has been taken away from us. She was carried off by cholera, as in a moment. I will give the particulars in the words of Mr. and Mrs. McCartie, who, by a kind Providence, were with our brother and sister in the hour of their trial.

"Mrs. McCartie writes, under date of July 14th, 1862: 'Mr. Smith begs me to write a few lines to tell you of the unexpected and severe bereavement which has befallen him. Dear Mrs. Smith 'sleeps in Jesus.' She died of cholera, this morning. Dr. McCartie was providentially here, and it is a comfort to feel that everything was done for her that could be, although God has taken her to Himself. Mrs. Smith had been two weeks in Yentai (Chifoo), and was expecting to come home Friday, but was prevented. However, she sent her little Fannie and Johnnie, hoping to come the next day, but the very heavy rains prevented. Sabbath P. M. Mr. Smith went for her; she was delighted to reach home once more, but had suffered from headache all day, and after tea and prayers retired early. About nine o'clock she asked for some medicine for diarrhœa, as she feared she might disturb us in the night. About midnight Dr. McCartie was called, as she had cramps in her limbs; and from that time Dr. McCartie and Mr. Smith carefully watched and nursed her till six this morning. I find my husband has already written you a note, so I will not add more.'

"Dr. McCartie writes under the same date, Monday, the 14th July. He writes from Mr. Smith's house: 'My dear Bishop Boone: Mrs. McCartie and I accepted Mr. and Mrs. Smith's kind invitation to come out here on Friday P. M., although Mrs. Smith was obliged to remain in Yentai, in attendance on Mrs. Holmes, who had been sick for some ten or twelve days previously. The *rains* and the *Sabbath* kept us from starting from Larry-chow, and last evening Mrs. Smith was enabled to get out here, much worn out and ailing, owing to fatigue and care in nursing, which was too much for her in her state of health. Last night, about eleven P. M., she was taken with cholera, and, in her weak and exhausted state, a few hours have been sufficient to loose the silver cord, and while I am now writing (in hope to catch the mail) her spirit is just leaving the earthly house of her tabernacle, we trust to be clothed upon with her house which is from heaven.

"'Six A. M. She is gone. Poor brother Smith is heart-broken, but leans on Jesus. It is a comfort to us all that Mrs. McCartie and I are with him, although we have been able to do but little for our departed sister. Mrs. Smith said but little, but her answers to my questions indicated a calm reliance upon Christ, and a willing and cheerful submission to God's holy will. I said, 'You are willing to leave the issue with him?' She said, 'Yes.' 'Are you able to rely peacefully upon him?' 'Yes, I think so.' Mr. S. wishes her buried at Larry-chow. As soon as the friends can get here from Yentai we will determine upon the plans to be pursued. As the mail is expected in an hour or two, I have been obliged to write in great haste.'

"This is all the information we have received, and I have copied it for you, my dear brother, as I know every line will have a deep interest for you. We have not yet heard from Mr. Smith, and do not know if any news went home to you by the last mail.

"Mrs. Boone has written to Mr. Smith, begging him to send little Fanny to us, as we can perhaps take better care of her than any of his other friends. Jane, our Irish nurse, promises to do her best for her, and our little Robbie pleads very hard for a little companion. It will benefit both the children to be together, and I have no doubt Mr. S. will send her to us if he can make up his mind to the separation. I will write to him and advise him to come down himself, as it is too much for him to undertake a mission by himself. We may probably get a line from him before the mail leaves, and I will keep this letter open to communicate any further information we may receive. We are an afflicted mission, and we mourn deeply the loss of your dear daughter; but we know that 'He doeth all things well' who has taken her away from us, and we say to Him, 'Thy will be done.' It is *infinite wisdom* and *love* that have ordered this dispensation, and we want to be under just these two infinite attributes.

"August 2. We have just received news from Mr. S. as late as the 27th of July. He and the baby were both well. There has been sad mortality at Chi-foo. A Mr. Hall and child, Mrs. Bonheur, and the last remaining child of the Mills' have died. It is sad, sad; enough to make us all weep. God in mercy sanctify it to us all. You must all live under a dreadful tension, with so many dear ones daily exposed to a violent death. God in mercy grant us peace, on those terms He sees to be best for all. Mrs. Boone joins me in kind regards to Mrs. Sparrow and all your family.

"With much sympathy,

"Affectionately yours, WM. J. BOONE.

"*Rev. Dr. Sparrow.*"

In the spring of 1863, the year after, during the Diocesan Council, the writer visited, with the Doctor, the Bishop's grave, in Hollywood Cemetery, near Richmond. In the course of the walk he spoke of his daughter who was resting in the same locality, and of the other who soon followed her, and when he came to the grave of the Bishop, it was with deep emotion that he contemplated and spoke of it. His feelings toward the Bishop were very peculiar; those not only of high admiration and regard, but of obligation and deep affection. And when, some four or five years afterward, he was assailed as a teacher of false doctrine, one part of his reply was, that so far as two independent minds, seeking the truth, could be said to have the same opinions, the Bishop's and his were the same; that between them there was no substantial difference.

The return to Staunton took place, as we have seen, in the fall or winter of 1862–3. And with the exception of brief visits in the neighborhood, to preach, and the annual call to the Diocesan Council, in Richmond, his residence there continued until the summer of 1865, when he returned to the Seminary. His own memorandum, in the Record Book of the proceedings of the Faculty, made in 1865, gives us the material for this period:—

"In the month of May, 1861, the officers and students of the Theological Seminary were interrupted in their duties by the national calamities which fell upon them. The students dispersed to their homes, North and South; the Rev. Dr. May went to his relations in Philadelphia; the Rev. Dr. Packard to his, in Fauquier County, Virginia; and the Rev. Dr. Sparrow to Staunton, Augusta County. In Staunton, with the sanction of the Board of Trustees, was made the temporary location of the Seminary; some students assembled for instruction, and for five months Dr. Sparrow and Dr. Packard taught them in conjunction. This was during the months of December, 1861, and January, February, March, and April, 1862. After that, the former returned to his family, in Fauquier, and the latter retired, to avoid the dangers and excitements of war, to Halifax County, and there taught for five months. After that he returned to Staunton again, and there remained with the students which conscription left him, to the close of the war."

The life in Staunton would naturally be one of little striking incident. Reports of raiding parties, and military movements, especially toward the close, would, at times, abound, and be productive of their due excitement. With these exceptions, and making allowance for the common burden which rested upon all hearts, the little theological circle of professors and students went on without disturbance in their peculiar duties. Dr. Packard was not able to rejoin them after the return to Staunton, and Dr. Sparrow, therefore, in the work of instruction, went on alone. The recitations, part of the time, were held in the vestry-room of the church, sometimes in the Doctor's study; at times, when he was feeble, with the teacher on a lounge, in a reclining position—his "clinical lectures," as he himself humorously called them. As the number of students, for a large portion of the time, was very small, he took one or two pupils in the classics. With these were varied, as we have seen, his occasional duties in the pulpit. He always bore in warm and grateful remembrance the kindness and hospitality with which he was treated by this community; spoke of their thoughtful attention and aid, during a portion of his residence among them. And the impression made by him upon them was most salutary. To a degree shared by very few, he appreciated the great calamity which had fallen alike upon the country and upon himself. The length, and breadth, and depth, and height of that calamity, in all its consequences, material, social, moral, and especially spiritual, were painfully recognized. As a refugee, the peculiarities of this season of trial were especially wrought into his own experience. He was thus thoroughly sympathetic with those around him, but not overcome by despondency. He endeavored to be cheerful, and others were sustained and cheered by his presence and influence. "I saw a great deal," is the language of a correspondent, "of our departed friend during the war, and greatly enjoyed intercourse with him. He bore his trials, that of pecuniary pressure included, with Christian fortitude. Indeed, his cheerfulness was truly to be admired. I never heard him express himself at all as regarded the causes of the war; but only felt that it was a privilege to hear him converse, and that it was well to have been with him." "I saw Dr. Sparrow," says Col. Skinner, "during the last year of the war, very frequently, and I need not say I enjoyed greatly his kind visits. He wrote me a letter from the Seminary, shortly after his return there, expressive of his sense of obligation, and full of warm utterances toward the people of Staunton for their many kindnesses to him. I wish, very much, now, that I had preserved it." "The war, as you no doubt know, was a great trial to him; and the secular papers of the day, I think I heard him say, he never read. His heart was full of the tenderest sympathy for the people of the South in their sufferings. But, as a follower of the Prince of Peace, he deprecated all war; and my impression is—I would not like to speak with entire positiveness about this—that his opinion was, so far as our struggle involved and turned upon the maintenance of slavery, that we were hopelessly contending with the spirit of the age. He rather shrank from conversation on these subjects. I think it always greatly pained him; but I shall never forget his deep emotion one summer afternoon, as he paced my front porch, in full view of woods, and waving fields, and serene mountains in the distance, and poured forth his soul in holy regrets at the internecine strife in which our country was involved; so that even when, perhaps, I did not altogether coincide with him, I did not hesitate to admire his Christian earnestness, nor could I fail to discern that his spirit dwelt in the beauty of holiness. Could one but be favored with a record of his inner life during those years of trial, there are but few of us, I imagine, who would not derive spiritual benefit therefrom."

"He occupied," says another, Mrs. Sheffey, "a portion of the house of Mrs. K., but kept a separate establishment, furniture being provided for himself and family, and, as was, doubtless, always the case, he greatly enjoyed his domestic life. He endured some of the privations incident to the war. It was, however, the pleasure of the people to remember him in many acts of kindness and loving consideration. And it is a sweet pleasure to those whose privilege it was to share with him what God had bestowed on them, to recur to those troubled times, and to recall the memory of his grateful appreciation of the goodness of God in opening the people's hearts toward him. He was much beloved in the congregation, among whom he frequently ministered in holy things, in the pulpit and otherwise. He visited many families frequently, and systematically; and in some of them he was a household favorite. He was everywhere a welcome guest. His sympathy, his interest, and tender oneness with many of us in our sorrows, in connection with the trials of the times, can never be forgotten. His heart overflowed with tender feeling and grief as he witnessed the afflictions of our people; and to the sorrowing and anxious he always brought the precious balm of Christian consolation.

"His health was not robust; he suffered much from languor; but he abated not his work. He was afflicted with sleeplessness;

the noise on the streets, and the barkings of dogs at night, affecting his delicate nervous temperament, so as to drive away refreshing slumber. Indeed, to the writer of this he once remarked that he scarcely ever became fully unconscious in sleep. His favorite theme in religious conversation was, 'The Heavenly Rest.' On one occasion, he started from his seat, walked the floor hurriedly, and exclaimed: 'O, think what it will be to serve Him unclogged by these bodies!'

"He frequently spoke of death, and expressed the desire that he might not have to endure a long and wasting sickness, but that, if it were God's will, he might go quickly to his eternal home! And his Heavenly Father heard him, and 'so He gave His beloved rest.'

"Unselfishness and self-sacrifice were traits of character prominently brought forward during his stay with us. He was an exile from his once pleasant and congenial home, and exposed to many trials; but no murmur or complaint ever escaped his lips. He found God everywhere, and realized fully that for him all that was was full of blessing. He was calm and trustful in the midst of the most exciting events, greatly wise as a counsellor, and brotherly as a comforter. On one occasion he left his own place of abode, and, with his family, spent a week in a friend's household, to comfort and protect its inmates, who were deprived of the protection of the exiled head of the family.

"There were no busy, startling incidents connected with his stay in Staunton. But there was left behind him, when he went from our midst, profound sorrow at his departure, and the sweet influence of a thousand remembered acts of kindness and of love which make the sum of a good man's life. And among none will his memory be kept green and fresh longer than among his loving friends of old Trinity."

The following letter to Dr. Packard, who, at this time, was in Alexandria, belongs here. It contains a beautiful tribute to their departed colleague, Dr. May; and it affords, incidentally, evidence of the difficulties of communication between friends across the lines of the opposing armies.

"STAUNTON, March 25, 1864.

"REV. AND VERY DEAR BROTHER:—

"I do not know when I have been more agreeably surprised than by a visit, this morning, from Dr. P.; and I gladly embrace the opportunity of writing. I have written you several times during the last twelve months, but know not that you have got any of my letters. The last from you was November the fifth, and for many a month before I had heard nothing. I am thankful to learn that your health is decidedly improving, and that you are getting on pretty comfortably.

"I am in my old place, 'room-keeping,' as the phrase is. I have, at the present, Mr. Gardner, whom you know, Mr. McKim and Mr. Mitchell, from Maryland, and Mr. Hutchinson, who was in the preparatory department when we broke up. Between them all, I have a hard time. Ingle has been ordained, and is gone; Mitchell has, also, been ordained, and will, probably, soon go; and Gardner and McKim expect to be ordained in seven weeks. Others are talking of joining the Seminary.

"All your old friends here are as usual. Bishop Johns is going, in a fortnight, to Halifax, to keep house, at least for the summer. Do you know anything about my son William, or my daughter Mary? I have got but one letter from W., and I wonder at his silence.

"Your last letter did not reach me for two months after its date. Before it arrived I had been shocked and grieved, more than I can express, by the news of Dr. May's death. Few such Christians have gone to heaven of late years. It was specially sad to me that in his sickness his mind was unhinged by disease most of the time. I should like to have heard of his last moments if lucid.

"My family are, in point of health, about as usual. L., who made us a visit of a fortnight, the first in a year and a half, is quite well. T. is in Petersburg, but not at all well; and as to W., you know more of him than I do, most probably.

"My family here desire to be most affectionately remembered to Mrs. P. Write as soon as you can, and believe me, truly,

"Your affectionate brother, W. SPARROW."

"On the first day of January, 1865," writes Rev. Mr. Hayden, describing the last four months in Staunton, "I went to Staunton to enter the theological Seminary. I found a seminary in name, but hardly in fact, since it consisted of only one professor, Rev. Dr. Sparrow, and one student, Mr. Thomas C. Hutchinson, of Canada, a discharged soldier. Mr. H. was a man of considerable promise and great earnestness. He had entered in the fall of

1864, and died, I think, of typhoid pneumonia, on the 12th of March, 1865, leaving the Seminary once more with the one professor, and one student, myself. Dr. Sparrow was then living at Mrs. Porterfield Kenney's, and Mr. Hutchinson and myself boarded ourselves, at the house of Mrs. Wm. Kinney. Of the life of Dr. Sparrow during this time and the following months, until he removed to Alexandria, I suppose little could be learned from any one. Mr. Hutchinson and myself were in different classes, and, therefore, recited separately. I am sure Dr. Sparrow took the same interest in our studies, and lectured to us as earnestly, and with the same faithful devotion to his duties, as he manifested afterward when the Seminary was fuller and his classes more interesting. Excepting in the lecture, we saw but little of the Doctor; enough, however, to be deeply impressed with the saintly character of the man, and to learn to love him. His sons were all in the army, and one in a United States prison. As I knew them, he frequently spoke of them and of the war, but studiously kept himself in ignorance of much that occurred, hardly ever reading a secular paper. His purpose, doubtless, was to keep his mind free from the anxieties and excitements which such reading would produce.

"I remember, as a little incident, on one occasion taking him a plate of butter, I having learned that he had none; it was then worth $8.00 a pound. After thanking me warmly, he asked, 'How did you bring it—in a basket?' I replied, 'No, Doctor, I carried the plate in my hand.' Opening his eyes, as he was accustomed to do at anything peculiar, he said, 'I must congratulate you, sir, upon the absence of that false pride that would make many a man ashamed to carry a plate through the street.' As the thought of shame had not entered my mind, his manner and words I have not been able to forget. The Doctor had warm ties to bind him to the North, yet that his deep sympathies were with our people in their severe struggle, no one could fail to know from his spirit and conversation. My impression of such fact was deepened by everything he said on the subject. He had, however, peculiar views about wars. He seemed to think that no man should use weapons of carnal warfare, even in his own defence, and was accustomed to say that if his life were in danger he would not strike a blow. This sentiment the Doctor acted out, as he several times told us, even in respect to his property; that he had lost it rather than sue for his rights."

With the close of the war was the almost immediate presentation of the question of the restoration of the Seminary. The buildings had escaped destruction, but were still in use as hospitals, and in the hands of the military authorities. Even if turned over to their original owners, the expenses involved in necessary repairs and refurnishing constituted a serious obstacle. The buildings were a good deal injured, the furniture of the rooms entirely gone, the enclosures and out-houses had disappeared, and large portions of the grounds were covered with temporary structures for the accommodation of the sick and wounded. Still, it was deemed advisable to make a beginning; and this was entered upon in the effort to obtain possession. Success crowned this effort; and when, after a few months' delay, the Seminary buildings and grounds were turned over to the representatives of the Board of Trustees, it was resolved to attempt reorganization. In anticipation of this, Dr. Sparrow left Staunton soon after the close of hostilities. It was with feelings of affectionate interest in a community with which he had passed through the trials of a common calamity, as of grateful regard for kindnesses of which he had been a recipient, that he was prepared to take his departure. That departure was characterized by an act of thoughtful attention on one side, and of grateful appreciation on the other, which may well find place in this record; a closing token and evidence of friendship and regard, in a present, most delicately tendered, of the means to meet the expenses of his journey and removal. Dr. Sparrow would have been deeply affected by such an expression of kindness at any time, and under any circumstances; but, as coming from that community, in their circumstances of the spring of 1865, it was recognized as an abounding "of their liberality out of the depth of their poverty," and was, therefore, still more cordially appreciated.

After leaving Staunton, he stopped for a short time in Richmond, and from thence went to Baltimore and the Seminary. From Baltimore we have a brief letter to one of his former pupils, to whom we are indebted for portions of correspondence in the chapters preceding.

"BALTIMORE, July 8, 1865.

"REV. AND DEAR BROTHER:—

"I lately saw, for a few moments, a pamphlet by you, and what

I saw I was much pleased with. It has put me in the notion of scribbling these lines, though with a rheumatic hand, for 'auld lang syne;' though I confess I stand in doubt how such as I will be regarded, even by old friends at the North. If you can exercise no more flattering feeling toward us, I trust that, in your magnanimity, you will, at least, pity us! Do tell us how the Bishop's pastoral is going to affect you all. Should there be any 'Alexander-the-coppersmith' in your city, you may have trouble, and the next thing may be an *ecclesiastical* secession—*I hope with a successful issue.*

"I am here with Mrs. S. and my daughter Frances, and two sons, the latter looking for something to do. As soon as the Seminary is vacated, I return to it, and begin life anew, furnishing my house afresh with everything but a cradle! It seems strange to find myself so situated, but it does not dishearten me. If my strength were equal to my spirits, I should not mind it. If I can, I shall visit New York before the autumn, and shall take real pleasure in talking over old times, and being posted up for the past four years. You may judge how ignorant I am, from the fact that I never read the papers during the war. But in the meanwhile, steal a half hour, and write me at this place, telling all about yourself, and directing the letter to the care of Rev. Julius E. Grammer, St. Peter's Church, Baltimore.

"Ever yours, affectionately, W. SPARROW.

"*Rev. Dr. Canfield.*"

The event contemplated in this letter, the evacuation of the Seminary by its military occupants, took place very soon after it was written; and within the next six weeks the Doctor and his family were in their old residence. Dr. Packard was also present, having reached there before him. The prospect, indeed, was not at all assuring. Of the endowment of the Seminary, at least half had become worthless, and of that remaining a considerable portion was bearing no interest. The Seminary had to be refurnished, as also the houses of the professors; and for all, repairs, expensive and thorough, were urgently needed. It was all doubtful as to what might be anticipated in the material of men for the classes, and quite as much so as to the capacity of the Education Society to afford such pecuniary aid as might be needed. Still, the effort had to be made, and it was determined to begin at the usual time.

Providentially, there came relief just when it was most needed, in the shape of a legacy, made to the Institution not long before the war, and this secured temporary provision for the undertaking. Things were righted up as far as possible. Some few rooms were furnished in the Seminary; furniture enough, of the simplest kind, to enable them to live, was obtained by the professors; temporary buildings connected with previous occupants were removed, a rough enclosure for the grounds was put up, and the anticipated opening anxiously awaited. During a part of this interval, in the month of September, Dr. Sparrow was in Richmond, at the special Diocesan Council, called, in view of the condition of things which had prevented its meeting at the usual time, in the month of May. He was exceedingly anxious, in view of the interests of the Seminary, as of those of peace and love, that initiatory movements should be made for reunion with the General Convention. But to this, with the large majority of the Council, there were decided objections; and the whole subject was postponed until the next Council. With the termination of this Council came the time of commencement for the exercises at the Seminary.

During the preparations for this, or rather, just as they were beginning, and before the Seminary had been restored to its authorities, an issue, of very serious interest, both for himself and the Institution, was presented to Dr. Sparrow for decision: another invitation to Gambier. The authorities there, probably regarding the prospect of the restoration of the Virginia Seminary as a hopeless one, extended to him an invitation to a professorship in that Institution, and outwardly there were very considerable inducements in favor of the change. His account of its reception, and of his decision and reply, are contained in the following note to his old friend, Mr. Cassius F. Lee, who was then working with him for restoration at Alexandria.

"BALTIMORE, June 26, 1865.

"MY DEAR SIR:—

"I have just received your letter. I got here yesterday morning, by steamer from Richmond, after a most fatiguing journey from Staunton. But though wearied in body, Mrs. S., F. and myself have been refreshed in spirit by seeing our children.

"Immediately on the receipt of the proposition from Ohio, I declined it. I have no disposition to leave Virginia while she thinks my services worth having. Her being in distress is a reason with me, if I can live at all, to abide with her, and share her lot.

"Truly and affectionately yours, W. SPARROW.

"*C. F. Lee, Esq., Alexandria, Va.*"

With this determination, and with the feeling expressed a week or two after, in the letter to Dr. Canfield—"It seems strange to find myself so situated, but it does not dishearten me. If my strength were equal to my spirits, I should not mind it"—he was prepared to take his part in rebuilding what had been thrown down. The degree of success connected with that effort will form one of the subjects of the chapter following.

CHAPTER VIII.

THE WORK OF RESTORATION.

It was, as already hinted, under very discouraging circumstances that the session of 1865–6 was begun. Apart from unallayed excitement in one portion of the country, and hopeless depression in the other, the consequent feeling of uncertainty as to the political, social, and ecclesiastical future, there were, in the peculiar circumstances of the Seminary itself, certain features well calculated to produce discouragement. The loss of so large a part of the endowment, already mentioned, had its necessary influence. This, under the most favorable circumstances, would have been a serious calamity. It was, of course, greatly aggravated by those of the time. In the Diocese of Virginia, from which contributions might have seemed due, individuals and congregations, hitherto most liberal friends of the Seminary, were struggling with poverty. The diocese, moreover, had not, as yet, adjusted her relations to the General Convention; and there was, manifestly, a difficulty in seeking aid in that direction. In the other Southern dioceses there were the same difficulties, pecuniary and ecclesiastical; and, with the exception of Kentucky and South Carolina, but little sympathy, theological or ecclesiastical, with the Seminary of Virginia. The Johns legacy, which had come in opportunely for the special emergency of making the start, could last but for a short time. Contrasted with these prospects were the most pressing necessities, mentioned in the close of the last chapter, arising from the dilapidation and emptiness of the buildings, and want of enclosures for the grounds. As, however, the beginnings were expected to be small, provision was made to the extent possible for necessities as they might arise. The Prayer Hall was furnished, to be used for morning and evening worship, as also for Sunday services during the first four or five months of the session. It served, also, during the week, as a recitation room for Dr. Packard. Dr. Sparrow's classes were provided for in his study, the recitation rooms not being, as yet, furnished. The chapel having been used for religious services during the military occupation, was in somewhat better condition than the other buildings. In view, however, of the difficulty and expense of heating it, as also of the small congregation, it was not used until the following spring.

From the necessities of the case, and the material at hand, there were but two theological classes, a junior and middle class, and one of preparatories. Some of those who had been in Staunton, with one or two additions, formed the middle class, and the other two classes were made up of new material. Dr. Sparrow taught Church History, in addition to his usual course, and gave instruction, also, to some of the students in the Preparatory Department. Dr. Packard, also, had extra classes; and toward the close of the session one of the students, Mr. Dudley, now assistant Bishop of Kentucky, rendered very efficient aid in teaching preparatory classes. The number was quite as large, if not larger than had been anticipated; and the effect of getting under way was to give encouragement to all concerned. We have but a few letters of Dr. Sparrow's during this session. Accounts from some of his pupils give interesting particulars. The writer visited the Seminary twice during this session. During the first visit the Doctor was absent, called away by the illness, terminating in the death of his eldest daughter, Mrs. Jerome. At this time, the first of April, 1866, the appearance of things, especially of the grounds, was peculiarly discouraging. The very grass had, in many places, in the succession of camps, been killed to the roots, leaving the fields full of bare places. This, indeed, was very much the appearance of things in the country between the Seminary and Alexandria, as there had been no cultivation, except in small garden-patches, since the spring of 1861, and the ground occupied by the camps had been thus cleared of vegetation. The writer remembers, during this visit, standing in Dr. Packard's porch, on the bright April Sunday morning, and as he looked over the grounds and neighborhood in sight, it was with the involuntary question, can there be a restoration? Can any one hereafter have an idea as to how this place looked in former times? Wonderful it was how soon that restoration came. The very causes of the evil ministered to its removal. As soon as the camps were gone, the residue of those camps, the scattered seed of their forage, the enriching influence of human and animal occupation, hastened restoration. Grass, in an unusual amount, covered the country, and very soon the bareness had disappeared.

The second of these visits was immediately after the Council in Alexandria, nearly two months later, when he walked out with Dr. Sparrow on Sunday afternoon, and shared with him in the hopeful anticipation of restored prosperity to the Institution. The Council had just settled the question of the relations of the diocese to the General Convention. The board of Trustees had elected an additional professor, to take the duties of the lamented Dr. May, and there were favorable intimations that the number of students, for the next session, would be considerably increased. During this Council, the Doctor was still wearing a suit of Confederate homespun, one of the memorials of the season of trial through which he had been passing.

A brief extract from one of his letters of this session will show that, while hastily engaged in his work at the Seminary, his interest in the general affairs of the Church was undiminished. "I regretted," says he to Dr. Canfield, "that you were not in New York when I passed through. I should have liked much to have talked about old times, and got posted up for the years that I have lost in exile. There is one thing I exceedingly want to know in regard to the present, and that is the effect of the controversy between Bishop P. and his presbyters, in which you were *magna pars*. If you should have ten minutes' leisure at any time, do write me, and let me know. Why have not trials come? What is the influence of the whole affair on Presbyterial liberty? Have we secured by the movement anything in time to come? Do you ever come to the Capital? If so, do not fail to visit us here."

To Rev. J. A. Jerome.

"Theological Seminary, October 2, 1865.

"My Dear J.:—

"Having nothing very special to do to-night, I am disposed to drop you a line. Day after to-morrow my work begins. Two students are on the ground, and there is a fair prospect of several more. It would be absurd in us to look for any but the humblest beginnings. You have heard how we have all been sick, of the intermittent; but I doubt not we are all through the worst of it. I hope, therefore, that neither that, nor anything else, will call you back till your errand is accomplished. We shall take good care of M. and the children. I suppose you will want to be at the General Convention. J. has just written me; he will be there if possible. I wish I could be there, chiefly, however, to see the brethren from whom I have been cut off for five years. As to the Convention, the most expressive and efficient course they can pursue in regard to reunion is to be silent. Any one who really knows the South, must be aware that there is no separatist, schismatical spirit in the Episcopal Church thereof; all want to re-establish their old ecclesiastical relations. It is already done in spirit, and soon will be done in form, if loquacious political Churchmen throw no obstacle in the way. But why talk thus? The Lord liveth. Let me hear from you. Love to all the brethren you meet that will accept it.

"Your affectionate father, WM. SPARROW."

"THEOLOGICAL SEMINARY, October 25, 1865.

"DEAR J.:—

"Though I have so recently written to you, I am disposed to write again. I thank Mr. B. for his suggestion, and may, hereafter, turn it to account. I am glad to hear Mr. G. P. spoke about us before the Church Missionary Society, and was listened to favorably. It grieves me, however, to think that the liberality of so good a man as Mr. W. should be turned away from us by what occurred in the Convention. Be they right or wrong, we are not the Convention; and while we are not the Convention, we are ourselves, *i. e.*, the Seminary, the same we ever were. As long as I am connected with it, the Seminary shall always be what it was when dear Dr. May was of our number.

"Between him and me, and, so far as I know, between him and others who controlled the Seminary and determined its character, there never was the slightest difference of opinion. He supposed our calling was to teach theology, and not politics, and from the latter we all kept aloof. As regards war, oh, how earnestly did we deprecate it! He would gladly have given, I believe, all he was worth in this world to avert it, and so would I. As to slavery, while he and we all deprecated its sudden abolition as productive of mischief all round, we never regarded it as anything else than an evil, sooner or later, in the providence of God, to be removed. If the Seminary ever did work which was acceptable to God, and beneficial to the Church, there is no reason now, so far as its tone and principles are concerned, why it should not continue so to do. And for the same reason, therefore, the class of men who befriended us in former years may very consistently aid us in our present great necessity. When the Seminary ceases to sustain Evangelical principles, or presumes directly or indirectly to encourage disloyalty to the government under which we live, I shall consider it to have departed from its calling and original design, and I am done with it.

"The doings of the Convention, which you say produced such excitement, admit, on all sides, of a better and fairer interpretation than passion can at present give them. As you say, there was no 'dictation' in the conduct of Bishops Atkinson and Lay. Whatever their own private opinions on the subject in its political relations, they might very well wish that the thanksgiving should be confined to the restoration of peace. Under that word every man might surely be allowed to comprehend more or less, according to his own private opinions. If thankful for peace, especially under the circumstances, they must be opposed to war, and set against a return of it. They must, also, have acquiesced in the decision of Providence as seen in the finale of that war. In the present sore state of their feelings, then, why insist on more? What *spiritual* good can come of it? It is not for legislation of this kind to set the heart right, if it is wrong. And should it be thought that every member should adopt certain political *principles* under pain of virtual excommunication, let it be remembered that, so far as the *theological enunciation* of these principles is concerned, all parties are already agreed. It is only in the *practical application* of them they differ; and to insist that they practically agree in this regard, is to identify church and state, religion and politics. But I did not mean to say so much. I only add, that ten years hence many among us will wonder how we could be so biased by feeling. Thank God, it is very much precluded in my case by my position.

"Do you hear anything of the New York troubles? As I said in my last, that, in my view, is vastly more important to us as a Church than much that is now exciting them in Philadelphia. I am curious to see how the missionary bishops will come out, and whether they will give us one out of the batch. I hope C. is a sound man, *for a High-Churchman.*

"I have done as you directed with the bond, and returned it to the company. Return my kind regards to the brethren that wished to be remembered to me. I know nothing of D. By the way, late as it is in the year, if the E. K. S. has an almanac for this year or the next, or both, send or bring them with you. Mrs. S. made us a visit to-day, with her children, and all were well enough to receive them. Love to Dudley.

"Your affectionate father, WM. SPARROW.

"*Rev. J. A. Jerome.*"

"THEOLOGICAL SEMINARY, November 27, 1865.

"REV. AND DEAR BROTHER:—

"Your letter was a great cordial to my heart. The older I grow the more I value my friends; and now that my own proper contemporaries are passing away so fast, I must cultivate the good will of the next generation, else I shall be left a friendless man in the world.

"Since I came here I have been as busy as my health would allow. Seminary duties, some of them extra; domestic duties, specially pressing; and the duties of beggar-general for the Institution, something new to my experience, all put together, have tried me not a little. Had it all come upon me in warm weather, I should have broken down. As things are, I get along as well as I could expect. The last three months in the year have always been the best of the twelve for me.

"We have seven students, and expect before New Year's Day to have three more. We have two classes in theology, and a class in preparatory studies. They take as much time, as you know, as if each class numbered thirty; while they do not afford the healthful and invigorating stimulus which relieves and sustains the teacher. Our great difficulty, however, is to find means to support them, and to furnish them rooms, for the rooms were left empty when the buildings were vacated. Should you come across any moneyed and liberal soul who would be, probably, willing to help a young man in preparation for the ministry by a scholarship of $200 at his pleasure, you will render a great service to that needy young man, and our so needy Seminary. Owing to the unhappy position of our diocese, we have to do whatever we do in this matter in a private way, that is, by private application. Mr. A. sent us $500, for which we were most thankful. Except this, we have received nothing from north of Baltimore, which is fairly overrun with Southern beggars! But I did not mean to run on in this way. Dear F. was very sensible of your kind remembrance of her, sent by D.; and we feel it vastly more than if we were the objects of it. Please remember me most kindly to Mrs. H., whom I hope to know better than I yet do, if we both are spared so long.

"Ever affectionately yours, W. SPARROW.

"*Rev. John P. Hubbard.*"

As this first session was one, in many respects, very peculiar, both in its circumstances and prospects, and the manner in which it went on, the account of it from some of those who were present will not be without its interest, especially in its bearing upon the subject of our narrative.

"It would be difficult," is the language of one of these, the Rev. David Barr, "to find a much more desolate-looking place than the Seminary and its surroundings on the chilly and bleak November evening of my first acquaintance with it. It stood in the centre of a desolate region, in which a fence could not be seen for miles, excepting around a house here and there, and upon which the sod had not been turned, seemingly, for years, saving, now and then, a small patch or garden. In striking contrast with this was the cordial greeting given me by the good Doctor upon my arrival. He had re-established himself in his long-deserted home, and was then working and praying for the bright days soon to come for his beloved Seminary.

"I found five students present, viz., Horace E. Hayden, now in the diocese of Pittsburg; James H. Williams, now rector of Grace Memorial Church, Lynchburg, Virginia; Benjamin E. Reed, now rector of a church in St. Louis, Missouri; Edward W. Hubbard, now rector of Brandon parish, Virginia; and Nicholas H. Lewis, who labored in the ministry but a few months in Matthews county, Virginia, and then rested from his labors forever. Dear Lewis! so gentle, so earnestly pious, and so pure!

"I was the sixth arrival. In a few weeks William H. Laird, now rector of Leeds parish, Fauquier, arrived; and before many weeks had passed came the lamented Bruce Davis, son of the late blind Bishop of South Carolina, a young man of singular sweetness and meekness of temper. Next came, I think, George H. Fitzhugh, now of the diocese of Easton; then young Davidson, of Missouri, who remained but a few weeks; then Thomas U. Dudley, Jr., now Assistant Bishop of Kentucky; then Walter Q. Hullihen, now rector of Trinity Church, Staunton; and lastly, a Mr. Phelps, who professed to have been, at one time, a Baptist minister, and had renounced that persuasion for our ministry. Mr. Phelps remained but a few weeks. I never heard what became of either him or Mr. Davidson.

"It would be impossible to describe the spirit of the little flock gathered there from different quarters, and in connection with them the few returned inhabitants of the Hill, during that first never-to-be-forgotten year after the resuscitation of the Seminary. What prayerful diligence on the part of the students! What unity, what love, what sweet Christian fellowship among all! What joy such a state of things must have afforded to our teachers, especially to the Doctor, who had, as it were, therein, an earnest of the future glory of the Seminary, the object not only of his affections, but of his most ardent wishes and single-minded exertions. And, considering his health and age, what exertions he made. During that first winter we had no means of riding into Alexandria, but had to walk the distance of three miles, and at that time over a very rough road. Mr. Sparrow walked to Alexandria and back, nearly every day, for several weeks, if not months, and generally alone. Frequently he would be so long detained in town as to be in the night getting home; and it was during these night trips, through the mud, and water, and snow, finding his way alone, that, as he once told me, he underwent no little suffering. On one occasion he said he was detained in Alexandria till about dark, and the weather was extremely cold, so cold, indeed, as to render it necessary to guard against freezing. When within a mile of the Seminary, his attention was attracted by groans, he could not tell whence. After listening awhile, he called, and was answered by some one near him. With some difficulty he found the sufferer, who proved to be a poor old negro man, so nearly frozen as to be unable to walk. The Doctor immediately determined to get him home, or sheltered elsewhere, if possible; and soon had the happiness of hailing a passing wagon, upon which the old man was placed, and taken home. When, with difficulty, the Doctor himself reached home, he found his own eyelids frozen together. He had, in a great measure, actually felt his way home.

"It was my privilege, on one of those cold evenings, to accompany him from Alexandria to the Seminary. He made the time pass rapidly by his conversation, mingled with anecdote, always pointed and appropriate. As we walked up the avenue in the front of the Seminary, he turned to me and said, in his genial manner, 'Well, Mr. B., I am reminded of an anecdote I once heard of a couple of Irishmen. The first of them, arriving in America, settled down near some great natural curiosity. When his friend arrived, he proposed that they should make this curiosity a visit. 'How far is it, thin?' 'Twinty miles!' was the answer. 'Och, mon, it's too far.' 'No,' said Pat, 'there are two of us, and we'll make it tin apiece!' 'Now,' continued the Doctor, 'your young eyes have enabled us, as it were, to shorten the distance from town, and make it one and a half apiece.' On another occasion, he, one of our clergy and myself, came over the same road together. Among other topics was that of exercise, the Doctor remarking upon the difficulty of taking just enough, neither too much nor too little. 'This subject we are upon,' said he, 'reminds me of an anecdote that Bishop Chase used to tell with great gusto. Some years ago, the Legislature of Vermont had under discussion the charter of a railroad. Some wanted it to run through one township, and some through another. Finally, a green Irishman, from one of the back counties, jumped to his feet, and cried, 'Misther Prisident, when I studied Vargil, I was taught to go through nather Cyrus nor Carabozus, but between the two. So I now say, sir, let the road go nather through this nor that township, but between the two.' Take the middle extreme!'

"As to the work of the Seminary, the theological classes, at his lectures, recited, at first, if I rightly remember, in either Dr. Sparrow's study or in one of the students' rooms. Perhaps they did so the whole of the session. Dr. Packard's classes recited either in his study or in the Prayer Hall. The preparatory classes in Greek and the sciences recited to Dr. Sparrow in his study. His fondness for Greek made him a pains-taking teacher in it, and he was so instructive a teacher, that things which others might consider dry were invested by him with interest and freshness. I think of those 'Greek days' with Dr. Sparrow in his study as among the most pleasant and instructive spent at the Seminary. It was after one of those hours that a fellow-student remarked that Dr. Sparrow went more naturally to prayer than any one he ever knew. He seemed so completely lost, in a moment, to all around him, and in such close, childlike and loving communion with God as his Father.

"The Faculty meetings were not restored at once; not, indeed, I think, until toward the end of the session. Lewis had been there before the Seminary closed in 1861, and retained sweetest impressions of the Faculty meetings in which the lowly-minded Dr. May participated, and he aroused my desires for their speedy beginning. Upon their revival I found that the half had not been told me concerning them. The remembrance of them is refreshing and edifying. In them Dr. Sparrow was a spiritual and intellectual power; so that the heart was indifferent that was not then roused and made more earnest by his appeals and exhortations. His closing prayers were as sweetest manna, for he seemed to carry us with him, and besiege the mercy-seat for grace and blessing.

"During the first half of the session we used one of the second-story rooms in Aspinwall Hall as our dining-room, our number being too small and our arrangements too simple to require so large a room as the dining-room under Bohlen Hall. We messed, as it is called, each man paying about twelve dollars and a half a month, and had one of our number as caterer. In the early spring of 1866 we were favored with the services of Miss Jones as our matron, a change for the better decidedly, in many respects; and this change was followed by our removal to the dining-room under Bohlen Hall.

"We were scattered, as regarded our accommodations, in the three principal halls, Aspinwall, Meade, and Bohlen, one or more sleeping in each. Aspinwall was principally occupied, however, as affording better rooms and rendering things more cheerful and home-like. Prayer Hall was used for public services till the early spring of 1866, I think, the chapel being out of repairs, perhaps, and certainly very cold and without stoves. And as those were days of poverty, we used what we had.

"I never heard the Doctor allude to his affliction in the loss of Mrs. Jerome. But I know that the God whom he served in his heart of hearts caused His consolation to abound toward His servant, yes, even over all his sorrow. Yes! A man of heavy afflictions, he was, also, one of much consolation."

"Never," says another student of this session, "never before I heard Dr. Sparrow was I able to listen to a discourse so attentively as to remember the entire substance of it. But some of his Faculty-meeting lectures have so burned themselves into my brain, that I have gone to my room and have written them down from my notes, without, I am sure, losing a word. Poor P., whom I knew well, said to me, shortly before his death, that he had gone to the Seminary to enter the ministry simply as a profession in which he thought he could excel; but that Dr. Sparrow, in the Faculty meeting, had spoken words that revealed to him his condition as a sinner, and that to these lectures he owed, under God, his conversion. After that I know he entered the ministry to win souls, and it was in doing this he met his death.

"One little note of the Doctor, as a memento of that session, is by me. It is connected with the boarding establishment. Fortunately for us, while messing, during the first few months of the session, all had been in the army and knew how to endure hardness. Our fare for some weeks was very little better than the rations we had received in the field. We discovered, after a time, that the cook boiled the potatoes in the coffee-pot, and made the coffee afterward. The peculiar flavor thus imparted to the coffee led to the discovery, and caused a change in our household arrangements. The butcher failed one day to bring out our supply, and we sent to borrow from the Doctor. The answer was as follows: 'Dear Mr. H. It just now occurred to me to ask Mrs. S. if she had any fresh beef. Her reply was, 'Yes, but it is in the oven for to-morrow.' She sends some of it 'with the smell of fire on its skirts,' hoping it may, nevertheless, answer.'

"He once told me of his advice to a young friend, in whom he felt a deep interest, on the eve of her marriage. 'Doctor,' was her request, 'you know that I am soon to be married; won't you give me some good advice about my new life?' 'I replied, I have only one piece of advice to give you, and that is, keep alive the spirituality of your husband; and I believe she did so,' he added."

At the Council, a short time before the close of this first session, it was determined by the Board of Trustees that an appeal should be made to the friends of the Seminary, to enable it to go on, especially in view of the needed support for the new professorship. Dr. Sparrow was appointed and requested to make this appeal, and, in accordance with this action, visited Baltimore, Philadelphia, and New York, on his mission. His effort to raise $5000, for five years, to be paid in annual installments, proved successful, and he returned home greatly cheered. A second short visit perfected his work, and he began to prepare for the work of the ensuing session. A couple of letters, one written while upon his errand, and another very soon after his return home, describe, among other things, a part of his experience while his work was going on, and show his gratification in view of the manner in which his appeal met reception.

"No. 3 Bible House, New York, August, 1866.

"My Dear Mr. Lee :—

"I have longed to write you, because I know you were anxious to hear from me, sympathizing with me and my errand. I have been silent only because I feared to say anything, lest there be utter disappointment, but I now write *in good hope.* A more unfortunate time I could not have chosen for my trip. Everybody is from home. In addition to the bareness of the field, comes the pressing demand occasioned by the Portland fire. Lastly, and chief, there stood up before me the Council speeches.* Still, I am confident I can raise the salary. Indeed, I am determined to try for $2000, instead of $1500. Yesterday I met Mr. ——, and before we parted he pledged $250 per annum for five years. It may be that I shall get as much from a couple of other gentlemen of this city. Besides the necessary annual subscriptions to make up the salary, it may be that I shall get a little something for the endowment. Some may give out and out who will not pledge themselves ahead. You see I speak cautiously, because I am nervously timid. Still, I can say to you with confidence, *the salary will be made up.* It takes time, and it is very trying to the patience, but I am prepared for anything that will secure the end.

"I am confident I can get $350 a year in Baltimore, as much in Philadelphia, more here, with subscriptions of $100 in scattered parishes. Dr. Dyer has taken a great interest in our affairs. We are under great obligations to him.

"I find I have to move very slowly, or I am made sick. I was very unwell in Baltimore, from over exertion, but am determined to be more moderate in my movements in future. The very noise and confusion of this city break me down. It is well called 'Babel.'

"I ought to say that Mr. —— received me very kindly, but seemed fixed in his purpose of lending us no further aid. However, he said, as warden of his congregation, he would favor an annual subscription of $100 for five years. Perhaps it may be increased. Before parish pledges can be secured, the rector and wardens, if not the vestry, must come together, but such meetings are now impossible. I can meet the one or the other, but not both together. Dr. —— was manifestly ready, but he must first talk with his wardens. So others.

* In the discussion as to whether the Diocese of Virginia should resume its former relations to the General Convention.

"Excuse this scrawl. I am so nervous I can hardly hold my pen, and my head is as unsteady—not with strong drink—as my hand. But these are small matters, if the Lord will be pleased to prosper us, and put the Seminary on its feet again, and in a sphere of usefulness.

"Please remember me kindly to Mrs. L., and believe me

"Ever yours, WM. SPARROW.

"*C. F. L.*"

"THEOLOGICAL SEMINARY, P. O., September 2, 1866.

"MY DEAR BROTHER:—

"Last night I got your letter. Let me assure you it afforded me great pleasure. I am thankful to God that you are so blessed in your work, and that amidst all your health has been preserved to you. May the same Divine blessing rest upon your person and your labors, even to the end.

"Doubtless, nominally, there ought to be more sponsors than one, and these sponsors ought to be communicants. The former regulation seems to have sprung ex abundante cautela; and the latter out of the manifest propriety of the case, and the spirit of the service in regard to the sponsorial feature. But neither is of Divine prescription, and the time was, I think until the eighth century, when no more than one was required, and that might be a woman, in the case of a male or female child alike. But, doubtless, in all ages, the *norm* of the case had to yield to necessity; *that*, in a matter of this kind, has no law. The Bishops of our Church have never called the clergy to account for accommodating themselves to a necessity *which is real*. To my mind, it is a great deal better to acknowledge the necessity, and yield to it, than resort to private baptism. That would be violating the spirit of the one service, that we may not violate the other. For though the word *expedient* is used about bringing the child privately baptized to the church, so is the word *exigence*, some other than a want of proper sponsors, used as the proper ground of private baptism in any case. I have spoken of our Bishops. The English Bishops also openly sanction such views. Archbishop Whateley, I remember, in one of his very last charges, when he had become an authority in the British Church, says, 'Ministers are bound to do *the best they can* toward complying with the prescriptions of the Church, in every way guarding against the thoughtless carelessness and the irregularities which are apt to find their way into the administration of this holy ordinance.' As to the case you propose, of the pious, *professing* mother who wishes to bring her child to baptism, *I* should have no difficulty about it. If she can get a second sponsor, well; if not, in the name of Him who 'suffers little children to come' (children brought each one by its mother), let her child be dedicated to God in that sacred rite. The main point is, where necessity compels us to depart from the usual order of procedure, to take care to show, as you are prepared to do, that the departure does not grow out of any superstitious opere operato notions of the ordinance, but that we deem it profitless unless accompanied with religious training.

"Let me correct a mistake. You draw an inference from the words, 'wilt thou be baptized in this faith,' as to what the sponsor may be. It strikes me these questions indicate nothing in regard to the religious condition of the sponsor, one way or the other. He merely answers for the child *because* it cannot answer for itself. It is a kind of legal fiction. He thereby indicates no character, assumes no responsibility; that is done by his standing and receiving the charge that he see the little one religiously brought up. Though it should afterward turn infidel, he is clear if he has seen that it was brought up in the nurture and admonition of the Lord.

"You ask after some book on the subject. Libraries have been written, chiefly controversial, each writer looking at it in one or two points of view; hence no one, or two, or three books, do it full justice. I suppose you can learn more of the subject from Goode than any one author. You can get it almost anywhere. You inquire about my 'Rationale.' Are you not confounding two things that are very different; a bishop and a presbyter; a man of the Seventeenth century and a man of the Nineteenth; a High-Churchman and a thorough-paced Low-Churchman? The 'Rationale' which I suppose you refer to was on the whole Prayer-book, a small work by Bishop Sparrow, who was concerned in the last revision of the English Liturgy, in Charles II's time. Is it possible you have so poor an opinion of my discretion as to suppose I ever published a book? I have been so far guilty of folly as to publish a pamphlet or two; this I confess, and can only plead human infirmity; but a book!

"You ask after my success at the North. The time was most unpropitious; nobody was at home, and I left my task unfinished. But still I had such success, that on the strength of it Dr. Walker is coming. I go North again this month or the next. I was treated most kindly. The alumni of the Institution have shown the very best feelings. I was received by them with open arms. But one, in a situation to help, declined. There may be much Christian character under the repulsive disguise of political and military hostility both North and South. A man may be a Christian, yea, a lovely Christian, though a Monarchist, an Oligarchist, or a Democrat, and though ready to go to the extreme of blood for the maintenance of his principles. This the world's history shows. It comes of our fallen state that there should be such anomalies and contradictions among us. What is the part and duty of one who belongs to the kingdom which is not of this world, is a nice question in some respects. One point is certain, it is not for the followers of the Prince of peace, at least after the sword is laid down, to throw oil upon the fire, but rather water.

"Assuring you I shall always be glad to hear from you, I am,

"Most affectionately yours, W. S.

"*Rev. Randolph H. McKim.*"

"THEOLOGICAL SEMINARY, October 4, 1866.

"MY DEAR J.:—

"It was my purpose, when I left home the last time, to make you a visit before my return; but circumstances compelled me to change my plans, and to be back at the opening of the term. It has just begun, with twenty-one students, all theologicals but four. This, you will say, is doing well. I have been busy all the summer in raising money to support the professors. It is not the new Professor only that has to be maintained. The Trustees, at present, have enough only to support one. I have done nothing in Philadelphia yet, but hope for something from Brooks, Parven, and Matlack, and the gentlemen whom they control. Of course it won't be much. Besides salaries for the professors, we need means to repair roofs, etc., and to support indigent young men. But I trust the Lord will provide.

"My trips North have increased my anxiety for the prosperity of this, and of every other Evangelical Institution. Ritualism seems to be sweeping over the Church. Not that I care so much about forms, and gestures, and garments, etc.; it is the principles out of which these things grow, and which are, under their cover, gradually introduced, that trouble me. The Bishop is in New

York now, helping in the consecration and election. I am curious to know how things will strike him.

"Do write soon, and tell me all about yourself, and the children, and your parish. Be assured of the tenderest love of all under this roof.

"Affectionately, W. SPARROW.

"*Rev. J. A. Jerome.*"

As had been anticipated, the number of students at the opening of the session, 1866–7, was found to have increased upon that of the previous year, and before the close of the session ran up to twenty-five. One of the recitation rooms was furnished, and from this time the classes met in that, and in the Prayer Hall. The arrangement of studies, as in the time of Dr. May before the war, was resumed; Dr. Sparrow taking his former course of Evidences, Systematic Divinity, and Creeds and Confessions. Monthly missionary meetings were re-established, and the students vigorously resumed operations at the various mission stations in the country around; and as most of the chapels had been destroyed or burned, their first effort was to rebuild them. The extra work of the preparatory classes, for the first third of the session, was divided among the professors; after this other arrangements were made. The material of this session was remarkably homogeneous, socially and ecclesiastically, and there was very little of a stirring character in the way of ecclesiastical discussion. In truth, the angry waves of another and more fearful controversy had not yet entirely subsided; and the feelings of anxiety and uncertainty as to many of its results, kept out of sight issues which in other parts of the Church were more earnestly contested. The Ritualistic controversy, for instance, becoming of interest and importance elsewhere, was only, in the diocese and Seminary of Virginia, looked at as from a distance. The session, therefore, partaking, in many respects, of the characteristics of the one preceding, was passed in great harmony and satisfaction.

One portion of Dr. Sparrow's work for this session, and, indeed, for the next four or five years, needs here distinctly to be presented, that of keeping up pecuniary supplies for the Seminary. Under God its continued existence depended very largely upon those efforts. These were twofold: first, to keep himself in communication with the contributors to the $5000 fund for five years, reminding them of the time when installments were needed; secondly, in any case where these failed, through death of the contributor, or from other causes, to find a supply to the deficiency, and then, further, to seek new contributions. How much depended upon him in these respects will be made manifest by a single fact. The first contribution of the $5000 was all paid for the five years, and there was an overplus. A second contribution of the same nature, to the extent of $7000 or $8000, pledged during the last few weeks of his life, has not, to more than about one-fourth of its amount, been realized. Other reasons, and good ones, may be given for this difference. But one, and a most important reason for that difference, was the fact of his lamented departure. His relations to the two classes of sectional feeling were unique and peculiar, and as they bear upon his work for the Seminary, a work which no other man, at that time, could have performed, it will not be out of place to exhibit them. His sympathies and affections were deeply enlisted for the community in which his lot was cast. He had, also, affectionate relations with many of those with whom they were in conflict. He believed, moreover, that both of them were largely blamable; one for making no effort, by prospective legislation or otherwise, to get rid of a social and moral evil, the irritating cause of much of the trouble; the other, for the resort to violence when the moral influences of truth and reason were the only proper weapons. But these views were held without sectional feeling, and without bitterness; because, although born in this country, he was not an American. He never knew, and could not be made to understand, how an American, on either side, say like Bishop Meade in one section and Bishop McIlvaine in the other, felt in this great contest. The associations, and impressions, and agencies, and influences of his life, up to his seventeenth year, would seem to have rendered this impossible. As to the question which of the two parties was more in the right or the wrong, he put it aside, refused to entertain it. Whether, under the circumstances, that issue ought not have been resolutely faced and decided, is another question; which would, probably, by both parties in the case, be answered in the affirmative. Without going into any such question, it is sufficient, for our purpose, to recognize how, from this his peculiar position, he was able to exercise the influence which he did in both directions. He loved both parties; was beloved and respected by both in return. His whole effort and desire, therefore, when the war ended, was to reconcile them fully; to work through such reconciliation for the great objects to which his life was devoted.

Returning to this work, in its specific form, as it went on in the duties of the Seminary, it, of course, found but little variation from that of previous sessions. There would necessarily be the adaptation of the material of his instruction to the peculiar aspects of contending truth and error, as established in the prevalent current of theological or ecclesiastical opinion. As already hinted, the pressure from other sources had kept from view some of the forms of controversy elsewhere becoming very prominent. With one feature of the existing state of religious controversy he at that time expressed great gratification, the manifest fact that Christianity, whether as defended or attacked, perhaps most clearly shown as attacked, occupied so large a share of the thought and heart of cultivated men. This opinion was especially called forth in connection with his perusal of Ecce Homo, and in it he saw an augury of good. He was persuaded that if men could be induced seriously and earnestly to discuss the problems of Scripture, and of Christian truth, their discussions would eventually be productive of benefit. And as a favorable indication, he gratefully recognized the improvement in the tone of infidel writers upon those of an earlier period.

Very soon after this session opened, the following letter was written. It was called forth by the sudden death, by violence, of a friend, with whom, as a fellow-refugee, he had passed through the trials of the war, at Staunton, and was addressed to his sorrowing companion:—

"THEOLOGICAL SEMINARY, NEAR ALEXANDRIA, VA.,
"October 13, 1866.

"MY DEAR FRIEND:—

"It is with a distress I cannot express that I have just heard of the terrible calamity which has fallen upon you. My first impulse was to take my pen. But wherefore? Why intrude upon the sacredness of your grief, while your heart is bleeding so profusely? This is not the time for the ordinary attentions of friendship, nor for ordinary sympathy of merely human kind. Such things seem only to mock a sorrow so deep as yours. Even though I might be well incited to write, by the recollection of our intercourse in Staunton, and of the substantial kindness of your departed husband to me and my family, from the day he came to Augusta County till the very day he left it, still it is only as a Christian friend I presume to send these lines. In God's name, as a minister of Christ, I would fain offer consolation, not by speaking of my feelings of friendship and sympathy, but by turning your thoughts to Him whose friendship was tested unto death, and whose sympathy is not, as that of mortals, inefficient, however sincere, but is mighty through God. With Him is strong consolation. Let His word be implicitly taken, when He says: '*Come unto me all ye that are weary and heavy laden, and I will give you rest.*' He is the Great, the Infallible Physician of the Spirit, and can staunch and heal every wound, however deep. His word is with power. His grace is sufficient for every emergency, even yours. 'Cast your care upon Him; He careth for you.' We are already assured of His interest in us; only He would have us make trial of His love. Take occasion from this dark and mysterious Providence to go to your Saviour as you never went before; submitting everything into His hands, and desiring to know no law of life, or purpose, or feeling, but His gracious will, and you will prove, in your own personal experience, that all His promises are yea and amen, and that

> 'Behind a frowning Providence
> He hides a smiling face.'

It may tax our faith to believe this; but—'Lord, we believe; help Thou our unbelief.'

"My dear Madam, it might, perhaps, almost seem as if I could not talk thus if I really felt the greatness of your calamity. But the more I think upon it, the more it grows upon me. My heart sinks within me when I think of the *widow and the orphan children*, the *cause* that made them such, and the *consequences* which may follow the bereavement. And it is because of my thorough conviction that this affliction is, in many respects, above the common lot, that I thus forego all earthly considerations, and would turn your heart heavenward. Mortals cannot help you, but God can, and God will. Was He not in Christ, and did not Christ go about doing good, delighting especially to visit *the house of mourning?* May His presence be with you and your family; and dark as this dispensation is, may the time soon come when you will see it all in the clear light of His everlasting love.

"Of course I expect no response to this. It would be wrong in me to do so. I write that you may gather from my letter that there are many Christian friends, afar off, who are thinking of you, and praying for you.

"Affectionately your servant in Christ,

"WILLIAM SPARROW."

During the spring of 1867, and toward the close of the session, Dr. Sparrow had an opportunity of again visiting Staunton, and taking part in the election of the Assistant Bishop, held at the Council in that place. In this election he felt the deepest interest; and while recognizing the qualifications of the other candidates, especially those of that eminent man who was elected by the clergy, and who has just passed away from us, Dr. Andrews, his judgment and his preferences were decidedly in favor of the candidate actually elected. One little incident of this election may be noted; it was the last appearance and the last ecclesiastical action of Dr. Sparrow's old colleague in the Seminary, Professor Lippitt. As one of the oldest clergy of the diocese, he made one of the first nominations, that which eventually received the vote of the majority.

"'Has it occurred to you,' said the Doctor, leaning back, with a comical expression, and in a half whisper," writes a lay delegate, who sat behind him as the election was going on, "'has it occurred to you how many here are speaking, and will vote presently, for only their second choice?' Seeing my slowness in taking, he added, with a twinkle, 'modesty forbids their bringing forward their first.'"

At the close of the previous session there had been no graduating class, and, of course, very little in the way of exercises of commencement. With this of 1866–7, the old order was resumed. The essays were read by the senior class; the ordinary address by one of the Faculty; and the address and delivery of diplomas by the Bishop. A catalogue of the Seminary, the first since 1860–1, had been gotten out during the session, and the prospect, in various respects, was exceedingly favorable, that, in due time, the Seminary would be going forward in full and successful operation.

Part of the vacation was spent in a visit to the West, in a visit, among others, to his old friend and colleague, then residing in Pittsburg, Dr. Preston. This friendship went back to those early days at Worthington and Gambier, when they worked and counseled together, and it only terminated, or was, rather, for a short time suspended, by the death of Dr. Sparrow. In the earlier part of this volume extracts from letters of Dr. Preston, as to his departed friend and associate, will be found. In a very little time, however, his own departure came; and we may now think of the sanctified friendship of almost half a century, as blessed with endless renewal.

With the next two sessions, those of 1867-8 and 1868-9, the agitation of the Ritualistic controversy went on, and, of course, made itself felt in the theological community of the Seminary. This controversy demanded and received from Dr. Sparrow his deepest attention. He felt himself, and he felt that the Institution with which he was connected was, pledged to the principles and views of evangelical truth for the support of which it had been originally established. A departure from these principles he regarded as not only a departure from the truth, and a sacrifice of that truth, but as a departure from the object for which the Seminary had been established and supported; as, therefore, involving a fraudulent misappropriation of sacred funds from the specific purpose for which they were given. "Our flag," said he, in speaking of the possibility of the extensive prevalence of a different class of views—not as extreme as those of the Ritualists, but those in opposition to which the Seminary was founded, of the school of Seabury and Hobart—"our flag is nailed to the mast; and if it goes down, we must go down with it." With these convictions he watched this new movement, or rather this new form of the old Tractarian movement, with the deepest interest. From the beginning he recognized its real character. Knowing, moreover, as he did, how the same errors, essentially, had been toyed with by a large party, perhaps the ruling majority of our Church, he was anxious to see whether in this new aspect they would have the same reception. He was therefore highly gratified with the first declaration of the Bishops in regard to Ritualism, and with what seemed a very extensive indisposition to accept the views put forth in the little volume of Bishop Hopkins. It was not so much with Dr. Sparrow a question of æsthetics, as of doctrinal teaching; not of flowers, or crosses, or dresses, or processions, but of truths obscured or falsehoods symbolized; of one system of doctrine put aside and another elevated. In itself, therefore, and in its doctrinal results, the controversy was to him of the deepest importance.

But this controversy was watched by Dr. Sparrow with peculiar interest, as to its bearing upon another practical question, that of the real toleration of men of Evangelical views, in what they had always claimed as an exercise of their lawful liberty. Supposing, without admitting, that some of these things were irregularities, would or could the dominant party allow and tolerate greater irregularities to those engaged in the new movement, and go on in their former intolerant course toward Evangelicals? The result of the Tyng trial, of the Cheney case, and the loud condemnation of Episcopal clergymen who communed with other Protestant clergymen during the meeting of the Evangelical Alliance—indeed, the general drift of ecclesiastical legislation, to the time of his death—impressed him painfully as to what might be the final result. His conviction was that there ought to be greater freedom of action and of ritual, to all classes, or greater stringency in demand as to doctrine. The former would secure peace, in the way of dissentients agreeing to differ, the latter in the real unity of inward agreement. That the latter mode of settling the difficulty would be adopted he had very little hope; and events seemed to show that the former, for one class, was as far off as ever. As to the doctrinal views involved in the new movement, Dr. Sparrow was too profound a theologian not to recognize that it was the old enemy in a new uniform, a materialized Christianity, against which his whole life and teaching had been directed. Its specific importance was that it was more open. There was less effort to hide its essential character. And it had associated with itself additional elements which, to certain classes, were making it more attractive.

But while thus deeply interested with this form of development, and its anticipated results, he was not wanting in like interest as to others. Allusion has been made as to his estimate of the moral and religious significance of such works as Ecce Homo, and its various replies and defences; to the evidence which he gratefully recognized, even in semi-Christian and positively anti-Christian works, of the hold which revealed truth and its issues had upon the mind and heart of the age, and upon men of certain classes, and of a certain kind of culture, beyond anything of the kind in previous experience. Of course such evidence was heightened in the appearance of works decidedly defensive of the great principles of revealed truth, such, for instance, as the Duke of Argyle's "reign of law." The more outspoken forms of unbelief, those especially connected with investigations in the department of material nature, had not assumed the prominence with which they have since come before the world. There were, however, clear indications of their approach; that the materialized Christianity which was vexing the Church would find its support in a materialized philosophy which was seeking to debauch the intellect of the world. The former, as more directly affecting the life and doctrine of the Church, as coming in conflict with principles of Christian truth, more naturally became, with him, the object of attention.

With these feelings it was that he attended, as a delegate, the General Convention of 1868. It was scarcely with the hope, but still with the question as a possibility, will anything, in the way of legislation, take place through which the existing and increasing evils of symbolized Romanism in our midst can be reached and arrested? As a member of the Convention, he took no part beyond his vote, and conference with his friends and colleagues. With the results he was not encouraged; indeed, he regarded the change in the Canon, as to those who could minister in congregations, as not only unnecessary, but as positively damaging to the Protestant spirit and cause in our Church. Fully appreciating the reasons presented by some of his ecclesiastical friends and leaders in favor of the change, he still believed that it had injured the great cause to which he and they were alike devoted. It was, in his estimation, another onward step in the process of dissociating the Protestant Episcopal Church from sympathy, feeling, and interest with the non-Episcopal Churches of Christendom—in other words, from Protestantism; and that it would be accepted by them, and by a large portion of the Episcopal Church, as meaning that they had no right to exist, had, in truth, no proper ecclesiastical existence. To this last dogma, that of excluding communities from the very name of Christian Churches, not on moral, religious or theological grounds, but upon those of mere outward order and arrangement, he stood in the most uncompromising antagonism. His theological nature repudiated it as a monstrous absurdity; his moral nature, as a great moral and religious outrage. The progress of this dogma, the implicit form in which it was accepted and acted upon, were facts which gave him pain, not merely in view of the error involved, but of its dwarfing and debilitating influence upon ecclesiastical and religious life. His most unsparing attack upon it, the Commencement address of 1869, was, not improbably, suggested by the results of this Convention.

Before leaving these few opening sessions, we may touch upon two points of interest which, at the time, were productive to Dr. Sparrow of some considerable anxiety, requiring tact and good feeling to deal with them successfully. The number of students for the session 1867–8 doubled that of the year previous, ran up from twenty-five to fifty. With this increase, in a little time were developed two sources of anxiety, of which a large portion fell to his share, as presiding official of the Institution. One of these was the feeling or suspicion of a portion, not of all, of the students from the North, that there was a strong prejudice and animosity against them in the Seminary, and in the community around. In some cases the impression was removed. In others it proved ineradicable, and those entertaining it finally left the Institution; although in no single instance could there be ascertained by the Faculty, through personal inquiry of the complainants, a specific case of positive incivility. The most hopeless form in which these impressions existed, hopeless as to the prospect of their removal, was that which took the direction of alarm, fear of personal violence from imagined lawless combinations investing the Seminary grounds, or lying in ambush for students on their way to Alexandria. This, at the time, by those resident at the Seminary, was seen to be utterly absurd and without foundation. Never, perhaps, was its quiet neighborhood more free from elements of disturbance.

But these impressions, however absurd in themselves, were anything but absurd as to be dealt with and disposed of—anything but absurd in their consequences. Some of them were communicated to friends of the Seminary at a distance, and at this season of her peculiar need closed their hearts to her appeals, or led them to contribute to her aid with the feeling that in all probability it was to the promotion of sectional animosity. The whole matter, to Dr. Sparrow in particular, was a source of the deepest annoyance and anxiety. The kindness and courteous liberality with which he had been met in his appeal for aid in Northern cities, he felt, had placed him and the Institution under great obligations. He was anxious to express his sense of such obligation. The arrival of every student from the North was welcomed, therefore, not only as an indication of returning confidence and good feeling, but as affording opportunity for such expression, as also of making returns, in some form, for benefits received. Everything of the kind indicated in these difficulties interfered with the attainment of his desires; and he was ever on the alert to explain differences, and remove apprehensions. In most cases he was successful; and it is due to the students from both sections to say that their admirable spirit sustained and aided him in his endeavors. So much so, that within the course of two or three sessions this element of anxiety entirely disappeared; may be said, at the present time, to be unknown.

Connected with this source of anxiety, in the increase of the number of the students, was another, having to do with a portion of them, those constituting the Preparatory Department. The peculiar object and idea of that department was to provide instruction for a certain class desiring to enter the Seminary, candidates for the ministry not sufficiently advanced in knowledge to enter a college class, and yet too far advanced in years to be classed with boys in an ordinary school. As, however, the instructors provided for these could, without additional labor or expense, instruct others, the department was enlarged so as to take any who were preparing for the ministry, above the age of eighteen, that at which students were admitted to the theological classes. But it was never intended as a grammar school for college classes, or as a place of preparation for other Institutions. Misapprehension upon both of these points seemed to find place with pupils of this earlier period, some of whom went to other seminaries, and others to secular institutions. The distinct manifestation of this abuse soon wrought its own remedy. But it had its effect in another direction; increased existing fears and doubts of some of the friends and governors of the Institution, as to the expediency or propriety of such department in connection with the Seminary. By some the objection was urged that the two years in the Preparatory Department, and the three in the theological, was too long a period to be at any one institution, though it was admitted that at the University, or any other secular institution, such prolonged residence would be eminently desirable. Then, again, it was objected that such arrangement would secularize the members of the theological classes; though it was admitted that in all other institutions class influences were from above upon those below, rather than from below upon those above. In reference to this whole subject, Dr. Sparrow took a most decided position. Most of the plans proposed by the objectors and doubters he had himself tried, or seen tried by others. Most of the difficulties he had carefully considered. And, while distinctly recognizing that there were cases in which this initial preparation could go on more advantageously elsewhere, he, at the same time, felt assured that there were many others, the majority, for whom the Preparatory Department constituted the best, and, indeed, the only effective provision that could be made. His appeal always was to its successful operation; that, since originated in the Virginia Seminary, it had been adopted in other institutions, and that the real question was, not whether the authorities could dictate, to material with which they were in no relation, other and better courses elsewhere, but whether, if it came, should it be provided for? The continued effectiveness of this department, and the gradual recognition of its real character and work, eventually disposed of most, if not all, of these objections. Dr. Sparrow was permitted to see its successful operation. Its material at the time of his death was equal, if not superior, to that of any former period; and he had the gratification of knowing that, of the graduates of the three or four preceding years, some of the most promising, as to efficiency, were among those who had received their preliminary training in the Preparatory Department.

His last performance of duty in this department, in the way of active instruction, was during the spring of 1869, through the sickness of the regular tutor. This necessitated a division of his work among the professors; and for three months Dr. Sparrow taught the class in Greek, very greatly to the delight of his pupils. Subsequent to this, as Dean of the Faculty, he (occasionally) was present at recitations of the classes, and made it a point to show his deep interest in their advancement, as in the thoroughness of the process by which it was made.

These duties and labors were pleasantly relieved toward the close of this session, by an event of a most gratifying nature, and one which for a time removed from him a source of anxiety. This was the munificent donation of $100,000, from A. G. P. Dodge, Esq., to the endowment of the Seminary, relieving it very largely from its pecuniary embarrassments. Mention has already been made of the five years' subscription secured by Dr. Sparrow, in 1866, and of the task falling upon him in the way of its collection.

As the active medium between the trustees and the subscribers, it was a matter constantly upon his mind, involving continuous correspondence. At the same time, he was making effort for an increase of the permanent endowment. Three of the five years over which the subscription extended had passed. The question as to what would supply its place with the close of the remaining two, naturally presented itself, and these efforts had in view its practical solution. All these anxious questions seemed, in this donation, to be satisfactorily answered, and the Doctor was thus enabled to rejoice in the assurance to the Seminary of relief from its embarrassments. The writer well remembers his beaming countenance as he walked in and announced the unanticipated but agreeable intelligence; how, as he walked to and fro, he gave expression to his feelings of relief, gratification, and of gratitude to his God for its bestowal. Those bright anticipations, in all respects, were not fully realized. They were, however, in many.

The Board of Trustees were thus enabled, at once, to put in repair the buildings of the Seminary and the residences of the Professors, as also to make provision for a fourth Professorship. The benefit of the donation in these forms was immediately realized; and although it did not go to the extent and desires of its donor, yet, in its actual reception and use, to the amount of nearly $30,000, before the reverses of 1872, it constituted by far the largest contribution which the Seminary has ever received from any one individual. It may thus properly constitute a ground of obligation and of grateful acknowledgment to its recipients, as it may of gratification to its donor.

Mention has been made of the Commencement Address of this session—1868–69. It is one of the most striking of Dr. Sparrow's productions, a tract for the times, the earnest outpouring of the author's heart in reference to evils which he recognized as injuring and destroying the real life of the Church, and against which he would desire to warn his brethren. It was listened to with deep interest by the Alumni and clergy present, and the delivery was followed by a request for its publication. As this will probably be given in full in the present volume, or in a volume of the Doctor's sermons, no further account of it just here is given. There are several letters to pupils, on matters of interest at the time, which may at this point be inserted. One of them will very naturally constitute the introduction to a topic by which they are followed.

On a Minister's Receiving the Title of "D. D."

"Theological Seminary, July 9, 1867.

"My Dear ——:—

"My pen has been laid by for nearly a fortnight, in consequence of sickness. I now resume it to say that I have lately heard of your great titular distinction. And so you are one of the great fraternity of doctors—doctors of law, and medicine, and farriery, and rain, and witchcraft, and theology! I hardly know how to treat you in the premises; to rejoice or sympathize with you; to act as the bridegroom's friend, or as one of Job's comforters! On the whole, I am disposed to regard it as a calamity. So it was to me when it befell me; so at the time I regarded it. That it should mean nothing I did not like, for I loathe all humbugs; and if it meant something, and that something was anything, I felt I could not fill it out; and so, instead of serving, it would do a disservice, raising expectations only to disappoint them, and make my deficiencies the more apparent. Thus, you see, I am, in view of my own experience, quite at a loss how to address you on this 'interesting occasion.' However, to come down from these heights and take a common sense view of the subject, I would fain hope it is a matter of small account every way. Doctorates, after all, it should be remembered, are as numerous and cheap as blackberries, and are thought no more of than the title of professor; and professors we have of dancing, and the extraction of corns. While this is the fact, I do not think you need be much elated or depressed by the action of your alma mater. The only tangible and available idea I can gather from the whole affair is the suggestion that, as it comes from a learned institution, and has reference to the highest of all sciences, it may well set us striving after solid information and well-considered opinions.

"Yours affectionately, Wm. Sparrow."

"Theological Seminary, October 19, 1867.

"Rev. and Dear Brother:—

"I am sorry to learn your fears about the godlessness of your town, though there are so many churches in it. It is a sad fact that there seems so great a disproportion between the means of grace and the effects of grace; between the light enjoyed and the resulting holiness. The perception of this enters into the motives of some in favoring ritualism, and multiplying ceremonies, emblems, forms, postures, processions, colors, paintings, statuary and music. But the yellow fever, or the plague, is not to be cured by pepper-mint. It is not by such might or power that the work is to be done, but by 'my Spirit, saith the Lord.' And the Spirit does not call for such means and appliances, such channels through which to reach the human heart; there are enough of these already. What was the instrumentality through which, in Apostolic times, such moral wonders were effected? It was not the Church, as a great and well-organized and perfected system of ingeniously contrived means, brought to bear in a very complex way upon society. Religion was a simple thing, and it came, of course, to society; but much more to the individual, and took hold of him with power, and made him, consciously to himself and manifestly to others, 'a new man.' And the medium through which the Spirit of the Gospel thus reached him, and transformed him, I believe, was *the highly spiritual character of the first preachers themselves.* That is the instrumentality which God has always chiefly employed for introducing a new dispensation of religion into the world, or for reforming an old one, or for any way 'reviving His work' in the world. We have, I was going to say, churches enough, and ministers enough, in point of numbers; but ah! the quality is by no means what it ought to be. Till that is improved, I despair of much progress in the number of Christian disciples. When the 'head' of supply is high, the waters will flow further and stand deeper. When it is low, they will be both circumscribed and shallow; the latter, I will venture to assert, is the case in your town. Not that the ministers who are and have been there are not able and educated men. So we think of our ministers, of course, and as to others, we can hardly say their 'pulpit' is more 'imbecile' than ours. What we all want, to advance the cause of Christ, and convert 'godless' villages into pious communities, is more of the simple 'truth as it is in Jesus,' putting itself forth through a living ministry, thoroughly imbued and informed by it. This, and this alone, will restore to us Pentecostal blessing and prosperity.

"Dear brother, you will say 'this is the old thing over again; the old man is garrulous with his pen as with his tongue.' I plead guilty. I had no thought of filling my sheet of paper in this way when I began. You will forgive me. I speak from the abundance of my heart. It is all the time, more and more, as I watch the state and progress of things in the Christian world, overflowing with these convictions and sentiments.

"You have heard that Mr. McKim has accepted Christ Church, Alexandria. It is a great satisfaction to me to know that he will soon be in our midst.

"We have forty students on the Seminary Hill, and look confidently for two or three more. When I see them thus multiplying, I am sometimes ready to wish the vigor of former years were restored to me, that I might better discharge my duty. But He who put me here knew the imperfection of His instrument, and decreed its gradual failure and decay, and that should be enough for me. Oh, that we could lose ourselves always in His sovereign authority and infinite glory!

"*Rev. T. U. Dudley, Jr.*"

TO THE SAME.

"THEOLOGICAL SEMINARY, November 14, 1868.

"DEAR BROTHER:—

"I received your letter, and thank you heartily for it. You were not mistaken in the interest I took in regard to your determination about going South. It had been much in my mind from the hour you mentioned it in New York. I feel persuaded you have done wisely, and that God will bless you in what you have done. As you hint, the mere effort, by prayer and self-examination, to find out the will of God, cannot fail to benefit. The further we can get into that temper of mind in which all is referred to God, and nothing reserved for ourselves in independence of Him, the happier, the more spiritually powerful, and the more useful shall we be. As to anything other than you have got in your present position, it will come in due season. Only wait the Lord's leisure; the Lord's, I say, not the world's, or the Church's, or man's leisure, but the Lord's.

"I do hope I shall be able some time to write that letter about Baptism I heard you speak of. I firmly believe the subject admits of being clearly and satisfactorily set forth. The main requisite to a right and easy understanding of it is, that we approach it in the proper attitude of mind, and from the right direction. Method is everything in such matters. For instance, we ought to begin our examination of the subject with the true normal case, the case of adult baptism, the only case that is undoubtedly mentioned and clearly exemplified in the New Testament. Then, again, we should descend from the general to the particular, not inversely. By this I mean, we ought first to settle in our minds, on grounds of reason, the teaching of the Old Testament, and the spirit of the New as compared with the Old. What is the relation of things external in general, in the Church of Christ, to things internal, and what, consequently, is the design and use of sacraments in particular. Thirdly, we ought to familiarize our minds with the strong Oriental way, throughout the Bible, of representing all spiritual exercises and subjects in material language. Occidentals have blundered because they have forgotten the first law of all sound interpretation, namely, to place themselves in the mental and ethical attitude of the authors; and so, having started wrong, have landed, at last, it may be most logically, in the grossest superstition and the rankest absurdity.

"Yours affectionately, WILLIAM SPARROW.

"*To Rev. T. U. Dudley, Jr.*"

"THEOLOGICAL SEMINARY, January 16, 1869.

"REV. AND DEAR BROTHER :—

"When I look at the date of your letter, I am ashamed. And yet I can safely say, my silence has not sprung from indifference. On the contrary, I feel a thrill of interest passing over me when I reflect that to-morrow you enter on your duties in Christ Church. Absent in body, I will be with you in spirit on the occasion. My heart goes forth in most earnest prayer that God may abundantly bless you in that new and important enterprise.

"Dear brother, God has given you talents, educational culture, qualities of temperament, providential discipline in the way of trial and occupation, which, as means and instrumentalities, authorize us to hope that you may do much for the glory of God and the good of man. And if your life is long spared, I shall look confidently for it, provided all these gifts and facilities are sanctified of the Holy Ghost. In saying this I am not enunciating an abstract dogma. There is no vital doctrine of the Gospel so constantly in words expressed, and yet, practically, which is so habitually shelved, as that of the presence and power of the Spirit. Men labor and toil to realize the very body and blood of Jesus Christ as present in the elements of the Lord's Supper, and they contend for, and never lose sight of, the supposed power of the priesthood to forgive sin! But, alas! the presence about which, theoretically, there is no dispute, and the power to which, in words, it is confessed all efficiency in the things of God properly belongs, are not sought, and counted, and involved, and habitually leaned upon, as they should be. In saying what I have said above, therefore, I am expressing a deep, practical conviction, which I want to see deepened more and more every day in myself, and those whom I love, and to whom I look as fitted to be useful in my Master's service. Most clearly do I see, in my own case and history, that if I have ever done anything for my Saviour's cause, it was just so far as and so long as I lived in His Spirit as my element, listened to His Spirit as my prompter, leaned upon His Spirit as my strength, and prayed in His Spirit as the unfailing procurement of needed, real good. And wherein I have failed—and my life has been, to a sad extent, a grievous failure—how clearly do I also see it has come of self-dependence, and self-seeking, and self-sufficiency. *In* ourselves we are weak; *out* of ourselves, strong. As the Apostle has it, 'when I am weak (in feeling) then am I strong' (in fact). But when the Apostle said this, he was living very nigh to God. One who did not so live, could not in truth speak thus. It would not be truth to him in fact or feeling. It might be in some sense his creed, but it would not be his life. Let us, dear brother, live nigh to God, and carefully drive away anything that would put itself between us and Him. How much there is thus to interpose between us and Him! The world in its various forms of fashion, and beauty, and eclat, and popularity, and prominence, and high life, and luxury, and pride, will push between us. Even the Church may exercise an intervention of hindrance rather than help, and by its organizations, and offices and forms, hinder that ultimate and loving intercourse of the soul with God which constitutes the character of the Christian and the power of the Christian minister.

"I did not mean to run to the end of my paper before I had begun to answer your letter. Yet so have I done. I hope you will pardon the error, as it was one of weakness, not intention. In reply to yours, I had many things to say, but I cannot say them now. Indeed, Weldon has just come to take letters to the office, and I must close. I may write my answer at another time, either on paper or viva voce. In the meanwhile, accept this random outpouring of my heart, from

"Your affectionate friend, WM. SPARROW.

"*Rev. T. U. Dudley, Jr.*"

"THEOLOGICAL SEMINARY, July 26, 1869.

"REV. AND DEAR BROTHER:—

"I have been on the point of writing you every day for a week, but have put it off, partly because I have been expecting to hear from you, and partly because I have thought you might be in Norfolk. My business is that redoubtable address, or discourse, or discourses, or sermon, or homily, or baccalaureate exhortation, or whatever else you may choose to call it (?). You may think it much ado about nothing; but a hen that lays an egg, however small, once in ten years, may be allowed to cackle over it. Have you got the manuscript for Mr. Pridham, and have you sent it to New York? That is all.

"I suppose Cheney's trial is nearly over. However it is determined it will prove important. If he is acquitted, it will help to deliver us from that rubrical martinetism which has of late been in a course of imposition on our Church, while latitudinarianism is allowed in the infinitely more important matter of doctrine. If he is condemned, it will lead to the establishment of a number of independent Episcopal Churches, till at length they get a Bishop at their head, and so we shall have another Episcopal Church in these United States! We already have the Romish, the Moravian, the Greek, perhaps the Swedish, and the Protestant Episcopal; why not the *Reformed Protestant Episcopal?* Oh, when will Churches learn wisdom? The world is wiser in its generation than they. The one great defect in our leading men is, they do not enlarge their ideas enough. They are using the microscope, when they ought to be employing the telescope.

"Ever yours, WILLIAM SPARROW.

"*Rev. T. U. Dudley, Jr.*"

EXTRACT FROM LETTER DATED JULY 7, 1869, IN REFERENCE TO ADDRESS ALLUDED TO IN LAST LETTER.

"After writing, delivering, and then reading in print, a man's own productions—oh, how he loathes them! To go through the correcting of the proof has been like taking nauseous medicine. I have felt at every turn ready to 'throw up,' in every sense of the expression.

"Ever since you told me about that little piece of poetry which has touched so many people's hearts on this and the other side of the Atlantic, I have felt a desire to see it, and have inquired for it in vain. What is its title, and where is it to be had? My heart is frozen, even in this hot weather, and I want to thaw it.

"Affectionately yours, W. SPARROW."

"July 28, 1869.

"REV. AND DEAR BROTHER:—

"Our correspondence, or at least mine, is becoming quite active. It can hardly be necessary to send another title page. On the one you sent did you put the authority by which the *thing* was published? On no account can I be responsible for *exposing* such a bantling to the public gaze! I am more than willing to *father* it, but I can't *vaunt* it. Publication looks a good deal like vaunting. In yesterday's letter I inquired, at the printer's request, about the number of copies to be published. You will please answer the question to him.

"I have been amused at the requests already received for copies of the Address. That I have spoken out on the notion of the value of tactual succession, seems to be the point of interest. Perhaps it would have been well if I had made that the sole topic of discourse, instead of crowding in so many others.

"Affectionately yours, W. S.

"*Rev. T. U. Dudley, Jr.*"

"THEOLOGICAL SEMINARY, FAIRFAX CO.,
"November 22, 1867.

"REV. AND DEAR BROTHER:—

"I received your letter and the inclosure last night, but regret to say I can do nothing for your friend in the matter about which he writes. No one of our young men is prepared to enter on the field indicated. This is to me especially sad, seeing the people crave ministrations of an evangelical stamp.

"I was not a little pleased to receive your letter; it brought up many old recollections which were very pleasant, among the rest the trip I made with you long years ago to your sister's in Detroit. I was then young, and, though sickly, vigorous; now I am old, and though I still work, my energy is not as exhaustless as it was. My hope is, if I live, to visit Gambier next summer. I should have done it this year, but the res angusta domi prevented. Should I accomplish my purpose, I shall hope to have a long chat with you. Our Seminary, thank God, is prospering beyond our expectations; we have upward of forty students; but though numerically we prosper, *nummularily*—pecuniarily, we are very much straitened. Still, we are very hopeful.

"Mrs. S. desires to reciprocate your kind remembrance. My family is now small. Out of nine children but one is with me, and she an invalid—Frances. These changes forewarn us that the last change is near.

"With kind regards to all who remember me, I am, very truly,

"Your friend and brother, WILLIAM SPARROW.

"*Rev. Mr. Blake, Gambier, Ohio.*"

"THEOLOGICAL SEMINARY, November 11, 1868.

"MY DEAR J.:—

"On the whole, the Convention, if it did little good, also did little harm. The Bishop's Pastoral is as outspoken as the famous Declaration.

"Dr. B. spent last Sunday with us, and preached two most excellent sermons. I think he is somewhat liberalized in his theological views, though perhaps morbidly sensitive about 'the germs.' Large bodies move slowly, and we are a specially slow, if not large coach. In due time, by patience and kindly discussion, and, above all, diligence in the preaching of the Gospel to sinners and saints, our wishes in regard to the Prayer-book must be gratified. The prospect at this time is better than it ever was. I am only anxious about the *temper* of the brethren. This point must be carried by love and good works, not by polemic bitterness and party tactics. Do write me soon. All send their love. With love to the children,

"Your affectionate father, W. SPARROW.

"*Rev. J. A. Jerome.*"

"THEOLOGICAL SEMINARY, December 17, 1868.

"MY DEAR J.:—

"What startling and distressing events we have been called to experience recently. The removal of Parven and Rising is certainly a mysterious event. It would seem as if they were the very two men whom we could not spare. I look upon it as a call to Evangelical men to cultivate personal religion more. It is by this only the Evangelical *party* can flourish. It began in this, and in this must continue. What a blessed thing if such should be the result of this trying dispensation. Two taken to heaven, and the rest left upon the earth advanced in their preparation for heaven.

"Your affectionate father, WILLIAM SPARROW.

"*Rev. John A. Jerome.*"

"THEOLOGICAL SEMINARY, February 24, 1869.

"REV. AND DEAR BROTHER:—

"Ten days ago, Mrs. Sparrow said to me: 'You never hear from Mr. H. now; why is it?' Before this, I had purposed, from the time of the 'verdict,' to write to you, and soon after she thus spoke your parochial pamphlet arrived. Ever since, I have been waiting a moment's disengagement to take pen in hand. You know, dear brother, how deeply I sympathized with you and watched the progress of your troubles. When I came to have an interview with you in New York (too brief, by the way), and saw how sleek, and fat and flourishing you had come out of your trials, I was almost ready to say to myself that I had fallen into the error of a needless waste of feeling! But, on second thoughts, I looked at it as a matter of thankfulness that you were kept in such peace, and especially that matters were likely to reach such an issue as they have since reached. Your pamphlet makes me further grateful to our heavenly Father that He has borne such testimony, by the fruits of your labors, to the soundness of your principles and the singleness of your views. His name be praised!

"Do write me at some leisure moments about you and yours. I want to learn about *each one* of the family. I have been grieved to hear that Mrs. H's health is not good. I had a letter not long since from dear Mr. S., sending money for the Seminary, but he told me nothing about M. He invited our Bishops on to Boston, kindly promising that he would do what he could, but not otherwise speaking encouragingly. They did not go, and I regret it. Finding that, personally, they could do so little in New York, perhaps they thought it a wild-goose chase to go further North. They were treated with much personal kindness in the great city; but because Virginia is still unreconstructed, I fear there is a want of confidence in *us*. Our Northern friends ought to distinguish between three classes—the Faculty and the Bishops, the Students, and Society at large—in these parts. The first class confess themselves bound by every obligation, as men and Christians, to cultivate kindly feeling toward those from whom they were separated by the war, and to do so not only in form, but in deed and in truth. As to the students from the two sections of the country, they are living in wonderful harmony and brotherly love. The questions growing out of the war are tabooed universally. Now and again, I suppose, a word may be uttered on one side which the other may not like to hear, but it must be a very rare thing indeed, otherwise they could not live so fraternally as they do, and the good feeling is increasing every day. Even in reference to the third class, outsiders, this last remark is true. Feeling in society is generally softened, and I trust, before long, we shall be as we once were, and in even a far healthier condition.

"To hasten on the day there is but one way, the way of forbearance and love. Evil is to be overcome by good. But why do I thus *prose?* Forgive the impertinence. With much love to Mrs. H. and all the family, I am ever truly,

"Your affectionate brother, W. SPARROW.

"*Rev. J. P. Hubbard.*"

"THEOLOGICAL SEMINARY, July 1, 1869.

"MY DEAR J.:—

"Though I have nothing very special to communicate, yet, as it is vacation, I am disposed to spend a few moments in writing you a brief epistle.

"Our commencement week passed off very pleasantly, examinations, sermons, essays, and all. Dr. Potter, from Grace Church, preached before the Missionary Society very acceptably, the essays of the students pleased, and my address, though terribly Low-Church, so commended itself to the judgment of the forty clergymen present, that they requested a copy for publication. You shall have a copy. To tell the truth, I feared it would not go down; but I wanted to deliver my conscience by a testimony against Apostolical, tactual succession, and I am thankful it was so well received.

"The Hill is as still as the wilderness. Nothing to be heard but the song of birds, or the low of a cow. I go to-day to Washington, and to-morrow to Baltimore, to spend Sunday there and preach. That, and a trip to Fauquier, are all the expeditions I have planned for the summer.

"H. was with us about three weeks, to our great delight, and to his own also. He preached once for us. When leaving he expressed himself as very thankful that he had come. He was cordially received everywhere. He is a dear, good man. Religion is an all-pervading reality with him.

"Write me soon. With much love,

"Ever yours, affectionately, WM. SPARROW."

"THEOLOGICAL SEMINARY, July 26, 1869.

"REV. AND DEAR BROTHER:—

"Accept my thanks for your two most welcome letters. It afforded me real pleasure to know that you were pleased with your visit here. I hope it will lead to many a similar visit in time to come.

"In regard to Church matters, what shall I say? There is so much to be said, and every day brings up such new considerations, that it is perfectly vain to attempt anything by pen. In regard to yourself, one idea was continually occurring as I read your two letters, the fear that you might be disposed to hurry too much. You are naturally impatient! But that is not the main point. The main point is that 'large bodies move slow,' and of all, large bodies Episcopal! Now, to get them to move at all, you must not be in a hurry; you must be patient, be willing to apply force, moral force, argument, for a length of time. It is thus only that the desired effect can be produced. No matter what is in the future, whether such a revision as will satisfy, or, which God forefend, result in a secession, it is best accomplished by letting patience have its perfect work. Whatever is done, to be well done, the people must be instructed; they must be so aroused as to be at the pains to learn. When the clergy and laity who are sound thoroughly understand the issue, then we shall move with power, whatever the direction. Until then, it will only precipitate matters to a disastrous result to take any revolutionary steps.

"Cheney's trial is going on, I suppose. Whilst I am deeply pained that he should be subjected to such anxiety and mortification, I think it will result in good. If he is condemned, it will wake up slumbering Low-Churchmen; and if he is acquitted, it will be one step toward delivering us from that ecclesiastical martinetism which would make a man answerable with his life for a verbal departure from a formulary prescribed, while, at the same time, there is the utmost latitude allowed in regard to postures, gestures, and costumes, and all kinds of ceremonies, and greater still, if possible, in regard to the doctrines of the Gospel to be preached.

"I am glad you did not rise and rebuke the preacher that held forth on altars, priests, and sacrifices. Anything of the kind just now would not add to the strength of the good cause, and would have confirmed men in an utterly false estimate of your spiritual character. You have, I trust, a good work yet to do in the Church—the Church! and I am unwilling to see you, by anything that is not clear duty, disqualify yourself for it.

"With affectionate regards to Mrs. H., and the girls and the boys, I am ever,

"Truly yours, W. Sparrow.

"*Rev. J. P. Hubbard.*"

The allusion in one of these letters to a matter now too well known and remembered, the trial then going on in Illinois, has, in many respects, its importance. The anticipation as to the ultimate consequences, in view of what then seemed as an immediate probable result, has been strikingly realized, even to the name of the new organization. It shows, too, with whom the writer of that letter regarded the responsibility of these troubles as ultimately resting. His own relations to this whole matter, as to the different parties, have, in some respects, been misunderstood. These relations were simply those of sympathy with a brother in the ministry, formerly a pupil, and holding the same views as himself, in trouble, upon a question of conscience. This trouble, to his view, was caused through a straining of the law and of legal principle, against the tenor of ordinary practice and allowed official discretion, not in the direction of mercy and forbearance, but in that of harshness and oppression. In other words, he looked upon the prosecution as a persecution. The harshness of this, moreover, was heightened in view of the fact that it was thus carried on against clergymen of one school of theology and Church views, upon the slightest allegations of irregularity in rubric and ritual, while, at the same time, the most startling irregularities of a different school, both of ritual and of doctrine, were allowed to go on without rebuke. Dr. Sparrow has left on record the opinion that the act in question was not properly a subject of discipline, that it was really within the limits of official discretion. This opinion, written at the time, at the request of Dr. Andrews, whose views in regard to the merits of the case were somewhat different, is here given. It was, of course, not prepared for the press; and the thoughts, rather than their form, were his object in its preparation. Whether assented to or not, it will make manifest his position with reference to the whole subject.

"When Dr. Cheney was tried, condemned, and deposed, because he could not conscientiously use the word 'regenerate' in one particular place in the Baptismal service for Infants, though he had used it everywhere else in that service, and did not otherwise depart from the prescribed form; though the omission no way affected the validity of the rite; and though he was acknowledged on all hands personally sound in the faith, irreproachable in morals, successful as a minister, and much beloved by his people; when all this took place, and all this appeared, every impartial person in our Church, and persons that were not impartial, but opposed in their opinions to Dr. C., felt that the whole affair looked very much like a piece of ecclesiastical persecution, and in their hearts despised the instigators of the proceeding. But while the *movers* in this matter were so generally condemned, inside and outside of our Church, the *employees*, on the other hand, were approved, or at least apologized for.

"It was said that the man ought not to have been tried, treated as an offender, for such a trifle; but that once brought into court as a reus, on the charge of omitting habitually any jot or tittle in the service of the Prayer-book, he must be condemned. *Is it so?*

"When we become ministers of religion we bind ourselves by *subscription* to render loyal obedience and service to the Protestant Episcopal Church. This practice of subscription we derived from our Mother-Church of England.

"There, at ordination, ministers used to make three distinct subscriptions, viz.: to the king's supremacy; to all and singular the Thirty-nine Articles, as agreeable to the Word of God; and to the Book of Common Prayer, as not contrary thereto. But in the progress of time, and the development of thought, these subscriptions came to mean much more than they did at first, and consequently began to gall, in some respects, the conscience of men, even of those who were and felt themselves to be the true doctrinal descendants of the framers of the subscription forms, and of the documents subscribed. To ease the consciences of such men, therefore, it was felt for a long time, and by many persons, that something must be done. At length, accordingly, in the reign of William and Mary, it was proposed, in what was called the 'Comprehension Bill,' to substitute for the old threefold subscription a simpler form of words, viz.: 'I do approve the doctrine, and worship, and government of the Church of England as by law established.' Had this bill been carried through there is no knowing what good it might have effected, preventing the State Church from becoming so reduced as to hold, as it now does, only a 'divided empire' over the nation. We American Episcopalians, at least, are constrained to think it would have been a wise and beneficial measure, judging from subsequent events, for, as soon as we in these American colonies were called on by the Revolution to organize ourselves as an independent Church, we at once adopted the liberal and conservative subscription which the authorities of the English Church had rejected. This was done very much at the instance of Bishop White. We do not mean by his personal influence, overbearing private opinion, for it was only in harmony with the prevalent sentiment among the Episcopal colonists of that day. He was only the leader of a willing and hearty following. In the Constitution of our Church, where the requirement and form of clerical subscription may be found, the person about to be ordained is made to put his hands to these words: 'I do solemnly engage to conform to the doctrines and worship of the Protestant Episcopal Church in the United States.'

"Thus we see that the style of subscription which was rejected by the authorities of the English Church in the Seventeenth century, was adopted by us at the beginning of our history, as right and expedient, though it ought to be added that that Church has, within the present decade of years, revised and corrected her own action on the subject, encouraged, perhaps, in some measure, by our example. But what now is the nature or import of this change in the form of subscription, for we cannot suppose it nugatory. In one word, it was *relaxation.* It was meant to abate stringency, to enlarge liberty, to lessen compulsion, to widen the sphere of choice. It was felt the world had made some progress in the previous two hundred years, and might be treated as a little further advanced toward its majority, especially the Christian part of it, and of the Christian, especially the *ministerial* part.

"Such was virtually the view of those who changed the form of subscription. Bishop White, when asked if our subscription is as stringent as that of the English clergy used to be, answered, with a vehemence quite unusual with him, 'God forbid.' He clearly intimates that we have more liberty than they had. But we need no man's opinion here; the charge, in the language, speaks for itself.

"Now the relaxation thus granted pertains to two things, doctrine and worship, and to both of these alike. To separate them is most unwarrantable. The same language is used in reference to both. Both stand in the same construction. That the old stringency in regard to doctrine is abated, no one will deny. If it be not abated, then the whole change of form in the subscription is idle and unmeaning, yea deceptive.

"Bishop White is very clear on the point. He says we subscribe only 'for substance of doctrine;' and distinctly intimates that Church of England ministers did not formerly enjoy the same liberty. If, then, there is relaxation in regard to doctrine, is there none in regard to worship? Is the old stringency removed in the one case, and not removed in the other? Thus to separate them is an unwarrantable piece of arbitrariness, which would not be tolerated a moment in legal hermeneutics. No mere exegete, looking at the language, would say that any distinction could be justly made. If there is relaxation in regard to 'doctrine,' there must be also in regard to 'worship.' Besides this parallelism between the two things in the prescribed form, it may be worth while to notice that one *manner* characterizes the *process* of the change in both cases, from the old to the new form. In regard to both, the change is from *particulars* to *generals*. In the one 'doctrine' is substituted for the 'Thirty-nine Articles;' in the other 'worship' for the offices of the Prayer-book. By this altered phraseology we are not by any means left at liberty to depart from the doctrine of our Articles or from the worship of our Liturgical forms; we are still held to the 'substance,' in each case, but, nevertheless, most indubitably, a liberty is conceded to the consciences of individuals, which was not accorded under the old form; unless, indeed, we can suppose the Church to be 'keeping the word of promise to the ear,' while 'breaking it to our hope.' We say, be it observed, 'the *con-*

sciences of individuals.' The relaxation was never designed, we maintain, to sanction wanton, frivolous and light-minded departures from things established, or a capricious and crotchety disposition in sacred things. It was designed to relieve the conscience, when solemnly pleaded by men of unimpeachable character, in the less important points of doctrine, and in the minutiæ of forms. It was not to give unlimited range to the *judgment*, as to what is expedient, or to the *taste*, as to what is most fitting. That 'doctrine' and 'worship' are under the same law of relaxation, is further manifest from the relation of one to the other. One cannot be without the other. How shall men be able to exercise the liberty wherewith the Church, so far as she is concerned, has set them free in their *opinions*, if they are compelled in every jot and tittle to use the same language, however their opinions vary? We cannot believe the Church would have a man in words say one thing, while in thought he is saying another. She does not require her servants thus to falter. Nay, she must desire, above all things, to have those who minister at her altars stand fair with their own consciences before God and before men. She must desire, above all things, to see in them 'simplicity and Godly sincerity,' not fleshly wisdom, or worldly policy, or ecclesiastical craft. But surely her wishes cannot be realized, if there is one rule for the *man's thinking* and another for the *official's saying*. We conclude, therefore, that there *is* liberty in *both* cases.

"Moreover, is it not passing strange that liberty should be accorded so freely in 'doctrine,' and that it should be practically exercised to such an extent, that men may believe any opinion almost, if only the Trinity is retained; and yet that they should be bound so strictly, have their feet bound so fast in the stocks, in regard to every word used in the offices of the Church? Is doctrine of so little importance as this? Did not Christianity begin with doctrine? Did not the Master say, 'To this end was I born, and for this cause came I into the world, that I might bear witness to the truth'? Did not Christianity appear among men first of all as truth preached; and is not its realization in individual souls begun and continued to the end in the reception of the 'truth in the love thereof'? Other things may be dispensed with, but this may not. There may be truth where Christianity is not, but there can be no Christianity without truth; the truth as it is in Jesus.

"Being, then, thus vitally important, why should there be such laxness in regard to the language of truth, and at the same time such extreme martinetism in regard to the language of forms?

"This disproportion in the caution exercised in the two cases is a striking phenomenon; and mischievous withal; for it misdirects the mind, and is itself a great untruth. How such a temper and state of opinion could come to exist is a question which might lead to curious conclusions, if it were worth while to pursue it. But this by the way.

"After all, however, it is said if you allow the omission of a word, or the misplacing of a point in the use of a liturgy, on the plea of conscience, to one man, you must allow the change of two words to another, and ten to a third, and a hundred to a fourth, and so on; whole systems of forms would be broken down. This plea, doubtless, influences many, and is with them a sufficient apology for the most Draconian spirit and conduct, on the part of ecclesiastical prosecutors and courts. Yet it is utterly delusive and dangerous.

"In the first place, it should be distinctly understood that its purpose is unconstitutional; it aims to take from us a liberty which the fundamental law of the Church concedes to her ministers, when they subscribe with a view to ordination. In the next place this plea, in the spirit of it, is the ostensible motive for all the despotism ever practiced in the world, whether in politics or religion. No tyrant ever yet curtailed the liberties of the people, except on the pretext that it was necessary, to prevent anarchy. But there is that in man, as a few have long known, and the world is now at length discovering, by which, when duly developed by education, he may be governed, without being enslaved. And, *a fortiori*, there is that in the Christian, at least the Christian in a Church which makes the Scripture its rule of faith and practice, and which consequently must have attained some considerable development, which will justify such Church in allowing the clergy some little liberty, as in doctrine so in forms, for the relief of individual minds when *harassed* by conscientious scruples; for, be it observed, it is for *conscience* only we plead, not for mere taste, not for mere expediency, not for whimsical idiosyncrasy.

"In the third place, does it not almost look like an affectation in us, when, feeling so perfectly secure, as we seem to do, against the greater peril of false doctrine, we show ourselves so terribly apprehensive that if a man is left silently to omit, for the relief of his conscience, one word, in one place, in one formulary, the result will be that the whole liturgical fabric will tumble about our ears; and therefore, to prevent such disastrous consequences, the offender must be at once seized and ecclesiastically put to death. For surely, if there is anything in their whole system which has made a lodgment in the affections of Protestant Episcopalians, it is their Prayer-book. If there is an attachment of our people that may be relied on without suspicion or fear, it is their attachment to the Liturgy; first as *a* liturgy, and next as *our* liturgy, originated by the reformers under Edward VI, used from time to time afterward, and so transmitted to us by our fathers for many generations. Standing on its own merits, and used in its own spirit, the Book of Common Prayer has never occupied a tottering position in the hearts of English or American Episcopalians. A liturgy will always be found to commend itself to the Christian world at large, and of all liturgies, among English-speaking Protestants, ours is confessedly the best. In times of peace there has been no lack of love and reverence for it; on the contrary, there has been sometimes an excessive devotion and deference to it. Tractarians and Ritualists have charged Protestants with Bibliolatry; liturgeolatry is a far greater and more probable sin. Of this liability we all partake, and, if self-observant, must be quite conscious. Things being so, how comes it to pass that we cannot, in the smallest degree, confide in its intrinsic merits to protect it, but put it into the hands of the clergy, as adults would put a delicate and precious vase of exquisitely wrought glass into the hands of little children, watching over them at every step, and chiding them lest they let it fall and break?

"Made use of by us, as the Prayer-book is, from week to week, and oftener; transmitted to us, as it has been, by our ancestors for many generations back; surrounded with associations, ecclesiastical, domestic, and personal, of deepest interest; familiar to our tongues and ears, as ministers and people, from early childhood, and incomparably excellent in matter and manner, as we maintain, fitting into all the demands of religious human life with wondrous judgment and good taste, and commending itself to all as a vehicle for the expression of devout affection, never yet surpassed by man; surely we might practically trust it a little to the keeping of its own merits, and not act as though we supposed it could not stand a moment on its own foundation, unless propped and shored up at every point by the terrible sanctions of penal law.

"But still the old objection comes back upon us, 'if you give an inch they will take an ell.'

"Be the danger even so. This argument has been already met in part. To guard against possible evil, shall we introduce the spirit and practices of despotism? But further and more directly: the liability to evil is legislatively allowed to exist in other things in which men claim liberty of conscience, and speech, and action. For example, to allow us any liberty of speech about our neighbor, is to expose his character to defamation, yet it is thought best it should be so. Some men will, indeed, in such case take advantage of this liberty, and will say many things in idle gossip which they ought not. Yet it is not thought wise to seal up men's lips altogether. It is deemed best to let the danger continue, and provide against it in another way. When the resulting evil in any case becomes serious, the matter may be referred to the courts. Let the judge and jury between them determine *not* whether the accused is a discreet man, or whether he spoke rashly with his lips, but whether he was *guilty of the malicious uttering of falsehood, with a view to destroy the good name of his neighbor.* Beyond such an appeal and such a verdict there is no legitimate resort in this world, and as it is the last resort of the individual, so is it the highest protection of civil society. To seek any higher or more effective, is to forfeit that which gives to society all its sweetness—liberty.

"The application of this to the liberty accorded us by the form of our clerical subscription, in 'doctrine and worship,' is obvious. If any man is found to violate the measured and generalized vow involved therein, let him be called solemnly to account, and made to take all the consequences of his offence; but let him not be tried by the court so assembled upon some principle totally opposed to the terms and spirit of that vow. Let it not be said that they are bound to bring him in guilty, if he be found deviating from the forms a hair's breadth; that they must adhere, in their judgment, to the minutest letter, though it be a letter that killeth, and *that* unreasonably and cruelly. Let it rather be maintained, and that firmly, that there is a liberty secured us by the terms of our subscription; that, say what partisans may, conscience, after all, *is* a reality with some men; that it is as sacred and deserving of respect as it is real; yea, the most sacred thing about man, because by it he comes into closest communion with God; and that it should be presumed to exist where it is solemnly asserted, *unless* the general *character* of the man is suspicious, his general conduct alien from the spirit of a liturgical Church, and the liberties taken by him reckless and not for self-relief, but manifestly capricious, disrespectful to our ecclesiastical peculiarities, and revolutionary.

"Had the present writer been a member of the court which tried Dr. Cheney, he would have unhesitatingly voted for his acquittal, *not* because of any doubt of the solitary fact laid to his charge, or because, admitting the fact, he chose to lean to mercy's side, or because, however guilty, it was inexpedient, under the circumstances; but *because* he had violated no law of the Church, and was entitled, by the terms of the subscription which he had made at his ordination, to the verdict 'Not Guilty.'"

The views thus indicated he freely expressed, and, as opportunity presented, used such means as he possessed to remedy the evils already produced, and to avert others which were seen to be in prospect. To one or two petitions to the General Convention, having these objects in view, he appended his signature, and to Dr. Cheney himself gave expression of his sympathy. Nor were these views, as to the wrong and outrage of the first proceedings on the part of the prosecution, at all changed by the subsequent and peculiar course of the defendant. These two issues he refused to confound. Whether the defendant, in this case, had been harshly and cruelly treated, was one question. Whether his course subsequent to such treatment was to be defended or imitated, was another. The latter of these questions was one comparatively of very slight importance. The former, as constituting a precedent, which might work infinite trouble and mischief, was that which specially claimed his regard and attention. And it was to him a matter of amazement, the perfect apathy with which this, the main and absorbing issue, by the great body of the clergy, was met and put aside; the disposition to forget and lose sight of it entirely in the other and subordinate issue, which had to do with only one of its consequences, and that not the most important. It will be seen from the above letter that he anticipated such consequences, and others, which have since made their appearance. How strongly that letter of 1869 reads in the light of events now in 1875! And yet, human nature being as it is, how could anything very different be anticipated?

But we turn to another and a more grateful topic. Just after the close of the Council of 1871, and while the session of the Seminary was still going on, a movement, under, it is believed, the suggestion of Cassius F. Lee, Esq., was made among the pupils of Dr. Sparrow, having in view provision for another voyage across the Atlantic. This was successful; and with a grateful appreciation of the feelings by which it was dictated, he began to make his preparations for departure. The change and relaxation involved were of a kind especially likely to prove beneficial, and he thankfully availed himself of the opportunity for them which had been afforded.

With a few characteristic letters of this period we bring this chapter to its close. The titles and contents of these letters contain their own explanation. One of them, to the students of the classes of 1871, we are sure will be read with interest and pleasure, not only by those to whom it was originally addressed, but by many others of his pupils. It constitutes an exhibition of the feelings of interest and affection with which he regarded those who came under his instruction, and it helps to explain the warmth of affection with which those feelings were reciprocated.

TO A CANDIDATE FOR THE MINISTRY AT THE UNIVERSITY.

"THEOLOGICAL SEMINARY, January 29, 1870.

"MY DEAR F.:—

"You may well think it strange I have not written you ere this, especially as I asked you to write me, and I think promised a reply. My excuse is, much work, little strength, and of late rather serious sickness.

"The account you have given of yourself is very interesting to me. I have felt some little anxiety lest you should attempt too much. Whilst there are some who will *do* nothing, the fault of our times, amongst those who are really disposed to do, is that they often overburden themselves and are in too great a hurry. We should not 'haste' to be learned, any more than 'to be rich.' It comes of evil and leads to evil. It is really injurious to the *discipline* of the mind, for which the knowledge acquired is no compensation; and then it is likely to interfere with the paramount interest of life, the care of the soul. This with the Christian is first, is last, is everything, whether at home or abroad, in business or at college.

Some pleasing and instructive illustrations of this idea are found in John Newton's correspondence with Dr. Buchanan, while the latter was pursuing his studies at Cambridge.

"I am pleased to learn you have joined the Young Men's Christian Association at the University, and pray you may be strengthened and helped along in the divine life by such intercourse. If it should help you to *sanctify wholly* the Lord's day, that alone will be an immense blessing to body, mind, and spirit. A *holy* Sabbath is quite as necessary to the student as the mechanic, while the obligation to observe it is far greater, seeing the student may be presumed to have more knowledge of God's will in the matter.

"Since I am in the way of giving hints just now, let me further suggest that you do *not* study for *the diploma*. The world seldom asks to see the "sheepskin;" but they expect to see in the minister discipline of mind and an adequate store of knowledge, and finding these they are content, as they may well be! This thought is in harmony with the suggestion about haste. It helps to make us value the present, to improve the present, to *enjoy* the present. The exercise is sweet and the acquisition precious in and of themselves, and for that reason have a more beneficial and more permanent effect upon the mind. But enough. All things remain here, I believe, pretty much as you used to see them, or if there have been any changes, doubtless you have been apprized of them. My dear F., let me say, I take a deep interest in you, as my dearest friend's son, as a Christian youth, and as a Christian youth looking forward to the ministry as the business of your life; and that the Lord may have you in his holy keeping and sanctify all your attainments, and prepare you in body, soul, and spirit for this high calling, is and shall be the prayer of,

"Yours affectionately, W. SPARROW."

TO REV. J. P. HUBBARD.

"THEOLOGICAL SEMINARY, March 28, 1871.

"REV. AND DEAR BROTHER:—

"Ever since you sent your last contribution to the Seminary, there has been lying on my portfolio a half-finished letter to you. Being interrupted in the writing, I have left it unfinished to this hour, and now replace it by a letter de novo. Even this ought to have been written and sent off long ago, or, at least, since the arrival of Mr. E. I ought to add, that even before your money-letter arrived I had been ineffectually purposing to write to you. I had begun to feel a strong desire to know how the Lord was dealing with you and yours. For, silent or not, be assured I ever think of you all with true affection.

"Mr. E. has taken hold of study, and, so far as I can learn, is quite contented in his new position. To one who has lived always at the North, a residence down here must be a great change. But all the more beneficial; it must help to cure narrow-mindedness, to which we are all so prone.

"We were all pleased to find you remembered the old Seminary, and felt a disposition to send us men as well as send us money. Would that the tide which once set in this direction from the North might so set again! Our number has been less this year than last; but we have got along, with a fair share of the Divine presence and blessing among us. I think that there has been much searching of heart among many of our students, which I trust will result in making many of them able ministers of the New Testament. Of course, we feel the influence of the prevailing sentiment in our Church. It is like a malarious atmosphere, and all have to breathe, and some are affected by it, but they are only a few, and I trust that some of these will have such principles lodged in them as will lead them hereafter to slough off the evil influence.

"Cheney's case has troubled me much. It is terrible to be made an offender for a word, to the degree of forfeiting a man's clerical standing, and that a word which is in no way essential to the rite, which comes after the rite is performed, which is omitted for conscience sake, which was omitted quietly, without any bravado or desire for notoriety. May God in infinite mercy bring good out of this evil!

"I deeply regretted I did not visit you last summer. I wasted my vacation in heat and inactivity at home. If I am spared till next summer, I shall, Deo volente, make you a visit; and if I can induce you to accompany me, I may be disposed to go to Canada, and visit Quebec and Montreal, which places I have never seen.

"I have entered on my seventy-first year, and it behooves me not to calculate far ahead, nor count with any confidence on the accomplishment of such little plans. There is another journey before me which must soon be taken; may the Saviour be my companion to help and cheer.

"With kindest regards to Mrs. H. and all the family,

"Your affectionate brother, W. SPARROW."

Acknowledgment of present of a study-lamp from the students, as a token of their esteem and affection, on his seventieth birthday:

"THEOLOGICAL SEMINARY, March 12, 1871.

"MY VERY DEAR BRETHREN:—

"This evening, as I returned from tea to my study, I found a student's lamp burning brilliantly upon my table. I was bewildered. Old men, as you know, are given to 'waking dreams,' 'brown studies,' 'hallucinations,' and all manner of absences of mind; and I, therefore, began to question, asking, 'Am I awake?' I had left my study a short time before, and nothing of the kind was to be seen. In my confusion I overlooked the card which was fixed to the lamp, and hurried back to the tea-room to get an explanation. I saw at once they were all in the secret, and as much delighted as I was bewildered. I was taken back to the study and shown the card which I had overlooked: 'From the students.'

"Dear brethren, from none on earth could such a token of good-will have come so acceptably as from you. I accept it with an overflowing heart, and with thankfulness to you and our common Father in heaven. Your kind wishes cheer me at this important crisis of my life. May your gift be to me a token of what I ought, above all things, seek as a man, and as a functionary, namely, LIGHT, especially as it comes from Him who is the light of the soul, and 'the light of the world.' Ever, affectionately,

"Your friend and servant, WM. SPARROW."

Within a week or two after the close of the session, the Doctor sailed for Europe, spending the vacation in Ireland and England, with a brief visit to Paris. With some of the particulars of this journey we shall be occupied in the next chapter.

CHAPTER IX.

TOUR TO EUROPE—DEATH—CONCLUSION.

The tour across the Atlantic, extending through vacation and into a few weeks of October, was confined to Ireland and England, with a short visit to Paris. The first part of the visit was to Dr. Sparrow's relations in Ireland, where he found an aunt, one of the sisters of his mother, more than fourscore, still living, but whose death took place within the next two years. After remaining with these a few weeks, he went over to London and Paris, and returned to Ireland, on his way homeward. He seems to have failed in finding suitable companions for a more extended tour in Europe, the state of his health, moreover, making it undesirable that he should be subjected to special exertion. One or two letters to friends on this side the Atlantic, as also a few written from this country on his return, and within the next two years, to his relatives in Ireland, are here inserted. They afford information as to his movements, as also in regard to the feelings with which he revisited the scenes of early life, and contemplated some of the localities coming under his observation. The last of these letters, that to Ireland in 1873, taken in connection with the circumstances which called it forth, as of those at that time of the writer himself, is exceedingly touching and beautiful. The "home feelings" of which he speaks, for that home above to which he was so very near, were manifestly strong and increasing.

Preceding these is a brief letter from Ireland, written in 1874, by one of his relatives, descriptive of his arrival and intercourse with them:—

"On the 26th of July, 1871, at an early hour, we were surprised by a visit from your father. He was stopping at the Shelborne Hotel, in Stephen's Green, having arrived there the day before from Cork, where he had landed from New York. We induced him to leave the hotel and come and stay with us. This he accordingly did in the course of the day, and remained with us till the eleventh of August, when he started for London. He remained there some time, and then visited Paris in company with a friend he met in London. He returned to us on the twenty-first of September, to Sandymount, a pretty locality about two miles from Dublin, facing the sea, where we had taken lodgings for the benefit of my mother's health. But his sojourn with us was but short, as on the twenty-seventh he left by rail for Killarney, which he wished to see. From there he went to Cork, where he embarked for New York.

"During his visit to us your father went by rail to visit Gorey, in hopes of meeting some acquaintances of early days and reviving the memory of old localities. The localities were there, but most of the acquaintances were gone."

"DUBLIN, July 31, 1871.

"MY DEAR MR. LEE:—

"After having communicated with my family, my first debt in letter-writing is due to you. I arrived in Cork on the 15th, after a pleasant enough voyage, if any voyage can be pleasant. It was ten days long, nearly, almost entirely by steam, the winds being light and not favorable. It was a very uneventful passage. We were two Sundays on board, and had the morning service of the Church of England, by the Captain. Such is the law of the Cunard line. He manifestly knew more of navigation than Liturgies! From Cork I came directly here; and from here I have been to Gorey, the scene of my boyhood, and walked the streets unknowing and unknown. Of course the visit was sad and even solemn, but I hope it has proved salutary. At least it ought. It was comforting to see, there, and in all the country I passed through by rail from Cork to Dublin, a manifest and great improvement in the condition of the people. Of course every inch of land is cultivated, and, what I did not look for, they are introducing our agricultural implements. The tenements of the poor are much improved; they are better clad, and mendicancy, which used to sadden every benevolent heart, and disgrace the land, is very much diminished. I speak only of the parts I have been in. I include Dublin, where I am. Dublin, you know, has no commerce or manufactures worth speaking of. After the Union in 1801, when it lost its Parliament, of course it declined; but they say it is reviving. It is a beautiful city, and where not beautiful, solid and substantial. It was greatly moved yesterday by a visit from the Prince of Wales, and other members of the Royal family, including the Marquis of Lorne and his royal wife. There was a fair show of Irish enthusiasm. As they passed by the College Green (where I stood), moving at a trot, preceded by a squadron of cavalry, and sitting in open barouches, they received a most enthusiastic cheering. How much heart was in it would be difficult to say. I fear there is a growing desire, even among Protestants, for a restoration of their lost legislative powers, and what that would lead to it is hard to say.

"I have formed no very definite plans of travel yet. My only desire in that line was to visit Rome and Naples, but I fear that cannot be accomplished. I shall go this week or next to London; and from there may go on the Continent. I hope my health is improving. I certainly am not oppressed with heat. Except yesterday, it has rained every day since I came on the coast. It is, indeed, a land of rains and showers, alternating rapidly with gleams of sunshine. If we had so much rain, our roads would be impassable, but the roads here are all macadamized with the finest, *i.e.*, the smallest stone, and hard and smooth, and, therefore, only washed by the showers. The perfection of the roads is the best feature of Ireland.

"Though only three weeks since I left my home, it really seems a very long time. Constant change, great distance, and novelty of appearance, all unknown to Seminary life, make me feel as if it were a year since I left the 'Hill.' However much further I may go, or whatever I may see, I expect to experience nothing so much to my mind as what our country, and especially our Seminary life, furnishes. We see and complain of the defects of our government and country, and they are not a few, but really, if they would only not grow and increase, but remain as they are, nothing to be seen this side the water is to be compared to what we have at home. There is an independence and individuality in society among us which seems infinitely precious, in view of the air of courtly sentiment and dependence which you see in the papers, and notice in the tone of conversation. Spokes in a wheel do not look more and more incessantly to the hub, than do thought, and language, and expectation, among the people, to the government and the Court.

"I am staying with my aunt, an old lady of eighty-four, or rather with my cousin, her son, who, on a moderate income, lives here. They were overwhelmed with surprise when I came in upon them. My aged aunt, the last remnant of a large family, could not, for some time, recover herself from the flood of feeling occasioned by my arrival. My mother, her sister, died more than fifty years ago. My presence brought back her image, and revived other recollections buried for long years. If you should feel disposed to write me, please direct to care of Jay Cooke, McCulloch & Co., 41 Lombard street, London.

"Remember me most affectionately to Mrs. Lee, and all the 'boys and girls.' It grieves me I could not go and bid them good bye. I would rather have omitted any other visit.

"Ever your affectionate friend, W. SPARROW."

"DUBLIN, August 2, 1871.

"MY DEAR J.:—

"I received your letter before I sailed, and thinking you would be glad to hear of my safe arrival, I drop you a few lines. I left New York on the 15th ult., and reached Cork and Dublin on the 25th. I am staying with an aged aunt, eighty-four years old, or rather with her son, who keeps house, and with whom she lives. He studied law, but, having enough to live on decently without labor, does nothing. He has an English wife, and a boy about nine; an only child.

"Ireland is wondrously improved since I left it. There is much less poverty. An air of comfort and of neatness prevails, not seen formerly. The roads are admirable everywhere. You see none such with us, except in the suburbs of large cities. One consequence is, that the poor can make use of donkeys. Small as they are, looking like rats, they carry huge loads. In our roads they could not drag them a foot. But how rainy the climate! It is shower and sunshine, alternately, all the time. When here before I used to joke my relatives, saying I was satisfied it rained every day in the year here. This time, it has rained every day since I arrived. A compensation is, perpetual verdure and a temperate climate. It is, however, too temperate, so to say, for me. This city is at this time greatly moved by the visit of the Prince of Wales, Prince Arthur, and the Marquis of Lorne and his royal or princely wife. Like everybody else, I have seen them as they rode along the street; but that, of course, is all. The Marchioness is the favorite. The Irish hope the Queen may marry another of her daughters to an Irish lord some of these days.

"I was at church at the Cathedral here on Sunday. It has been renovated at the expense of Guinness, the brewer, whose porter and ale are imported among us. It is an old firm, and the present head of it has a baronetcy. The cost of the improvements was nearly a half million of dollars. It is a noble building, full of ancient monuments. A modern one of Archbishop Whateley, of course, arrested my attention. The music magnificent, of course, far beyond me. Not so in the church which I attended in the morning. All was plain and proper, with an extemporary discourse of an expository nature. Except, of course, in the Cathedral, the singing in the Church is far more congregational than with us. At night I attended lay preaching in Merion Hall. A Mr. Dewly built and sustains the house for religious and benevolent purposes. It has three galleries all round. The preacher on this occasion was not an Irishman.

"Let me say, I met Mr. D. in New York for a moment. I was pleased with the account which he gave of the boys. At first I did not know it was Mr. D. the teacher. I supposed it was his brother.

"I must conclude, simply adding, I shall probably go to London in two days. Give my love to the four boys. Let me have your prayers. I am, my dear John, ever, affectionately,

"Your father, W. SPARROW.

"*Rev. J. A. Jerome.*"

"LONDON, August 14, 1871.

"MY DEAR COUSIN:—

"Have I or have I not written you since my arrival here? It may seem a strange question, but it is a sincere one. You and your dear family have been so much in my thoughts since I left you, and I have been writing home so much since, mentioning things pertaining to you and yours, and have so firmly resolved to write *promptly* to you, and I have thought of it so often in my wakeful hours at night, that when you add to all this the oblivion which is coming over me by reason of age, you need hardly wonder that I stand in doubt whether this will not prove a 'crambe repetita.' Still, it can do no harm.

"My passage across was smooth, for the Channel was as a mill-pond. I was recognized on board by a clergyman of New York, who had, when young, been to my house with a common friend, with whom he was traveling. To my grief we parted at Chester. I am now lodging in 2 Euston Square. I was recognized through the window by another New Yorker before the door was opened!

This, also, was an agreeable surprise. I am pleased with my abode, only the company is so intensely worldly. It is a terrible thing for men to live only to themselves, and to make number one the object of all they think, and say, and do, eating, drinking, sleeping; excesses of all kinds and the uses of remedies for these excesses; excitement and ennui rapidly alternating; no high thoughts; no benevolent plans and doings; what a condition for an immortal creature! And how inane the conversation of such people; concerts, plays, and the news of the day, these constitute the pabulum by which their souls are fed. Oh, how I long for the quiet, rational, Christian converse I enjoyed under your roof! But all this is vain.

"Yesterday I went to *St. Alban's* and the *Tabernacle.* What a contrast! The one all form, and show, and superstition; the other, life, power, truth, practicalness. I hoped to hear Maconochie, but was disappointed. I heard a Mr. Angel. Is he the angel, one is tempted to ask, who 'preached another gospel'? It was extemporaneous, and he tried to be animated; but what a jumble of doctrine, not only inconsistent with the New Testament, but with himself. As to *Spurgeon,* do not let folk delude you into the idea that he is a common man, or that his preaching is vulgar clap-trap. I venture to say that there is not another man in this city that could hold so intelligent an audience as he had yesterday, spellbound as we were, for so long a time. From my heart I thank God that He has raised up such a man to do His work. Spurgeon is a great blessing to this city; such a city needs such a man. Do sublime cathedrals, with their sublime worship, make religion, to say the least, *respectable* in the world? Much more does such a man make it *respected.* People carry home from such preaching impressions and ideas which are remembered in daily duty, at the fireside and in the shop. But I can say no more. If I were with you, I should delight to make verbally a full report of that wonderful man's performance. I shall expect a line in answer, telling me of your country trip. Give my love to my cousin, and tell her, though our acquaintance was so short, it is very precious and ever to be remembered. Let S. have a full share of my regard; and for his sake I even send a greeting to Midge.* Name me with true affection to all at Molesworth Street.

"Ever your affectionate cousin, WM. SPARROW."

* The pet dog of S., the little son of Mr. G.

"2 EUSTON SQUARE, LONDON, August 19, 1871.

"MY DEAR AUNT MINA:—

"I have just received a very welcome letter from John Henry, and feel disposed to answer it by a line to you. I have, indeed, nothing special to communicate. Though professedly a traveler, I have no adventures to record. I came here a week ago last night, but there has been little to distinguish one day from another. Still, it is pleasant for me to write, if I can only thereby convey to you the profound satisfaction with which I made my visit to Dublin, and talked with the sister of my dear mother, whose memory, after fifty years, is still fresh and precious. If ever youth loved his mother, I did; and though I was not permitted to spend the last two years of her life with her, nor to be present at her death, yet that affection lived on, and endeared to me every one connected with her; so that now in my old age I still cling to my Irish kindred. Among them all, of course, you stand first. My remembrance of you, as a young lady in Gorey, is still distinct and vivid; I saw you in the Isle of Man, in 1838, in Dublin, in 1848, and now again I have been permitted another interview, when both of us are well advanced in years, and can never expect to meet again in this world. Well, dear Aunt, what a blessed thing there is another world, where the friends of Jesus will meet again after the separation of death, a world where all tears will be wiped from all eyes. Oh, why is it that we do not more thoroughly comfort ourselves with this reflection; and rest in faith, and hope, and love, and joy, on the rich promises given us through grace in the Word of God!

"It is a great pleasure to me to reflect that you are so pleasantly situated in the evening of your days, and that you have a son and daughter so gratified to minister to your comfort; and a grandson, by his mercurial temper, to keep you and his parents constantly on the 'qui vive!'

"When I get home, if it pleases God to restore me to my own family, I shall write John Henry, and tell him how I have fared. At present, I stand in doubt whether I shall go on the Continent or not. Having been there before, not feeling strong and enterprising, and finding no companion, I am indisposed to go further than through the British Islands, or even through them fully.

"And now, my dear Aunt, I must bid you farewell. Let me have your prayers that I may finish my course with joy. That the Lord may bless you, and keep you; that He may make His face to shine upon you, and be gracious with you; that He may lift up the light of His countenance upon you and give you peace, now and forever, is the prayer of

"Your affectionate nephew, W. SPARROW.

"P. S. Love to all under your roof, and at Molesworth Street.

"W. S."

"LONDON, September 12, 1871.

"MY DEAR MR. LEE:—

"As my trip is drawing to a close, I feel disposed to drop you a line. I received your letter in due time, and cordially thank you for it. The news it conveyed was very acceptable. Since the receipt of it I have been over to Paris, just to see the havoc made by Prussian invasion and Communal insurrection, the last inexpressibly the worst. It was sad indeed to see the ruins; but far sadder still to see the moral condition of the people. I was there on a Sunday. The calendar told me it was Sunday, but little else besides. I went to the American Episcopal Chapel in the morning, heard a good sermon from some Englishman, and partook of the Lord's supper. Thence I went to Notre Dame, where they keep up the celebration of the Mass, one celebration after the other, on Sundays. It was painful to see Christianity so caricatured. The marchings and counter-marchings by boys and men, in gorgeous dresses, and carrying lights, were endless. But St. Alban's, in this city, is, on a small scale, a close imitation. I also went, in Paris, to the Madelaine, a famous chapel of the Roman Catholics, and heard a French priest hold forth in a sermon. In all these churches the chief worshipers were the women. I tried to get into the Greek church, but failed. But in reference to the great mass of the people, it is a godless city. It is painful to think it should boast itself (and all the world should virtually sanction the boast) of being the most civilized spot in the world. Polished it is, but oh, how much rottenness beneath! There is but one object of pursuit, that is, pleasure; and one object of worship, that is, man. You have seen the confession of Favre, I suppose; counted one of the best of their public men. But I only took my pen to let you know about my return. I do not expect to leave before the 28th. I shall then, Deo volente, sail in the Atlantic, from Liverpool. I may cross over to Dublin again, and see once more in the world my Irish relatives, and thence proceed to Queenstown, and embark there. I hope nobody will censure me for extending my time of absence so far. I am anxious to get the benefit of this climate as long as possible. It has certainly been a service, to spend the last two months where there has been no sun to oppress me with its heat. Providence has hung a very thick awning between the English and Irish people and that luminary. As to sight-seeing, I have had enough of it long ago. I have sent you a few newspapers; I hope you have got them. I send you *The Times* to-day. Please remember me affectionately to Mrs. Lee and all the family, to Drs. Packard and Walker, and theirs, and to the three brethren in Alexandria. I am, dear sir,

"Ever truly yours, W. SPARROW.

"*To C. F. Lee, Esq., Alexandria, Va., U. S. A.*"

"LONDON, September 16, 1871.

"REV. AND DEAR BROTHER:—

"I confess this is very much pro forma. I cannot, however, permit it to be said that I have never written to yourself or Dr. P. during my whole absence. I write to save appearances, nothing more. I have had for *pretext* that you both were absent from home, especially Dr. P.; and for *reason*, my good-for-nothingness, and the fact that I have had no startling adventures by flood or field, and no interesting incidents of social life to record. I came for health alone, and I soon saw that it was by no means conducive to that end to be traveling much and far without some one to bear the burden of a 'commissioner' for me. I spent a fortnight in Ireland, and am going back to spend a last week there, meeting the steamer at Queenstown on the way to the United States. The few incidents of these periods and the interval we shall talk of when we meet.

"I have just written a letter to go with this to Dr. P., expressing my regret that I could not be with you at the beginning of the term, and also my hope that you will be strict at the examinations. Few things, in my humble judgment, tend more to sustain the reputation of the Seminary, and to make the students patient for a long term of study and submission to rules of all kinds, than to show them their ignorance and make them feel it. It is especially important in regard to our preparatories.

"The Atlantic steamer is to sail from Liverpool on the 28th

instant, and I expect to join her at Queenstown on the day following. Let me have your prayers for a propitious voyage.

"With kind regards to all your family,

"Your friend and brother, W. S.

"*Rev. C. Walker, D. D.*"

"THEOLOGICAL SEMINARY, FAIRFAX CO., VA.,
"October 18, 1871.

"MY DEAR COUSIN:—

"It is time that I let you know how a kind Providence has dealt with me since we parted. We parted Wednesday, 27th ult. That day I got to Killarney, in company with the very pleasant gentleman whom I found in the coach at the station, a Mr. M., I think a lawyer of that city, and one of the commissioners with Master Brooke and others on Church affairs. The next day I viewed the Lakes, and in the evening reached Queenstown about midnight, not finding a resting-place for the sole (or soal) of my foot in Cork, by reason of the races. So, Friday I embarked on board of the Atlantic, about two o'clock, and found my young friend Roper, and four Episcopal clergymen and two Presbyterians! That day we had a fine run, but after that, for two days and a night, we had a heavy gale, in which two of our ten boats were driven from their fastenings, and five of our sailors disabled, one by the fracture of his skull, another of his thigh, another of his arm, and so on. It was an anxious time; but the Lord delivered us from all our fears. The anxiety of the passengers was increased by the extreme length of the vessel, by her having a flat bottom, by the new construction of her engine, and by the fact that she had never experienced bad weather before. Our winds were ahead almost all the time, so that we did not reach New York till Tuesday, the 10th inst., about the same hour I sailed from Queenstown. To my delight, dear Dudley D. Smith was on the wharf to receive me and help me through the Custom House. The next day I spent in New York, and the day after set out for home, not stopping in Baltimore, though the General Convention was sitting, and though I had children and grandchildren in the city. I was in my perihelion and could not; the centripetal force was too strong. I arrived at home, in the evening; one of my married daughters had left in the morning of that day. However, Ma and Frances were at home, and quite ready to make me welcome.

"I preached last Sunday. It was very pleasant after a silence of three months. (I declined preaching on ship-board.) It was pleasant, too, to be greeted by so many pleasant faces, and warm hand-grasps. I am now engaged in my daily routine of duty. I will scarcely have finished this before the bell will summon me to two hours' duty.

"And now, my dear cousin, having indulged in these egotistical details, let me hope that they will reach you in good health. You have long since returned to Harcourt Terrace. I trust my dear aunt has recruited her strength, and that you all feel prepared to enjoy the blessings and discharge the duties of life. I feel truly thankful that I have been permitted to see you in the flesh once more. The recollection of my visits to Dublin will brighten many an hour, and furnish many a topic of conversation at the fireside. My heart overflows with love to you all, and prayers for God's blessing on you. Write me soon.

"Your affectionate cousin, W. SPARROW.

"*J. H. Going, Esq., Dublin.*"

"THEOLOGICAL SEMINARY, July 8, 1873.

"MY DEAR COUSIN:—

"The first glance of your letter told its tale to me. Every letter received from you since I left Ireland, I conceived might bring tidings of my dear aunt's departure. Well, the mystery of life is ended for her. She has reached a world of light and peace. Oh, how dark a thing death would be, but for the good hope which Christ imparts, both in reference to ourselves and those we love. Thanks be to God, who giveth us the victory over this fear, through Jesus Christ our Lord! One of the advantages I find, connected with the removal of those we love, is that it helps to create a home feeling in regard to the other world, and to wean us from this. Our home is wherever those we love abide. This land has been a home to me, and Ireland has been a home to me, and often so called, because it has been the residence of dear relations; but, as these relations have been steadily passing, for the last sixty years of my remembrance, from both continents to a yet 'better country' than either, why should not our hearts find a home with them there also? There is nothing to prevent it but that fear of death from which Christ came to relieve us, that lack of spirituality which He gives His Spirit to supply. Let us pray for one another, dear cousin, that when our hour comes we may feel we are going home.

"I am glad to hear you and M. J. and S. are in good health. Should the death of my dear aunt make any change in the mode of your life, I hope you will inform me. I am rejoiced to learn that Mr. M. is going to be relieved of the Post Office. I hope it will not be attended with any unpleasant straitening of his circumstances. Remember me affectionately to him and all the family.

"I got the papers you sent me, and read them with much interest. With you, I was annoyed at the position taken by some who were deemed pillars among you. I thought very considerable ability was displayed in the discussions, and that the laity displayed more zeal and knowledge in these matters than the same class would have done among us. But that fundamental regulation of a two-thirds vote of both orders, as necessary to the carrying of any important point, was suicidal. You are organizing as an independent, disestablished church, but the spell of the Establishment is upon you. Hinc illæ lacrymæ.

"You speak of my work. I have lectured, since my sickness, but three times a week, for five or six weeks. It is now vacation with us, and will be till the 24th of September. The Board that rules this Institution have been very kind in lightening my burdens, and providing for my lack of service. My family consists of myself, dear invalid F., a housekeeper, and a maid and man-servant, with occasional visits from my distant children. The duties of those who live far off do not allow their visiting us often or long. If I could be in the midst of my children, it would lessen the loneliness of my feeling. But, thank God, I can in some comforting measure believe it is all for the best.

"With much love to M. J. and S., and hoping to hear from you in due time, I am truly,

"Your affectionate cousin, W. SPARROW.

"*John Henry Going, Esq.*, 10 *Harcourt Terrace, Dublin.*"

During this tour, the death of the Hon. Thomas Sparrow, the youngest brother of the Doctor, took place in Ohio. It was very sudden, and its occurrence formed an element of sadness connected with his absence from home. In all other respects his journey appears to have given him great gratification. Soon after his return home, if not, in fact, just as he was returning, he ascertained that pleasant arrangements might have been made by which he could have had a more extended visit to the Continent. Perhaps it was better that this was not known earlier, and his visit thus confined to more familiar localities, those connected with early and affectionate association.

The return home was during the session of the General Convention, that year held in Baltimore. He did not, however, stop, passing through on his way home from New York. The session of the Seminary had already opened, and he was anxious to get under way with his work. If present at the Convention at all, therefore, it was only for a few days toward its close. Basing his expectations upon the action and the material of the preceding Convention of 1868, he did not anticipate a great deal from this of 1871. He was not, therefore, greatly surprised or disappointed at the failure to pass a canon against ritualism, and he was not at all hopeful as to the effects of the Declaration in regard to the Baptismal service. To the writer, as to others who were expressing their gratification and their hope that something had been gained by it to the cause of truth and sound doctrine, he expressed himself to the effect, that so far as regarded the peace of the Church and the relief of perplexed and tender consciences, it left the difficulties just where they were, and that after a momentary lull these difficulties would again be making their appearance. The practice, moreover, of settling questions of doctrine and ritual by an authority extra-legal, not by the whole Church in its representative action through all its orders, but by the act of one of those orders, the Episcopate, he deprecated as wrong in principle, and, as a precedent, full of mischief. His views, in regard to the difficulties involved in the use of certain forms of expression in the Prayer-book, had been given not long before, in connection with a tract on "Romanizing Germs," which, in its publication had been productive of angry controversy. The paper in which those views were presented it has been impossible to recover. Indeed, it is not at all improbable that it was destroyed, at the time of the sudden death of the lamented author of the tract, to whom it was sent. But as those views were expressed at the time, in other words, they may here be briefly indicated.

"The Prayer-book, as a whole, and interpreted, as to its particulars, by its leading principles, is thoroughly Protestant. It contains and exhibits a certain system of doctrinal truth; a system which, whatever may be said of exceptional inconsistencies, apparent or real, is that of the leading English Reformers of Edward and Elizabeth, of those in the Lutheran and Reformed Churches on the Continent, as of the Evangelical portion of the Church of England and of our Church in this country at the present time. But, like all the works of man, the Prayer-book is not perfect. It bears upon its face, to the intelligent reader, traces of the process through which it reached its present form. And while, as a whole, and in its controlling principles, it is Protestant and Evangelical, it has expressions, particularly some put in by later revisers, not thoroughly in sympathy with the first Reformers of Edward and Elizabeth, which are not perfectly in accord with this general system of the book, and which, if taken by themselves, would only lead astray. Some of these admit of explanations which make them congruous with the whole book. Others, at the time of their first usage, were harmless, and had not the significance which they have acquired under the light of subsequent discussion. And others, again, as familiar expressions in forms of devotion, and upon the principle of making no unnecessary changes (as capable of a Protestant meaning), were allowed to remain. But there they are, whatever the explanation of their presence. And this is their relation to the whole book, to its general tenor, its Protestant, Evangelical, organic structure.

"Indicated in these facts, we have, first, a principle of interpretation; secondly, a practical and consistent course of action. The principle of interpretation is that the homogeneous general tenor must control the exceptional and heterogeneous particular. The course of action is frankly to admit the existence of any such inconsistency, whether real or apparent, and make effort to get rid of it. In the meantime, and until such effort prove successful, the book is ours. We are the true representatives of the men who drew it up, and may, therefore, consistently use it, even when seeking, by all lawful means, to remove from it everything that is or seems like an inconsistency. As one mode of securing these results, we should insist upon alternate forms, such as may relieve perplexed and weak consciences, consciences offended and disturbed, not by the general tenor of the book, but by these, its exceptional particulars."

The substance of the opinion thus given was stated by Dr. Sparrow to the writer, immediately after its preparation, with the further statement of the circumstances calling it forth, and his object in writing it. The above, of course, is only an outline. As it was communicated with an unusual degree of particularity, and portions of it discussed at the time, the account of it is believed to be substantially correct. It will thus be seen that his object, with one class of Evangelical men, was to show that, without any sacrifice of principle, they could continue the use of the Prayer-book. Affectionately sympathizing with this class, and fully realizing their difficulties, those especially connected with known perversions of certain portions of the Prayer-book, he did not recognize in those difficulties a sufficient cause to stop any one in his work. At the same time, in opposition to another class, of the same school of theology and Church sentiment, he was not content to abide in this condition; to remain satisfied with the continued existence of these offences and causes of stumbling. Truth and principle, in his view of it, required that the real facts of the case should be honestly recognized, and frankly admitted; and that unintermitting effort should be made, until, in some mode or other, relief in the matters complained of could be obtained. The mode, in all respects, of such effort he did not undertake to point out. But he had a strong assurance that if those with whom he sympathized in theological and ecclesiastical opinion proved true to their principles, that is, to those embodied and set forth in the general tenor of the Prayer-book, there could be but little doubt of their ultimate success.

Cognate in subject with the above is a letter to one of his pupils, here appended, and written about the same time. His views of the perverting influences of the doctrine alluded to are brought out more fully in the Commencement Address of 1869.

Apart, moreover, from its sacerdotal connections, this opinion was one to which he was repugnant upon other accounts; especially in view of its tendency to foster a spirit of narrow denominationalism, to tempt men, even of Protestant and Evangelical views, in our Church, to indulge in feelings of alienation and contempt toward ministers and members of non-Episcopal Churches. The great principle of his sermon to the Virginia Convention in 1845, "Grace be with all that love the Lord Jesus Christ in sincerity," was one in regard to which he felt very deeply. Everything seeming to limit or oppose that principle he regarded with suspicion; and when such opposition became clearly manifest, he strenuously opposed it. The letter which follows will indicate his position in reference to this particular form of erroneous doctrine.

"THEOLOGICAL SEMINARY, January 9, 1872.

"MY DEAR BROTHER:—

"In reply to your welcome letter, I hardly know what to say that will quite meet your wants. I know of no work written by an Episcopalian against the figment of 'tactual succession;' as, indeed, I know of none but Haddan's, a recent publication in England, in favor of it. Besides these, Powell and Boardman, non-Episcopalians, have, I think, written about the 'Apostolical Succession,' so called, and against it. Most of the matter on the subject, both pro and con, is to be found scattered up and down in larger works, on other, and it may be larger topics. Thus you will find in Goode's Rule of Faith and Practice a very excellent discussion of Apostolical Succession, as far as it goes. It is quite enough to convince any one that unbroken tactual succession cannot be shown to be essential; and that it was not so regarded in primitive times; was practically disregarded and so far condemned in the very prominent Church of Alexandria, from the time of St. Mark till the Nicene Council. It will be found in Goode's eighth chapter. Turretin's Theology contains, also, something upon it.

"The whole theory is an assumption, for which the general mind has been prepared by centuries of Sacerdotalism and priestly domination, and which, being once approved, the general mind, from a mistaken conservatism, is afraid to give up; especially as it seems to be countenanced by 'as my Father hath sent me.' Just as Transubstantiation is favored by 'This is my body.' People do not stop to consider the consequences of their doctrine; nor how inconsistent it is with some of the first principles of the Gospel; nor how subversive of the whole Reform movement; nor what rigidly precise doctrines they are building on expressions of the most general character, like those of our Lord here quoted.

"Neither do men consider how superfluous this theory, except upon the principle that the ministry is the conduit—the personal conduit—through which grace flows to guilty man. If we are appointed simply to teach and rule in the house of God, unbroken digital succession is like a wind-mill in a cave, or a water-mill in an arid desert, as a necessary thing. Succession is everywhere in human affairs, and everywhere valued in one form and another. In the monarchs of England and the Presidents of the United States, succession is valued as a conservative expedient, but not as an essential element of social order and real government. The succession has been changed in the land of our fathers, but it did not cease, therefore, to be a nation, nor its rulers a government. And so unbroken continuity is not necessary in the Church of Christ; though it ought not causelessly be broken. In telegraph wires there must be no break; but grace is not electricity; and as to authority and instruction, they can, for they have been, used and maintained in other ways.

"But I must stop. I am glad to see that you are aware of the danger of this doctrine. Many Evangelical men are weak, and wavering, and inconstant, from not perceiving it. I would encourage no man to enter the ministry of our Church with such notions in his head. His proper home is some ecclesiastical enclosure into whose title the term Protestant does not enter.

"Affectionately your friend and servant, W. S.

"*Rev. C. C. Penick.*"

"THEOLOGICAL SEMINARY, December 23, 1871.

"MY DEAR J.:—

"I regretted much I did not see you on my return home, and have a talk with you about the boys, and your parish, and your diocese, and your church at large. I rejoice that you did not get Dr. ——— for your Bishop. As to the effect of the Convention, I could not give you my thoughts in the space of a letter. No denomination in Christendom is so anomalously situated as ours. But there is no wood from which there is no issue. What the finale here is to be, it is hard to conjecture. But the state of things is such that our manifest duty is, leaving events in God's hands, and doing, also, ecclesiastically, whatever our hand findeth to do, to give ourselves to the proper work of the ministry, preaching Christ, and making prayer and supplication for all men. Labor of this kind can never be lost.

"I am, my dear J., ever,

"Your affectionate father, WM. SPARROW."

As already mentioned, the studies of the session of 1871–2 were so arranged that Dr. Sparrow had only one recitation daily, and for the first five months he was enabled to go on in his work efficiently and comfortably. About the middle of February he was taken with a deep-seated cold, and confined to his chamber for several weeks. As the months of spring drew on he slowly recovered; but had scarcely gotten into his study and at his recitations, when he received a terrible shock in the sickness of Mrs. Sparrow, and the development of its character, as disease of the heart. She had been a sufferer for years, but no serious disease was suspected, and the announcement of the nature of her attack was very greatly a surprise. Soon after this announcement the attack became very severe, for several days so alarmingly serious that the Doctor was afraid to leave the house long enough for service or recitation, and on one occasion, after having ventured to meet a class, was called home by a sudden change which threatened a fatal termination. It is with feelings of peculiar interest and gratification that the writer can look back to his visits to the Doctor's study during this hour of his trial; that he can recall the deeply solemnized yet acquiescent spirit with which he awaited the Divine dealings. Beyond his expectations, he was for a time spared from the impending trial. After some five or six weeks Mrs. Sparrow again rallied, and, although still very much an invalid, was enabled to resume many of her household duties. Of course, there was always, after this, the knowledge and depressing conviction, from the nature of her disease, that it might at any moment reach its termination. Of this, however, for the next eight or ten months, there was no immediate threatening.

These two things together, the sickness of Mrs. Sparrow and his debility from his own attack, prevented his attendance upon the Diocesân Council, held this year in Norfolk. The Board of Trustees, at their meeting during this Council, added another professor, the Rev. Dr. McElhinney, to the Faculty. This made the temporary arrangement, by which Dr. Sparrow had been relieved in the department of Evidences, a permanent one. At the same time, it took a weight of anxiety from his mind, as to the going on of the work of the Seminary in case of his own sickness or departure. By the first of June he seemed to be restored to his usual condition of health, and was thus enabled to prepare and deliver the address at the Commencement. This address, entitled "Our Times and Our Duties," like that of 1869, was immediately asked for publication by alumni and clergy present. Its closing sentences, the last in which their author came before the Church and the world, are peculiarly characteristic:—

"I have done. I have said what I have said, first, of course, because I believe it true; secondly, because, as I think, it is not untimely on an occasion like this; thirdly, because, if true, it is important truth; and lastly, because it is not proclaimed by those who hold it as often as it should be. If I am not mistaken on these points, then I would humbly ask God to add His blessing to what has been said, for Christ's sake. Amen."

Most of the vacation following this address was spent at home. A visit of a few days, soon after the next session, 1872–3, commenced, was made to New York, to the meeting of the Evangelical Societies. It involved but a few days' deviation from the ordinary round of Seminary life and duty. This was characterized by very little change of any kind for the first six months of the session. With the arrangement of studies already mentioned, the Doctor was enabled to go on quite comfortably, taking his time for preaching in the ordinary course, as, also, in the Thursday evening meetings. His health seemed to be very much as it had been for several years previous; in one most important respect it was better than at an earlier period. He was very little troubled with the dyspeptic headaches from which at Gambier, and during his early residence in Virginia, he had been so great a sufferer. He was disturbed during these later years more through want of comfortable sleep, the sleep of natural and refreshing rest. His usual complaint was as to his head, and he often expressed the wish, after a night of disturbed or uncomfortable sleep, that he could have the professional knowledge which would enable him to understand the exact nature of his ailment. This, however, did not seem to affect his general spirits, or his efficiency. These remained the same, and the promise of work at the beginning of the session was quite as favorable as at any time since the close of the war. Indeed, the relief afforded by the addition to the Faculty seemed to give more life and vigor to his exertions.

A letter, at this point, properly comes in, which has its interest, in connection with an exciting issue presented within the next twelve months, by the movement of Bishop Cummins. Postponing the subject of Dr. Sparrow's relations to that movement until it comes up in the order of time for its consideration, the letter is here inserted, as showing the feelings and views with which a question of this serious character was regarded, as also the sympathy with which he could enter into difficulties of his pupils and brethren in the ministry.

"THEOLOGICAL SEMINARY, November 8, 1872.

"REV. AND DEAR BROTHER:—

"You have wondered at my silence. It has not been indifference. I do not think a day has passed since we met in Boston that I have not thought of you, and that, I may venture to say, with the affection and anxiety of true friendship.

"I cannot attempt a response to the many things in your letter that have touched my heart. Indeed, I am almost unfit, from a violent cold, to write at all. The one point upon which I can only speak, and that but a word, is, your leaving our Church. Such a step would be fraught with so many consequences, to your usefulness in life, to your personal comfort, to the comfort and future of your family, and to a great many other interests that might be named, that it ought not to be taken without *long*, as well as earnest, deliberation and prayer. A man of your temperament is liable to impatience. You are intensely active in your turn, and cannot well brook being laid by for a time. But you know it is sometimes the Lord's will, and is only designed to increase our usefulness afterward; and it is eventually found that the time supposed to be lost was so much placed in usury at a high interest. Moses was forty years in Midian, and was thereby prepared for the forty years spent in leading Israel into the land of promise.

"It was a real grief to me that we could not shake hands in Boston. I went the other day to New York, to attend the Evangelical anniversaries, and hoped to meet you there, but was disappointed. I went by night and returned by night, so, you may judge, saw none but members of the Societies, and we were in session most of the time, but not seeing you there, the next best thing is to see you here. You spoke a word about a trip to the South when we met at the funeral; can't you make us a visit? I need not say how delighted I should be to see you under my unpretentious roof. Does not your care of your Virginia lands call for a visit in this direction?

"I wish now with all my heart I had not wasted my past vacation on this Hill, but had gone North early enough to allow me to visit your family. They are now pretty well grown up, and I want to see what sort of men and women time is making of them. It would also have been a great gratification to me to have seen Mrs. H. and talk to her about sundry matters. If I am spared to another summer, I think I shall be more wise. But summers and winters many cannot be for me. Time flies, and my end must soon come. Thank God, I can contemplate it as in early life I did not.

"Last night I received Dr. C.'s annual report of the Home for Consumptives, and saw your name (with some remarks) among the speakers at the dedication. Work on irregularly till something permanent offers.

"With true Christian love for you and yours,

"Your old friend and brother, W. SPARROW."

One or two sentences in this letter claim notice, as connected with a topic to which they allude, the changed feelings with which his approach to the world of realities was contemplated. "Summers and winters many cannot be for me. Time flies, and my end must soon come. Thank God, I can contemplate it as in early life I did not." The change thus alluded to was very remarkable, very noticeable in the change of tone, the language and manner, in which during these last years, especially the last five or six, with which he spoke of his departure, from what it was at an earlier period. The intensity of awe, not fear, for of this there was no manifestation, but the deep solemnity of a spirit thoroughly awed in its contemplation of a world of eternal realities, and of the great change by which the soul was introduced into that world, was almost painful as it became a subject of conversation. Distinct remembrances come to the mind of the writer, of allusions by the Doctor to this subject many years ago; of the manner of such allusion at the time of the death of Albert Duy; when, again, in 1862, he visited the grave of Bishop Meade, and even as late as the year after the restoration of the Seminary, in 1865. Not long after this last date, it was, that he noticed a difference. And then on, and to the end, every allusion showed, and they were not unfrequently made, that the awe of contemplation as to the great change had lost its oppressiveness; that in childlike acquiescence, and without anxiety, he was waiting the summons of a reconciled Father and Saviour; ready to depart and be with Christ, as far better.

Thus the session was wearing on in its usual round of study and duty, when the writer received a message, about sunrise on Friday, February 14th, requesting him to come over to Dr. Sparrow's study. Mrs. Sparrow had been taken suddenly ill in the course of the night, and the indications were very alarming. The day previous had been the anniversary of her marriage, forty-six years before, and although not well, she had made a special effort to recognize its recurrence. "During the day," said the Doctor, "she came into my study, and sat there," pointing to a chair, "but she told me that she did not anticipate that we should be together again on a like occasion." As the day wore on, she became too sick to keep up with the family, and between bedtime and sunrise became desperately ill. In this condition she continued until the time of her death, the Tuesday afterward. The first few days the Doctor was able to be with her, and share in the sad privilege of endeavoring to alleviate her suffering. His strength, however, was soon exhausted, and he was compelled to seek rest. From some inadvertence, in the confusion occasioned by Mrs. Sparrow's sickness, he went to sleep in a room in which there had been no fire for several days, and thus took a severe cold, by which he was confined to his bed for more than a month following. This, although serious, was not regarded at first as alarming. He was unable, however, to leave his room, to take any further part in attendance upon his dying wife, or even to see her after his attack commenced. Her departure was announced to the writer while conducting a recitation in the Seminary; dismissing the class, he went immediately to the chamber of the Doctor. The sad announcement had already been made to him; and he was staying himself upon that consolation which is to be found in the Divine promises, the Divine assurances of blessing to the departed children of God. "Death," said he, in his impressive manner, in reply to a question intended to ascertain whether he knew what had taken place, "death has been here. But she is in Heaven—certainly she is in Heaven." The bereavement, mournful and severe under any circumstances, was peculiarly so under those actually existing. The most bereaved of all could not be present at the hour of departure, the chief mourner compelled to be absent from the last rites of friendship and affection.

A couple of letters, to sympathizing pupils, written not long after, are here inserted. They show the spirit in which this dispensation was received, his grateful appreciation of the affection and sympathy which had been expressed for him in his affliction.

"THEOLOGICAL SEMINARY, March 31, 1873.

"REV. AND DEAR BROTHER:—

"Your kind and comforting letter would not have remained so

long unanswered but for the debility which still hangs upon me. I have not yet got out of doors; and my nerves have been so weakened that it costs an effort to hold a pen steadily five minutes.

"You speak of your nearness to your *silver* wedding. Mrs. Sparrow and myself had come within four years of our *golden*. We had been in the habit of celebrating, in a simple way, the day of our wedding, which was the thirteenth of February. As the last wedding day was approaching, conversing together alone, she solemnly remarked, 'We shall never celebrate another.' When the day came, she appeared at the breakfast-table, but could not come down to dinner, though some guests had been invited. Oh, that I could have known how near the end was! I cannot help giving utterance to the thought, though I know that it is not one which should be indulged. Another vain regret, which has caused great bitterness of grief, is, that I was taken down sick myself some days before the end, and I never saw her afterward, either dying or dead. My heart bleeds at the thought, and I might almost say refuses to be comforted. But I know it is wrong, and I bow my head to Sovereign wisdom and love. But I stop. You will forgive all this, dear brother. If my weakness is great, so is my loss. I say nothing of her many traits of character which made her the best of wives and mothers, kinswoman and neighbor; truthful, unselfish, wise and benevolent to a remarkable degree; but truly I can say I know not what I would have been as a Christian and Christian minister but for her devout example, and wise and faithful counsels. Being dead, may the remembrance of her spirit, and life, and wise suggestions, still speak to me. But I forbear. It is with very few that I could be so obtrusive of myself and my sorrows.

"F., thank God, has stood her trial wonderfully. Last fall my dear wife was so feeble we had to get a housekeeper; but she has left us. We have got another, who promises well; by which I mean that dear F. seems to be much pleased with the arrangement.

"As to myself, my sickness has left me very feeble, and to how much work, or whether to any, it will please the Lord to restore me, is not yet clear. I await His good pleasure, sometimes with submission, but also sometimes with anxious heart. Pray for me, and let my dear friend M. pray for me, that I may be able to leave myself and mine with peaceful confidence in the hands of my heavenly Father.

"With much love to your precious wife, and many thanks for your kind letter, I am ever,

"Your affectionate friend and brother, W. SPARROW."

"THEOLOGICAL SEMINARY, April 21, 1873.

"MY DEAR ——:—

"Sickness and sorrow must account for my long silence in regard to your letter. Some days before Mrs. Sparrow was taken from us I was seized with a violent attack of sickness myself, so that I was not permitted to be present at her departure, nor to see her afterward. From that sickness, through God's goodness, I am now convalescing, but I have not yet been able to resume my duties. It has, moreover, left me with a deafness so severe that I hope to go to-morrow with Dr. M., our resident physician, to consult an aurist. Yesterday was the first day that I have been at church since our affliction; but it was profitless, so far as the hearing of the sermon was concerned. Be assured, therefore, that your letter and those of many others have not remained unnoticed from indifference, but from necessity. I was truly thankful for your words of kindness and Christian sympathy. Such condolence helps one to realize more fully the meaning of the 'communion of saints,' which, as a mere outward association, is a small matter; but as a thing of the Spirit, built on divine truths, and entering into the precious and glorious things of eternity, is most elevating, as well as soothing, and aids us in entering more fully into that fellowship with the Father, and His Son Jesus Christ, which is the basis of all Christian association.

"I wish you had told me something about yourself, and your situation. My heart's desire and prayer is that you may be abundantly blessed in your person, your family, and your works, and that whenever it may please God to send affliction upon you, you may be sustained and cheered by the consolation wherewith you have sought to comfort me.

"Faithfully and affectionately yours, WILLIAM SPARROW."

"Such a bereavement," is his language in another letter on the same topic, "is the severest, I suppose, that an old man can be called on to endure. Thanks be to God, I have every consolation which a surviving Christian can have in reference to one departed. Forty-six years of intercourse disclosed to me a character such as the Church of God seldom sees this side of the grave; a precious legacy to her husband and to her children."

This eulogy, from him who had known her worth, precludes the necessity, and almost the propriety, of anything of the same kind from any one else. Her characteristic remark, as she gave up a beloved child to the work of a missionary among the heathen, and as expressive of her own, and what ought to be the feelings of her household, "God loveth a cheerful giver," constitutes one illustration of the language of these letters. "There is," says Dr. Grammer, "one thing to be remembered in Dr. Sparrow's estimate of his wife, which I doubt not is familiar to you. It is his frequent mention of the fact that he intended to put a monument or stone over her grave, and on it inscribe these words, 'Sic vos, non vobis.' You recollect the allusion. In the life of Virgil the whole story is given: 'The bees make their honey, but not for themselves. The sheep have their wool, but not for themselves. The oxen plow, but not for themselves. The birds build their nests, but not for themselves.' I have often heard the Doctor recite the words in Latin, as applicable to the self-denying character of Mrs. Sparrow." During the continuance of his sickness, after her death, there were times when the indications became very serious of a fatal termination. His objections to the use of stimulants were very great, and it was only upon the assurance that it was absolutely necessary that he was induced to yield them. For a considerable portion of the time it was necessary that he should have attendance through the night, and this was rendered by the students, who arranged among themselves for the purpose, the attendance of the day being in the hands of the family. It was a source of gratification to be able in this way to express their affection and regard, the difficulty being not to get attendants, but to select those of most experience in nursing. After some weeks, as mentioned in one of the letters above, it became manifest that the sickness had very seriously affected his hearing. The degree of this would vary from time to time, but at the best it was quite serious, and a source of annoyance and depression. His classes, after the first few weeks, were divided among his colleagues, so as in that respect to relieve his mind of anxiety.

About the first of May, however, he was enabled to resume his duties, and to the close of the session, saving the trouble of his deafness, was almost restored to his ordinary condition. "His enforced inactivity," says Miss B., "during his lengthened convalescence, was extremely irksome to his active spirit. At times, to a casual observer, he might have seemed rebellious. But those who knew him most, felt that his restlessness was rather the dissatisfaction of a disabled soldier than the petulance of suffering. He was a worker, and there was work to do. He was fond of his special work, and it was waiting for him. His deafness was a constant source of annoyance, and from his description of his sensations, it must at times have been painful. It distressed him to know that people were obliged to make an effort to be heard by him. Sometimes, he said, he believed he would cease trying to talk to us, because we were spoiling our voices raising them so high to reply to him. He was very fond of the clerical and other society with which it was his privilege to associate. One of his dearest pleasures was the receipt of letters, and during his season of trial and mourning they were doubly precious. They had accumulated greatly when I came; but afterward scarcely a day passed that he did not congratulate himself upon having answered one or two more of them. He always seemed pleased when able to spend a portion of each day in letter-writing."

He did not venture to attend the Diocesan Council held in Winchester. The Trustees having, in their meeting at this Council, decided to have a semi-centennial celebration of the founding of the Seminary, it became his duty to co-operate with them in carrying their purpose into execution. The occasion was one in which he felt deep interest, and he roused himself for the consultations and efforts preparatory. As a member of the committee he took part in framing the plan of commemoration and aiding to its completion before the session terminated. A new interest in the Semi-Centennial was called forth in view of the loss, at this time, of the $100,000 donation already mentioned. It was hoped that in the gathering of the Alumni and friends of the Institution some plan could be devised and some effort originated by which the deficiency thus made might be remedied.

The vacation was spent largely at home. The effects of his sickness in the spring had not entirely passed away, and he was therefore little disposed to the exertion of travel, or to encounter the bustle incident to change of location. One brief visit to Fauquier, where he met with several clerical brethren, formed an exception, as also a longer one in New York, during the last weeks of the vacation. The beginning of the session was one of unusual interest, as connected with the Semi-Centennial, and found him in his place, prepared to welcome his brethren from a distance, and rejoice with them in the event which had called them together. It is peculiarly grateful to feel that he was spared to be present, to enjoy the services of the meeting, and to afford to so many of his former pupils the opportunity of again meeting him amid the associations of the place and occasion. The various incidents of the jubilee, its services, and addresses, and discussions, were exceedingly pleasant. The attendance was most gratifyingly large, the weather favorable, and the spirit pervading most delightful. It was a season to be remembered with feelings of gratitude. And among all those who were present, no one more appreciated and enjoyed what was going on than Dr. Sparrow. More than once afterwards he alluded to it, expressing his gratification, especially in view of its bearing upon the future welfare and interests of the Seminary, with its great work of furthering the cause of sound theological education. It was a grateful recompense, in many respects, for years of labor and responsibility.

The letters here inserted were written during this year, the one in January, and the other in August, 1873. The first contains its own explanation, and is valuable as a partial discussion of a subject which has been lately occupying the public mind. The second was to a gentleman eminent in his profession, and as a public man, but not a communicant, in whose welfare the Doctor felt a very deep interest. That interest, as thus expressed, it is grateful to know, was thankfully appreciated.

"THEOLOGICAL SEMINARY, January 20, 1873.

"Should you attempt the revision, you will doubtless see many things which you will want to introduce, but cannot, for lack of space. Let me suggest that if among these you select any, one might be the inconsistency of scientists among themselves, and with their own declarations on former occasions, in proposing this test of prayer. As scientists, they deal with matter, while Divines (and Metaphysicians) deal with spirit. The former employ the senses; the latter, consciousness and reason only. The former are questioning nature; the latter are humbly inquiring after the will of God. The sphere of the one is the laboratory, where the experimentalist is the god of the place; the sphere of the other is the temple of the moral universe, where the true and living God presides to give light and peace, all others being worshipers. The object of the one is to discover some quality by the help of furnaces and retorts; the object of the other, to learn the will of God as ruler, as God over all, blessed forever. In fine, the one is torturing a piece of inert matter, a passive creature of God, as unconscious as it is passive, with a view to some material interest, and nothing beyond; whilst the other is inquiring (if in the right spirit) most reverently what are the laws of the Supreme, as they concern all creatures, conscious and unconscious, in their mutual relations, and that not only in reference to time, but much more in reference to eternity; laying the chief stress on the moral relations of the intelligent creature to his Creator, knowing if they are properly adjusted all else will come right, seeing that matter is ancillary to mind. Thus are scientists on the one side, and theologians and philosophers on the other. The contrast is complete. A great gulf is fixed between.

"Now it is said that these antithetical parties have, at different times, interfered with one another; and, doubtless, it has been so. It is said, especially by scientists, that theologians have all through the ages acted the part of 'busy-bodies' in other men's matters; attempting to settle scientific questions by theological principles, carrying out the principles and rules of judgment which belong to the one, and applying them to the other; committing the same kind of blunder as learned men when they determine points in physiology by mathematics. The stock example here is, of course, the case of Galileo and his contemporaries. But now all that is changed. We may say to Tyndall and his friend, 'De *te* fabula narratur.' They call on Christians to leave the sphere in which, as such, they live, and move, and have their being, and come down into the arena of *physical nature,* and there test their views of God and immortality, of all moral affections, of faith, of hope, of love, and manipulate them as if they were earths or metals, acids or alkalies, and constituted according to some law of 'definite proportions,' and subject to measurement of weight and volume. Surely this is a mixing of things which ought not to be so confounded. It is an intrusion of the physical into the moral department, which ought to be rebuked, not only as dry, hard, harsh, unfeeling, and irreverent, but as utterly *unphilosophical.* We say to those who betray such lack of self-knowledge, stick to your last, gentlemen; ne sutor ultra crepidam. Abstract science is one thing, and concrete quite another. Much more is physical science one thing, and moral science quite another. And if you do not use the same process to look for the same results in the one case, why should you in the other? There is no common measure that applies to mind and matter, and he who subjects mind, the finite and the infinite, to the same laws of calculation and judgment which he recognizes in matter, virtually annihilates that mind, leaving us a physical world, and nothing beside.

"All this leads to the conclusion that it is not really a scientific result that is sought, but an atheistic argument. And if this be so, what are we to think of the way in which Christians are treated in the proposing of this test of prayer? Christians believe in a God who controls all things, material laws included, and, therefore, that he can answer prayer, and does answer prayer, without let or hindrance, whenever he pleases. On this their whole moral being is based. This is not a theory with them, it is their life. Think otherwise, and their life and character are instantly and necessarily changed. The Christian is not a headful of notions—bare notions, right or wrong, taken in connection with a decently regulated conduct. In him right notions and proper conduct must be connected by and with a body of emotions, sentiments, ethical tendencies, devout affections, volitions and will, which make him what he is; and, therefore, to suppose no such connections thus formed, is to suppose no Christian in the case. Yet these men have the audacity to propose to us that we put off this character, that we become other than ourselves, that we place ourselves in the condition of those who doubt whether there is a God, a God that can control all things, such a God as can alone satisfy the convictions and cravings of the Christian mind and heart; and then in this state of profane doubt offer the prayer of faith, *i. e.*, such prayer as the Christian believes to be alone acceptable to God through Christ! Was there ever such a jumble of seeming reverence and real profanity? such a contradiction in terms and in ideas as is thus presented! Surely the animus of such a proposition, coming from men of understanding and education, cannot be considered ingenuous, frank, kindly, or respectful.

"But the apology for all this is, that it is impossible God should answer prayer when the laws of physical nature are concerned, for that they are immutable in their very being and must flow on in their resistless course far beyond and above any impediment or control from mind or will. God may be asked to do other things, with the hope of success, perhaps; but nature is beyond his reach, and prayer, therefore, is unavailing. If this be so, then there is no God! First of all, if miracles are impossible, there is no consolation for us; we are given over to hopeless atheism, for they are entirely possible on the supposition of a personal God, and an impersonal nature, and that the latter is the work of His hands. Perhaps this is the view of these gentlemen; and in that case candor required their statement of it, and fairness also.

"But, in the second place, if the being of God as personal be admitted, and it is also admitted that as he set the machine of nature agoing, so he can also stop it when he pleases, and that *visible miracles* are possible to him; what forbids us to believe that the wisdom and power which made the machine, and can suspend its operation in the sight of all men, at will, can also, with an unseen hand, make it work out his purposes just as effectually? Whether we call a miracle a suspension, or violation, or interruption of the laws of nature, surely, if he can thus break in upon the orderly agencies of the physical world, he can, in a more quiet and gradual way, modify the working of these laws, so that in any given case the result will be according to his will, acting in compliance with some suppliant's prayer. The laws of nature are instrumentalities which God made and ordinarily uses. They are His servants, not His masters. They exist because He wills it, and as He wills it. Their working, and the results thereof, are equally His, and of His appointment. If God be God, He can create agents, laws, operations, and results. If He be God, He can work thus the natural laws He has created, or He can suspend them openly, or modify their efficiency secretly, all in answer to prayer. It is one of the glories of God thus to *conceal* a matter. But why run on in this random way? Excuse my garrulity. I ought to have read your sermon over again, and then I would have been more brief, not repeating what you have already said, and that better.

"Yours, affectionately, W. SPARROW.

"*Rev. Mr. McKim.*"

"THEOLOGICAL SEMINARY, July 31, 1873.

"MY DEAR J.:—

"The Hill is almost entirely deserted. So we have a very quiet time, indeed. Except one short trip for three days into an adjoining county, I have not been abroad anywhere, and I am not likely to be during the vacation. I have not enterprise enough to leave home.

"F.'s health is as good as usual. Our housekeeper, Miss B., is getting on very well. You have received the postal card inviting you to the jubilee. I hope you will be able to be with us. The loss of our donation has thrown us into much anxiety. Perhaps the jubilee may prove a gathering providentially ordered to meet this exigency.

"I hope the boys are still diligent and prosperous in their studies. Anything you can tell about them, or they will tell about themselves, will always be acceptable.

"I lately had a letter from Ireland, announcing the death of my aunt, my mother's youngest sister. The last of a large family. My connection with Ireland is nearly severed. But so also is my connection with the world! Yet I love the one and enjoy the other, in ways for which I *ought to be thankful.* With love and blessing to the boys,

"I am your affectionate father, W. SPARROW.

"*Rev. J. A. Jerome.*"

The following letter contains its own explanation. It was addressed to an eminent public man, with whom the Doctor, during the war, if not earlier, had formed an acquaintance:—

"THEOLOGICAL SEMINARY, FAIRFAX CO., VA.,
"August 31, 1873.

"MY DEAR ——:—

"Just returned home from a fortnight's trip, I learn by private hand of your severe indisposition, and cannot refrain from dropping this line in expression of true sympathy. Our personal intercourse has not been great; nevertheless it has been such as to give me an affectionate interest in your welfare. Your public services to the State and community at large, though I highly appreciated them in the time of our war troubles, and know how they are appreciated by all competent judges now, I do not speak of. At the present time I am specially moved by the recollection of your prompt attention to a request or two on my part of a personal nature, and also your civility and kindness to my son. He has often spoken of it.

"I hope, my dear sir, that this will find you rapidly convalescing, or, if such be not the will of our heavenly Father, that you are enjoying that higher order of 'health and spirits' which flows from the assurance of God's love in Christ. I understand your attack came upon you in the house of God. I take it as a good augury, so to say, of a beneficent result, whatever may be the outward form of that result.

"I write this, not expecting an answer. It is done only to satisfy a feeling of respect and earnest good wishes.

"I am, dear sir, truly your friend and servant,

"WILLIAM SPARROW."

Immediately following upon the jubilee was the work of the session. The Evangelical Alliance, within a few weeks, commenced its sessions in New York, and Dr. Sparrow went on for a few days, to be present at the opening services. His anticipations as to the pleasure and interest connected with the presence and conferences of the members of this body were very high, and they were not at all disappointed. He enjoyed them intensely, and his heart was overflowing, when he returned, with varied emotion; with gratitude to God that Christendom afforded such material as was there congregated; that he had been permitted to witness such an exhibition (amid so many unessential diversities) of essential Christian unity. While, to use his own strong expression, in one of the Faculty meetings, soon after, he "was not such a fool as to imagine that the enthusiasm called forth by those meetings would do away with all the evils of denominationalism or exclusiveness;" that while it might, as on former occasions, evoke peculiar exhibitions of such evils in the way of antagonism, yet still it promised to do a great work; that it had indeed already accomplished a great work; and that, whatever might be the fears of timid sympathizers, or the abuse of angry opposers, it was a practical exhibition of Christian unity, of moral and intellectual power for Christian truth and work, unique and unexampled. The antagonism which he thus predicted was not long in making itself manifest; and as it had been anticipated, so it made no change of estimation with him as to the object against which it was directed. That such movement could affect the highest interests of the Episcopal Church in any other than a beneficial manner, he never believed. Fully convinced of the essential unity of the great Protestant churches of modern Christendom, and consequently of their reciprocal action upon each other, whether legislatively connected together or not; that any extensive outpouring of Divine grace upon any one of such Christian communities must be productive of blessing to the other, he rejoiced in every real manifestation of Christian unity and affection.

"I am glad," is his language in a letter to a friend, "you begin to relish the New York "Observer." I hope your father gets it on Saturday, for I almost always mail it on Friday. From its pages you may gather something of the Evangelical Alliance; but nothing but personal presence, ocular observation, and the hearing of the ear, can convey anything like an adequate conception of the great reality. It is no exaggeration to say, there has never been such a gathering of religious men in this world! No council of old ever compared with it in numbers, in interest, in talent, in learning, in religious character, in spirit and living power, and in immediate influence upon the Church of Christ, and upon the world. Wicked, secular and money-making New York was moved as one man. Day after day were assembled in its halls and churches thousands of men, in disregard of the panic and all such things, who showed by their whole air, appearance, and conduct, that they were at once highly cultivated and profoundly in earnest on the subject of religion. Their zeal never flagged for a moment. Indeed, I see not how it could. Some of the very first minds in Christendom were there, with their wondrous gifts of speech, their vast learning, and their big hearts; and how could they put forth their strength, and the great mass of mind within their reach not be powerfully moved? Dr. Norton, who did not go there, from reading the reports was led to preach last Sunday afternoon about the Alliance; and Mr. McKim, who was at the meeting two days, could not satisfy himself by one sermon only, but took the same subject at night also!"

This subject has its connection with an event soon following, the excitement of which has not yet entirely passed away; the consequences of which, as yet, are but partially exhibited: the secession of Bishop Cummins. Dr. Sparrow, as may be seen from his letter, in 1869, to Mr. Dudley, had seriously and thoughtfully contemplated the probability of such movement. As will be seen, also, from his letters to Rev. Messrs. Jerome and Hubbard, (pages 299, 302) it was a movement the necessity of which he earnestly deprecated. And yet he believed that if a certain policy should be pressed by the ruling majority in the Church, it could not be avoided. At the same time, it will be seen that this was to be thought of as the extreme resort, and when conscientious conviction was disregarded and outraged. The decision as to when this point was reached, he earnestly insisted, must and could only be properly made by the conscientious action of the individual, deciding for himself, and for no one else. What was Bishop Cummins' duty, or that of any acting with him, he did not pretend to decide; he refused, indeed, to entertain the question. What was his own duty was very clear, and the course indicated he conscientiously followed. His views on the subject were quite fully expressed, soon after his visit to New York in December of 1874, and in connection with his account of an accidental meeting with Bishop Cummins in the study of a common friend and brother in the ministry. "I had been told," said he, "that Bishop Cummins had expressed surprise that he had not heard from me since his movement. When, therefore, he came in where I was sitting, I remembering this, and he also probably thinking of something of the kind, there was a little embarrassment in our meeting. Our host, however, Dr. S. H. Tyng, Jr., was in fine spirits, and with considerable talk, and we were soon, all three of us, engaged in conversation, largely on ordinary topics." "I was often asked," said he again, speaking of this visit to the North, "what we intended doing with reference to the new movement, and further, what would be its probable effect upon the future of the Episcopal Church." His answer, in substance, to the first of these questions was, that he could only undertake to speak for himself; that he could not take part in the movement save under the contingency of legislation which would compel violation of conscience, a contingency not probable to one, like himself, in almost daily expectation of departure. His view in regard to the second of these inquiries was very hopeful, his language very strong: that "the prospect for the Episcopal Church, so far as regarded its real spiritual interests and work, was more hopeful than he had known it for fifty years." His feeling and hope seemed to be, that in some mode this movement would be providentially overruled to the breaking of a power against which, during his whole life, he had been struggling. The evils of Ritualism, as symbolical of false doctrine, and as an agency to its dissemination, he fully recognized. But those evils, great as they were, in his estimation, were greatly aggravated by the course of the ruling majority, in two respects. First, in the too common misrepresentation, which, admitting the existence and character of the radical extreme of

Ritualism, immediately offsetted this admission, and took away all the grace of it, in the assertion that Evangelical men, such men, for instance, as Bishop Eastburn, Dr. Andrews, and Dr. Sparrow himself, constituted an extreme of equal radicalism in a different direction, and deserved the same kind of treatment. Secondly, that unjust as was this misrepresentation, the practice under it was more unjust still; that there was a freedom to the offending Ritualist, and a stringency of canon and rubric to the offending Evangelical, which were wholly inexcusable; that while such men as Ewer and Curtis were allowed to add or take away in their services with perfect freedom, others, like Tyng and Cheney, upon a slight indiscretion, or for the omission of a word, were immediately under the Episcopal maul, for discipline or for destruction. It was the prospect of seeing a power thus wielded broken that he regarded as an omen of good.

Connected with this, was his deprecation of the language of many Evangelical men, in regard to the seceders, the harsh judgments, the unloving words, in which the motives of these latter were questioned, and the impropriety of their course asserted. Such judgments, on the part of others, he would not allow in reference to his own course of conscientious conviction. And as he would not be judged by others in such matters, so he would not venture to judge others, left them to their own Master, and was deeply grieved to find so many of those with whom he agreed in other respects forgetting this law, alike of Christian love and Christian conscience. Questions as to the expediency, the wisdom, the opportuneness of such movement, he was ready enough to consider. But the question which touched the principle of the Christian liberty of his brethren, or more properly that of their Christian subjection to clear convictions of duty, this was one with which he refused to have concern. There, every one must be fully persuaded, as to his own course, "in his own mind."

No less strongly did he object to the course of some of his Evangelical brethren in another respect, as inconsistent alike with their principles, and with those upon which the Reformation itself can alone be justified: that of committing themselves, in the excitement of recoil from a movement which they feared, to a course which they might be compelled to abandon. The public declaration of certain Evangelical clergymen, that the movement was one in which they had no sympathy, he regarded, under the circumstances, as gratuitous, as, indeed, seeming to involve the confession that they were properly suspected, and needed such a purge to take away the suspicion. The declarations, again, of others, by which they substantially pledged themselves, unconditionally, for the future, to passive obedience to all possible legislation of the General Convention, he regarded as not only unwise and inconsistent, but as calculated to increase the evils out of which this movement originated. Those evils, to his mind, were palpable, and by no means trifling. And while no one had a right to say what course another ought to pursue, in view of them, at the same time it was wrong and unwise for any one to speak and act as if those evils had no real existence. This was the last conversation of any length had with Dr. Sparrow upon subjects of this character. He had just written a letter upon the subject, to a brother in the ministry, touching these same topics, and it was in speaking of them that he was led to enlarge in the manner above indicated.

Since writing the preceding sketch of the conversation in question, a couple of letters upon the subject, one of them two or three weeks earlier in date, and the other a few days before his death, have been received. It will be seen that they touch some of the points that have been mentioned. A portion of one of these letters has been already published, and at the time was followed by a brief discussion in one of our Church papers as to the meaning of one of its paragraphs. The entire letter, especially taken in connection with others (see pages 299, 302,) will best exhibit the correct interpretation of that paragraph, or of any other. It will be seen that it was written in great hurry, and confidentially; and it is only in view of the fact that a portion of it has been already published, that it is here inserted.

"December 12, 1873.

"Rev. and Dear Brother:—

"I am not sure what volume of Whateley's you saw upon my shelves, to which you refer. Besides his text-books, and Cautions for the times, there are, you know, two or three series of Essays; these I had, but lost during the war; also a volume of miscellaneous Lectures, which you may have noticed in my library, and a volume made up of his Bampton Lectures, Archbishop King's discourse on Predestination and an Appendix, and Five University Sermons. This must have been the volume you inquire about.

There has never been a complete collection of Archbishop Whateley's works published. According to Allibone, he issued, during his life, about ninety distinct publications! He was a wondrously active man, and as accurate and lucid as he was prolific. Any I have I shall be happy to loan you.

"I agree with you in your sentiments about Bishop Cummins. I am, of course, often questioned, 'Well, Doctor, what do you think of the Bishop Cummins movement?' My uniform answer is the *counsel of Gamaliel.* It is painful to me to see how Evangelical men, so-called, join in the hue and cry against him, just as if there never had been any agreement between him and them. That declaration! The life, for long years, of its signers, proves the reverse of that disclaimer. All Evangelical Episcopalians have had and professed the same grievances, and have contemplated the possibility of a secession in consequence. How, then, when one of their number makes the possibility actual, can they, in a moment, reverse the engine and move backward? They might think Cummins' mode of procedure unwise, but the procedure itself is only what their hearts have been craving for a quarter of a century. I had a letter from New York, this evening, saying this movement is likely to spread. If it should, it will certainly ease the yoke from our neck. Some fear that the next General Convention will tighten the screws yet further. I hold the very opposite. Who knows but God means to use Bishop Cummins as an instrument for our release from the bondage imposed by a heartless majority, who will not believe in the *scruples of tender consciences*? His success might liberalize *us*, and bring him and us together again, and put an end to the schism. If, on the other hand, our General Convention should become more stringent toward Low-Churchmen, and more indulgent toward High-Churchmen, then the Reformed Episcopal Church would be a city of refuge, and soon overshadow its rival. The Protestant Episcopal Church needs only to be liberalized, and rid of Romish germs, to overspread this Continent, at least in the upper and middle state of society.

"The false and exaggerated notions about schism do us much harm. There are already at least four Episcopal Churches in the United States. Where is the great harm if a fifth should be added, especially when it would give peace where there is now war, and where the Gospel would be better suited to the varied wants of society thereby? But I stop. I have written in a great hurry, and for you alone. In my hurry I have written on two sheets as one.

"Affectionately, WILLIAM SPARROW."

"I suppose," is his language to another of his pupils in a different direction, "I suppose you Bostonians are not moved by Bishop Cummins' movement as are the New Yorkers. Massachusetts, like Virginia, is far away from the vortex of the whirlpool. Still, to all Episcopalians, it is a matter of no little interest whether it prove a success or a failure. For myself, I am disposed to regard the prospects of our Church brighter now than they have ever been in my day. If this schism is a good (as schisms may be), it is a good; if it is an evil, I am sanguine that God will bring good out of it. At least, so ought we to pray."

Thus trustingly and hopefully he left this movement and all the complications connected with it to the Divine disposal. The letter containing this extract was written on the fourteenth of January, only three days before his death. As respects our undertaking, it closes his correspondence; the last expression of his spirit of faith and hopeful prayer, that in the movements and troubles spoken of, as in all others, God would overrule them for good, and to the advancement of His kingdom.

At the Semi-Centennial a plan had been proposed by which $100,000 could be collected, so as to place the funds of the Seminary in the same condition as before their loss during the earlier portion of the year. The peculiar depression in the financial state of the country seemed to render it inexpedient to carry out this plan at the time, and there was, therefore, a necessity for some provisional effort until this could be done. At the request of the Board of Trustees, Dr. Sparrow undertook this by seeking subscriptions, for the next three years, to the extent of the deficiency. This work he began in Washington and Georgetown, prosecuted afterward in Baltimore, Philadelphia, and New York, successfully ending it with a subscription between $7000 and $8000 more, indeed, than he had expected. The writer remembers with peculiar interest the Doctor's farewell call, before starting, a little after sunrise, on the nineteenth of December. He was in fine spirits, telling of the omens of success already received, and of his expectations through certain agencies and in certain localities; and while not at all liking the kind of work upon which he was going, was very hopeful as to the final result. During his tour, which extended through the next three weeks, terminating on the seventh of January, letters were received which created some uneasiness, lest he might be over-exerting himself; and this was increased by reports of his appearance from persons who had seen him in New York. His own letters were cheerful, although speaking of his weakness; and just before his return he wrote, announcing the successful result. The special danger feared by friends at home was that he might contract a cold like that of the spring of 1872, and 1873, which would trouble him for the remainder of the winter. But when he got back, suffering, apparently, only the effects of travel and exertion, the expectation was that in a few days he would be able to resume his duties. This was on Thursday, the eighth of January. The writer saw him the next day, jaded by his travel, but up at his desk upon a letter, and very cheerful in view of his success. His account of some of the incidents of his trip was full of interest, as were some of his descriptions of the different moods in which he was met by different contributors. All, however, received him pleasantly; from none had he met a rebuff. "When," said he, speaking, during the next few days, to some of the ladies on the Hill, of his going on his rounds in New York, "when I walked up the marble steps of some of those private palaces, I used sometimes to think of the lines in the beggar's petition:—

> "Pity the sorrows of a poor old man,
> Whose trembling limbs have borne him to your door."

"Why, Doctor," said one of his listeners, "did not Dr. M. go with you?" "Oh, he was begging for himself," was the reply; "beggars never travel in company."

On Saturday afternoon, January 10th, I called to see whether he would not prefer that I should take his place in the pulpit of the chapel next day, it being his Sunday in regular course, so as to allow him fully to recruit, and preach on my day, the Sunday following. He was lying upon a lounge in his study, but only for temporary change of position; and decided that, as he had been away so long, he would undertake the morning sermon, but exchange for the night. My visit was very brief, as there was a call in a different direction.

His sermon on Sunday morning, his last, was from the text,

"This is a faithful saying, and worthy of all acceptation, that Jesus Christ came into the world to save sinners." Portions of it were delivered apparently with comfort and freedom. There was one part in which there was something of hesitation, and one or two of his hearers supposed it was from failing to recognize the contents of the manuscript, or from passing over portions, as he was often in the habit of doing. His own explanation, after finishing, was that of his weakness; that he had not entirely recovered from the fatigue of his journey. He did not venture out any more during the day.

On Monday he went to Alexandria, to meet some visitors from a distance, as also Dr. Riley, from Mexico, who had promised to address the students in regard to the mission in that country. Filling his carriage with his visitors, he started homeward on foot, but was taken up very soon by a neighbor. He was apparently well, and in good spirits, during Dr. Riley's lecture, and, at the request of Bishop Johns, closed the meeting with prayer. He had made arrangements, in view of his fatigue, that this should be done by another member of the Faculty, and when the Bishop called upon him was taken by surprise, and showed greater evidence of languor than at any time during the evening. It was indeed the first and only time, in thirty-four years' acquaintanceship, that the writer had witnessed anything like it, in which the effort of prayer did not seem to elevate the spirit above the conditions of bodily infirmity. Looking at it now, it can be recognized as a reason for alarm. But the explanation afforded in the fatigues of the day seemed perfectly satisfactory.

The next afternoon, after the recitation of the day, he went to Alexandria to hear a second lecture from Dr. Riley, in one of the churches; and on Thursday night, at the Faculty meeting, he opened, after prayer, with remarks upon the passage: "Not slothful in business, fervent in spirit, serving the Lord." This, like the sermon of the Sunday preceding, was most appropriate, as terminating a course so beautifully described in this passage; the sermon exhibiting the mode of salvation to lost sinners; the address, the work of these sinners redeemed from death, in a state of gracious life and salvation. After the prayer-meeting, there was a brief, informal conference of the Faculty, in regard to excusing a member of the Seminary from a part of the course. This he opposed, in view of the interests of the petitioner, as of those of the Seminary, and the excuse was not granted. On Friday, the recitation was as usual; the subject of an essay on the bearing of Titus, chapter ii, verse 13, on the Deity of Christ, given out, in course, to a member of the class for the next recitation; and the week's work, the life's work, of teaching—the last recitation—had ended!

During the evening of that day Mr. Cassius Lee called on him, and had a long conversation, finding him cheerful and apparently well. He received by the mail of this evening a letter from Rev. D. D. Smith, describing his settlement in a new and pleasant parish, with which he was greatly pleased. The Doctor had advised the move; hence his delight in that, as in other things connected.

On Saturday morning, January 17th, he determined to go to Alexandria. Mr. Nelson, a member of the senior class, having a matter of business, saw him just before he started, his spirits buoyant, and illustrating in his conversation, as was often his wont, some of the matters spoken of, by incidents of his boyhood in Ireland. The morning was very bright and clear, but extremely cold. It was, indeed, a part of the coldest season of that winter; and as the ground was covered with snow, there was a very peculiar sharpness in the atmosphere. "The Doctor," says Miss B., "rose that morning as well, apparently, as usual. He said that he had slept better than he usually did. During breakfast he was led to speak of Dr. Muhlenburg's hymn, 'I would not live alway,' and remarked that it had made the name of Dr. M. immortal, aside from Saint Luke's Hospital and his other great works. After eating quite a hearty breakfast, he held family prayer. The morning was cold. As was his frequent custom, he prayed especially for the poor, asking God's care and comfort for them according to their need. He prayed for the heathen world, and thanked God, with more than usual fervor, for the unparalleled blessings of our own favored country, resulting from the light of Christianity, asking for aid to work faithfully in that light to the end. Then he prayed for his scattered family, and for their spiritual interest. We joined, as ever, in the Lord's prayer, and he ended with the benediction, which he never omitted. I feel that the prayer and benediction abide with us.

"About nine o'clock we started for Alexandria. It was his frequent custom to go in to town with me when I went to market on Saturday morning. We chatted all the way. During the ride, in speaking of a clergyman of Philadelphia, Dr. M., he remarked that, as a class, the clergy were, of all men, the most hard-worked.

'Others,' said he, 'work from a more tangible motive, some desire or ambition that will not let the laboring powers rest. A minister of the gospel must often labor when these are against him.' I ventured to reply that 'he ought to remember that his work is the greatest of all works.' 'And yet,' said he, 'this, his best incentive to the particular kind of work, is often the chief cause of his depression. The incomparable magnitude and importance of the work, and the weakness of the instrument, is, to say the least, rather humbling when reflected upon. But the humble instrument is in the hands of the great Master Workman.' He seemed less abstracted and more talkative than he usually was, and I rather exerted myself to keep up the flow, with the news and gossip of the neighborhood, and this and that that had accumulated during his absence at the North, and the following busy week. He appeared interested, and told me some of his traveling experiences. I remember nothing remarkable in them, or in his conversation, except that just mentioned, about the work of the clergy.

"Before I left him," after getting to Alexandria, "at Mr. Entwisle's, he spoke of a pain in his chest. I feared he had taken cold; he thought not." After Miss B. left him, he attempted to warm himself at the stove, and became apparently more comfortable. Leaving the store, with a pleasant remark to Mr. E. that he had no money to pay him a little account due, but would have some when he got back, he pursued his way to the bank, with the intent of getting cashed a check in his possession. On his way there he became very much indisposed, and making his condition known to his friend Mr. H., the cashier, he was aided by him to an apartment in the building, and a physician sent for immediately. "When I arrived," said Dr. B., "I found him perfectly intelligent, but with little or no warmth upon the surface of the skin, and almost pulseless. He remarked that he supposed, from the description of it in the books, his attack must be angina pectoris; and upon my prescribing stimulant, made some objection, but yielded and took it. I sent immediately for other remedies, to produce reaction, but a spasm came on, and in a few moments he was gone." To use his own language, applied to the sudden departure of a brother in the ministry, a few years before, "it was like an apotheosis." Saving the fulfillment of one desire he had been known to express, that "he might be permitted to go to Heaven from his home on the Seminary Hill," his departure was just what he would have chosen.

Dr. B. was rather disposed to acquiesce in the opinion of the patient as to the nature of his attack. No suspicion of such disease had previously existed. The specific knowledge of its symptoms was probably acquired within the year or two previous, and in connection with Mrs. Sparrow's sickness. Whatever the nature of the attack, whether this or something else, it is not improbable that the extreme cold of the morning had its share in bringing it on. Most merciful it was, in the manner of his departure, as in its attendant circumstances.

The whole progress of the attack was so rapid and brief that there was no opportunity of summoning the only member of his family at the Seminary, three miles off, his fellow Professors or brethren of the ministry, residing in Alexandria. Rev. Dr. Sprigg got to the house a short time after death; others soon followed, and in a little while the sad intelligence spread through the community.

"When," says Miss B., "we parted at Mr. Entwisle's, I asked him if I should find him there when ready to return home. He answered rather absently in the affirmative; and I parted from him never to see him alive again in this world. When my business was finished, and I stopped for him at the appointed place, two of the students met me. I soon gathered from their pale faces and rather incoherent words that the Doctor was very ill at the bank. I alighted from the laden carriage, and walked down there as rapidly as possible. The friends that were with him were just closing his eyes."

The sad intelligence reached the Seminary between eleven and twelve o'clock, and in the course of the next few hours his remains were brought out and deposited in the parlor of his residence. A change meantime had taken place in the atmosphere. The sharpness of the morning had passed away, and it had become one of those bright, mild, spring days in winter, so beautiful, but so inexpressibly sad, in the shadow of the great grief which had fallen upon us. That Saturday of surprise, and bereavement, and difficulty of realization as to what had taken place, and the following Sunday of sorrowful assurance of loss, may better be imagined than described; will scarcely, by those who were present, ever be forgotten. It was felt to be a sorrow common to all, and yet personal to each one; to his family, and colleagues, and students, to his aged Diocesan, as to his brethren and pupils in the ministry, to the neighborhood, including the youths of the neighboring Institution, and the young of all classes, among his acquaintance. Very peculiar feelings of reverence and affection, in his intercourse with all these, he had called forth. And the suddenness of his departure only seemed to deepen the feelings with which it was connected. Those feelings were not, indeed, entirely sorrowful. There were others of gratitude to God, and to him, for all that he had been in the past, as a teacher, and friend, and counsellor; of solemn joy in the assurance that the endless future would be even better with him than the past; that the few mysterious moments of pain to him, and of shock and surprise to those who remained, had been really a blessed translation; a translation to a higher sphere of excellence, and of employment in the service of a Heavenly Master. "Absent from the body, at home with Christ the Lord."

Appropriate tributes to his memory were rendered in the churches of Alexandria and elsewhere, on Sunday and the Sunday following. In the Seminary chapel, which had been draped by the students, there was no regular sermon; but the Bishop, after the reading of the service in the morning, made an address, appropriate to the time and occasion. The Psalter for the day, the eighteenth of the month, began with the ninetieth Psalm, and the Epistle for the day, the second Sunday after Epiphany, contained the passage upon which the Doctor had remarked on the Thursday night preceding. The tears were near the surface, and even flowing more than once, with many, as the whole service went on. It was only, indeed, with effort that those officiating, as those listening, were able, at times, to restrain them. But in the surprise of the passage from the Epistle, and the rush of feeling which it produced, it seemed, for a few seconds, as if it would be difficult to go on. The Bishop, however, who was reading, recovered himself, and the service proceeded. There was again service at night, and sermon on the translation of Enoch.

The funeral took place on Tuesday morning. Opportunity had thus been given for the arrival of distant members of the family, as also of many of the Alumni from neighboring cities and parishes. The services were conducted and addresses made by the Bishop and by Dr. Andrews, so soon himself to follow, and the mournful procession, consisting of the students of the Seminary and the pupils of the High School, the clergy from a distance, and friends from

Alexandria and the neighborhood, took its way to the place appointed for all living. Temporarily only, we trust, his remains were deposited in one of the cemeteries of Alexandria, to be removed to the grounds of that Seminary which he loved so well, and for which, during more than the third of a century, he so successfully and abundantly labored.

Our task has reached its close. A few words, in the way of summary, will not be out of place, especially as calling attention to traits of character, incidentally brought to view in the preceding narrative, but not, in any one of such incidents, fully exhibited. The portraiture of individual character is, of course, most apt to be reflected from the faithful record of individual action and feeling. Peculiarly is this the case where such record is made in the form of correspondence, the spontaneous outflow of heart and character in the unreserve of friendly communication. Such record, with the material at command, we have attempted to give. One or two features, not contained in such material, or brought out but imperfectly, may, for a brief space, and as closing our undertaking, be dwelt upon. And, here, as in previous portions of our undertaking, we gladly use the language and impressions of others.

Among these, and, perhaps, one of the first recognized, and ever afterward felt, was his genuine humanity, his genial and cordial interest in his fellow-creatures, of all classes, with whom he was brought in contact. "Dr. Sparrow," to use the language of Dr. McKim, "loved his kind as truly as any man I ever knew. Notwithstanding his elevation of mind, and his reach and compass of thought, he was truly a man among men. He could, and did, descend from the lofty region of reflection and speculation in which he dwelt, easily and cheerfully, to mingle with the humblest, to converse with the most unlearned, and all with a simplicity of heart and genuine human sympathy which charmed all who met him." "What a difference," was his remark once to a friend, as they were riding together in a funeral procession, and some children were seen hurrying by to the place of burial, "what a difference in their views of life and ours." In a few moments afterward he was helping some of them into the vehicle, and with pleasant words making room for their accommodation. Different as might have been his views of life from many of those around him, there were always points of sympathetic contact and pleasant feeling, which he immediately recognized. In this there was no condescension —none actually—none in the appearance. It was the expression of his real feelings, a cordial interest in his fellow-creatures, really entering into their objects and interests, and, so far as they could be approved, desiring their advancement. This constituted very largely the charm of intercourse with his pupils. Few of these pupils will forget their first interview, and the impressions then received, those impressions as confirmed and deepened by subsequent acquaintance. He was ever ready to hear of their difficulties, intellectual, spiritual, pecuniary; prompt to plan for them, and aid them to the extent of his ability. And, when no such difficulty had existence, he was at all times ready to be in communication with them, to listen to their views and questions, whether as to facts or opinions, and to respond freely with his own. So, too, outside of the circle of Seminary association. There was a warmth of sunshine in his presence that made itself felt alike in his social intercourse and with his brethren of the ministry everywhere. "Which of the humblest or youngest of these latter ever carried to him his perplexities, or doubts, or anxieties, or disappointments, and failed to find a ready, responsive sympathy? What appeal for the relief of the poor or the suffering ever met a rebuff from that kind heart? When did that liberal hand, poor though it was, close against the call of a sister or brother in distress? The stranger from a foreign land, the missionary babe whose mother had found a grave beneath the burning sands of Africa, found a home beneath that humble but hospitable roof, and shared the best that a meagre purse could give. No wonder that strong men stood by his lifeless clay and wept as little children weep when their father is taken away from them! No wonder that they who sat at his feet in the class-room, who leaned on his arm in their earliest trembling steps in the work of the ministry, and took sweet counsel in a time of subsequent need, felt that, for this world, the loss was irreparable! Mere intellectual power, capacity of suggesting thought or imparting knowledge, skill in teaching, would never have called forth such feelings. They constituted the heart-felt response to a heart-felt kindliness and cordiality."

The same may be said, in many respects, as to his teaching. The same spirit of perfect naturalness might ever be recognized. To use the language of one of his pupils already quoted, "he placed himself abreast of those whom he taught. He did not stand on the heights of truth and say, 'Come up hither to this lofty eminence I have reached,' but he came down into the valley where we stood, and helped us to climb. And he was able to do this, partly by reason of his childlike humility, partly by reason of his genuine sympathy with the young, and partly by reason of the fact that truth never became trite to him, but, however often repeated, continued fresh and living, the desire and rejoicing of his heart." "As I look back," says Rev. Phillips Brooks, "upon our Seminary days, I am much impressed with the way in which Dr. Sparrow led us naturally and easily into a study which was so unfamiliar to most of us when we went there. It was not anything peculiar in his way of teaching. It was no professor's skillful trick. It must have been something very human about the man, which made his scholars feel that in studying theology they were doing reasonable work, and finding the highest use for their best faculties. In Dr. Sparrow's class-room no serious question was ever left unanswered. No student was ever silenced in an earnest inquiry by a charge of irreverence. Every man was bidden to use his powers. The result was that the whole field of theology at once had an open and real look to us. It was not a region of technicalities, where we were to use a set of faculties unknown in ordinary life. The same powers which we had employed as students elsewhere to study lower things, were to be used here with deeper solemnity and purity, but the same powers still to learn the things of God. All his influence led us to a rational theology, and his daily spirit taught us that such a theology was beautifully consistent with a deep and tender piety."

"Dr. Sparrow was a timid man about some things. In social and political matters he let the circumstances in which he found himself direct his action, even when they did not convince his judgment. But when he felt himself on his own ground, there was nothing at all of this. There was not a particle of cant or the saying of other people's words in his religion. Everything he said was real to him, and whether we accepted and held it permanently as true or not, the reality with which he said and believed it did us good. The best of all things which he did for his students, was to teach them, so far as one man can teach another, to think naturally and earnestly, and never, out of fear or fancied piety, to say a thing they did not mean. The degree to which we learned this lesson of him, or rather the sense of how earnestly he tried to teach it to us, constitutes the deep indebtedness that many of us will always feel to Dr. Sparrow."

"I might speak of other traits which were very delightful in him; his kindliness, his self-forgetfulness, his cordial enjoyment of any good thing that any student did, his humor, and simplicity, and child-likeness. All his students remember these; but what gave the charm to them all, and makes the Seminary always a place of sacred associations, is the genuineness and thorough truthfulness of him under whom it was our privilege to begin the study of theology." "He sought," says another, "to lead men to the investigation of Scripture, as far as prescribed, unbiased by prejudice, unshackled by a previously adopted set of opinions. For himself, he was as far from latitudinarianism as from vacillation of mind in theological opinion. He saw clearly the danger of attempting to be wise above what is written upon many points; and these, therefore, whatever his speculations concerning them, he held in suspense, sub judice, as he himself would express it. He saw also the temptation to which the adherents of a system were exposed, of straining the sense of Scripture to make it square with their system, and thus making human philosophizings the measure of Divine verities." And we may add, that he knew nothing in his investigations, and in the suggestions of his teaching, for purposes of mere speculation. Truths and principles were exhibited and handled with reference to their practical bearing. They were living truths, life-giving principles, pressing upon the minds and hearts, and through these, pervading and controlling, the life and conduct.

One other trait, having its place in the thorough development of his own character, as in the influence of that character upon others, may be briefly indicated: his carefulness in reference to what are often regarded as little matters. "He lived and labored," as has been said of him, "in the light of *great principles*. These were, to him, ever the solvents of every difficulty and perplexity, whether in philosophy or in theology." And the power and thoroughly pervading influence of these principles were seen in the minutest details to which they were properly applicable. It was the substance of a part of his annual matriculating address to the students, that they should give conscience its full place and power in all matters of Seminary arrangement. But the most effective mode in which that exhortation was presented was in his own constant example. No class ever found him unprepared for the particular matter, in its details as in the general, which were properly the subject of recitation. The conscientious and careful mastery of the details in their place and order had given him his mastery of those details as a whole.

Incidents illustrative of the same spirit and habit will recur to the memory of his pupils. We may mention, for instance, his singular retentiveness of memory in pecuniary matters, as to anything, the smallest trifle, due from him to others, and this, too, while often forgetful of what was due from others to him. Not less illustrative of the same trait, may be mentioned his anxiety in his estimate of his household property for taxation, lest he might make it below the proper value; his solicitude as to the influence upon the students of certain associations, not positively evil, but still tending to worldliness and levity; his carefulness as to the observance of the Lord's day, and to the discouragement of everything interfering with the idea of its sacredness. These are but illustrations. The spirit which dictated them was to be seen everywhere. Duty, like truth, was recognized as a sacred thing. His constant and manifest effort was so to discharge that duty that every obligation, and in all its details, should be fully met and honored. He was emphatically a man of principle, high moral principle, sanctified and elevated by a spirit of genuine devotion. "Fifty years ago," says Dr. McKim, "he had put away earthly ambition, and ever since, with single eye and steadfast purpose, had sought those things which are above. He had committed his ways to the Lord, and left the direction of his steps in His hands, cheerfully and trustfully following wheresoever His providence led. He once told me that it was a source of unspeakable satisfaction, in the review of his life, to be able to say that he had never sought a position which he had occupied." It is not possible to over-estimate the influence of this upon those with whom he came in contact, particularly those who were under his instruction and government. This gave direction and consistency to other features of his character already mentioned. His power of intellect, his geniality, his naturalness, so attractive in themselves, were thus steadied and directed to the exercise of the highest form of beneficial influence. That, after all, which was of most value to his pupils, and through them, in their varied spheres of labor, to the Church, was the impress, not of his intellect, of his theology, or of his social nature, but of his character, the pervading and controlling spirit of duty, of sacred principle, by which he was ever manifestly actuated. If, to any degree, we have succeeded in exhibiting that character, and thus extending its influence, our object will have been accomplished. "The path of the just, as a shining light, shining more and more to the perfect day," may thus become a light to the footsteps of others, leading them to a world of heavenly blessedness.

ADDRESS.*

To those of us who, during the last thirty years or more, on occasions like the present, have been preparing to leave this place for their first fields of ministerial trial, as to those who, temporarily coming back from those fields, have renewed, for a few days, the associations of Seminary life, there comes up spontaneously one revered and familiar form, as almost a necessary accompaniment, as, indeed, that of the presiding genius of our Commencement exercises. Here, it may be, as on special occasions, when it became his duty to enunciate and enforce some of those great principles which controlled his own thinking and action. There, at that chancel, presenting some of his pupils for their reception of the ministerial commission. Or there, in that neighboring study, with genial welcome for former pupils and friends, with pleasant reminiscence of previous Seminary intercourse, or with profitable converse, and wise suggestion as to future ministerial labor. With many, indeed, it was the distinct anticipation of such converse that helped to bring them here; sometimes to seek advice and counsel for pastoral work, sometimes as needed for issues of personal duty. It was felt that his sympathy was ever ready and cordial, that his advice was not apt to lead astray, and that personal communion with him was not only pleasant, but full of improvement and elevation. As we passed from this brief intercourse to our respective homes, we had something more to think about. Old truths were seen in a new light, and with new applications, or new truths and duties were recognized, to quicken our sense of obligation, to enliven our hearts, and to call into more vigorous exercise our practical activities. "As iron brighteneth iron," so were our countenances brightened by that of our teacher and friend.

That revered and familiar form we no longer see. Very suddenly was he taken from our midst. So suddenly was it with him,

* At the Annual Commencement of the Seminary, June 25, 1874.

that in all probability he had passed through the dark valley before he was distinctly aware that he was in it. So suddenly was it with us, that before danger was known, or apprehension felt, our calamity was overpassed, his translation and our bereavement had been accomplished. Without any break of work, the week's recitations had closed the day before; he had fulfilled his appointment in the pulpit the previous Sunday, and opened the Faculty meeting on Thursday evening; on his day of weekly relaxation, "a time to die," the summons came for speedy departure. Like Elisha and the sons of the Prophets, we found that our teacher had been taken from us, had himself passed into the higher school of heavenly acquisition. I need not speak of the shadow of that day, and of the days following, which rested upon our hearts and in our homes; of that bright Sunday morning, the darkest that was ever known on this Hill, when, as a bereaved community, we first met for worship in this building; of the sadness in view of our loss, and yet of the solemn joy in view of the legacy of his example, as of his endless gain, with which, a few days afterward, we followed his remains to the place appointed for all living. Of these things we do not now need to speak. Our task is rather with the present moment. We stand to-day, as we did on that day of his departure, mindful, indeed, of our loss, but at the same time grateful to the Giver of all good for what permanently remains; for what, through him who has gone, many of us have received; those "truths," awakened in us through his instrumentality, "to perish never;" that example of Christian simplicity, of godly sincerity, of diligent effort, of cheerful exertion, in its influence so powerful and quickening. It is as introductory to the contemplation of that example, and of some of the features of character thus exhibited, that these remarks have been made. The portion of time ordinarily devoted to the present exercise may be made use of for this purpose. And I feel that in thus using it I am consulting not only my own inclinations, but those of my hearers. It will not, moreover, be unprofitable, nor alien from the usual purpose of these occasions, to give our attention to this topic; to look at some of those features, and to contemplate some of those elements, intellectual and moral, which made our departed preceptor what he was, which enabled him to impress himself so powerfully upon the men of his day and generation, especially upon those under his instruction. When "a great man falls in Israel," it is well for Israel to pause, and ask, and try to find out, what constitutes his greatness; wherein was the secret of his power, of his influence, so widely and beneficially exerted. The answer to these and similar questions will usually be found in such investigation as has been suggested. The man did what he did because he was what he was. If we would know the secret of his power, we must know the secret of his character, the peculiar elements of his moral personality.

We thus naturally have our topic, the Theological Instructor, the elements which give success to him in his work of teaching those who are themselves to be teachers, enabling him successfully to train and fit men for the gospel ministry. This topic, in the circumstances of the present moment, we can look at in the concrete. We can thus recognize the correctness of certain general principles, can verify those principles in their personal illustration.

First, then, as essential to the highest success in this high vocation, the theological teacher, as the teacher of science, of art, or literature, must have, in a most important sense of the word, a call to his work; not that Divine call which comes through the special influence of the Holy Ghost upon the heart and life, but that Divine call which comes through the natural, that is, the Divine endowment of special tastes and capacities. In other words, he must be a born teacher, must have a natural aptness and capacity for his calling. It is just as true, the maxim of Horace, with reference to the teacher as it is to the poet, the artist, or the orator. If the Divine gift be not in him, you cannot by any amount of cultivation evolve it out of him, or by any process of impartation put it in him. This, of course, does not by itself constitute the effective teacher. It may, as with the gift of natural eloquence, tempt its possessor to neglect requisite cultivation; and if we were obliged to choose between the instruction of untrained genius and that of carefully and conscientiously cultivated average talent, we should, without hesitation, take the latter. The question just now, however, is not of the better between two instruments, both of them defective, but as to what constitutes the best instrument, the highest element of efficiency. All other things being equal, the man naturally apt to teach is the man for his work. The desirable basis of all training and preparation for this work is this natural fitness and talent for it. This may not, either to the individual himself or to any one else, be immediately manifest. It may require the appropriate stimuli of circumstances to call it forth and give it exercise. It does not dispense with cultivation, but carefully takes it on, makes diligent and conscientious use of it, recognizes its importance, its absolute necessity. Its own previous existence, however, gives to such cultivation its highest value. Here in this natural aptitude and capacity we have the proper beginning. When we have this, we may, in the use of the proper means, anticipate a successful continuation. When we are led to contemplate the past career of an eminently successful man, we may look, and we shall find that this was one of his qualifications.

Need I remind you of the personal illustration of this portion of our subject? Need I describe to those who so well have known, that rare power of impartation, that aptness not only to teach but to quicken thought in the recipient, to set men to thinking and investigating, so as to enable them to reach conclusions really their own, and, therefore, of permanent value! Whatever may be said of William Sparrow in other respects, this was peculiarly his gift, pre-eminently his power. It was not merely that he was endowed by nature with the regal prerogative of a superb intellect, an imagination adequate to all the demands of that intellect for illustrative and embodying power to vivify its conceptions to others, an emotional structure promptly and thoroughly responsive. With all this, there was something more, the power of living communication, of stimulating thought, of quickening intellectual activity. He was a teacher! Teaching was his work. It was natural to him; and whenever and wherever he was brought in converse with his fellow-men, it was to impart to them information: either to tell them something which they had not previously known, or to freshen their impression of truths already familiar. It was thus in the pulpit, in the Faculty meeting, in social converse, in epistolary correspondence. Many of his pupils have received almost as much from his letters as from his regular instructions. Teaching with him was not only the spontaneous outgoing of his personality, but it was the definitely selected work to which his highest energies were sacredly consecrated, and with which, during the larger portion of his career, he was diligently occupied. In his eighteenth year, he began life as an instructor of youth, with a considerable share of governing the Academy in which he was employed; and from the start his career was a successful one. That brief and successful essay was followed by a course of additional study, and the work of life was then fairly entered upon: first as tutor at Worthington, at Cincinnati, and Miami University; then as full Professor at the last of these institutions; then as Senior Literary and Theological Professor at Worthington and Gambier; then strictly Theological at the latter place; and finally, in the same capacity, for nearly one-third of a century, in this institution. During most of the time, moreover, of his professional life, both literary and theological, the government of the institutions with which he was connected was placed in his hands. Confining our attention, for the present, simply to his power as a teacher, I need only remind some of those before me what that power was; what some of us, in those fresh days of student enthusiasm, have witnessed of its exhibitions. Some, doubtless, came under those instructions incapable of appreciating them. Others, again, fearful of being changed in their theological and ecclesiastical views, kept themselves in such habitual attitude of self-defence and non-receptivity as but partially to understand them. Others, again, wanting in moral and spiritual sympathy, met them, so far as understood, with positive aversion. But even with these imperfectly receptive classes, there was always the impression of power, of transcendent skill in the mode of handling the material of thought and information, of placing it before the minds of others, and quickening their activity, even though it might be in the way of opposition. While to another class, the pupil-minded, the real learners, those anxious to know, those willing to test and try everything in the light of that Divine truth to which he constantly appealed, his quickening influence cannot be described. It was recognized and felt to be that of a master. "I had just graduated at Yale," is the language of one of his associates in Ohio, describing him as he was in those first, almost youthful, days at Worthington, "and I knew of no one there whom I regarded as his equal." The same remark, in substance, was made to me some years later by a fellow-student, a graduate of Pennsylvania University. And I have since heard it from another, in reference to a still different institution. Men who had graduated upon Butler elsewhere, came to him and found out that they had yet to learn the full meaning of his argument. And as in Butler, so in other things. Whether in Divinity, in Evidences, in Mental and Moral Science, or in Language, there was the same peculiarity of power: the aptness of suggestion, the ease, and freedom, and promptitude of movement, the fertility of resource and of illustration, the distinctness of contemplation as to facts and principles presented or illustrated, the clearness of outline in such presentation. These, to the real student, constituted the removal of his worst difficulties. At the same time, they quickened his energies, increased his information, made clear and definite his previous knowledge, revealing its defects and opening the way for their removal. In the recitation room, whatever he was elsewhere, he was on his throne! His sovereignty was indisputable, a sovereignty exercised in its most beneficial form, and in such exercise full of delight and benefit to the subject. I do not know, brethren, how it was, in all respects, with you or with others, on those occasions, and as sitting in the seat of the learner. I may, however, judge from expressions, at different times, and from different sources, that your experience was not altogether unlike my own; and that, by comparison, may be very briefly stated. In looking back upon my experiences of intellectual satisfaction and enjoyment, I recognize none such, in kind or in degree, as I derived from those recitations, unless it was in the reception of the same truths and illustrations, in a more practical form, from the pulpit, and brought to bear upon the heart and conscience. Well do I remember a walk with Albert Duy and Owen Thackara, one pleasant June evening, to Alexandria, during our middle year, when our conversation turned upon the recitations and discussions of the few days preceding, and the glowing language in which the former described his enjoyment of them. No less distinctly do I remember the numberless and curious questions, on such occasions, of another classmate, fresh from a German university, full of distinctions and queries as to entities and quiddities, the σῶμα, the φυχη, and the πνευμα, but never finding his instructor embarrassed, the clearness of the reply often lighting up the obscurity of the question. "How often," to use the language of one of his pupils of later years, "how often have we seen his eyes dilate, and his countenance shine, and his whole mien take on a certain majesty, as the very oracle of truth, as he sat in the class-room and spoke to us of the things of God. By what a subtle, irresistible magnetism have we sometimes felt ourselves drawn, while listening to his fervent words." These are but illustrations. They serve to make manifest the peculiar gift now under discussion, its place and importance, with the theological as with the scientific or the literary teacher, that of the natural, the Divinely conferred capacity of conveying the contents of our own minds into the minds of others.

But this is merely the beginning, the foundation; and it must be carefully and diligently built upon. This capacity of communication, this power of conveyance and of quickening exerted by one mind upon another, to be exerted beneficially, must be in connection with something else, material to be communicated. The teacher must himself be taught, must consent to be a learner, and this, too, not merely as introductory to the beginning of his work, but all along, and to the end of his course. If he ever reaches a point in which he stops learning, it will be time for him to stop teaching. The freshness which comes, and comes only in the process of constant reception, is always needed, as giving vitality and interest to that of impartation. The subject-matter, of course, is exhaustless. The language of poetry here is not at all that of exaggeration:

> "Were man to live coeval with the sun,
> The patriarch-pupil would be learning still,
> And dying, leave his lessons half unlearned."

The pupil spirit is ever the proper spirit of the teacher, which recognizes how much is still to be known, and is, therefore, ever ready with the confession of imperfect knowledge. Most strikingly, and in each of these respects, was the spirit exhibited by our departed instructor. While ever learning, he was ever ready to confess his want of learning; not in such a manner as to extort the compliment from others that such was the case, but manifestly as expressive of his real convictions, an entire absence of all pretension, of everything like assumption of intellectual superiority. More than once, as I have heard him speak of his want of knowledge, or of his imperfect knowledge upon certain subjects, have I been reminded of Dr. Johnson's disclaimer as to Greek scholarship, and the explanation of an intelligent friend as to how far this disclaimer, a thoroughly honest one, gave a correct view of the case: "He does not possess that mastery of it which, in his estimation, would justify him in claiming to be a Greek scholar; but he knows more of it than do most of those who are called so. Any one else who had his knowledge would not hesitate to claim the title which he declines." But whether thus intelligent or not in certain cognate departments of knowledge—and there were some in which he distinctly recognized that there must be a division of abor—in his own proper sphere, the constant process went on of fresh acquisition, of systematic adjustment of every such new acquisition, in its relation to material already in possession. And while upon this topic, let me direct attention to two characteristics in his efforts for self-culture, and in his mode of intellectual acquisition. One of these was the thorough mastery of the subject under investigation. During the latter years of his life he spoke of his special obligations, in the way of intellectual training, to a mathematical teacher who would never accept a hazy or halting demonstration; of the habit of study acquired under this strict regimen. "Too many students," was another of his remarks which some of us have heard, "too many students are satisfied merely to *understand* a thing; they do not *possess* it." The difference thus indicated, between understanding and possessing, may be said to have constituted the difference between his mode of cultivation and that of the great majority. First of all, by thorough discriminative analysis, to distinguish and separate the subject-matter of investigation from all others, to look at it, and to know it in all its various portions and particulars; then, by the process of synthetic reconstruction, fully to possess it, to know it as a whole, each part in itself and in relation to others, and all in its relations to other things. Whatever the direction of his study, this seems to have been his effort and habit. And the result was seen in the thoroughness and definiteness of his information. What he undertook to impart he was careful to know. Where his knowledge was not definite and satisfactory he refused to speak, or he spoke in such a manner as to give no wrong impression; as to involve no pretensions to a knowledge of which he was not in actual possession.

The other of these characteristics was that of the order in which these acquisitions were made, the relation in this process of self-culture of various studies to each other. Just as we shall find, when we come to his theological course in the task of imparting, that there was a natural order, the various parts adapted to each other, and sustaining each other as they were severally mastered, so do we find the same feature in the course of acquisition. Among these departments of acquisition was one which, if we would estimate his peculiar power, must never be forgotten, his metaphysical studies. By this, too, we mean not merely the psychological investigation of the various powers and faculties of the human mind, their laws and modes of operation, intellectual, emotional, and volitional, but the problems with which they come in contact, the great problems of ontological speculation, of existence, of God, of duty, and of immortality, over which the human mind, with imperfect knowledge and imperfect capacity, has so long wrestled in the dark, but which it cannot consent to leave without attempting some kind of solution. In this field it was, so barren to ordinary cultivators, so empty in ordinary estimation, that he gathered some of his richest intellectual treasures, that he made one of his most important acquisitions, for the special work of teaching theology — that of ascertaining how far, or rather how short a distance, the human mind is really able to go in certain directions. He became thus able himself to say to others, a most important qualification to the instructor, "Thus far, and no further!" *Here* is knowledge, science, the material of their construction! *There* is speculation, imagination, fancy, nonsense! If Dr. Sparrow had not been something greater and better, he would have been a great metaphysician. As it was, his metaphysical power made his greatness manifest in other respects. If not among the first, it was at a very early period that his cultivation in these studies began. And his peculiar capacity, as also his mastery of material, were very soon recognized. "He was," says Dr. McElroy, describing him at Gambier, in his twenty-seventh or eighth year, "he was specially able, even at that early age, in the mental and moral philosophies. He had thoroughly mastered every able book on those subjects that had at that time been published; and my impression was, that he was fully able to write, on either, a better book than any on the subject extant." Nor can this portion of his attainments be over-estimated either as to its influence upon his general training, or upon his efficiency as a teacher of divinity. "It used to be a common remark," says the biographer of another eminent teacher of this country, Dr. Archibald Alexander, "it used to be a common remark, in the days of Church controversy, that students who had been imbued with Dr. Alexander's metaphysics were sure to swallow his entire theological system." "Perhaps," continues the biographer, "perhaps the same is true of every theological instructor who deduces a concatenated system from any clearly defined principles." The prevalent tendency, just now, is to despise and underrate this class of studies; to a materialized religion, to a materialized science. There is a disposition to get rid, in science and religion alike, of everything which does not come under the cognizance of the senses, which cannot be referred to sensible verification. Even where this tendency does not manifest itself in the grosser forms of a Pantheistic science or a materialized religion, it sometimes does in depreciative statements as to the uselessness of intellectual science, of philosophical investigation. This, too, by a wonderful inconsistency in connection with statements as to the importance of intellectual cultivation. Intellectual cultivation! The cultivation of a field, the size of which and the capacities and properties of the soil of which you are profoundly ignorant! The effective and skillful employment of a tool which you have never handled, the adaptations of which you know nothing! He who would instruct other minds, and control them for good, must first know something of his own, of the facts and laws common to all minds; must carefully observe his own intellectual operations, and test these by the experiences of others. A large share of the material of human knowledge, as also the capacity of using it, is only to be gotten in this way. It was the training here, in metaphysics, in mental and moral science, which, so far as mere intellect was concerned, prepared the way for all that followed. The habits thus formed, of discrimination in thought and expression, were carried into all other studies, those of language, of political economy, of history, of his chosen vocation and work, theology. In all the departments of this latter he at different times gave instruction. But for most of his time in Ohio, and for the whole of it, saving a few months, in this Institution, it was in the chair of Systematic Divinity and Christian Evidences, including in the latter the Analogy of Butler. His mastery of this last work, and his development of many of its principles, have already been alluded to. But the same mastery was seen elsewhere, the same result exhibited of careful and thorough acquisition. He was a learner to the last. The first volumes of Dr. Hodge's great work were read in the unbound sheets on his journey to Europe. Dorner's work on the Protestant Reformation, almost immediately upon its appearance, was subjected to like examination. And I have little doubt that on that last Saturday morning, before his ride to Alexandria, and while many of us were in the arms of sleep, a portion of the Greek text of the New Testament, with the latest critical aids and appliances, received his careful and devout examination. How grateful the thought, how precious to us the assurance, of that blessed transition, so near at hand; a transition which was a translation, when all human aids, no longer needed, would be forever laid aside. That which had been seen as in a mirror, obscurely reflected, being now perfectly seen with open face, in the very presence of his Lord!

And here, before leaving this sphere, the almost purely intellectual, let me indicate the order, not only of his acquisition, but of his impartation, the relations of the several portions of his course to each other. The stages of that course were fourfold, the first opening the way to that which followed, those subsequent dependent upon this, and adding to it, all forming one complete and systematic whole. The first of these was that of simple fact, the historic facts and evidences connected with the coming into the world, under certain circumstances, of the Divine Author of Christianity, the origin of the books in which are contained the truths of the Christian system, with the removal of difficulties and the replies to objections. The second was that of the general philosophy of this revealed system, the tracing out of the essential resemblance between this supernatural revelation and that which is natural, the analogy of nature and religion. The third was occupied with the particular examination of the contents of inspired revelation, the dictates of the Divine Word, Biblical Theology. And the fourth, and last, had reference to creeds and confessions, Christian doctrines formulated by human agency, expressive of the position of the whole Church, or of portions of it, at different stages of its existence, especially those of our own Church, and all these in their relation to the Supreme authority of Scripture. Putting aside the two former, the course adopted in reference to the others is well worthy of note; may for a few moments, be considered. This was to make Scripture not only supreme, but alone; not only ultimate, but all-sufficient. Adopting the motto, "Bonus textuarius est bonus theologus," he was willing to rest everything in Christian theology proper upon the simple teaching of the inspired Word. Upon the foundation and with the material of this word was his structure; and then, by the results of that word he tested all mere human systems and confessions. The questions, what is the teaching of the early Church, of the Augsburg Confession, of the Council of Trent, of the Prayer-book and Thirty-nine Articles had, indeed, their proper time and place in his instruction. But they were touched only incidentally in the study of Divinity proper. It was his constant effort to keep before the minds of others, and to act for himself upon the great principle, not to allow any of these, or anything else human, to be a measure and circumscribing limit in the process of theological investigation. He refused to know anything as authority, to hear of anything in theology, until, in a spirit of childlike reliance upon its Divine Author, he had patiently and carefully sought His own revealed meaning. This, as most of us are aware, is one of the characteristics of the text-book in that department, introduced by Dr. Keith, but adopted by his successor; and in this its main principle cordially accepted. Not, of course, slavishly to adopt any man's textual analysis or exegesis, any more than his theory of doctrine. But, still, to recognize the fundamental principle of a Scriptural theology, preceding all other theologies, and by which all others must be tested. There was, as already hinted, a later part of his course, and with different text-books, when this question of human standards, and their uses, was distinctly raised; when the question of our own standards, those in England and of our own country, as related to the teaching of Scripture, was carefully investigated. Creeds and confessions, in his estimation, had their place, and that by no means an unimportant one. He had no sympathy with the loose, wild talk of which we now hear so much, that dogma is the source of all the evils of Christendom. The men who babble this nonsense have their dogma, which they are all the time preaching: "That nothing particular ought to be insisted upon!" To use his own striking illustration, "a Church without a creed or confession is like a ship on the high seas without a flag—an ecclesiastical pirate." But while all this, in its place, was thus insisted upon, the great Protestant principle, already mentioned, was never lost sight of, was firmly grasped and unshrinkingly adhered to; in the study of Scriptural theology, Scripture itself and alone must decide all issues. The striking thought of Coleridge, in reference to truth in general, was recognized as specially applicable in the domain of theological inquiry. He who begins by studying the word of God by the measure of this or that human standard, will soon bring it into accord with that standard; and it will not be very long before he brings that standard and the word of God alike into accord with himself, to the measure of his own individual ideas of truth and duty. It is the man loving his Church better than the truth, and loving himself better than either. There is a constant tendency to this, even in Protestant communities, or rather in human nature itself. But no pupil of Dr. Sparrow ever failed to receive his warning against it.

But these intellectual prerequisites, however important to the theological teacher, must be connected with others which are needed as rendering him apt and fit for the work which he has undertaken. When, as in the instance before us, you find the peculiar gift for the peculiar task, the teacher born, not made for his office; when, moreover, you find, superadded upon this, careful and systematic cultivation; when, still further, you have a love for the work, a pleasure in the doing it, and a clear perception of what is to be done; even with all this, you need something more for this high vocation. Thus far we have seen the furnishment mainly, if not entirely, of the teacher's head, his provision for the furnishment of the heads of his pupils. That which gives direction, and steadiness, and elevation, to each of these, alike to the teacher and the taught, is a high moral purpose, the regulative influence of a high moral principle in the reception and in the dispensation of knowledge, whatever its character or applications. If, for the attainment of the highest object of his calling, "the orator must be a good man," much more must the teacher, much more the teacher of theology. There must be in him that upon which his pupils can rely, which they will profoundly respect, or the full benefit of his instruction cannot be enjoyed, if, indeed, there be not positive mischief and injury. Illustrations of the power of this moral element, and the weakness incident to its absence, in individual cases, might be easily adduced. I mention only a few. Take, for instance, the celebrated Hebraist, the benefit of whose text books we have some of us enjoyed—but for whom we have no respect—as, in his lecture-room, with frivolity and sneer, he undermined, or endeavored to undermine, the faith to which his position and office were pledged, and by which he got his bread. Is it possible for such a man properly to instruct students of theology, or, indeed, students of any kind? Take, again, the case of any man who fails to recognize the responsibilities of his position; who does not deal with truth as a sacred thing, and impress it with the same spirit upon those who come under his influence; who indulges in a spirit of levity or indifference in reference to those great moral issues which are constantly presenting themselves, and which must have a decision; who suggests the impression that these are matters in which he feels but little or a subordinate interest; who thus shows that he himself, morally, is a bending reed, shivering and shaking in every passing wind of incidental circumstance, and you have a man who is wanting in the main element of human power to beneficial purposes. I care not what may be his intellectual capacity, his stores of acquisition, his gifts of impartation. He is still wanting in one of the highest qualifications for his work. That qualification being absent, the teacher will, as to the highest culture of his pupils, prove a failure. "He," says Bishop Berkeley, "who has not meditated much upon God, upon the human soul, and upon man's ultimate good, may possibly make a thriving earth-worm; but he will be a blundering patriot, and a sorry statesman." The statement, with a change in terms, is quite as applicable to the office of which we are speaking. A large portion of its power is a moral one, the power of character, of thorough, high-toned integrity. It was the presence of this, the felt presence of this, immediately felt and constantly recognized, which added so much to the qualities already described in the subject of our discussion; its distinct and abundant manifestation, which gave him such hold upon his pupils. He was admired and respected for his intellectual power. He was revered for his moral power. His appeal to men's conscientious convictions, to the supremacy of conscience in their studies, as in their intercourse with each other and the world around them, came with the power of his own example and spirit to sustain them. Nothing that was mean, or little, or crooked, or sidewise, could live in his presence; was instantly withered and consumed in the glance of his indignation. Everything pure, and noble, and elevating, dwelt within and before him, a source of delight wherever and whenever exhibited. Putting aside, for the present, the high motive power of religious principle, and thinking of him only as he would be thought of by those who know nothing of the influence of such principle, these two unmistakable features of character were ever manifest: moral integrity in all things, high moral elevation in thought and precept, as in personal example. In these, to a great degree, was the secret of his power, that power which he so pre-eminently possessed, not only as a teacher, but as an administrator, as a man! His course was felt by himself, and seen by others, to be a thoroughly conscientious one. He was thus enabled to go forward without faltering; and others felt that they ought not, dare not, refuse to follow him.

And as there was this influence of high moral integrity, and this clear exhibition of pure moral principle in teaching and in life, so was all this, in turn, quickened, and purified, and elevated by a profoundly religious spirit, by the constant recognition and application of the great principle that all duty and obligation must be viewed in the light of Divine truth, that all truth and all duty must have reference to God. It was a morality, as a theology, baptized with the Holy Ghost. Christianity to him was a great moral and spiritual system to work upon the minds and hearts of men. Its various institutions, its ministry, its sacraments, its instructions, were recognized of value only as they attained spiritual results. They were but as scaffolding for the building, not something for which that building was erected. "Religion," to use almost his very words, "religion of some kind or other men must and will have. There is no trouble nor difficulty about that. The trouble, the difficulty is, not to make them have a religion, or to make them religious, but to make them have the right kind of religion; to make them religious in the right way; to make them have spiritual religion." This was the one word which expressed his idea of the essential nature of Christianity; as to what this right kind of religion was; which described the predominant element of his own personal religion, as it made itself manifest to others; spirituality, the Gospel dispensation, a dispensation of the spirit of Christ, for the moral and spiritual regeneration of man's whole nature. It was not, to his view, a dispensation of the Incarnate Christ by His bodily presence in the sacramental emblems, in His visibly organized Church, or in His outwardly consecrated ministry. It was one of the risen Christ, in the perfection of His divinity, as of His humanity, by His Spirit, the Comforter, the Holy Ghost, the Lord and Giver of spiritual life, making use of these various outward agencies for the sanctification of human spirits, for their transformation into Christ's divine image, for their fitting and preparation for the service of Christ's heavenly sanctuary. If there was any one truth which, more than others, may be said to have shaped his thinking and teaching, it was this: *Christianity a spiritual religion, a dispensation of the Spirit.* All, in some form or other, admit this. He fully believed it, realized it, and permanently rested in it. This it was which gave character and tone to his theology, which shaped his ecclesiastical system, which gave directness, force, and symmetry to his personal religion. To the test of this everything else was subjected; as it stood that test, was it cast aside as worthless, or cordially accepted. This at once explains his position to many of the issues of the last half century, to many of the tendencies now prevailing. All of those developments of materialized Christianity, of spiritualized materialism of the past and of the present, which have so much interfered with, and are so much interfering with spiritual religion, in the Church and in the world, were thus summarily and indignantly rejected. Those deeper views, as they are claimed to be, of the sacraments, circumscribing and localizing the omnipresent Spirit in the waters of baptism, the ascended Christ in the elements of the Supper, were thus recognized as anything but deep; as essentially degrading alike to the sacraments, their administrators, and their recipients. Those higher views, again, as they are claimed to be, of the Church or of the ministry, which make the validity of their action and their very existence depend upon the outward, the visible, and the tangible, were thus seen to be low, earthly, groveling. All these tendencies of unregenerate or partially regenerate human nature to get rid of the dispensation of the Spirit, and to have one of sense and of sight in its place, to bring back the visibilities and externalities of Judaism, or even worse, the fetich elements of a dead and putrescent Paganism; to all this he set himself in steady opposition. His whole teaching with reference to such matters might have been expressed in the language of the Master: "Take these things hence." Or in the reproachful question of the Apostle: "Are ye so foolish; having begun in the Spirit, are ye made perfect in the flesh?" Against everything of this nature he set his face as a flint. It was an issue of essential Christianity, and there could be no compromise. The conflict must be to the death. For other differences he made large allowance, in reference to other issues was disposed to much tolerance. But here, the faith, its very kernel and life, must be earnestly contended for. To make spirit flesh, and flesh spirit, to materialize Christianity, was to change its nature, was to betray Christianity, was to betray Christ Himself, and misrepresent Him and His cause before the world. This was the theology of the recitation-room. It was the burden of the Thursday evening exhortation. And it rang out from this place in tones clear and distinct, and that could not be misunderstood: Christianity a system of spiritual truth, seeking spiritual results depending upon spiritual instrumentalities!

And this, his high spirituality, let it be distinctly noted, rested upon certain well-defined objective truths, out of those truths derived its power and vitality. His teaching, and thinking, and living were distinctively Evangelical. He cordially accepted the system known by that name, and as represented by such men as Leigh Richmond and Charles Simeon, in England, Alexander Griswold and William Meade, in this country. Probably the first decidedly theological influence brought to bear upon his mind was that of a relative, the Rev. Peter Roe, of Ireland, a clergyman of this school. He listened to the same truths, drank in the same influences, as a lonely student, in his weekly attendance upon the lectures of Dr. Milnor. The principles thus brought before him became those of his life, more philosophically arranged, better expressed than by some with whom he sympathized, more elaborated than by others, more carefully guarded in certain points, especially those involving the issues of Divine agency and human accountability, but still essentially in thorough accord with the system thus described, and the leaders just mentioned, by whom it was represented. He candidly accepted that view of Christianity which humbles man, which abases the sinner and exalts Christ; which finds that "Christ is all" in all the spiritual wants of men as lost and ruined creatures; which, therefore, brings every imagination and every capacity in captivity to the will of Christ, in humble dependence upon His grace, in loving obedience to His will. These were the great truths in which he himself lived, and moved, and had his spiritual being, and which, therefore, constituted the staple of his instruction. For, while accepting heartily the maxim of one great theologian, already quoted, that thorough scriptural knowledge is the basis of all real theological knowledge, he no less heartily, as a moral correlate, accepted that of another, that such knowledge, to be of any value, must be examined and received in a certain state of the heart. It was not merely, therefore, natural talent, culture, high moral tone, spirituality. All these were increased as to their value by Evangelical truth. Some of them found their value, and even their source, in that truth. In these respects, Dr. Sparrow, like another great thinker and preacher of this century, Robert Hall, was a remarkable exemplification of the fact that this Evangelical system is entirely consistent not only with the most thorough training and culture, but with the highest order of metaphysical acumen, of philosophical intellect, and that, in these as in other classes, it was combined with high spirituality. These two things, Evangelical truth and spirituality, are naturally connected. The whole history of the Church shows that the amount of either one, in any age or country, constitutes an indication of the presence and a measure of the amount of the other. I do not mean by this to say that there is no spirituality outside of and beyond the limits of the Evangelical portion of our Church, or those of the same views in other churches. A great many men are better than their creed, and a great many are not as good. Professedly Evangelical men are sometimes formalists and legalists, narrow in themselves and harsh in their thoughts and judgments of others, even worse than this, Antinomians. There are others, again, who repudiate this name, are ashamed of it, or who positively hate and revile it; but, by a blessed inconsistency, as individuals, are in the cordial reception of Evangelical truth and in the diligent cultivation of Evangelical graces. In all such cases we would rejoice that so much of the substance is in possession, whatever may be done or said as to the name. The issue now is not between individuals, but systems; those systems intelligently accepted and consistently worked; individuals only to be thought of as they consistently represent those systems. We cannot venture to say of any individual who is identifying himself with the materialistic or legalistic movements of our day, with the Sacramental or Sacerdotal systems, now so industriously advocated, we cannot venture to say of any such individual that he is not one of Christ's people. But this we must and ought to say, that the system which he is working and the doctrine which he is advocating is not Christianity, is not that of the Gospel of salvation. It does behoove us at this time, those who are set for the defence of the truth, especially, in view of the tremendous odds against it, an ecclesiastical atmosphere reeking with the contagion of its opposite, it is incumbent upon us to be open and square as to this our position; meekly and lovingly, but firmly and decidedly, retaining not only the thing, but the name by which that thing is known among men. Names are often things, and he who wishes to get rid of the name by which certain principles have been described, and recognized, and known, is in a fair way to get rid of the principles themselves. There *is* an Evangelical system, that of the leading Reformers in England and on the Continent; that of the first two or three generations of theological leaders in the English Church; that of Venn, and Richmond, and Wilberforce; that of Meade, and Milnor, and McIlvaine. And there is another system: you may call it the Church system, or the Legal system, or the Sacramental system, or the Tractarian system, or the Ritualistic system, just as it modifies itself at different times to these distinct forms of manifestation. But in all these modifications it has one unifying principle: it ever fronts and opposes the Evangelical. Between them there can be no real cordiality. It is, to use the striking thought of another, the wrestle of Luther and Cyprian in the womb of the same ecclesiastical mother. Eventually one must overcome and cast out the other; not, necessarily, by force, by ecclesiastical legislation, or by outward machinery of any kind, but by argument and by truth. I have no doubt as to where the argument and truth are, and therefore none as to the final result. We may properly fear for individuals, and even for generations. Certainly, there are just grounds of fear for many of the men of this generation. But there need be no such fear whatever as to the final triumph of Evangelical truth. In the meantime, however, and while the struggle is going on and the great issue pending, it behooves us to stand in our lot, to recognize our position, and to do what we may for the accomplishment of the great result. And here, in the example of our departed preceptor and leader, we have an indication as to our proper duty. It was ever his wish to be understood as identified with these Evangelical principles, as an upholder of the Evangelical system. While it was his effort to impress upon those under his tuition the responsibility for themselves to "prove all things," to "hold only that which was true and" good, there could be no doubt what he regarded as good, what he had proved, to his own satisfaction, to be true. His main interest in this Institution, which he served so long and which he loved so well, was as it was identified with the principles of its original founders. It was his effort to keep it and to leave it in these respects as he found it, a place in which men might learn Evangelical truth and be brought under its responsibilities, whatever use or perversion they might make of it afterward. "Our flag," said he, some eight years ago, while the Institution was struggling with the difficulties of its fresh start, after the calamities through which it had been passing, and in speaking of its anticipated future work, "our flag of Evangelical principles is nailed to the mast; and if it goes down, we had better go down with it." How grateful the thought that those efforts were successful; that he was permitted to survive and to witness so much of that success; that he was able to welcome on our Semi-Centennial so many of his old friends and pupils, and to rejoice with them in the assurance that his labors had not been in vain. It was this, coupled with the additional assurance that the Institution was to go on more vigorously than ever in its old work, resting upon its old foundations and witnessing for the same old precious truths, which constituted the special grounds of his rejoicing. For this he had labored. In these assurances he was already receiving the fruit of his labors.

And as there was this hope and assurance to him, so does it contain an important practical suggestion to us: our duty and work for this Institution, with which he was so closely identified and which so long enjoyed the benefit of his labors. Is it not our part to actualize his anticipations, to see that his hopes receive fulfillment? And when I say "our," I do not mean those only who are engaged in the work of instruction, or in that of control and administration. They act efficiently and successfully only as sustained and encouraged by others. Our Alumni, those here present with us, those elsewhere, who are interested in our work, those of our members who are just leaving us, those who expect for a brief period to return, all these have their work for its advancement and welfare. In these, our respective positions, we are now especially reminded of our duty to fill up, so far as we can, the gap that has been made, to supply the place of what has been taken away. Individuals die, but principles, and institutions representing principles, live. When an individual, identified with such an institution and its principles, who has occupied a large sphere of effort and of usefulness, is taken from it by death, or otherwise, the providential call to those who remain is not to despond, but to be up and doing more actively, to be more determined and more abundant than ever in their labors and exertions. The dying words of one of our Alumni, on the coast of Africa, in regard to the work to which he had given his life, are expressive of what ought to be our feelings under our present circumstances: "Let the Mission," our work, "go forward; let it go forward more than ever." Such, I am persuaded, would be the exhortation of our departed teacher, if he could now appear in our midst. Such is the providential appeal and charge to us under the circumstances of the present moment. Let our Seminary go forward. Let it go forward, not for its own sake, but for its work's sake, and for the Master's sake; let it go forward more than ever. If we would effectively respond to this appeal, we must remember that it can be done only through definite and earnest exertion. We want, brethren, a great many things. But I put aside, for the present, mention of all but three, that are almost indispensable, that ought to be distinctly placed before us, as claiming our exertions. We want, first, the material of men, to be ready to take hold of and to carry on the work of the Institution when those now engaged in it follow their departed colleague, are laid aside, or in their graves. Our younger clergy, especially, ought to see to this, that they are fully abreast of the culture of our age, so that, if necessary, they can fill the teacher's place. We want, again, the material, in the way of full endowment, to work the Institution comfortably, efficiently, thoroughly, and without embarrassment. And, last of all, and most important of all, we need material for our classes, that there should be a full supply of men, and of the right kind of men, to be enjoying the benefit of such provision. In this last item there is great deficiency, deficiency which involves great culpability. There are congregations in this Diocese, and elsewhere, large congregations, which have been going on for years, which have used up and worn out two or three generations of ministerial laborers, and yet have not themselves sent a single laborer into the field. This ought not so to be. It would not if there were distinct, specific, and earnest pastoral effort and prayer, not only to save souls, but to find, and call out, and develop men who will consecrate themselves to the same great undertaking. I would leave these three points, especially the last, for your reflection, and as suggesting some of the modes in which you may aid our Institution; in which you may take up and carry on the work to which the life and energies of our departed teacher were so long and faithfully devoted.

I have thus endeavored, very imperfectly, to recall some of those features which we delighted to contemplate; amid the associations of this hour, to dwell for a little time longer, mournfully, reverently, and lovingly, upon those traits of character, intellectual, moral, and spiritual, which, through the force of example, have impressed themselves upon so many others, have so greatly shaped and moulded the character and ministerial work of so many, during the last half century. Let us remember that these traits, while those of the successful theological teacher, are also those of the teacher everywhere: in the pulpit, in the Bible-class, in the sphere of pastoral life, in the intercourse of ministerial contact with our fellow-men. There are not many men who possess the combination of rare qualities with which he was endowed. Few, indeed, possess any one of those qualities in the same degree. But to some degree, all have most of them. They can all be cultivated, and, in our work, they all have their proper place. We honor him most highly, so far as in these traits we closely imitate his example; his diligent, and careful, and thorough cultivation, his high moral tone, his deep and all-pervading spirituality, his thorough appreciation, and love, and zeal for the essential truths of the Gospel. All these constitute elements of power in the ministerial work, elements which may well become to us objects of earnest attainment. "Not slothful in business, fervent in spirit, serving the Lord." That was his last message, the last pouring out of that heart and intellect for our benefit and welfare, as for the honor of the Master. Let us take that precept as illustrated in his personal example; follow him, as he would have had us do, only "as he followed Christ."

REMINISCENCES OF DR. SPARROW.

BY REV. E. W. SYLE.

"YEDO, JAPAN, July 13, 1875.

"REV. AND DEAR BROTHER:—

"From your own experience you can understand that the time of entering on a new professorship is not one of literary leisure; and you may imagine that in adapting one's lecture to the mental status of a class of young Japanese students, on such subjects as History and Moral Philosophy, I have had, if not a difficult, yet an absorbing task, during the past few months.

"Now, however, the examinations are over, and after one day of mental relaxation I set myself to use my leisure in complying with your request for some reminiscences of Dr. Sparrow.

"I have already sent you a few pages, and have referred you to my son for letters, which he was authorized to put at your service, so that you might have the material for that 'unconscious autobiography' which is to be found in the correspondence of one who writes, as Dr. Sparrow did, fully, and earnestly, and ingenuously. Indeed, it was this gift, or habit (with him it was both), of conscientious letter-writing, as a part of his ministry, which I should fix upon as one of the most marked and valuable of his characteristics. I never knew of his writing a foolish letter, although he sometimes, not often, however, indulged in pleasantry; while he was far from despising wit, or regarding it as wickedness. He *was*, however, conscientious about it; and I remember one occasion, when, in a company of friends, I had myself said something which failed to be as pleasant as was intended, and as pleasantries should be, to deserve the name, he volunteered the remark afterward, when we were alone: 'I know nothing more difficult or delicate than the right use of wit, a sanctified wit. It is a talent, but a very rare one.'

"Let me return, however, to his letters, of which I have a few with me, the last of a long series, extending from 1840, when I left Ohio, after having been under his instruction for five years at Gambier (part of that time acting as private tutor in his family), down to the date of October, 1873, when he wrote the most touching of all, some short time after Mrs. Sparrow's death.

"I find it difficult to make extracts without bringing myself more prominently into notice than I could wish; but as you particularly request me to send you 'personal' traits, I can only do so by giving what he wrote and did, as I personally was connected with him.

"The first extract is from a letter dated January 3, 1868, and refers to a claim I had against a certain parish for balance of salary.

"'I had declined, not very long ago, to act as a referee at the request of a clerical brother; and yet I would have made your case an exception to my rule, if I felt myself competent to such duty, or standing in a state of indifference to both the parties. But that is not the case, and therefore I have been compelled to decline.'

"This calls to mind his characteristic delicacy and sensitiveness as to money-matters. His mind recoiled from rough contact, of any kind, with others, and especially from an assertion of his own rights. I feel sure he never could have written such a passage as 2 Cor. xi, 12; he would have shrunk from saying so much about himself.

"For this reason he was apt to be a disappointing—I might as well say it, for I am sure he would have said it himself—a disappointing and an *ineffective* member of conventions, boards, etc., in cases where it might be necessary 'earnestly to contend' for some plan or principle; so that even a good cause in his hands was apt to suffer, because he hated anything like strife among brethren.

"The idea of *soliciting* any position of honor or emolument was entirely at variance with his feelings and principles, however much he might know that he deserved the honor and needed the emolument.

"After a suggestion that he might very properly do something of this kind in regard to the presidency of Kenyon College, then vacant, his answer was, 'No, sir, no; I could never do so.' And then, after a pause, 'I might do it for my children's sake, but never for my own.'

"In speaking of that Institution, he once said: 'I have stood by it through all its struggles, from the time it was commenced at Worthington till now, when Bexley Hall is being built. In this place my best years of labor have been spent, and here my children have been born. Mr. Syle, *I love the very stones upon the road!'*

"Just at that juncture, when he had determined to leave Kenyon, the rectorship of St. Andrew's, Pittsburg, was pressed upon him, and he was well minded to accept it; but he doubted his ability to do pastoral work with satisfaction to himself; and he dreaded the task of clearing off a $10,000 debt which was then weighing on the congregation.

"In the wear and tear of the struggling work of the first days of the College, none took a heavier share than Dr. Sparrow. He and Professor Wing were the veterans of those early battles which were fought against obloquy, poverty, and, as the trustees were apt to think, Episcopal encroachment.

"Many were the contests on this latter point, in Bishop Chase's time, and Dr. Sparrow was, in most cases, I believe, the spokesman of the trustees, though greatly against his wishes. It is thoroughly characteristic of him that, on one occasion, he wrote a very powerful pamphlet, and had it printed; and then, having relieved his mind by this advocacy of what he felt to be right and true, his aversion to strife returned, like a tide, and his heart failed him as soon as a few copies were put in circulation. The greater part were, as he told me himself, bundled up and stowed away in the garret of his house at Gambier; to be brought out, I doubt not, at the time of his removal, to be treated as waste paper.

"He had always, as you know, an extreme jealousy of the *undefined* prerogatives of the Episcopal office, maintaining that these were limited strictly by the written laws of the Church; and his view of the 'Divine Right' was, that it stood in the category of all governments, as such; not exclusive, as to any one form, but binding, like the injunction, 'Honor the king,' as an obedience due on the part of Christians to the 'powers that be,' general, not restricted in its application.

"I cannot say that his arguments of this subject were satisfactory to my own mind; my feeling was that they *fell short* of the mark; but in those college days I had not been led to study the matter very fully, and I do not think I am competent to state fairly what he really held, or even what he declined to hold, though I am sure he demurred, after the manner of Archbishop Whately, to extreme High-Church claims, and had a most hearty contempt for the man-millinery of Ritualism, while he relished greatly Sidney

Smith's description of the Oxford movement, as consisting of 'Posture and Imposture;' as also that epithet of 'The Times,' which stigmatized the whole system as 'Pernicious Nonsense.'

"Before leaving Gambier and its associations, I must mention one or two of Dr. Sparrow's characteristic engagements there. I call them *characteristic*, because, though they were things which other men might do, yet his way of doing them had an air of freshness, and a flavor of originality about it which makes the memory of them as distinct as the experience of them was enjoyable.

"For instance: When giving us undergraduates, as his custom was, a Bible Lecture, on Thursday evenings, on one occasion he dwelt upon what he called the 'invaluable tenth chapter of Genesis,' in such a manner as to make us feel that wonderful collection of unaccustomed names was one of the most interesting passages of history that had ever been written; and when he dwelt on the expression 'before the Lord,' as added to the designation of 'Nimrod, the mighty hunter,' we were made to feel that it was the searching something of God's sight which made things to appear what they *really are.* What power of vivid portraiture he had will be well known to all who attended the 'Faculty' prayer-meetings at Alexandria.

"At Kenyon, toward the end of his residence, he introduced the custom of holding a recitation in the Greek New Testament, on Monday mornings, for the Junior and Senior classes. These were remarkably instructive and impressive. I shall never forget the amount of emotion he evoked when dwelling on Acts v, 41, and showing, first, what a powerful feeling *shame* was, and then, how great must have been the grace which enabled the Apostles not only to *bear* the shame, but to *rejoice* in it!

"A connecting link in my mind, between his work at Gambier and at Alexandria, was his exceptional kindness in permitting me to make a copy of his manuscripts: Questions and Notes on Butler's Analogy, Christian Evidences, and Systematic Divinity. This favor was accorded to me on the ground that I was going abroad as a Missionary, and it might be especially helpful to me in my far-off field of labor, removed from all libraries and from intercourse with studious and scholarly minds. And greatly helpful have I found them; for on missionary ground we find the heresies of old springing up almost in their original order, Arianism first, and Sabellianism not long after; Corinthian confusion and ascetic self-righteousness filling up the intervals of serious doctrinal departures.

"As to the Questions themselves, the very process of copying them (which occupied me about two months, the whole of a long vacation), brought its own benediction; for they were so suggestive, and the notes and extracts appended to them were so full of the choicest matter, that I doubt if any other method of dwelling on the several topics which passed under review could have been more advantageous to a student. It made me understand that in the days when books were fewer, and copying more common, thoroughness in scholarship might be looked for rather than in these times when the book-trade has so much to do with common-school education. At all events, this experience of mine has had its effect in moulding the method I pursue in carrying my students at the Imperial College through the lessons of Moral Philosophy which I myself learned under Dr. Sparrow. Our text-book at Gambier was Wayland, and we found it satisfactory, as amplified by our admired Professor.

"The Questions above referred to were re-cast at about the time when he removed to Alexandria; reduced in amount, and expressed with more terseness—perhaps with more accuracy; but not, as I thought, improved upon the whole; especially as he omitted many of the extracts and references to current literature, as well as to unusual authorities, which are so invaluable to a young student, who has not yet learned where to find what he wants.

"And now farewell to Gambier, a place where there was a strange blending of the old and new; of refined ideas and primitive manners; of literary life and country customs. Some of the contrasts and transitions were bordering on the ludicrous; and of this there was no lack of appreciation on the part of our good Doctor. Those very preaching excursions, to which I have referred as so full of impressiveness and profit, were sometimes preceded by endeavors to borrow a horse for the occasion, which were anything but propitious and promotive of 'a quiet mind.' Riding up to his house one day, for the purpose of escorting him out into the wilderness—for such it was—his description of what he had just gone through was of the most graphic kind, concluding with, 'You see, Mr. Syle, that when one has borrowed a horse from one neighbor, and a saddle from another, and then goes out, bridle in hand, to catch the "critter," who dodges about in every fence-corner in the field; then, when you have led him up to the door and saddled him, you have had about enough of the ride!' Most certainly, in his case; for his feeble, attenuated physique was an unceasing source of distress to him, and his constant tendency to headache a veritable thorn in the flesh; though he was accustomed to work on, and work through all such ailments, very seldom giving up except from sheer exhaustion and actual inability. Once, I remember, myself, bringing him—unintentionally, of course—to the breaking-down point, by making him a visit to inquire what his views were as to *how far* a man might differ from the Articles, to which he made a general subscription. His answer I well remember, perhaps all the better for its having been given at the moment of exhaustion: 'As far,' he said, 'as his own conscience will permit, and the existing authorities of the Church, duly informed, will tolerate.'

"This answer was a specimen of many we used to receive to questions we were in the habit of putting to him. He would generally close his eyes while listening to a question (sometimes quoting the Arabic proverb, 'Shut the windows that there may be light in the house'), and never answering until he had made the questioner state the *precise point* of his inquiry; and then his answer would be simple, and careful, and generally rather disappointing *at the moment;* but the more you thought over it, the more you appreciated its judiciousness and adequacy. In this matter of answering his student's questions, he would seem to have been in marked contrast to his predecessor at the Seminary, Dr. Keith, who had the faculty of replying to questions, pertinent or *otherwise,* in a manner which made the young man 'wish he had not spoken.' With Dr. Sparrow, however, it was otherwise. I never remember, but once, his reproving a student in class, and that he did by pointing and looking at the offender in silence, until he felt as if he wished the earth would open and swallow him up. But, as a general thing, he was eminently patient with the difficulties of young inquiring minds, and would take much pains to put them on the right track when he found them wandering.

"As to those frightful headaches, from which he suffered so much, and which were induced by such slight causes (I have heard him say that three grains of black pepper would suffice to put him in misery), they were induced, he told me, by his inordinate and irregular habits of study when he was an undergraduate at Columbia College, where, after the occupations of the day, he would read far into the night, under the stimulus of strong coffee. For this imprudence he paid a heavy, life-long penalty. I should rank him among the many men of note, such as Baxter and Leighton, who have accomplished much work, and done much good in the world, in spite of permanent bodily suffering and infirmity.

"Sometimes the students would apply to him more formally, and in writing. As an instance, I remember my dear friend and fellow-student, Stephen Gassaway, who had been brought under deep convictions during a revival which was experienced at Kenyon in the year 1838–39.

"The question Mr. Gassaway submitted was as to whether or not he ought to seek the ministry; and the answer of Dr. Sparrow, if it is extant, will be found to be one of the most judicious and most thorough that was ever written on the subject. In a word, he was always accessible to his students, patient and pains-taking in considering their difficulties, and eminently wise and satisfactory in his answers and practical advice.

"In connection with Gambier, I may mention one more of the occasions when Dr. Sparrow's willingness to be 'about his Master's work' showed itself in an interesting manner, and brought out traits of character which are not often found in combination with the learning and acumen, the meditative mood and studious habit, which he undoubtedly possessed.

"It was the custom of the religious students at Gambier to set off early on Sunday mornings and distribute themselves among the numerous school-houses, generally log cabins, which were scattered through all the country round about; and when circumstances permitted, they made preaching appointments for the several professors who might be disengaged. I had two such schools under my care, and succeeded in frequently securing Dr. Sparrow to preach in one or other of them.

"Those were the days of very primitive arrangements: rough slabs for benches; a tin bucket of water and a dipper, near the door, for thirsty children; babies in arms, or (when asleep) laid on the floor; candles, when it was an 'early candle-light preaching,' stuck on hoops hung up, or on blocks of wood, set on the preaching-desk; men in summer costume of new vest and shirt-sleeves; women in an indescribable variety of home-made linsey-woolsey and store-bought dry goods; occasionally a hunter with the accustomed long, heavy rifle in his hand, or a traveler who would hitch his horse to a bough outside, and 'come in for a spell, to hear preaching.'

"It was in such circumstances as these, winter and summer, that our good Doctor would preach with a simplicity and directness, and at the same time with a wisdom and depth, that made his sermons a study and a model. Often have I myself reproduced to heathen congregations in China, as well as to Christian audiences in Brooklyn, Newark, Washington, Pelham, Shanghai, and Yokohama, the very thoughts and turns of expression which I have heard drop from him in 'Schenk's school-house,' or by 'Jones' Run,' in Ohio.

"Once, I remember his dwelling with much earnestness on the way in which many persons delude themselves by saying: 'I'm not a professor of religion, and therefore I'm not responsible for doing religious things.' His text, I think, was, 'Men ought always to pray,' and he was emphasizing the first word, as showing that prayer was the duty of men, *all* men, not of those only who professed themselves Christians. 'We must not,' he urged, 'get our convictions of duty only by going round through the door of a Christian profession.'

"On another occasion, when discussing the question, What is the right course to pursue when convinced of its being our duty to perform a certain act, but at the same time our state of mind is anything but suitable for its performance? 'Do the thing,' he said, 'and humble yourselves before God for being in such an unfit state of mind.'

"These are but specimens, and I give them as indicating that discriminating habit of thought which was so sure to appear in dealing with minds under all circumstances; and in mentioning, above, the several places to which I, as one of his hearers, have carried the seeds of thought he dropped, I wished to show how widespread his influence was. Moreover, I am satisfied that a large proportion of his students have done the same thing; and that not only China and Japan, but Africa and Greece, with many a parish and mission-station in the United States, have been enriched intellectually and theologically by the clear and forcible ideas which he had the peculiar faculty of impressing on his students, and which they, in turn, have imparted to others also. Not that all his thoughts were original, as being exclusively his own;

and yet original they were, as coming fresh from a mind which had made them completely its own, and reproduced them with all the freshness and force of vivid and sincere conviction.

"Perhaps the most exciting (and I am afraid I must add *enjoyable*) occasions on which the college students looked for a 'treat,' was when his gaunt form was seen walking up to the reading-desk at the time of evening prayers, and his air was that of one filled with gentlemanly indignation, and trying to repress it. Then every one knew that 'something was coming' in the way of castigation for some unhappy collegian who had been misbehaving himself. The little lectures that he gave on these occasions ranged over the whole field of college discipline, and I might say of active life; and very memorable were some of his sayings at such times, not always from their unusualness, but from the simple earnestness with which they were uttered. As, for instance, when, at the beginning of a term, he urged us to be good and diligent workers, he added, in his quiet, solemn tones, 'Young gentlemen, six months is a considerable portion of a lifetime.'

"So of his sermons in the college chapel; they were always looked forward to with the greatest interest, and no one dreamed of making the silly complaint of their being 'long;' we could have listened for an hour longer, and been thankful for it.

"When he preached the baccalaureate sermon at the time of our graduation, in 1840, he left an ineffaceable impression on our minds by the remark: 'It is the responsibility of educated men that they must think not only for themselves, but also for others.'

"Among extracts from letters, one of the first is from a letter dated December 7, 1867, and refers to my (then) approaching departure for China, on what I am accustomed to call my third missionary campaign:—

"'Your letter startled me, and on reflection gave me pleasure. Though I feel an old man's weakness in not liking to see early friends locally separated from me, yet, as I know it is according to your mind, and will give you a field of usefulness for which you are eminently qualified, I rejoice. I hope, too, if you should be so inclined, you may be put back into your old, and, as I suppose, your proper sphere of labor.'

"This last remark had reference to my being reappointed as a missionary of our Board. I was going out to Shanghai for two years, as seamen's chaplain.

"'It is a real satisfaction to me, that I shall once more have the opportunity of shaking hands with you, and that I shall be permitted to bid you and your dear wife "God speed," as you set out for that land which is full of profoundest interest to me as a field of Christian beneficence, and the depository of the remains of my dear Susan.'

"No one knows better than myself, perhaps none now living so well, what an amount of fatherly love and Christian resignation lay hidden in this reference to his 'dear Susan.' She was his very dear, I might almost say his favorite daughter; though it was not easy for him to distinguish between those, all of whom he loved so well.

"He had strong views of the value of home education, and a great horror of the evils to which all schools are liable; and certainly no family ever grew up more 'ignorant of evil' than his. Susan was eminently a 'child of nature,' and from the time when she was my pupil, at the age of nine, up to the day when she came out to China, as the wife of Rev. Dudley D. Smith, and took charge (for a season) of my motherless children, she showed herself one of the most devoted, cheerful, unselfish Christians I ever met with; perhaps the very most.

"This was a result (so far as education can produce such results) of the pure, unsophisticated home-training which she and her sisters had received, and of the impressions made by the character of mother as well as father. Mrs. Sparrow was absorbingly devoted to her children; to such a degree, indeed, as to make it difficult for any but the most intimate friends to attain to a due appreciation of her influence and attainments. Her reading was thorough and extensive, so that she sympathized intelligently in her husband's intellectual pursuits; and could (as I had occasion to know) co-operate earnestly in her children's advancement in all that goes under the name of 'schooling.' She had, also, the reputation of being a great Shakspearean, although, as before remarked, she mixed so little in general society that this fact could only be known to those who constituted the home circle.

"I lost the opportunity of seeing them all more intimately, by not accompanying the family when they 'took up their carriages' and migrated in a body from Gambier to Alexandria. Two 'stages' were chartered for the purpose, and it was more like the setting out of a caravan than anything one could witness now in the same region. Wheeling was to be a stopping-place, and I well remember the hearty letter of welcome and invitation received from good Dr. Armstrong on the occasion. It said: 'Come one, come all; we can easily put you up. You have but seven children, and I have only three, which altogether makes two less than the canonical number!' Which last remark caused Dr. Sparrow a hearty laugh. 'I never knew before,' he said, 'what the canonical number was!' He needed something to cheer him up at that time, for this moving was a painful trial.

"To return to his letter. I had suggested that a relative (one of his sons-in-law) might like to take the pleasant parish I was vacating, and to this Dr. Sparrow's answer was:—

"'I sent your letter to ——, but I have no idea he will accept. To say all in a word, there would not be enough of stirring work for him. If his *father-in-law* were offered it, he would be in much more of a temper to accept it than he.

"'With the very best wishes to Mrs. Syle, I am, dear brother,

"'Affectionately yours, W. SPARROW.'

"And when he said 'affectionately yours,' he meant it all.

"The next letter is without date of month or year; but it must have been when our good Doctor 'came North,' on an errand which must have been a martyrdom to him, an errand connected with the collection of money for restoring the Seminary property after the damage it had sustained during the war. I presume it was the knowledge of how repulsive to him was the office of money-gatherer that led to the considerate course of action to which he refers.

"'PHILADELPHIA, Wednesday Morning, 6 o'clock A. M.

"'REV. AND DEAR BROTHER:—

"'Here I am at Dudley's, having arrived in this city last night. It is almost the first leisure moment I have had since I left your pleasant abode, or I should have written you before. The brethren have printed a circular asking $5000 for the repair and fitting up of our tenements and grounds. They are to send this circular themselves, and receive the avails, and so relieve me of further trouble. It is signed by Dr. Dyer, Dr. Smith, and Messrs. Sabine, Tyng, Jr., and J. H. Smith. If they succeed, oh, what a relief it will be!

"'I enclose a dollar to pay for what I borrowed of you. It falls short of what I owe you, but I know not how much. We can adjust the matter when we meet; if it should be the Lord's will, we shall. 'If the Lord will' seems to be most appropriate everywhere now. I go back to my winter's work feeling very doubtful if I shall ever return North again. What a dream, a brief dream, life is! How long, and yet short, the time since you and I first met! The Lord prepare us for our change, be it far off or near.

"'Please present me most kindly to Mrs. Syle. I wish I could have had a quiet day's talk with her. Remember me to the children, and believe me, as ever,

"'Your friend and brother, WILLIAM SPARROW.

"'*Rev. E. W. Syle, Pelham Priory, N. Y.*'

"I give this letter entire, in spite of—or, rather, *because* of—its tone of domesticity, for this was one of his leading characteristics; love of home, and a profound sense of the importance of the Family, as distinguished from all other forms of human association. I remember his finding fault with some of my letters from China, because they were too exclusively occupied with public matters, and did not give the details of family life, what the Chinese ate and drank, and how the women and children occupied themselves, etc. Also, what was the daily, domestic life of the missionary and his wife: how they fared, and what intercourse they had with other families. He was much struck and pleased with a remark which I related to him as having heard fall from Archbishop Whately, in a conversation which turned on Macaulay's History of England, then recently published. The Archbishop said: 'Macaulay is right; we want to know the daily life of the common people. No one can prize Thucydides more than I do; yet I would give all Thucydides ever wrote for the diary of an Athenian fish-woman for one day: what she ate; what was the price of her fish; what orator she heard speak in the agora, etc.' Perhaps he was the more alive to these points, at that particular time, because they were then thinking of the dear daughter Susan, who was about to enter, herself, on the experiences of missionary life. Her early death was a very severe blow, and all the home-circle felt it keenly; but when I asked the tender-hearted father whether, all things considered, he had not regretted her going abroad, 'No,' he said, 'never; her's was a holy calling, and she fulfilled it. Neither myself nor Mrs. Sparrow ever regretted giving our consent.' This, to me, was a great satisfaction, for I knew that Susan's coming out to China had been partly through my influence.

"Reverting to the subject of family life, and its importance. On one occasion we were at Arlington together, and were looking over Mr. Custis' library, when Dr. Sparrow's eye fell on a copy of Bowdler's *Expurgated* edition of Shakspeare, the idea of which he praised warmly, as enabling us to read the great poet freely in our families, without the risk of encountering passages marred by obscenity and profaneness.

"It was his high esteem of the family, and his deep conviction of the advantages resulting to all parties concerned from the existence of a married, rather than a celibate ministry, that gave an extra edge to his severity against Rome; indeed, he hardly seemed to know which his heart and conscience most revolted against, Monasticism or Sacerdotalism. On one occasion we were engaged together in an examination of pupils in Virgil, and the teacher—who *had been* a Roman Catholic—while putting questions about the history and character of Dido, took occasion to make some disparaging remarks about women in general, especially married women. After the examination, and when we were alone, Dr. Sparrow remarked: 'Did you observe ——'s sneer about Dido? You see how the vice of Romanism—disparagement of the marriage state—clings to him, though he has come over to our Church; that miserable delusion and fallacy that the single life is something better, purer, holier than the married state; which is an idea derogatory to the wisdom and goodness of the Creator.'

"In thorough antagonism to all things which are rightly called *Romish*, as distinguished from *Catholic*, I believe Dr. Sparrow and myself were in perfect accord; even more than in regard to Missions, as the *supreme* work of the Christian Church. As a Missionary man he was not showy, or even ardent, but very thorough and reliable; witness the unregretted giving up to the work of his dearly-loved daughter.

"These remarks seemed necessary, as an introduction to the next letter, which was addressed to me after I had arrived in China:—

"'THEOLOGICAL SEMINARY, August 19, 1868.

"'REV. AND DEAR BROTHER:—

"'I am ashamed that your letter should have remained without an answer so long. I read it with much interest, and, in most respects, I take the same view of the condition of the world and of the cause of Missions, especially in our Church, that you do. I think, however, that your views are rather more sombre than they ought to be. Not only do I believe, on the Divine testimony, that all things are working steadily onward for good, but I fancy, amid the actual confusion, the abounding iniquity, and the seeming failure of well-meant effort, the beginnings of a better state of things. It is a long and laborious task to draw the seine around; but once done, then comes the great 'draught of fishes.' The one single thing that troubles me is the low state of religion among professing Christians. With Rome, it cannot improve; the system will not bear it; but among us it is not so; we are far, far below our system. "The Lord amend this blindness," and this hardness!

"'What you say about Hoffman's memoir is too true. So thinks the public. It does not sell. The preface is nothing. The author's *name*, however, may have helped it in England; but here, it experiences no aid from that particular. As a composition, the memoir may be lacking in skill, the biographer's comments in enlargement, and the work, as a whole, in condensation; and yet, to pious minds, that read for spiritual edification and exercise, it must be profitable. Hoffman's death was remarkable, and the style of his religious life truly evangelical. Few men "rejoiced in the Lord" more fully than he, or rose more uniformly above carnal despondency; and yet his elation was not of the kind that brings on reaction. In that view it was healthier, perhaps, than the religion of Martyn, of whom you speak.

"'Dear brother, I rejoice to think that you are now fairly engaged on heathen ground; and though your direct duty is to Christians, so called, yet that the heathen will also profit by your labors.

"'I have often heard D—— speak of your fitness for Chinese labor, and longed to see you returned to it. The cause of Foreign Missions seems at a low ebb among us. The Hartford paper pronounced Domestic Missions tenfold more important. But at present our Church is so taken up with little things—the millinery of religion, matters of color, and form, and sound, and gesture, and posture, and movement, with rubrics and canons—that no time, or space, or heart, is left for large ideas. But we pray, and look to see "this calamity overpast." How it is to be brought about, to be sure, we do not see, but we walk by faith. Individuals may go back and bury themselves in Romish superstition; but surely this Protestant Church is not going to eat its own words, condemn its own history, and bring back the Middle Ages as the Ages of Light, as Dr. Dix calls them. It is not to be believed; and yet the current is so strong in the direction of Rome, that it does not at all appear how it can be stayed.

"'Our mother Church of England has a twofold trouble, within and without. The Establishment is doomed. It is only a question of time, as with the Reform Bill, Catholic Emancipation, and the like. Oh, that English Episcopalians might know the day of their visitation! But they never have done so, and why should they now? To me there seems to be a singular want of ability among them to see themselves as others see them. They appear unable to grasp big ideas, and *stand to them*. Propriety and red-tape, and prescription and caste, are their dependence! Forgive me if I am treading on the toes of your opinions. [He could hardly have expressed them more exactly. E. W. S.]

"'Just *here* things go their old way. We closed a happy term in June, with fifty students, and hope, with God's blessing, to do as well next year. * * * * *

"'I have just come from Ohio. Saw my brother and sister and the graves of my parents. Kenyon is in difficulty again. President Stone preached ritualism, and retired to Hobart College, Geneva, where he was more at home. When your next letter comes it shall be answered more promptly. The family all join me in best wishes to you and Mrs. Syle.

"'Ever affectionately yours, WILLIAM SPARROW.

"'*Rev. Mr. Syle, Shanghai.*'

"Of the many suggestive topics in the foregoing letter, I will only remark on one, the position of the English Church and its clergy. On his return from a visit to England and Ireland, I remember asking Dr. Sparrow what things *most* struck him in the aspect of affairs, and among those he mentioned were the infatuated inability (above mentioned) to read the 'signs of the times' as regards the coming disestablishment, and also the remarkable clinging, on the part of the 'Evangelical' clergy, to the union of Church and State, for which Dr. Sparrow found it difficult to account. 'In consistency with their principles,' he said, 'they ought to sit loose from any such arrangement, but, on the contrary, they seem to be *especially* fond of it. Perhaps,' he added, 'they find themselves obliged to protest against so many things in the life and principles of their friends and patrons, that they are glad to have one point on which they find it possible to pull together, and this predisposes them to Establishmentarianism.'

"I leave the explanation for what it may be worth, and only mention one little matter connected with this home visit, which is an illustration of the childlike tenderness of his feelings:—

"'Nothing seems to me so perfectly beautiful as the scenery in North Wales. Early one morning I went out to walk by the hill-side, and there I saw a *daisy*, the first one I had seen for many, many years. I must confess, Mr. Syle, that then I made a fool of myself; I shed tears, just from the instinct of emotion.'

"His relatives, the Roes, of Dublin, were spoken of by him with the greatest regard and admiration, as having refreshed his spirit to an especial degree during this visit to his native land. He seemed to think the Christian family life he saw among them to be the loveliest and holiest he had ever met with; a little Paradise Regained, a heaven upon earth.

"Far otherwise was the impression made upon him by his short sojourn in France; 'there,' he said, 'the moral atmosphere oppressed and stifled' him. Yet he was charmed with the peasantry, and so much interested in their Evangelization, that he suggested my going to labor among them, thinking my characteristics suited for that field.*

"France and Italy are certainly now more accessible to true Christian influences than they have been in many centuries; nay,

* His daughter Susan was similarly affected by her sojourn in Italy. They both seemed to be persuaded that these fields were fast ripening for a great harvest. And is this not the case?

we almost see the 'beginning of the end,' when the man of sin is dethroned, and those who have pre-eminently 'given their power and strength unto the beast' are humbled and made weak.

"The school to which reference is made in the next extract, written in 1870, is one still in operation at Shanghai, established for the benefit of Chinese children, and supported by local contributions. It is now under the fostering care and charge of two of our own missionaries, and stands as a 'memorial' of Mrs. Bridgman, a lady who first went out to China in 1844, as a teacher under Bishop Boone.

"'I can truly say your letter afforded me real pleasure; partly because I am always glad to hear from you, and partly because you seem so happy in your work. The school enterprise strikes me as important for its own sake, and because it enlists the interests, and energies, and means of those on the spot, foreigners and natives. I was struck with the contributions of the latter.

"'It is delightful to think that, amid the confusions now prevailing in Christendom, and the cries we are hearing every day, "Lo, here, and lo, there," we know where we can find, and have, and hold, and enjoy the Divine Master—even in laboring for the individual men for whom He died—in ministering to the saints, and plucking brands from the burning.

"'Everything in the Church (universal) indicates to me great and beneficent changes. In the Sixteenth century the Reformation took place; but it was not to be expected that at one stroke, and in one generation, the then inveterate and multitudinous errors that had crept into Christianity could be abolished. The Reformers did much, but not all that was to be done. The residuum is about to be cared for and disposed of. They escaped out of the furnace, but they carried with them the smell of fire on their skirts. That foul odor is to be removed. The disestablishment of all churches is a great means to this end. I am glad the Church of Ireland is gone; it ought to have gone long ago. I pray that English Episcopalians may have wisdom to see the change coming on themselves, and, instead of striving to ward it off, try to prepare for it. They have not hitherto exhibited such wisdom. The Bishops are too far removed from the people to catch the true spirit of the times, and so to understand themselves and their duties. So long as Bishops think the Church was made for them (and by them), and not they for the Church, so long we may expect to see them act as infatuated, "demented" men. However, they have opportunities of learning, in this Nineteenth century, which their predecessors had not.

"'You English are a fine people when you get started in the right way; but when in the wrong—oh, you are terribly wrong-headed.

"'As to our own Church, we think and feel very much as does the Church of England—through our Bishops. We import annually a large measure of the sacerdotal, prelatical, and "Established" sentiment, through our traveling clergy, especially of the highest order. It is not only silk aprons and shorts, and shoe-buckles and shovel-hats they bring back. These are only the *deck* freight; the *hold* is full of high notions of spiritual power, utterly incompatible with the principles and spirit of the Gospel. Our Church will never be what she ought to be till these foreign notions are exorcised from our Bishops, and that large class which exists among us—aspirants to the Episcopate!

"'The Seminary is very much blessed, all things considered. Though my close approximation to threescore and ten makes me slow and increases my labor, yet, thus far, perhaps, I do my duty with very little diminution of my ordinary amount of efficiency. But it can't last long.

"'Bishop Johns continues to labor as much as could be expected for his years. Bishop Whittle is a most valuable assistant. Oh, that all our bishops were like him! Virginia has been much blessed in all her bishops except the first.

"'The next time I go to New York I will endeavor to see Henry. I shall always take an interest in him for your sake and his mother's.

"'If Mrs. Sparrow and Frances were at my elbow, they would send their warmest regards to you and Mrs. Syle. You can never be forgotten in my family, nor thought of but with an affectionate interest. Ever truly,

"'Your friend and brother.

"'P. S. With this I send a copy of my last Commencement Address. You will think me outspoken.'

"I take occasion, by the allusion to Bishops being 'far removed from the people,' to record Dr. Sparrow's extreme jealousy of everything that tended to set off the clergy by themselves, as a sacerdotal class. On one occasion, we were admiring a new church-building, I forget where, but I remember that it had an unusual number of 'steps to the altar,' and that all its chancel arrangements were elaborate and spacious, and deeply 'recessed.'

"'All this,' he said, 'tends in the wrong direction; it separates the minister from the congregation, and isolates him, so that he does not feel one with them. These architectural peculiarities all help to foster the sacerdotal temper, and are, therefore, not matters of indifference.'

"'THEOLOGICAL SEMINARY, July 26, 1872.

"'I am growing old very fast, but I do not find that it makes me forget old friends. It may unfit me for writing to them, but it does not indispose or disable my mind from recalling the years when, however far apart now, we were associated together.

"'Since I last wrote to you, many things have occurred to me. My friends, last summer, sent me for my health to Europe. I was absent about three months, chiefly in England and Ireland. Last spring, I had an attack of pneumonia, which tried me much.

"'As I was convalescing, Mrs. S. was taken down with heart-disease and rheumatism; and waiting upon us brought a severe attack upon dear Frances. She is now as usual, but Mrs. S. is very feeble, so that I have been compelled to employ a lady to take the burden of housekeeping off her shoulders. Thus continue we to this hour.'

* * * * * *

[More domestic details, showing his tender interest in children and grandchildren.]

* * * * * *

"'I have written all this, first, because it *may* be news to you; and, secondly, because I want to provoke you to make a return in kind. I very much desire to know "all about you." I hope the Lord has prospered you in your work, though you are not permitted to *see* the fruit of your labor as are pastors with settled congregations. But work that tells on eternity, for the present visible or invisible, is the work which we love to contemplate, the older we grow.

"'You see from the papers the state of this Church. Not very satisfactory! The ship has drifted from her course, according to the observation of the heavenly bodies, and yet we insist on sailing by the uncorrected log! Oh, that Providence would raise up a few great minds, spiritually taught and of large influence, to bring us out of this fog and darkness!

"'Do write me soon. Mrs. S. and Frances send their love.

"'Your old and unchanged friend.'

"And now I come to his last letter, the saddest and most touching of all I had ever received from him, as well it might be, for it tells of his *great* bereavement!

"I had written in ignorance of Mrs. Sparrow's death, yet fearing, from an allusion in one of the papers, that it might be the sorrow referred to, and this was his reply:—

"'October 14, 1873.

"'DEAR BROTHER SYLE:—

"'Your letter, 20th of August, reached me a few weeks ago. All that you inferred from the allusion in the "Southern Churchman" is true. Here I am alone, with dear Frances (who is about as she has been), and a housekeeper and two servants. Though poor Frances, with most touching diligence, takes care of me, the charge of the household was altogether beyond her strength. Though I have had eight months' sad experience, the feeling of loneliness is extreme. My mind almost recoils from the thought of winter, when I know the feeling must be tenfold. But of that enough.

"'My dear wife, who always took great interest in your letters and yourself, and always valued, more than you imagined, your wise and faithful instruction in our family, was unwell long before she was taken from us. The latter part of last year she was very sick, but partially recovered. In the beginning of this, as our wedding day was approaching, she told me we should never celebrate another. She hardly celebrated that one. She was down to breakfast, but could not appear at dinner, though a few friends had been invited to dine with us. After she had been most seriously sick for a fortnight, I was myself taken down, from exhaustion and anxiety, which brought on a fever. The bitter reflection in that retrospect is, that I never saw her again. My sickness was so severe and nigh unto death, that I was not permitted, in truth was not able, to go to her bedside. I only heard the feet that carried her to the hearse. When I last saw her, her consciousness was nearly gone. She knew nobody but myself; though she lingered several days. As to her spiritual state, thank God, there is no bitterness, but joy and full assurance. For forty-six years she lived before me, in matters great and small, such an example of intelligent conscientiousness, of true religious devotion, of self-control and self-denial, of laborious love, of delicate consideration, of truthfulness, fairness, and honesty, and, above all, of *entire unselfishness,* as I never saw anywhere else, and never expect to see in this world! Oh, how my soul blushes to think what a life I lived in her presence, and what a contrast it formed to her Christ-like character and conduct! I am humbled and ashamed before God that I learned so little from her marvelous character. I often ask myself, What sort of a man, Christian and minister, would I have proved if I had fallen into other hands, seeing, as things were, what I am? I am almost ready to use St. Paul's language and say, Surely I would have been a "castaway." But I must stop this. Excuse what I have written. I know it is unnecessary for you; but the moment I touch this subject the floodgates fly open. Many things which you have said have gone very near my heart, especially your reference to Sue, and the meeting of the mother and daughter in heaven. But here again I must stop. During all my trial of sickness and death, and protracted sickness in my own person afterward, my own children have been a great comfort to me. This, too, I owe to the departed!

"'The Seminary prospers very fairly. We have just celebrated our first jubilee, with much success. Our students are nearly fifty. We have four Professors, the addition being Dr. McElhinney, from Gambier. I have now but one lecture a day. That much I can do, perhaps, as well as ever. During my long trial and sickness, all, especially the Trustees, were very, very kind to me, for which I thank God.

"'I have been to New York within a week, to attend the Evangelical Alliance. It was the greatest, and most successful, and most extraordinary gathering of Christians ever held, I am not afraid to say, in the history of the Church of Christ. This country, the Church, and the world, has been moved by it. But you must see the papers and judge for yourself. New York surpassed all previous example in hospitality. Our European brethren have gone back to their homes amazed alike at the extent and progress of this country, and the largeness of its hospitality. So they said, again and again.

"'But I must close. Dear Mr. Syle, I thank you for your letter.

For the little while I can hope to remain in this world, do, now and again, cheer me with a letter. Long have we been friends. Let us keep the chain bright unto the end. My thanks and kindest regards to Mrs. Syle. Frances desires her truest love.

"'Your affectionate friend and brother, W. SPARROW.'

"There are no comments to be made on such a farewell letter as this. It forms a fitting close to my reminiscences of the most learned and most childlike, the wisest and the kindliest, the most high-minded and tender-hearted friend I have ever known.

"EDWARD W. SYLE."

FRAGMENTS.

DOCTRINAL PURITY.

"I have been inclined to think, for many years past, in looking at the condition of our Church, that we have been, and still are, entirely too lax on the subject of sound doctrine. I am well aware that it is possible to err in the opposite extreme, as I think I could name brethren of other denominations who have been faulty in this respect, enlarging their creeds and confessions to a voluminous extent, and, in the details of doctrine, running out into the nicest and most subtle metaphysical distinctions. If one of another denomination may be allowed to say it without offence, this is, in my judgment, the case with the Old and New School of the Presbyterian Church. They have indulged in the splitting of hairs too much; and, as a natural consequence, are now divided into two independent religious societies, for discrepancies of doctrinal opinion not one-tenth part as great as those existing in some denominations which still hold together. This of the Presbyterians is one extreme; may not ours be the opposite? We ought not always to assume that we, of course, travel the 'via media,' nor even that the 'via media' is the 'via recta.'

"The controversy now going on in the English Church and our own, and likely for some time to continue, confirms my apprehension that we have not sufficiently valued sound doctrine. No people can be more strict than we in regard to external arrangements; and nothing endangers a man's reputation amongst us more than a slight difference, on such points, from the majority. But I fear there is great supineness among many in regard to those truths which bear immediately upon the heart and life, and pertain to the office and work of our Divine Redeemer. If it were not so, could a people holding to the Bible, 'as containing all things necessary to salvation,' and believing it to be so perfect, as its Author declared, that we 'must not add thereto nor diminish from it,' and receiving also the Thirty-nine Articles as a true explanation and exhibition of Scriptural Divinity, receive so frequently and extensively the Oxford un-Protestant novelties, and speak about them as they do? It seems to me that many who subscribed the Articles, as a preliminary to orders, must have forgotten that solemn act, or else the doctrines to which their assent was given and their sign-manual affixed. That these new notions imported from Oxford do not, in general spirit or in particulars, agree with the Articles, it is not necessary to prove by specific quotations. Particulars have been adduced in sad abundance by writers on the Scriptural side of this controversy. But let any one observe how the Oxford Tractarians feel and speak in regard to the glorious Reformation, and it is enough. One of the very first of them (notwithstanding all his superstitions, I trust now a saint in heaven, and I fear a subject of prayer to his survivors of the same school) speaks in the most unmeasured language of the disastrousness of that event, and his brethren love to have it so. It is plain they look upon the Church of England as having reformed too much. The body of the Prayer-book is too much filled with the Reformation spirit; for they would prefer the one which preceded it, when the Reformation was as yet inchoate. Of course, the Articles, which go deeper into doctrine and the differences between us and Rome, must be more offensive. Now, is it not strange that a Church calling itself Protestant should listen so patiently to a condemnation of the Reformation, and not only so, but also back the censure, to a great extent, even with applause!"

THE MORAL CHARACTER OF EMULATION.

"The sources of proof are twofold, Scripture and analysis:

"1. Scripture, except in Galatians, c. v, v. 20, where emulations ζῆλοι are condemned, does not *directly* speak upon this subject. It exhorts us indeed to pursue 'those things which are lovely and of good report;' but the question arises, on what ground? Manifestly that the Christian may adorn his profession, and glorify Him that called him, not that he may have the unworthy gratification of looking down upon inferiors. Scripture may be said to consider emulation indirectly, perhaps. What is the spirit which, from the beginning to the end, it inculcates? Humility and contentment. These have reference one-half to our fellow-men. So far as these virtues have such reference to our fellow-men they are impeded by the spirit of emulation. The disciples once disputed who should be superior, 'Who is the greatest in the kingdom of heaven?' and Jesus set a little child in the midst of them to reprove their emulation. Their work was to 'provoke to love and good works.'

"2. All moral writers, nearly, especially since the days of Butler, set down emulation as one of our native and allowable desires. Plato seems to have thought otherwise, as he made Emulation the daughter of Envy; and, if language is any index to the mind, we may suppose the Latins thought so too, as they derived æmulatio, through æmulus, from ἁμιλλω. They define it, the love of superiority. Now, is this allowable? It is the love of superiority as such, not the love of power, or knowledge, or virtue, or usefulness, but the desire to be in a condition which will enable us to regard our fellow-creatures as inferiors. Now, if the same desire exist in them also, is there not direct collision? Is there not a want of harmony in the organization of the human mind and human society? Here one man's gain is another's loss, and that in the exercise of allowable feelings. Surely, we are not at liberty to seek that which is a good to us by being an evil to others.

"Admitting, for a moment, that emulation is innocent, per se, it seems to be so intimately connected with the selfish feelings that it is dangerous to excite it. They seem to run into one another, as the organs of taste and smell. It is prudent to seek some other mode of approaching the mind than one which leads so directly to the principle of selfishness.

"In determining what are the original desires, it is important to bear in mind that man is fallen, and that his heart is full of idols, otherwise we may be setting down as allowable what is actually sinful.

"Payne says that the desire of superiority is like the desire of knowledge, society, etc., having nothing moral in itself; and as we appeal to fear and shame, so we may appeal to emulation; that if we give up one, we must give up all. But it should be first shown that these emotions interfere with the desires of others, as does emulation.

"It is said that, like the desire of power, per se, emulation has no moral character. How, then, does it acquire it? By exciting it in view of motives? But would we feel justified in exciting it by an explicit description of itself? Would it not be better to use the many better arguments?"

TRANSUBSTANTIATION.

"When good men get into bad habits, we are loth to expose the latter, lest we weaken the authority of the former. When, again, systems of truth become corrupted with error, we are afraid to touch the latter, lest the former be overthrown. The ivy on the wall is eating out the cement and displacing the stones, yet we are afraid to pluck up and tear it away, lest the wall should totter. We think of the tares and the wheat in the field, like truth and error in systems. In France there must have been good men who lamented the corruptions of Christianity, and mourned the contempt which they occasioned, and feared the consequences. But they feared much more to disabuse the public mind by exposing the delusions:—Christianity must fall with priestcraft.

"This feeling is natural, and should be regarded. But it has its limits; and these limits are not always the same. The dishonest world sets no limits at all. Rash truthfulness would disregard them altogether. Prudence would observe a medium. The limits are not the same among an ignorant, and among a thinking people; in Protestant and in Popish countries; at the beginning or the end of a Reformation; among the friends and the enemies of religion. The error has usually been rather on the side of secrecy, than that of extensive exposure. Human nature is on that side.

"But the danger is less than is imagined. When the exposure comes from those who are true friends of the cause with which the error is connected, and is made in the proper spirit; not in hatred, but in love; not to indulge idle curiosity, but for instruction's sake; and when the truth is put where the error stood, and offered as a substitute for it, Protestantism and the Scriptures gain thereby. This is the characteristic of Protestantism, arising out of putting Scripture above the Church. When there is confidence in truth there will be boldness in this matter—boldness, not rashness.

"All this is apologetical for exposing a doctrine once considered an essential of Christianity, and still so considered by many. This doctrine is the glory and trust of the priesthood; the object of awe and reverence to the multitude; the test of faith, the task-master of reason. It is held to with tenacity by the greatest power the world ever saw. This doctrine I consider the greatest absurdity ever palmed on creatures called rational; especially because it is held by those who pretend to argue the matter.

Gnosticism had its errors and absurdities, but they were of the imagination. This doctrine is of men who pretend to reason and philosophy. Let us, then, take the language of this absurdity.

"First, we have a complete change of the whole substance of the bread into the substance of the body of Christ, that of the wine into that of the blood—*transubstantiation.*

"This substance thus changed into another substance, ceases to have the attributes or accidents of material substances.

"These attributes or accidents which remain, and which, to the senses, are, apparently, as they were before the change, are accidents inhering in no substance.*

"Here, then, we have annihilation—substitution. Nothing more or less. Individual existences *are* what *are.*

"What is annihilated seems to continue, and what is substituted does not appear. So all the senses testify.

"The explanation of this by substance and accidents is inconceivable.

"If the bread moulds, there is reverse action, and yet no evidence of this. What is it that moulds, accidents or substances? So of the wine. So, if before this the elements be consumed by a dumb animal, the body and blood of Christ are eaten! And all this in the face of the record of the first Institution. He held the bread and cup, the whole substance of His body and blood, in His hands."

ARE MEN RESPONSIBLE FOR THEIR OPINIONS?

"The human mind a pendulum, would swing into the boundless void unchecked by the gravitating power of the good providence of God. This power acts by laws which attach evil consequences to extremes. These revolt the mind. True wisdom usually consists in discovering and settling in the centre. 'Medio tutissimus ibis.' God hedges up our way.

"This propensity to extremes is manifest in the history of our subject. One extreme in the Romish Church not only considered certain opinions as criminal, but punished them as overt acts. This latter was the consequence which led to the reaction. Two things were confounded. Intolerance acquired a being and a name, and that an infamous one. Intolerance is an intolerable evil. How

* See Catechism of Trent, 39, 42, 43, Questions.

shall it be avoided? It came into being with the doctrine that we are responsible for our opinions. Banish the latter, and the former will expatriate itself.

"We find this latter doctrine largely sanctioned at the present day. Lord Brougham, Sir J. Macintosh, passim. 'The great truth, so pregnant with charity toward our fellow-men, that belief is independent of the will, was not, in those times, dreamt of' (the times of Cranmer, Sir T. More, etc).

"But, first, such a doctrine is not necessary to accomplish this object. It is not necessary to prove that opinions are not moral, in order to show that man should not punish his fellow for them. How is it with regard to character (not put forth in action)? Do we, to prevent men visiting one another with pains and penalties for evil tempers, impure passions, etc., maintain that they have no moral character? There is *another way of preventing persecution in both cases.*

This idea, moreover, is inconsistent with the relations between the several functions of the mind. It is inconsistent with the relation of opinions to actions. On what do we act if not on opinion? Brutes do not act on opinion, and therefore are not responsible. But men do act on opinion, and therefore are. Unless carried away by a whirlwind of passion (a case not contemplated here) man always acts on opinion. It may be good or bad, right or wrong, still it is opinion, and the ground of action.

"This doctrine, again, is contrary to the common sentiment of men. They say our belief is according to our wishes. Now, are these wishes or desires moral? If so, they involve accountability. If not, what does? Desires are especially moral when the will is determined by them; and is it not then that opinion is formed? To be sure, 'video meliora,' etc. But what does this prove? If he had not this opinion, if he did not see, then 'had he been without sin.' But he does see, has this opinion, and therefore purely in his relations to it acts rightly or wrongly. Suppose a man to see and approve the worse, this is only an aggravation of his guilt."

"PROBABILITIES AN AID TO FAITH."

"In this borrowed heading, we understand by faith that act and state of mind, as the intelligent principle, in which it apprehends the truths pertaining to the unseen world. So using the term, why should we not speak of probabilities as an aid thereto? Is there any incompatibility between them? May not the latter conduce to the former? May they not constitute its very groundwork and root? Suppose nothing but probabilities in the case, but that they preponderate strongly on one side; then, if forced by the exigencies with which we were surrounded to come to a conclusion in regard to things unseen and spiritual, would not that conclusion justly be called faith? Might it not be a religious act? Might it not be a strong persuasion? Might it not move us like a voice from heaven?

"But why ask these questions? We do not ask them because we believe there is any ground to doubt about the answer, but because we find some, in the new school, which has lately risen up among us, seeking to plant faith on some other than a *rational* foundation. One of the wisest philosophical divines has pronounced 'probability the very guide of life,' and argues that as it guides us in relation to this life, so ought it in relation to the next. And he, and almost all others who have attempted anything in logical science, have divided all the evidence which comes to man, of truths not intuitively seen, into demonstrative and probable; by demonstrative understanding that proof which belongs to the abstractions of mathematics, and by probable understanding that which establishes all facts not naturally known to man by original suggestion, such as the phenomena of the physical world, the events of secular history, and the miracles of inspired revelation. These all are alike supported by probable evidence, meaning by the term probable, it is hardly necessary to say, not any uncertainty in point of fact or deficiency in the amount of proof, but only that it is not what is conventionally and technically called demonstrative.

"Now, this almost universally received view of the matter is, by some, sought to be set aside. They would substitute a blind submission to human authority, or acquiescence in the doctrines of some official personage. They think it dangerous to encourage the common view, as it may foster self-sufficiency in man. If man is left to look for evidence aside from known authority, and to exercise his own private judgment upon the subjects for which his credence is challenged, 'he will become,' it has been said, 'arrogant and vain. His foolish heart will become darkened by pride, and he will adopt error just to show his independence of evidence, reason, and truth.' In the same spirit, those who take this view judge it wise to encourage the people to submit entirely for instruction to him whose lips keep knowledge professionally, dissuade them from searching the Scriptures to see if the things which they hear from their teachers be so. Instead of being desirous for the wider diffusion of knowledge, they are half disposed to think with the poet that 'a little learning is a dangerous thing.' On the whole, they manifestly feel that, as we have lawyers and physicians to take care of our health and property, so have we clergymen to take care of our souls; and that, as their callings are all three alike 'arts and mysteries,' our wisest course is to conduct ourselves, in regard to them, pretty much in the same way—to lie passively in their hands, afraid that, in attempting to mend, we may only mar."

DAILY SERVICE.

"In the Book of Common Prayer there are several days set apart for the commemoration, not only of the prominent events in the work of man's redemption, but also of the holy lives and glorious deaths of many of the more eminent saints mentioned in the New Testament. For each of these days, also, there is appointed a service adapted, in the matter or the spirit of it, to the history or character of the Apostle or Evangelist after whom the day is called. It would seem that this part of our Prayer-book was especially designed for the cathedrals, where provision is made for daily service. At all events, no general and long-continued attempt has ever been made to observe all these days, much less to have the Morning and Evening Prayer read in all the churches. When there is any special event calling for a week-day service, respect is had to the Collect, Gospel, and Epistle for the occasion, if there be such; but beyond this, our own Church, or the mother Church of England, has never gone.

"At the present day, however, a great effort is making to introduce a daily public service, and especially the observance of saints' days, into some of the churches here and in England.

"Now, God forbid that we should check any disposition in any one to resort to the house of God morning and evening, if it is open to him, and his circumstances are such as to allow him to attend. But it ought to be borne in mind that there is an 'Ecclesiastical' as well as a 'Political Economy,' and that as industry, to produce its proper effects, must be rightly directed, so must religious zeal. The question is not whether it is right or wrong to go to the house of God to worship, but whether, under the existing circumstances of the Church and the world, it is expedient for the minister to take upon him this peculiar mode and amount of duty, and for the people to be called on to worship, not *so often*, but so often in that *particular place*. We confess we have no confidence in the measures now proposed by some, who are so zealous for daily services in the Church, or for honoring the saints by signalizing every day called after their names by public worship. It is in vain that the ordinary mode of *dating* the advertisement of a printed sermon, or a communication to a daily journal, or the preface of a book, is abandoned, and that the work is consummated and put under the patronage of some saint, by being brought out on the day devoted to his memory, or on its eve or vigil. In vain, too, is the 'sacramental character' of sacred vestments and consecrated edifices urged as a reason why men should worship God in the church, rather than the closet, or at the family altar, every morning and evening. It will be found impracticable in the issue, and injurious in the attempt. Several reasons might be assigned for thinking it an injudicious and pernicious measure. We mention one or two:—

"1. In the first place, it is an arrangement for the benefit of the few, not the many. Those in more comfortable circumstances, with time at their command, and every other means necessary for appearing in public twice a day, may take advantage of these frequent services in the church; but the more limited in their living and their leisure, especially servants, must ordinarily stay at home. As society is now constituted, therefore, the advantage is for the advantage of the rich, not the poor; for the few, not the many.

"2. Besides, must it not be a positive loss to poor employees to be separated from their masters and mistresses in their religious exercises? Are not the latter less likely, in consequence, to take a spiritual interest in them, and to feel their obligation to attend to their religious instruction under such circumstances?

"3. Is not the direct tendency of the practice, so far as it may prevail, to interfere with family worship and religion, and with the religious training of the rising generation? At *family* prayer, scarce any one need be absent; not only the servants, but every child over twenty months old, may, at all seasons of the year, attend; but at *public* prayers, not only must servants be separated from their masters, but parents must also be separated from their children. The little ones cannot generally attend.

"4. Again, must not the introduction of daily public worship interfere, especially in the cases of persons who have to 'labor to get their own living,' with family worship altogether? The prayer of the closet stands first in the obligation; next, except on the days in which inspiration has required that we assemble ourselves together in the great congregation, comes family worship; and last stands the proposed daily morning and evening prayer."

EFFECT OF EXTRAVAGANT NOTIONS OF BAPTISM UPON THEOLOGICAL OPINION GENERALLY.

"1. If it is regeneration in any other than an external sense, it is made necessary to salvation, even in regard to infants; and, if so regarded, why should any one balk at the imputation of Adam's sin, and the condemnation of men for it alone?

"2. These extravagant notions caused it, at one time, to be postponed till late in life.

"3. It also led to Lay Baptism.

"4. It also occasioned the hypothesis of a limbus infantum.

"5. Also the doctrine of the damnation of the most virtuous heathen, or else that they are baptized in another world, in order to salvation.

"6. Though designed to make the sacraments very sacred, it leads to their profanation.

"7. The Jews magnified circumcision unduly, and the effects were seen, not in their view of one another, for it was a national rite, but of the neighboring nations."

CONVERSATION.

"1. Talk of things and events, rather than of persons, and of the departed rather than the living.

"2. Make others talk rather than talk yourself.

"3. If you talk, let it be conversation or colloquy, rather than discourse. Be sure your neighbor has his full share.

"4. Talk with others to get knowledge rather than to show it.

"5. If you are compelled to talk of little matters, do not dwell upon them. The bee's visit to each flower is short, though it might tarry long at a plate of honey.

"6. Avoid a habit of objecting. To assent to everything is insincere; to dispute everything is offensive. In most cases, neither is at all necessary. We can almost always find some point of agreement; we are seldom under the necessity of disputation. We may let most things to which we do not assent pass in silence; and this silence will often have more effect than refutation.

"7. Before you speak be sure you have something to say. This precept holds good even in little things. In little things, folks get into a way of talking at random, which, indulged in, must detract from their reputation for judgment, and even for strict truthfulness. Nervous persons are liable to this, and may aggravate it by indulgence, till it becomes a mental disease, called light-headedness.

"8. We may avoid dogmatism and controversy, often, by simply asking questions, and seeking for the opinions of others, which opinions may be received in silence. It is not necessary to give an opinion upon every other opinion.

"9. Remember you are not under obligation to know everything. You may expect to be ignorant of many, very many things, of which others are not so ignorant; and you need not attempt to hide your ignorance, or to make a show of knowledge where you have none—filling your library, as it were, with 'wooden Elzevirs.'"

"CONTRAST BETWEEN UNITARIANISM AND ROMANISM."

"Unitarianism for the learned; Romanism for the ignorant. Unitarianism, minimi fidian, rejecting mysteries; Romanism, maximi fidian, believing contradictions. Unitarianism is moral in its aims and efforts; Romanism is ceremonious and devout. Unitarianism is skeptical; Romanism is superstitious. Unitarianism exalts the people; Romanism, the clergy. Unitarianism rejects all authority, and would make a little child suspicious and jealous of the power and influence of its parent; Romanism makes human authority divine, and would teach kings it was a fitting employment to be broidering petticoats for images of the Virgin Mary. Unitarianism would make man over-confident, and induce him to feel self-sufficient in securing his soul's salvation; Romanism would not only refer man to a Saviour, but to his fellow-men in the character of priests, and make him not so much the humble servant of God as the abject slave of His creature. Unitarianism seeks the promotion of education and the enlightenment of society, so ever committing suicide; Romanism would exclude knowledge, and so build up its own authority, till that becomes so grinding and intolerable as to occasion a revolt in human nature. All evil and error in society is ultimately suicidal; that of Unitarianism more immediately so than Romanism."

"OUT OF THE CHURCH NO SALVATION."

"This maxim is a potent weapon for good or evil. Rightly understood, it embodies a truth which, the more explicitly it is promulgated and enforced, advances the more the glory of Christ and the salvation of men. So interpreted, it turns men from the shadow to the substance, from the judging of others to the examination of themselves, from reliance upon man to trust, exclusive trust, in God, through Christ. It enlarges rather than contracts, elevates rather than degrades. It enables a man to feel that he breathes the spirit of that religion which is from above, which is comprehensive, which is internal, which is real; that he serves that God, who, by revelation, more than by the wonders of nature or the gifts of Providence, proves that His mercy is over all His works, and that 'in every nation he that feareth God and worketh righteousness is accepted of Him.' With such views one can rejoice before God, through Christ, on his own account and on account of his fellow-creatures. They bring him and them directly to God, and make communion with God dependent directly and indispensably upon nothing created or which a creature can control. It supposes God's laws to be administered by men, but not as the civil laws are administered. So far as the office holder is concerned, nothing is absolute and definitive. They may acquit where the Supreme Power condemns; they may condemn where the Supreme Power acquits; their authority may be recognized, and yet no favor come from the source of that authority; and their authority may be mistakingly resisted, and yet the condemnation of God not finally follow. It supposes human agencies to be very needful, and particular forms of them very desirable; but that God reserves to Himself the power and privilege of recognizing souls, everywhere and under all circumstances, that truly look to Him. It teaches men to inquire, not whether they are children of Abraham by lineal descent, but whether they have the faith of Abraham, and to regard this first, and look upon everything else only as the outward exhibition of this inward principle. It teaches us, in short, in the arrangement of our principles, and in our judgment of men and things, to observe the great law of Proportion. All this comes of understanding the maxim, 'Extra ecclesiam nulla salus,' as having reference to that body which Christ controls by His Spirit, and which is, consequently, composed of 'all who love our Lord Jesus Christ in sincerity.'

"But, to suppose it has reference to some particular Ecclesiastical organization; and to repeat that article in the Creed, the 'Holy Catholic Church,' on every Sabbath-day, and to teach it to our children with that understanding! Oh, what a sad perversion; how opposed to the genius of our holy religion, how belittling to the soul, how hardening to the heart, how calculated to exalt man and degrade Christ the Saviour! It must pervert the judgment in reference to ourselves and to others. It must lead us to estimate others by their ecclesiastical connection rather than the soundness of their doctrine and the holiness of their lives; and must cause us to suppose that God has suspended the eternal destinies of man upon things positive and contingent, rather than things essential, and moral, and spiritual. And in reference to ourselves, it must foster one of the worst forms of self-righteousness. On each repetition of the Creed we virtually congratulate ourselves that we are of the corporation to which salvation exclusively belongs; so exclusively, that all without which wears the appearance of heaven-inspired virtue is to be considered suspicious, if not positively mischievous."

"CLOSE OF THE TERM."

"SADNESS CONNECTED WITH THE THOUGHT OF SEPARATION."

"Two travelers when they part. Two ships when they part after sailing in company. Two ships when they speak and part.

"We have been together one, two, three years. Some shall never meet in the same relation. This is a time of sad feelings, of serious reflection. Life is a journey.

"1. So to all. All men live, and 'It is appointed unto all men to die.' Cradle and grave. Short, long, cheerful, afflicted, conspicuous, obscure, but to all a journey.

"2. Difference between men of the world and Christians this: they are journeying unconsciously, Christians consciously.

"*a.* The world floats on a tide of which they are heedless. They are occupied with the present only. Dum vivimus vivamus? They are as men that dream. They are as men out of their right mind. When the journey is ended they come to themselves, they awake.

"*b.* Christians have so done. But they now realize what life is; 'What shadows we are, and what shadows we pursue.' This influences their whole nature. They see and feel this to be a transition state.

"3. This moderates all minor considerations. By fixing the mind intently on the end, the things by the way please but moderately. 'Let your moderation be known unto all men.' 'Be careful for nothing.'

"*a.* It moderates expectations of happiness. Such a state cannot be expected to afford more than foretastes, slight antepasts. Enjoyment, even in ministerial work, should not be counted on too sanguinely. The principle of happiness there is the principle of happiness everywhere. If not happy as Christian students, why happy as Christian ministers?

"*b.* Moderates fears, also, in regard to trials and afflictions. They are only disagreeable incidents by the way. They will soon be over, and only a subject of recollection as perils escaped. So a foil to happiness hereafter. More than that, they may be used somewhat in that way even here. If we are pilgrims, our afflictions are marks of sonship and adoption. Nay, more, they may 'work out for us a far more exceeding and eternal weight of glory.' How? 'Tribulation worketh patience, and patience experience, and experience hope.' If we find difficulty in viewing things thus, it only shows that we still linger, in heart, in Egypt.

"4. I began with *sadness*, let us end with *cheerfulness*."

"PROBATION AND SPEECH."

"Candidates were at first promptly admitted to the Church.

"Afterward they had a long probation.

"The reasons of the change various. Chief one, that the candidate might know himself and be known of others, so that the Church should not suffer.

"The Church has suffered from indiscriminate admissions.

"This example in regard to candidates for baptism too often followed in regard to those for the ministry.

"Probation with these even more needful. Less so, perhaps, in former times; more so now. Private Christians escaped when ministers were slain. The sharpshooters of persecution picked out the leaders. Now, the leaders have as little danger and more honor.

"Accordingly, the Church has appointed candidateship of three years.

"1. She would know those to whom she confides so much.

"2. She would let them know themselves.

"3. She would give them time to mature.

"This last view not sufficiently considered. The impatience of youth causes it to be overlooked. It is regarded as a curriculum to be passed through indeed, but as soon as possible. Rather a season of the year, not Autumn or Winter, but Spring and Summer, the growing season; season, if not improved for growing purposes, leaves an irreparable loss behind.

"It is our business to see that we are maturing. Oh, what maturity necessary here! Who sufficient for these things? Let raw recruits go into battle; if through the want of experience they perish, they shall revive again. The valley of dry bones shall be quickened. The whited battle-field shall give up its dead. Let the young physician, if it must be, tamper with the health and lives of men. Neither health nor life can last forever. Though one be cut down before his time, he will revive again, and may revive in immortal youth. Oh, what a solemn and delicate thing to minister to souls diseased! What thorough understanding of the heavenly science, and what skill in its application. What experimental knowledge of its power. If we had due sense of the importance of the work and our deficiency, how slow should we be in entering on its responsibilities. How anxious to improve every moment. And when we come to the end of our novitiate, we should proceed only constrained by the love of Christ, and the authority of Christian friends. Nolo Episcopari would not be a piece of affectation.

"Brethren, are we maturing?

"Different ways of answering this question:—

"1. Look directly in our hearts.

"2. Look at our actions.

"3. Look at our words. This, of outward means, the most important. Out of the abundance of the heart we *act*, much more speak. Speech the drapery of thought. Easier to speak as we think than otherwise. Hypocrisy is constraint. Speaking or forbearing, from mere duty, or regard to appearances, is constraint. What we say spontaneously, a clear indication. 'By thy words shalt thou be justified.' Once I thought this strange."

"SHOULD A MINISTER PREACH BEYOND HIS EXPERIENCE?"

"The Bible, remarkable for its truthfulness, says more about it, and makes more of it, than any other book. It calls religion truth; God, the God of truth; Christ, the Truth; the Spirit, the Spirit of truth; disciples, children of truth. It condemns all falsehood and lying; makes the confession of truth a duty. Men must lay down their lives for it. It has actually had more witnesses, under trying circumstances, to truth, martyrs, than any other book or religion. In contrast to all this, too, and making it stronger from such contrast, Satan is the father of lies.

"It sets high value on truth *objective*. Calls on men to seek it, to buy it, to take heed they fail not of it; not to turn from it, to love it, not to fail to follow after it.

"Much more does it set a value upon subjective truth, that is, an honest search of it and use of it. Truth in the head is immensely valuable, and it has a very important connection with truth in the heart; still, they are not always equal or parallel, and, of the two, decidedly the most important is truth in the heart. A truthful purpose is better than the best arranged system; an honest desire to know the truth, than an actual knowledge. Yes, it puts the highest value on true, honest persuasion, in one's own mind; not professing more than we do believe for any motive whatsoever, not withholding our own sincere conviction. Both are alike in divergence from that straight line, truth in heart and conduct, which, in the sight of God, is of great price. It is not enough that we speak the truth; we must speak it in truthfulness of soul, even as we must speak it in love.

"When I think of the vast deal to be found in the Bible in this strain, and reflect how much want of truth, objective and subjective, there is among Christians who adopt the Bible, I am led to ask how must it have been and be when this book does not prevail and preside over the mental operations of men. If there is anything the Book is emphatic about, it is this; and if there is any sin to which human nature, owing to its extreme facility, is given, more than another, it is this of its opposite.

"As an evidence of the power of the Bible to foster a truthful spirit, I would mention a question which Christian ministers have been led to make: Whether they should preach beyond their individual experience? This question would never be mooted where men did not feel that God required truth in the inward parts; that we have to do with God, and that He looketh on the heart, and will require of us the strictest and most transparent honesty."

TEMPTATION OF CHRIST.

"Our relations to God are twofold, personal and mundane.

"The first is through our individual unity. This personality the most perfect unity. How perfect? So that one may ascend to heaven, another go down to hell. How fearful. Though human, compatriotic, of the same family, yet this also may be. More than a distinction, a separation, as complete as between light and darkness, holiness and sin, and made by that gulf which lies between.

"This, then, the prime relation invariably found in moral agents, has reference to eternity, and involves eternal responsibility.

"The second is that which belongs to us in common with the race. This through Adam. It is not, like the other, connected with acts; is prior to all deeds done in the body, is involuntary, unconditional. We are born in the consequences of this relation, those of mortality and corruption.

"In this last we differ from angels. They were each one made, as Adam, in innocence and freedom. Each one bore his own burden only. Our Father ate sour grapes and our teeth are set on edge. It might seem as if mankind had a less share of God's mercy than angels. If it were so, God might do what He will with His own. But is it so? One thing is very observable: if we have a first, so we have a second Adam. If sin hath abounded, grace hath much more abounded. But our connection with the first is prior to our own act, with the second through it, and that act is faith.

"Moreover, this connection is proportioned to the intelligence and heartiness of faith. And the central object of faith is Christ, from birth to death, advent, incarnation to ascension; yea, from the fall to the end of all things.

"Temptation one part of His course, and an interesting subject of inquiry. We confine ourselves to the question why it was. Various answers made, displaying the wisdom and goodness of God.

"1. General answer. Why did Christ come in the flesh? As He was born, and grew, and labored, and hungered and thirsted, and felt weariness and pain, so was He tempted. It belongs to humanity. He suffered for men as they do for one another. Why not for evil spirits? 'It behooved Him in all things to be made like unto His brethren.' This, then, might suffice. This is part of a scheme; and if we ask the why of that scheme, we answer, 'Even so, Father, for so it seemed good in Thy sight.' Not sovereignty alone: mercy and goodness. In such a scheme, not every tittle intelligible; enough that it is so as a whole.

"2. More particularly. We have here an example of holiness, hatred of sin, and resistance to it. The importance of this example not realized, because we have always had it, and we have others also. But others are only the sequel of this, and would not have been without it. This is the significant figure, these are the cyphers. Religious biography is a library. These worthies shine with a borrowed light. So of living saints. If we profit by them, it is because they profit by Him. Suppose that this primary example, and all these secondary examples, were withdrawn, and we were left to abstract truths. Our moral atmosphere might be clear, but it would be cold. We should feel that our helps were fewer and less effectual. But here we have a peculiar advantage, the perfection of God in the form of humanity. God manifest in the flesh, in fallen humanity. The best example in the best form. How different the verbal descriptions of science from reality. So here.

"3. Example which assures us of sympathy in our temptations. 'He was in all points tempted like as we are.' 'Having suffered, being tempted, He is able to succor them that are tempted.' Though God, and as such impassible, though in heaven, and not likely to sympathize with earth, we have a feeling High Priest. On earth He showed this. The command to watch, the apology 'the spirit is willing;' 'Satan hath desired to have thee, but I have prayed for thee;' the assurance of this, or sympathy like this, every one has who resists the devil.

"4. Redounds to the glory of God, and comfort of men, as a triumph over Satan. In making free agents He made it possible for evil men to obtain an apparent temporary triumph. So with Satan—first parents—every sinner. 'Tush, God doth not regard.' 'Where is the promise of His coming?' But such triumph and exemption are only temporary. God owes it to Himself not to grant final impunity. Men's sins do find them out. Angels' also. The reprisals fearful. This defeat a signal one. Ever after the spirits stood in terror. 'Art thou come hither to torment us before our time?' And, though they attempted to renew the conflict, Jesus saw Satan as lightning fall from heaven. Here Satan was foiled. He felt it. It was known to him and his legions, and to the angels who kept them in check. If he once triumphed over man, man now triumphs over him.

"5. He shows, too, that man need not have fallen, and that when he fell, it was because he let go his hold of God.

"6. Meant to prove the perfect sinlessness of Christ. He came in personal conflict:—in a desert place—no human countenance—suffering from hunger and lassitude. Satan had tempted Adam successfully. Perhaps angels also. The odds fearful But though Satan thus came, he found nothing in Him. He must have gone away acknowledging, like Pilate, 'I find no fault in Him.' Yea, like the centurion at the cross, 'truly this is the Son of God.' It was a proof, then, that Christ was fit to be a lamb of sacrifice; and, like all resisted temptation, it confirmed Him in holiness.

"7. Meant to make Him *perfect through suffering.* 'He was wounded for our transgressions;' but not on Calvary alone, or Gethsemane, or the Judgment Hall. He bore His cross everywhere. His life one of vicarious suffering. And what His greatest suffering? His temptation. He had to taste of every cup. This the bitterest. We may not feel it. One who is but little jealous of God's honor, and has but a slight loathing of sin, will not understand this. Like everything else pertaining to Christ and His religion, it is unintelligible when religion is low in our hearts. So far as temptation dishonors God, cannot we understand it? We feel when we ourselves are dishonored. How much more when a friend is insulted? It is a dagger to one's own heart. On this account, and because of the intrinsic nature of sin, good men have always been made miserable by temptation in themselves and transgressions in others. 'Rivers of water,' says David, 'run down mine eyes, because men do not obey Thy law.' 'Who,' exclaims St. Paul, in the character of a Christian, or anxious inquirer, 'who shall deliver me from the body of this death?' Halyburton seems to have suffered a long martyrdom from that cause. Legh Richmond's last days were visited by a peculiar temptation. So Thomas Scott's. When Christ said, 'Get thee behind me,' it may be considered an expression of holy indignation and shuddering abhorrence. How must He have been shocked at the temptation! How would we feel, standing in the temple of Juggernaut, and seeing fellow-mortals, rational creatures, fall down before the idol, and to be tempted to unite with them! We, owing to our dim apprehensions and slight emotions, may only see it to be unreasonable; but it revolted His feelings, lacerated His heart. To such suffering He was exposed all through life, but on this occasion, and at the last, it was specially severe. It suggested, in part, that mournful confession: 'My soul is exceeding sorrowful, even unto death.'"

THE TEMPTATION.

"'Christ tempted of the devil.' This is a great truth not sufficiently considered. It might have been kept back, and yet the business of life, temporal and spiritual, be carried on. The temptations of Satan do not interfere with the laws of nature, any more than do the temptations of men. His agency is like the miasma which produces death. It is unseen, yet real; not miraculous, yet fatal. So, again, we might have been armed against him without knowing of his existence, even as the power of God might shield us against natural disease without any agency of our own, leaving us alike ignorant of our danger and of our deliverance. God has not so acted. He has been pleased to let us know of this danger, that with His aid we might guard ourselves against it. 'With the temptation,' He has 'made a way of escape, so that we may be able to bear it.'

"This knowledge widens our view, enlarges our conception, elevates the whole man. We understand nature better—ourselves—the purpose of this life, its importance, the value of the stake. It is well to know that 'we wrestle with principalities and powers;' 'with the powers of darkness.' Not being ignorant of Satan's devices, we can the better resist them. We are more ready to understand that the evil in the world is a spirit. The evil one is a person, and the evil person is a spirit, not acting palpably, but subtilely and secretly, like poison in a cup, or infection in the air. It makes the people of God more spiritual. As to its effect on others, it is the savor of life unto life with one class, of death unto death with another.

"This truth, it is to be observed, seems to have been revealed more fully as the dispensations of God advanced, if not in the fact, at least in its relations and peculiar meaning. Possessed by men, out of this proportion it only breeds superstition. Hence devil worship. To us the fact is much in place, and very needful.

"2. He was led up of the Spirit. There is something peculiar here, because He acted officially, and yet something common with all men under temptation. God has put us in this world to be tempted. He is pleased to see us act, in such circumstances, as becomes us. It was so with the Angels, so with Adam and Eve, so with all men, not excepting Christians. He takes them not out of the world, but promises to be with them in the world. So of all men, with the temptation He will make a way of escape. Let us, then, submit to our lot, and fight manfully under God's eye.

"3. After His Baptism. Christ's baptism had special reference to His work. Also an example 'fulfilling all righteousness.' These things called attention to Him, and made Satan more active against Him. Satan is always active, but finite; and, therefore, he husbands his resources, and displays what may be called skill in the use of the means of assault. He chooses his time, places, and persons. By baptism, and the visible tokens of the Divine favor which accompanied it, it was made manifest that Christ was some way largely connected with the kingdom of God. As Herod was jealous at Christ's birth, so was Satan at His baptism. Both feared for their kingdom. 'We are come to worship the king of the Jews,' troubled Herod. So the voice which said, 'This is my beloved Son, hear ye Him,' troubled Satan.

"From this we infer that Christians, professors of religion, if they are in earnest, are the chief objects of Satan's enmity. Worldly persons, without God, are all that he could desire. It is when they break away from him and turn to God that his wrath is roused. It was natural that he should make his assault at an early stage, and being defeated, should afterward wait for other opportunities. Nominal Christians are not troubled. That is not his policy. 'This arch-pirate,' says Leighton, 'lets the empty ship pass, but lays wait for them when they return richest laden.'

"A faithful minister not exempt, especially on his entrance into public life. He finds himself in a novel situation, perhaps one flattering to the vanity of the natural heart. All office is, when first assumed. This of the ministry especially. For Christ's sake good people show regard which, though well intentioned, is most pernicious. Worldly people, at the instance of different feelings, do the same thing. Hence a spirit of self-seeking and self-dependence. And when in such a frame, then is the hour of Satan's power. If he does not cause a fall before men, he causes a decline before God, which, perhaps, answers as well his malicious purpose.

"4. The temptations themselves. Christ was forty days in the wilderness. All that time we may suppose He was tempted. The particular solicitations recorded are but samples. It is not easy to classify these satisfactorily. At all events, He was called to resist 'the world, the flesh, and the devil.' Through the natural and allowable appetite of hunger, which we feel merely in virtue of possessing bodies, He was tempted in the first instance. Besides this, by the panoramic shows of this world He was further tempted to forsake God's allegiance. Once more, He was tempted to magnify Himself; was solicited to an act which would have its root chiefly in pride and self-sufficiency. All these temptations were plied and pressed by Satan. This last would seem more especially his own. It provoked to what we call spiritual sin, and may, with propriety, be fathered especially on the great evil Spirit. It did not come from the flesh, nor from the world; therefore, we must refer it, so far as it had an outward cause, to Satan himself.

"But the best way is to look at the temptation in the root of it. Satan would lead Christ to unbelief. The unbelief of supposing that His sufferings were not all right, and that His Father would not deliver Him out of them—that he was overlooked in them. The unbelief of thinking the world could make Him happy without God. Our Saviour says, 'What shall it profit a man if he gain the whole world, and lose his own soul?' The soul without God is lost. Satan would tempt to the belief that being without God in the world we may still be happy. The unbelief of thinking there can be any evidence better than God's word, or that when He has spoken from heaven any natural appearances can outweigh such testimony.

"5. The weapons with which Christ resisted Satan. Most striking. Who was He? With whom were the treasures of wisdom and knowledge? Even at twelve years of age what understanding! Yet He made the Scriptures the man of His counsel. At every call its language came. When encouraging to the search of truth, He says, 'Search the Scriptures.' When reproving error, 'Ye do err, not understanding the Scriptures.' He not only urged its use on others. He used it Himself. Every temptation was met by a text of Scripture.

"What honor on Holy Writ! How entirely adequate must He have deemed it, interpreted with the aid of the Holy Spirit! What a lesson to us, 'to read, mark, learn, and inwardly digest' its blessed truths. To have it in our memory ready for use. To be familiar with Scripture is to secure the presence of a friend at our side in the hour of temptation; whether we need consolation, doctrine, reproof, or instruction, to impart them. This friend is not Omnipotent (none that but God), but most helpful. Besides, what friend more suitable to direct us to this Higher Friend? A precept of man is comparatively of the earth, earthy. The Word of God, from Heaven, leads to Heaven directly; yea, to God. Let all honor, then, be put on God's Word. Not that which will lead us to pay it a nominal respect, but to use it. It is said, none so difficult to cope with in argument as a man of one book. Whatever the truth of the saying, or the philosophy of it, if true, the most successful man in resisting Satan is a man of one book, the Bible.

"6. 'The devil left Him, and angels came and ministered unto Him.' How pleasant this. So always under God's administration. Though heaviness may endure for a night, joy cometh in the morning. The Apostle says, 'Resist the devil, and he will flee from you.' How exhibited here. 'Christ was made like His brethren.' No final deliverance until death; yet respite. More than that, strength increased. 'Angels came to minister.' 'Well done, good and faithful servant.' This is not to foster pride, but to inculcate humility; therein lies all spiritual victory, and the congratulation fosters this. 'O Israel, thou hast destroyed thyself, but in Me is thy help.' 'Trust in the Lord with all thine heart, and lean not on thine own understanding.' 'Angels sent forth to minister to Him.' This intimated that we should know the extent of creation, the sympathy of other good beings with a soul struggling against temptation, not to call off our thoughts or dependence from God. In their exigencies they look to Him. At all times we move in Him. They ministered to Christ in the wilderness, in the garden, at the tomb, at the ascension. So, if we follow Jesus, 'in the regeneration' we shall be in all these things as He was."

WATER.*

"A favorite emblem of Gospel Truth. Because, 1st. It is *necessary* to human physical life; so the other to intellectual and moral life. They are alike cheap.

"2. An *emblem* of truth, as snow is. Who has seen the gush of pure water from some of the great springs of the Valley of Virginia. It seems to us stainless as the white covering of the highest Himalayas.

"3. Not only an emblem, but an *agent*. It is the great purifier of society. As it is necessary to slake man's thirst, so to cleanse his person, and all other things.

"4. Water, again, is refreshing, and so is truth. The universe was made on a principle of truth, and mind was made for it; it thirsts for it, often when it is in many respects condemnatory. When in a normal state, 'as the hart desireth the water-brooks,' so the human mind the truth of God.

"Truth *may* be death; but legitimately it is life, and health, and peace, and joy.

"Accordingly, the Prophets make much use of water to represent truth: 'Ho! every one that thirsteth.' So our Lord represents Himself as a fountain of living waters. In the last book of the New Testament the image is beautifully used."

* Found, in pencil, on the fly-leaf of his Life of Krummacher, and probably one of his last sketches.

www.ingramcontent.com/pod-product-compliance
Lightning Source LLC
LaVergne TN
LVHW011149110826
845150LV00006B/1200

* 9 7 8 1 4 2 5 5 4 7 1 3 4 *